Worse than the Devil

WORSE THAN THE DEVIL

Anarchists, Clarence Darrow, and Justice in a Time of Terror

Revised Edition

Dean A. Strang

The University of Wisconsin Press

The University of Wisconsin Press
1930 Monroe Street, 3rd Floor
Madison, Wisconsin 53711-2059
uwpress.wisc.edu

3 Henrietta Street
London WC2E 8LU, England
eurospanbookstore.com

Printed in the United States of America

The Library of Congress has cataloged the earlier edition as follows:

Strang, Dean A.
Worse than the devil: anarchists, Clarence Darrow, and
justice in a time of terror / Dean A. Strang.
p.   cm.
Includes bibliographical references and index.
ISBN 978-0-299-29394-9 (pbk.: alk. paper)
ISBN 978-0-299-29393-2 (e-book)
1. Trials (Riots)—Wisconsin—Milwaukee—History—20th century.
2. Judicial corruption—Wisconsin—Milwaukee—History—20th century.
3. Darrow, Clarence, 1857–1938.
4. Anarchists—Wisconsin—Milwaukee—History—20th century.
5. Italian Americans—Wisconsin—Milwaukee—History—20th century.
6. Bay View (Milwaukee, Wis.)—History—20th century.
7. Milwaukee (Wis.)—History—20th century.   I. Title.
HV6483.M55S77   2013
345.775'0243—dc23
2012032689

ISBN 978-0-299-30914-5 (pbk.: alk. paper)

In memory of

Alma Sieber Strang

Catharine McClelland Wedge

Per (Paul) Strang

Arthur H. Wedge

Contents

Illustrations

Preface

Usually, Chicago's Haymarket Square comes to mind first when the topic of radicals on trial arises or when we ask how justice fares in the heated atmosphere of political struggle, fear of foreign-born agitators, and grief over lives lost. Just maybe, though, events that took place ninety miles north of Chicago and thirty years after the Haymarket tragedy offer an even better moment for considering those questions. More police officers died in a Milwaukee bombing in November 1917 than died in the May 4, 1886, bombing in Chicago. Several of the Chicago defendants were immigrants; all of the Milwaukee defendants were. And, while both cases concerned anarchism, the dominant radical (and sometimes violent) ideology of that era, the Milwaukee case arose in the early months of this country's direct participation in an unprecedented world war, when the country was awash in nativist sentiment, patriotism, and intolerance of dissent.

The trials themselves provide even sharper contrast. After the bomb exploded in the ranks of police officers who were clearing Haymarket Square, the ensuing trial in Chicago directly concerned responsibility for that bombing. And that trial may not have been the failure that conventional wisdom has had it for decades.[1] The Milwaukee trial was different. It was but a proxy proceeding in two senses.

First, police and prosecutors never charged anyone with making or planting the bomb that eventually exploded in an assembly room at Milwaukee's central police station. The trial that began the very next week nominally concerned only a separate event, a disturbance in an Italian neighborhood that had resulted in gunplay and death more than two months before the bomb destroyed much of the police station. Because the trial began in Milwaukee just three days after that city buried nine fallen police officers whose deaths otherwise went unvindicated, it became a proxy for the bombing trial that never would be.

Second, the eleven defendants themselves were proxies for their supporters whom the public, police, and mainstream newspapers widely blamed for the bombing. When someone planted the bomb, these eleven already were in jail awaiting trial on the separate events two months earlier. Jail is exactly where they had been since that melee. They could not have made or planted the bomb had they wanted to. But because the intended target of the bomb was the man at the center of the neighborhood disturbance, an antagonist of the eleven defendants, it was easy, even natural, to assume that supporters of the eleven were responsible.

Even if not the travesty that many think, Chicago's Haymarket trial surely included a kind of corruption of the justice system. That corruption is the sort that festers in any opportunity for the selfish ambitions of lawyers and judges to overtake the selflessness that their official duties high-mindedly suggest. In the light of intense public interest, judges sometimes strut a path that they hope will lead to higher office, prosecutors preen for the same reason, and both defense lawyers and their clients resort to political theater designed to advance their personal fame or broad causes rather than their legal interests. The Milwaukee story includes corruption of the justice system in the same sense and possibly to an even greater degree. Specifically, it ends in an appeal that leaves one queasy even today. No less than Chicago's own Clarence Darrow is a central figure in that unsettling appeal.

This book explores all of this.

Uncoupled from its day and details, the book's story is a parable of the human frailty that necessarily weakens every link in any system of justice, including ours today. In its own time, the story concerned immigrants who were real or suspected anarchists. Thirty years later, after the next world war, it would have concerned actual and suspected communists, many of them also immigrants or the children of immigrants. Today, it might concern actual and suspected Islamist radicals, who again often are immigrants, the children of immigrants, or watching the West (and the United States especially) from afar.

So the accidental details of characters, creed, and catalyst change over time. But the underlying flaws, even failings, of our institutions of criminal justice stubbornly resist rectification. In a land that proposes to dispense equal justice under law, the alienated newcomer—the "other," whoever he or she is in a given day—remains at real risk of an outcome that has little to do with individual justice or even fair process and much to do with assuaging public fear and venting anger. The prejudices, superstitions, and plain fears that animated police officers, prosecutors, judges, and juries a century ago all persist today. Now, more than ten years after the September 11 attacks and the sometimes repressive or lawless responses of our institutions of criminal justice to those events, the parable is worth telling and remembering.

Beyond its value as parable, this story also has concrete historical importance. The most significant aspect is a previously unknown episode in which America's greatest trial lawyer, Clarence Darrow, perhaps tried directly to corrupt the justice system. Questions about Darrow's ethics and tactics are not new. He stood trial twice in Los Angeles on juror bribery charges after the 1912 McNamara brothers prosecution, and there are other documented, if hazier, incidents in which allegations arose about the lawfulness of his work. But no biographer or researcher ever has raised a question about his role in the 1918–19 appeal from the Milwaukee convictions of eleven Italians. While the evidence is not conclusive, it also is not weak: it begins with the sworn testimony of an ex-prosecutor who directly implicated himself in the illegal plot and continues with some corroboration of that lawyer's testimony.

Given the comparative rarity with which Darrow handled appeals at all and the fact that this was a one-off relationship with clients he had not known and never represented again, the mere fact that Darrow may have joined an effort to corrupt the appellate process casts his other likely wrongs in a different light. If Darrow in fact sought to bribe either of two jurors in the McNamara case, that was but one trial case among many hundreds in his long career. Further, the defendants were heroes of organized labor at a time when Darrow was labor's champion. And the two McNamara brothers faced hanging. Those facts might suggest that such a high-stakes gamble was a rare mistake, if Darrow was guilty at all. But Darrow appeared as counsel in fewer than sixty appeals in his long career, and he had no special stake in this one. That may suggest a different context entirely, if he in fact gambled his reputation and liberty in an effort to corrupt this appeal.

In all events, the transcribed testimony implicating Darrow, drawn from a secret grand jury proceeding in 1922–23, lay in Wisconsin Historical Society files for more than eighty years before seeing light here for the first time. Darrow researchers and all those with an interest in him have new questions to consider.

This tale has historical interest as well for the minor gaps it fills in our knowledge of Emma Goldman's last months in the United States. A letter in the papers of a nearly-forgotten Milwaukee lawyer, William Benjamin Rubin, locates the Chicago hotel in which Goldman likely hunkered down while she awaited deportation after losing an appeal to the U.S. Supreme Court from a federal conviction for opposing the World War I draft in New York. The historical record does not quite link Goldman directly to Darrow's appearance as counsel in the eleven Italians' appeal, but it makes a reasonable circumstantial case that it was she who intervened to secure the famed lawyer's services. And the record does support Goldman's active interest, both public and private, in the plight of the eleven Milwaukee Italians. Out of public sight, she anchored that interest in part in a touching concern for the welfare of one little boy whom she never met. Without making this a purely academic work, I have tried to locate Goldman's role and other events in the history of the Progressive era and World War I, as factually they are a piece of those times. The insights of scholars, where I have offered them, add to the story.

Finally, the fact that more American police officers died in a forgotten terrorist bombing in Milwaukee in 1917 than in any other single event until September 11, 2001, should be of some somber historical interest. In the frighteningly haphazard way that marks any act of terror, the Milwaukee bomb was more lethal than the Haymarket bomb. The police investigation, prosecution, trial, and appeal that all followed were themselves haphazard and frightening, too.

But these events were nearly a century ago. Have not the U.S. Supreme Court and advances in policing in fact rectified much since then? After all, we do not often hear today about random, dragnet searches and arrests, third-degree tactics, or the use of illegally gathered evidence in court, all of which were common in 1917 and on display here.

No doubt both court decisions and the increasingly professional ethos of policing and prosecuting over the intervening decades have improved procedural regularity. In the United States, in ordinary criminal investigative efforts, interrogation methods are more deftly psychological now; only rarely are they crudely physical.[2] The grossest sorts of warrantless, speculative searches also are rarer. In general, for example, the police have learned that *Miranda* need not prevent them from securing confessions (one major specter at the time the Supreme Court announced that decision). They also have come to know that the Fourth Amendment's warrant preference need not defeat many searches, for judges generally are quite compliant in issuing warrants.

So it is not that progress has been impossible or nonexistent. Yet our institutions of criminal justice continue stubbornly to resist rectification, the same way they did in 1917. Improvement, when it comes at all, comes in the teeth of resistance by thousands upon thousands of police officers, prosecutors, defense lawyers, and judges across the country, most of whom are deeply habituated to institutional inertia and suspicious of change. Their resistance often is fiercest when it is utterly silent. Progress does not come; it must overcome. And not uncommonly, the battle is unheard.

When progress does overcome, often it is at the procedural level that Americans rightly hold dear, but not necessarily at a substantive level. There is a linkage between the procedural and the substantive, to be sure. But procedural change often is incremental, and at best it mediates substantive advance. While the process of approaching a judge for a search warrant now may be more routine, the cozy relationship between judges and the police, and the tendency of judges to bend toward the concrete appeal of detecting crime rather than toward the abstract call of civil liberty, means that objectively questionable searches probably remain about as common as ever.[3] They just are more likely to occur now under cover of the procedural regularity that a warrant represents. And while psychological techniques of interrogation are not bloody or brutal, they too may lead to false confessions just like the physical abuse that was common in 1917.[4]

Consider one striking and obvious example of institutional defiance to progress in truth-finding. At a time when technology makes recording police interviews easy and cheap, many police departments stoutly resist creating a visual or audio record of their questioning of suspects. A police report of the suspect's words and the interaction between police officers and the suspect remains the only—and far more malleable—means of preserving a record of the interview. In that sense, some police departments still prefer the recording methods of 1917, not those of the twenty-first century.

There are other examples. Notwithstanding substantial research data on the unreliability of eyewitness identifications (especially cross-racial identifications) and on the problems of suggestiveness in police lineups, those lineups and identification procedures are now nearly as they would have been nine decades ago.[5] And jailhouse informants, no more reliable than they were in 1917, continue to find their places on prosecution witness lists. They still succeed in escaping part of the consequences for their own crimes by claiming to have overheard a cellmate's confession, just as they did almost a century ago.

At the level of legislative policy, two-thirds of this country's states, as well as its federal government, rely occasionally but tenaciously on a mode of criminal punishment—death—that has vanished in Europe and other Western nations.[6] Indeed, capital punishment practically disappeared in other first-world nations closer to 1917 than to today. Our *procedures* for meting out death are much more complex and cautious (improved, in a sense) than they were generations ago. But in the United States the death penalty persists substantively all the same.

Lastly, and perhaps most broadly, the rising numbers of exonerated prisoners, often but not always cleared by DNA evidence, expose the institutional resistance to rectification so common in American criminal justice. The essential point is not that mistaken convictions continue to happen; they will, in any human and thus fallible system of justice. Instead, the essential point is that it often is years after a trial court and one or more appellate courts have affirmed those convictions that the truth comes out—and then often only through the efforts of people who are, relatively speaking, outsiders. It is law students, volunteer lawyers, even journalism students who finally upset the wrongful conviction. Most damning, they typically do so only after months or years of determined resistance by the offices of attorneys general, trial court prosecutors, original defense lawyers, law enforcement agencies, and judges to whom the obligation of doing justice squarely was entrusted.

Apologists insist that such exonerations prove that, in the end, the system works. But a system that "works," when it works at all, only because volunteers and strangers persist in seeking justice long after duty-bound insiders have failed and quit is a system dependent on happy accidents to cure its unhappy ones. That is not rightly a system of justice at all: it is a system of chance, and a cruel one at that. It is an inverted system that sets self-justification for those on the inside above justice for those it should serve on the outside.

That, fundamentally, was the system that was operating in this story from 1917. It was a system that depended on accidents to fix its mistakes, even on offsetting corruption to redeem its corruption. In important ways, our criminal justice system still does.

Acknowledgments

A humbling number of people contributed to this book in many ways over the years that I worked on it. The staff at the Wisconsin Historical Society's archives reading room I relied upon most frequently. Likewise, the staff at the Milwaukee County Historical Society was unfailingly helpful. Candace Falk and Alice Hall, scholars and keepers of the Emma Goldman Papers at the University of California, Berkeley, were very kind with their help. Staff at the University of Wisconsin–Milwaukee's Golda Meir Library provided important early aid, as did the University of Wisconsin Law Library's capable staff.

Beverly Gage, Matthew Rothschild, Mike Mooney, and Athan Theoharis graciously read the entire manuscript. They corrected errors, suggested improvements, and offered valuable insight. Matt Rothschild's detailed editorial suggestions were an especially welcome gift. Tom Cannon gave freely of his time and his family history. Jeri Famighetti was a helpful copyeditor. Carol Roberts did the tedious but necessary job of indexing, for which I am grateful, and Sheila McMahon shepherded production and more. Throughout, Gwen C. Walker was a steady, smart, and extraordinarily skilled editor. She devoted much more time to this book than any obligation required.

If I have learned anything in writing this book, it is this: authors mean it when they thank those who have read and edited a book, and when they take the blame for remaining mistakes. Truly, the flaws that persist in this book are reflections of me, and of none other.

Like most of us, I needed encouragement over the years. Stanley Kutler, John Demos, Steve Glynn, Charles G. Curtis Jr., Jerald Podair, and Ellen Kozak provided that at important moments. From others, encouragement was constant. These include Mike Mooney, Lynn Adelman, Steve Hurley, Marcus Berghahn, the late Gilda B. Shellow, and my most demanding, devoted, and fearless mentor,

Jim Shellow. Finally, two people both encouraged and tolerated me; they lived not just with this book but with me. I owe Angela Kvidera and Jannea Wood my deepest gratitude. I did not earn what they gave.

Preface to the 2016 Edition

Nearly five years have passed since I wrote the preface to the first edition of this book. During that time, my clients and their cases have come and gone; many on to good things, some not. Some systemic change has come, too. We know more about juvenile brain development now than we did even five years ago, and police departments, lawyers, and courts all are moving in the direction of acknowledging the truths that neurobiologists have discovered. My sense, too, is that the nation's police agencies and courts are making real progress toward consistently recording in-custody interrogations. Indeed, as the nation has begun to examine more closely the violence that occurs between police officers and citizens, more encounters outside police stations are captured on video, whether by citizens or by police cameras.

But many of the systemic failings and weaknesses that the book explores remain resistant to change. That is no surprise. All the assembled institutions that make our system of justice are composed of human beings; no more, no less. Human beings resist change. We evade blame, we seek tenaciously to ratify our past conduct and choices, we continue to fear those whom we see as different. Appellate courts remain a chancy way to correct errors when they occur, for the standards of review they employ often reflect overt and stout confirmation bias, the cognitive error of shaping all information simply to ratify our choices.

Data on exonerations of the mistakenly convicted remind us that our progress is ambiguous. The National Registry of Exonerations, a project of the University of Michigan Law School, reported recently that 2015 saw the greatest number of exonerations since 1989, when reliable recordkeeping began. Some 149 innocent or probably innocent prisoners won release in 2015 alone. Most had been in prison for years, and many would have remained there much longer but for dogged efforts to prove their convictions mistaken: the greatest numbers of innocents were in prison for homicides. In a nation that has a population of African descent still hovering at just over 13 percent, more than 46 percent of all those exonerated between 1989 and February 2016—807 of the 1,733 total—were African American, which is even higher than the background disparity in that group's rate of confinement. During the same period, nearly one in seven of those convictions of the innocent involved a false confession; one third involved mistaken identifications; and over half, 56 percent, featured perjury or false accusation. On average over that nearly twenty-seven-year period, the wrongfully convicted spent almost exactly nine years in prison.

No one knows how many innocent prisoners sit moldering today, hoping that exoneration some day may come. The numbers of exonerations climb, though, with the steepest rate of climb since 2013. That means many innocents remain in United States prisons as you read this book.

The average delay also means that, very often, it was not the first appeal that uncovered the injustice. It was later efforts, often the work of volunteer lawyers, law students, undergraduates, or even the unrepresented inmates themselves, that finally freed the innocent. Judges, prosecutors, police officers, and defense lawyers whose first duty was to spare the innocent, while convicting only the guilty, failed that duty not just in the pretrial process and in the trial court but frequently on appeal. The exonerations suggest either hubris or incompetence, or a bit of both, of we who serve as officers of the justice system in one or another of these roles. When not overweening in our certitude—stubbornly insisting for years that we are right when we are wrong—we may be too careless or callow to discover the difference. Either way, a new commitment to humility must come.

Our advances, then, are no cause for complacency. But neither is the seeming intractability of the flaws cause for cynicism or despair. Yes, our institutions of justice fail and do harm, because human beings fail and do harm. But human beings also crave justice, innately I think, and human beings are capable of progress. We need but the moments when humility pairs with will—when we are able to admit a mistake and then act with resolve to fix it and take steps to prevent its recurrence—to make some progress.

A renewed national discussion of many aspects of criminal justice, from mandatory minimum sentences to police shootings to campaign finance rules in judicial elections to the role of lawyers, as well as the approaching centenary of the trial that this book chronicles, warranted a revised edition. I have taken the opportunity to fix some of my own mistakes in the book, where I found them. No doubt some remain. I am, like all of my courthouse colleagues, human.

Worse than the Devil

1

What the Scrubwoman Found

Detective Fred W. Kaiser's watch stopped at 7:43 on Saturday evening, November 24, 1917.[1] The bomb, loaded with screws, bolts, and other metal odds and ends intended specifically to kill, cost him his life in the same tick of the second hand. Nine other lives stopped just about that abruptly, too.

With a blinding flash, every window in Milwaukee's central police station on the Oneida Street side erupted onto the street in a jagged shower.[2] The clap was so loud that those in the building who survived felt more than heard it. The momentary spike in air pressure deafened them temporarily and blackened their vision for a few seconds. In the squad room, the violently expanding air at incinerating temperature had already completed its work and escaped through the ragged holes and gaps it had torn everywhere. Lights went out, pitch black dropping instantly in the building.[3]

In his office, the blast threw Lieutenant Robert Flood from his chair and left him stunned.[4] He staggered to the squad room across the entrance hall as soon as he could walk. On the street, smoke and plaster dust belched out the gaping window holes. Acrid smoke and dust and burnt fiber and flesh gagged those who still breathed. To the men inside who could hear only the ringing in their ears, the others who staggered or ran pell-mell with their mouths going furiously appeared like actors in an insane pantomime. Detective Bert Stout, not halfway across the street as he walked diagonally west toward the Pabst Theater, turned around to rush back in. Within minutes, firemen from the neighboring Broadway Engine House began a search by lantern light.[5]

The search party found Detective Kaiser's watch later. His diamond ring, blown off his finger, no searcher ever admitted finding. The finger itself the searchers did find. Directly above, on the second floor, telephone operator Edward Spindler slumped dying, still in his chair. Shrapnel had pierced the plaster ceiling that separated the first and second floors, ripped straight up through his abdomen, and left through his head. The many small clumps of Desk Sergeant Henry Deckert's body that rescuers gathered initially led them to believe that an eleventh person had died. But it was ten.[6]

Detective Charles Seehawer and Detective Stephen H. Stecker had started together on the police force the same day, December 1, 1899,[7] and were wounded mortally while just shoulders' width apart. Stecker landed near the doorway. "His arms and limbs were crushed to pulp and his body was mangled frightfully," the *Milwaukee Sentinel* reported.[8] Kaiser, whose stopped watch froze the moment, was dead. Spindler was in his death throes; next to him upstairs, other telephone operators were unhurt. Detective David G. O'Brien, the most experienced officer in the room and possessed of a splendid, thick mustache, died face down in the center of the room.[9] Not three weeks earlier, he had celebrated twenty years of service. Detective Albert H. Templin and Detective Paul J. Weiler perished. They had been together two months earlier during the Bay View riot, three miles south of the police station, on September 9. Templin had been shot that day, but his wound was minor and he had missed perhaps not a full day's work.[10] The pieces of Detective Weiler's revolver were twisted out of shape, its barrel lost altogether. The young plainclothesman Frank M. Caswin was lost, too.

And one civilian, Catherine Walker, who evidently had been just to the side of the open squad room door in the entrance way, would not make it. A few seconds more and she would have escaped unscathed. Instead, she was "beyond human aid."[11] She lay among most of the corpses, which were "piled in crushed heaps on the floor."[12] The coroner's gray ambulance took the dead to the county morgue.[13]

So Saturday ended.

In the weeks before, autumn had blanched to gray, soon to be white. A bleak Thanksgiving approached. The city had awakened to life in a minor key that Saturday morning. An icy wind gusted out of the northwest and the temperature would rise no higher than 36 degrees.[14] Milwaukee, huddled on the western shore of Lake Michigan around the mouth of the Milwaukee River, had turned inward for the winter. Ninety miles of farmland, stark after harvest, separated it from Chicago, with the industrial patches of Racine, Kenosha, and Waukegan lying between. In morning's low sun and again backlit at dusk, Milwaukee's irregular profile against the sky at first appeared all spikes of smokestacks and church spires, similar in that light. Below, on closer inspection, orderly gray sawtoothed rooftops of bungalows and workmen's cottages separated stack from steeple. Here and there, smoke arose, in meandering wisps from home furnaces and in purposeful dark plumes above factories. In the foundries, shutting down the furnaces would mean replacing the ceramic linings, so the fires burnt constantly.

Closer still, commercial buildings and more substantial homes built of Milwaukee's distinctive "cream city" brick lightened the grays of the city's clapboards. Eventually, though, soot of coal and coke darkened all to smudge and black. That same soot tinged the cheaper russet brick of the city's warehouses. At street level, trolleys of the Milwaukee Electric Road & Light Company plied cobbled streets webbed overhead in black wiring. Ornate street clocks stood sentinel at intervals between dingy street lamp posts. Leafless trees lined the streets, their branches spreading outward into the diffuse gray.

Winding down from the farms of Cedarburg and Thiensville several miles north of the city and gathering width as streams and creeks fed it, the Milwaukee River was muddy gray and smooth. It coursed southward and then bent east in the Third Ward, just south of downtown, to pour with the Menominee and Kinnickinnic Rivers from the west and southwest into steely cold, choppy Lake Michigan. Steamships and mercantile vessels were fewer on the river as the time of ice approached and the Great Lakes became too treacherous for trade. That morning the ships remaining sat listlessly at mooring.

Few of Milwaukee's Germans, Poles, Italians, and Irish, who mostly had drifted northward from Chicago in search of work, found reason to test the raw air outdoors on a Saturday morning in late November unless they had to work. Neither did the blacks who had clustered just north and west of downtown after migrating from rural Arkansas and Mississippi and Alabama for industrial work. Working men and women stayed indoors if they could.

Electric lights burned even at that hour, to banish November's gloom. Men smoked and read the morning *Milwaukee Sentinel*, the florid daily that was the city's oldest newspaper, dating to 1837, eleven years before statehood. The speculation of the day was that the New York Giants might trade their second baseman, Charley "Buck" Herzog, back to the Reds (they did not; he went to the Boston Braves).[15] Other men, women, and children puttered at their respective chores. Families played sheepshead, *Schafkopf* in its original German, the local card game with a thirty-two-card deck, around kitchen tables with extra chairs pulled close for nearby aunts and grandmothers and cousins. They busied themselves with early preparations for the coming Thanksgiving meal. Still, just as nature wore Wisconsin's washed grays of winter, the city's mood had a tint of tension.

Not because it was November, though, and surely not because it was Saturday, but because it was 1917 and the war was on. At least superficially, most Milwaukeeans supported the war and President Wilson. Good people made a show of the flag-bunted politics that they thought appropriate in wartime. Patriotism generally won public praise. Just eleven days earlier, November 13, the war had claimed its first Milwaukeean, a Polish immigrant. Six days before that, the Bolsheviks had seized power in Russia. The red scare loomed. Yet this also was a city with a history of electing a Socialist Party mayor, district attorney, and city officials. It was Victor L. Berger's city: he the stoutly sincere socialist editor of the *Milwaukee Leader* and a founder of the Social Democratic Party in 1900. That party merged with the Social Labor Party in 1901 to become the Socialist Party of America. Although never a firebrand, Berger in little more than a year would be both a re-elected U.S. congressman whom Congress would refuse to seat and an Espionage Act convict serving a twenty-year sentence for disloyalty. He and his intellectually imposing wife, Meta Berger, pled the case for pacifism in print, in speeches, and in meeting halls. They pled it in English. They pled it in German, which both spoke: Victor was an Austro-Hungarian Jew by birth. Seven weeks earlier, the postmaster general had revoked the second-class postage permit of the *Milwaukee Leader* in an effort to silence Berger. The disloyalty indictment would follow the next year.

Milwaukee was a city of fresh immigrants. From 1890 through 1908, of the twenty-eight leading cities in the United States, Milwaukee had the largest population with foreign-born parents. A staggering 82.7 percent of the city's people in 1908 had parents born abroad.[16] The largest group by far was German. Many in that group were torn between pride in the young nation to which they or their parents had immigrated and the ancestral tug of the kaiser's Germany. A substantial Austro-Hungarian population faced the same internal torment of crossed allegiances. The next largest immigrant group, Poles, perhaps had not the same ancestral conflict.

In smaller but still significant measure, Milwaukee also was a city of Italians.[17] The Italian population was more complicated than the German, Polish, or Austro-Hungarian. Two waves of immigrants had come from the Italian peninsula. The first, beginning in the 1870s during a famine in southern Italy, eventually filled Milwaukee's Third Ward. Sicilian and Italian immigrants began to replace the original Irish settlers of the Third Ward area after a disastrous 1892 fire that destroyed sixteen blocks and left 1,900 homeless.[18] The Italian influx brought the Third Ward the new produce district, known as Commission Row, that came to define it. This aldermanic ward was bounded on the south and the west by the elbow in the Milwaukee River and extended north into the downtown commercial district.

Many of the immigrants who settled in the Third Ward were Sicilian, not part of a unified Italian nation at the time. Others came from the southern boot of Italy. They had assimilated relatively well by the second decade of the twentieth century, and many had achieved an economic foothold as small merchants, grocers, bakers, and produce brokers. While some remained laborers in the city's factories and foundries, this group of Italian immigrants viewed themselves as Americans.

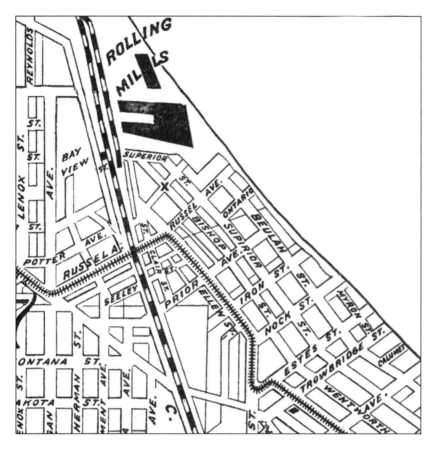

The Bay View intersection of Bishop and Potter Avenues (indicated by an X), ca. 1906. (map in author's collection)

The second wave of Italian immigrants, by comparison, came predominantly from central and northern Italy. They arrived later, in the waning years of the nineteenth century and the first years of the twentieth. In the main, this contingent settled three miles south of the Third Ward along the lake, in what had been the separate township of Bay View. Many, perhaps most, found work in or around the vast rolling mill that the Illinois Steel Company operated on the southern edge of the Milwaukee harbor. This sprawling plant, with a small forest of smokestacks serving its coke-fired furnaces, lay where the land swept southeast away from the terminus of the three rivers in Lake Michigan. The harbor, rivers, and tiny Jones Island all but severed Bay View from the city. The settlement of immigrants up the low sandy hill from the steel rolling mill became known as the Italian Colony.

These newer Italian immigrants were unassimilated. They spoke in their native tongue. They subsisted at the lowest rung of American workers, where the newest immigrants often start. Life in the mill was hellish. Puddlers, working with molten iron in puddling furnaces as impurities burned off, stirred the iron into clumps weighing hundreds of pounds before a crane lifted them. For Italians, the jobs went downhill from there. Because of their skills, puddlers merited small single-family cottages among the company homes in the colony. Furnacemen and less skilled workers had to settle for cramped quarters in rooming houses.

America could not match the imaginings that had led many to leave Italy. The newcomers were isolated in an unfamiliar land, thousands of miles from family and friends whom they never again might see. Work, if available at all, offered no hope of prosperity. The company recouped in rent for company housing much of what it paid in wages, trapping the new workers economically just as their lack of English trapped them culturally. Six days of work left little time in the week to study English, walk along the lake, or seek a mate in dance halls or the neighborhood.

The Bay View Italians also were a less uniformly religious lot than those in the Third Ward. Some were openly hostile to the Roman Catholic Church or to the notion of a God. A few subscribed to anarchist theory that rejected both state and Church. If they were religious at all, though, the Bay View Italians were Catholic. These clung to the Roman Catholic Church, whether out of conviction, need of refuge from the mill, or habit from birth. The Church of the Immaculate Conception, just a few blocks west of the Italian Colony, served them—although in uneasy relation with the Irish. Together, these immigrants filled the pews on Sundays, if perhaps at a cautious distance from one another. Protestant denominations had no foothold in Bay View among the Italians.

Politically, these new Italians lay furthest apart from the Third Ward. The earlier immigrants had fled famine; no resentment of Italy, its monarchy, or its Church had moved them. The more recent émigrés were different. These had fled not for food but for freedom from monarchy, Church, or both. They found much the same in America, though. A government girding for war may have seemed ominous and menacing by reason of basic competence and stability, more so in this new country than in the old. Americans also were a doggedly religious lot. While the Church in America was not a monolith as in Italy, to the irreligious it was here an omnipresent nuisance in its many splinters. And work at the bottom rungs of churning, mechanized, smoky America dulled body and soul if it did not break them, each ten- or twelve-hour shift in the mill like the one before. Not surprisingly, the sympathies of the newcomers often lay with those who challenged the injustices of capital or promised a brighter future for the working man.

Atop that, when Italy declared war in 1915 on the side of the Allies after more than a year of entente (and decades of alignment) with Austria-Hungary and Germany, some in Bay View took this perfidy as proof of the illegitimacy of the Allied cause. In 1917, their adopted country, America, was to join against Austria, as well.

These economic, religious, and political troughs together melded into an alloy of antipathy toward Woodrow Wilson, America's recent entry into the war, and American patriotism generally. That antipathy burned in corners of the Italian Colony.[19]

Saturday, November 24, 1917, was the day that Milwaukee confronted the reach and consequences of this anger. At 7:43 p.m., to be precise. That confrontation began inconspicuously enough with a scrubwoman, Erminia Spicciati.

Unlike the luckier ones, her circumstances bid her to bundle up and face the outdoors that raw, damp morning. She had to work. With her ten-year-old daughter Josie in tow, she was at work before 9 a.m. at the Italian Evangelical Mission Church, at 355 Van Buren Street, on the north edge of the Third Ward.

The church was the pride and domain of the Reverend August Giuliani. An Italian immigrant himself, Giuliani had been born in Vignanello, a town of a few thousand, on January 28, 1881. With a light complexion and brown hair, Giuliani had the fair appearance of Italy's central and northern reaches. By about the turn of the century, this young man with the blue eyes took his vows as a Catholic priest. The novice stood a compact five foot six at most, weighed in at 160 pounds, and bore a rakish scar on his forehead.

Sometime in 1909, when Giuliani already may have been living in Rome, he met an American missionary woman, Katherine Eyerick.[20] She was five years his senior, fluent in Italian, and had worked with Milwaukee's Italian immigrants for the Women's Missionary Society since 1908.[21] How exactly August came to know Katherine is lost. But the fragmentary historical record suggests that the priest confronted a crisis in his vocation after he met her. She steamed back to the United States from Palermo in November 1910 on the *Konig Albert*, arriving in New York on November 25.[22] On December 21, 1910, he boarded the *Oceania* in Palermo, bound for New York. He arrived at Ellis Island in dead winter, on January 5, 1911. Through Katherine's intervention, he was in Milwaukee a week later, on January 12.[23] By then, he had left the priesthood and the Catholic Church to convert to an evangelical stripe of Methodism.[24]

Katherine continued to exert a considerable influence. They married that very year.

August then plunged himself into evangelical work with the city's Italians alongside the established Katherine. Together they combed Roman Catholic believers in the Third Ward for Protestant converts, often appealing first to belly and basics with charitable meals and clothing. The mission church followed in time. By 1917, August Giuliani had the church on Van Buren and two other mission houses, one a block west and four north at 721 Jackson Street and the second in the industrial town of West Allis on Milwaukee's west side.[25]

The mission put August and Katherine Giuliani and their church squarely within the relatively new settlement house movement that the Progressive era brought. Although Jane Addams was not the first to start a settlement house, her Hull House in Chicago was the most noted example of this movement. Beginning in the 1890s, the rise of settlement houses in the nation's larger cities reflected the earnest wish of predominantly middle-class reformers to improve the education, the sanitary conditions, and, in general, the lives of the working classes by providing a variety of programs in one gathering place. This was hands-on, intensely local social work. A settlement house would reach out to the neighborhood's residents, pulling them in for night classes, day care, wholesome entertainment, warm meals, books, or perhaps just a bath. Eventually, workers in the settlement house would come from the neighborhood itself. Such efforts often were the particular interest of Protestant denominations, which gave birth to the Social Gospel movement that accompanied and fed the emergence of progressive political thought in the middle classes from the 1880s into the 1920s.[26] Reform-minded and collective in its orientation, the settlement house movement grew out of the progressive critique of Gilded Age excesses and the growing antipathy between the upper classes and the urban working classes. The Giulianis and their Protestant mission church fit comfortably into this mold of settlement work.

Giuliani's energy and fervor served him well in his calling, despite his fragile English. He also may have had a sense of humor; in 1916, he wrote a thank-you card in the voice of his three-month old son, saying, in part, "sometime I feel lonesome and I like party."[27] Giuliani became a successful minister, and his work took him well out of town. This particular Saturday, November 24, 1917, was such a day. He had traveled to the small town of Markesan, Wisconsin, for a preaching engagement the following morning.[28]

August left in charge his settlement worker and assistant, Maud Richter. Youthful but serious, she appears a soft but prim figure in newspaper photographs. Richter was not at the church when Erminia Spicciati, the scrubwoman, and her daughter arrived to start cleaning.

Probably it was Erminia's daughter Josie who first noticed the strange package outside the church, nestled in the space between the exterior wall and the fence on the south face of the church.[29] It was about 9 a.m. The child called her mother's attention to the find, and the harried charwoman apparently was nonplussed. She brought the paper-wrapped package into the church and left it. Erminia turned back to her work for hours until Richter appeared at the church that afternoon.

Hearing Erminia Spicciati's report upon her arrival, Richter went to investigate. Certainly the package looked like something that ought not be there; carefully wrapped, it was not rubbish or something a passerby had pitched carelessly. Police Captain John T. Sullivan later offered the most benign description, saying, "It looked like a big dinner pail, and innocent enough."[30] Perhaps. But a big dinner pail hardly should have found its way to that narrow, remote gap between wall and fence. For that matter, a more detailed description of the mysterious package suggested something substantially less innocent than a lunch pail. It was fourteen inches long, nine inches in both height and width, and "wound closely in a coil of wire"; to complete the effect, in the center sat a glass tube.[31] The contraption may have weighed as much as twenty pounds.

Richter suspected the worst. It was a bomb. More inquisitive than sensible, she lugged it to the basement and "began fingering the infernal machine, and even pulled the glass tube from it," she later admitted.[32] The glass tube contained brown liquid, and, after removing the vial, Richter could see a yellow powder inside the package.

Aside from the suspicious appearance of the package, Richter had good reason to consider the possibility of a bomb at her Third Ward workplace if ever she glanced at a newspaper. In the ten years up to October 1917, the papers reported, the Third Ward alone had accounted for sixteen murders—eleven of them unsolved.[33] These had occurred in one small district of a city that still numbered no more than about 440,000 inhabitants.[34] On the whole, Milwaukee had a modest murder rate. In 1917 the police had arrested only five people in the entire city for murder and one more for manslaughter.[35] The Third Ward also had seen at least ten bombings according to the *Milwaukee Journal*'s count.[36] Racial and ethnic attitudes of the day made it all seem so simple. Bombs were the "particular weapon of Sicilians," meaning Third Ward residents (not Italians; that was the code word for the Bay View colony), explained the *Milwaukee Journal*.[37] "The Italian may use a knife, but he leaves the bomb and the sawed off shotgun to the Sicilian."[38]

In spite of her suspicions, Richter dithered. The short afternoon turned dark, and supper hour approached. It was 5:20 p.m. before Richter went around the corner to the YWCA, which was equipped with a telephone, to call the police.[39]

Now the police dallied. Although the dispatcher promised to send an officer immediately, almost an hour passed while Richter waited at the church. No officer. Eventually, she decided to act. By this time, a sensible side prevailed, with a self-protective edge. She would send a neighborhood boy to the police station with the package. She summoned the church's teenage handyman and part-time cornetist, Sam Mazzone.[40] He was to go off with package in hand to the central police station several blocks to the northwest at Broadway and Oneida.[41]

Mazzone, then nineteen or twenty years old, was a "well dressed young man, smooth shaven, of average size, clear complexion and rather handsome appearance."[42] He rounded up a companion for the slow walk four blocks west and three north along streets only lightly traveled at that hour, the two young men gingerly cradling the heavy package found lying against the church wall nine hours earlier. They passed quietly in and out of pale spheres of light as street lamps shone. "Two Italian boys" appeared at the police station many minutes later.[43]

What neither Mazzone nor Richter knew was that a police officer at last had responded. Detective McKenney was walking from the central police station to the Italian Evangelical Mission Church at the same time.[44] He and Mazzone never crossed paths.

The central police station occupied the southeast corner of the intersection of Oneida (now Wells Street) and Broadway. An elaborate stone castle, the armory, adjoined it to the east. City Hall, a glorious Flemish Renaissance building housing the district court and the municipal court for criminal cases, stood one block west on Oneida and then a few strides north, its imposing stone arch opening south toward Oneida Street. The location was convenient, for the city jail occupied part of the second floor of the police station.

The night shift's roll call was under way when the boys arrived. Mazzone approached the night stationkeeper, Desk Sergeant Henry Deckert, who sat behind a massive desk at the far end of the public entry way. From this redoubt, Deckert dealt with the walk-in traffic. Operator Spindler worked dispatch and the telephones upstairs. Mazzone tendered the package to Deckert. At the moment, Deckert was occupied with Catherine Walker, a single woman of thirty-six who was there to make a delicate complaint of extortion against a former boyfriend. When he turned his attention to Mazzone and the package, Deckert either knew what it was or had a strong hunch. But he had not seen one like this before.[45]

Deckert told Mazzone to stay put, picked up the bomb, and took it to Lieutenant Flood, his supervisor, in Flood's office adjoining the entrance hall to the south. Flood reacted decisively. "Get rid of the damned thing at once!" he barked.[46]

Easier said than done. Where exactly would he go with it "at once"? Who would man the desk? No one suggested then to Deckert that he could dunk it in a pail of water, which might have been the best bet. Whatever his reasons, Deckert turned, crossed the hall to the north end of the station (the Oneida Street side), and carried the package into the squad room, also called the assembly room. Roll call now had concluded there, and patrolmen were straggling out to find peacoats, caps, and gear to begin their shifts. Upstairs, where the detectives had their separate roll call, Detective Henry Mangert had not yet reported, tardy for the first time in sixteen years.[47]

Deckert deposited the suspected bomb on the large table in the squad room.[48] Then he summoned the station house's detectives, who had no beats to walk. Seven wandered down. Detective Bert Stout, however, left almost as soon as he arrived to answer a new call, about an attempted suicide, from the Pabst Theater, just more than a block west on Oneida Street.[49]

Mazzone and his companion waited in the public reception area as Deckert had directed. Catherine Walker, though, ducked into the squad room herself momentarily to avoid an officer whom she knew, then entering the police station. Unmarried, she was embarrassed by her errand concerning the awkward situation with her former suitor.[50] What would the officer and her fellow workers at the Otto Pietsch Dye Company think of her? Deckert stood closest to the table, possibly with his hands on the curious package, as the six detectives clustered about. No one paid any attention to Walker near the door. She peeked out, eager for a chance to leave unobserved. Plainclothesman Frank M. Caswin, the newest officer in the assembly room, lingered out of interest. Three to six minutes or more, give or take, had passed since Mazzone had walked in the door.[51] The men peered.

Exactly then, the "infernal machine," as newspapers of the day often called bombs, did its work.[52]

Henry Mangert, tardy just this once, lived. Two other detectives, Louis Hartman and Herman Bergin, were in the building and badly hurt. But both escaped fatal injury.[53] Detective Burns had left the squad room almost immediately to go to Lieutenant Flood's office, there to suggest, sensibly but too late, immersing the bomb in a pail of water. He was unhurt.[54] And, in a bit of irony, the attempted suicide at the Pabst Theater saved Stout's life.

Ralph S. McPherran, the chief chemist at Allis-Chalmers, a vast manufacturer in neighboring West Allis, surmised later that the vial in the bomb held sulfuric acid, which dripped onto a zinc plate. That dripping generated heat. Eventually the heat ignited either cotton or black powder. McPherran considered it a very powerful bomb.[55] Its maker had packed the container with screws, bolts, tacks, and other metal slugs to make it more lethal.[56] The bomb stripped the assembly room walls of all plaster. One slug reportedly traveled a full city block, punched through a bedroom window, and still was hurtling fast enough to cut through an iron bed post.[57]

Four people actually made it out of the blackened squad room only half-dead. In part, their brief reprieve was the work of Detective Bert Stout and Lieutenant Robert Flood, who tried furiously to rescue their colleagues. Seehawer, Spindler, and Walker died en route to Emergency Hospital in a "wildly clanging" ambulance.[58] Stecker got to the operating table, but he was beyond help.[59] The quiet gray ambulance from the morgue came again.

The next day, Sunday, Police Chief John T. Janssen sat in his office on the second floor, his building partly destroyed and in chaos as hundreds of the morbid gathered outside and poked through the rubble. Lieutenant Flood was nearby. With melodramatic effect, a reporter wrote that Janssen held a list of the dead and injured in his hand. At least five detectives had left young and middle-aged widows.[60] "It is terrible," Janssen intoned. "I sympathize with the families. Their grief is a thousand times keener than ours."[61] Flood, although hard-bitten and an old hand, just sobbed.[62]

Thanksgiving indeed was bleak. It was gray, dirty, and cold. Purifying snow would come, but not just yet. No greater number of American police officers had ever died together before. Nine were lost that night; Chicago's Haymarket Square bombing on May 4, 1886, took but seven. No greater number would die together again until September 11, 2001.

2

Eleven

That week came the funerals. Seven took place on Tuesday, three on Wednesday. Fred Kaiser and Edward Spindler had a double funeral the first day. O'Brien was alone. Stephen Stecker's family laid him to rest then, too, with police officers as pallbearers. Later that afternoon, Paul Weiler and the sundered shreds of Henry Deckert went. Albert Templin was buried Tuesday as well, after a simple wake at his home.[1] His days had darkened recently: there was the gunshot wound in September during the Bay View melee, and also in the last months he had lost two children—the "greatest sorrow of his life," the Reverend A. Baebenroth told the bereaved at Saint Peter's Church.[2] Frank Caswin and Charles Seehawer were interred on Wednesday, Seehawer in a Masonic ceremony.[3]

The department afforded all nine police officers an honorary escort of twenty-five uniformed patrolmen.[4] Chief Janssen, Captain Sullivan, Milwaukee County District Attorney Winfred C. Zabel, and Judge August Charles Backus attended the funerals.[5] Backus presided over Milwaukee Municipal Court, which at the time had jurisdiction over felonies. He would have known the detectives well.

Amid the pageantry of grief, Catherine Walker almost was lost. She was not from Milwaukee. Rather, she had come down from DePere, Wisconsin, a small town along the Fox River just south of the raw city of Green Bay. Her parents had been dead for many years, although she was but thirty-six. By that age, this unmarried woman had worked fifteen years as an expert spot remover at the Otto Pietsch Dye Company. The company's president, Edgar Ulbricht, identified her ruined body at the county morgue on Saturday night.[6] Later, her siblings, Patrick and Maria, both also unmarried and living together in the family's DePere homestead, came to Milwaukee to carry her body home. On Wednesday, they buried her quietly in a Catholic ceremony.[7]

The night of the infernal machine, Spindler's wife had slumped in the chair of her neighbor, Jacob Grob, in the downstairs flat and cried, "What did Ed do that he had to die, and he was so young, too. Our poor children, what will they do? We were so happy and were getting along so nicely and now to think that he is dead."[8] The Spindler children, Eleanor and Robert, were just nine and six. David O'Brien's sons, on the other hand, were grown. But O'Brien had remarried just weeks earlier, about the time he passed twenty years on the police department, leaving a woman both bride and widow.[9]

Not just solitude would stalk the widows and children. Privation, too, would keep pace with them. Police wives were eligible for $3,000 compensation if their husbands died on duty—but the widows had to choose between that and the officer's pension.[10] They could not claim both. A separate relief fund for all nine families reached $4,066.10 by Tuesday; after that, the papers told little of it until late December, and then nothing at all.[11]

Thursday was Thanksgiving.

On Saturday, Archbishop Sebastian G. Messmer presided over a special Mass for all of the victims at Saint John's Cathedral.[12] The cathedral stood on the east flank of the county circuit court square, hardly more than three blocks north of the Italian Evangelical Mission Church.

Flags on the city's public buildings rose from half-mast only well after the last victims lay in freshly turned Wisconsin earth.[13]

Policing never paused, though. In the inexorable way of large city police departments even in 1917, men ended their shifts roughly as scheduled that first night. A new shift came on; another roll call. Day broke. So it went around the clock, the inertia of regular governmental function muting the reverberations of the bomb's physical and emotional chaos, damping toward predictability, monotony, and order. Individually, officers surely felt and acted on anger and turmoil and loss. Collectively, however, the numbing quality of routine helped.

From the very beginning of the bombing investigation, police and press and therefore much of the public pursued but one theory: Italians had planted the device—specifically, friends and supporters of eleven Bay View Italians then in the city jail for their alleged roles in a recent riot in the Bay View neighborhood. Newspaper accounts recited that theory without variation, often quoting the police.[14]

The reason for the hunch dated back three months, to late summer, when Milwaukee still was green and warm. Reverend Giuliani's work had always featured an evangelical edge. As the church and its satellite missions grew and as Maud Richter joined in settlement work with the Third Ward's Italian immigrants,

Giuliani naturally began to look south of the harbor to the new Italian immigrants filling Bay View. He organized within his congregation a group interested in recruiting new members and converts among these newly arrived émigrés from Italy's central and northern reaches. He particularly pressed for help from those members of the church who had musical talent. Sam Mazzone could play the cornet; loyal congregant and janitor that he was, he joined the evangelical troupe. A second cornetist played as well.[15] Maud Richter played the organ—today we would call it an accordion or concertina—and doubled as musical director.[16] Members who played no instrument could lend their voices to sing or at least lend their presence to make a more impressive showing for the church and its energetic minister.

On Sunday, August 26, after morning services, the troupe made its first trip by streetcar, traveling the three miles or so down to Bay View. There they assembled and struck up the small band. They then marched east from the streetcar stop on Kinnickinnic Avenue to the Italian Colony. In the warmth of a late-summer Sunday afternoon, women were out hanging clothes and talking with one another. Children played in the streets. Men on their day off strolled, smoked, or swapped stories, passing time on the stoop. Just as ice-cream trucks with organ-grinder recordings would draw children on muggy summer days in years to come, the sounds of accordion and cornet and song drew curious inhabitants of the colony that August day. The singing was in Italian.

But when the thick air finally allowed the colony's inhabitants to make out the words as the parade approached close, Giuliani and his troupe found that the Lord's work would be hard. More than just by birth, these new immigrants were by centuries of ancestry Roman Catholic if they were interested in God at all (and again, not a few were atheists or at least stoutly irreligious). Since the Gothic-Byzantine War in the mid-sixth century, Italy's many invaders had learned— if they wished to stay rather than just to sack—to strike compromises with the Bishop of Rome and to adopt his religion at least as a matter of show. In time, perhaps for their grandchildren and great-grandchildren, the faith became life itself. And more than a millennium's ancestors had lived and died Roman Catholic in Italy's hill villages and valleys since then. These tough new immigrants clustered around and under the menacing smokestacks of the rolling mill were a tough audience: a Protestant message would be a very hard sell.

To make matters dicier yet, Giuliani also had a sort of secular evangelization in mind. He was nothing if not determined. Mixed with the hymns were patriotic airs, and his own preaching included a heady dose of country along with God. Giuliani stood firmly behind President Wilson and America's recent entry into the Great War. To many of the Third Ward Italians, supporting their new country's war effort was an obvious course: after all, America was fighting on the side of Italy, and it was not antipathy toward their mother country but hunger that had driven them or their parents or grandparents to leave. Also, as relatively recent immigrants, some may have wished to make a show of patriotic allegiance to their adopted country, both out of genuine appreciation for its opportunities and to blunt nativist suspicions.

Many of the Bay View Italians saw it all very differently. They had no faith in the Italian government, where already fascism stirred, and they resented the Church. Some may have distrusted Church and state equally—not unreasonably, for at the time, the Church was still at least as important a presence in an ordinary Italian's life as was the state. Italy's entry into the war on the side of the Allies in 1915 had been an unwelcome betrayal of a long friendship with the Austro-Hungarian empire.[17] The United States, therefore, won no favor among these immigrants by joining the Italian side. Some among them would have seen this awful war, like any war, as a consequence of capitalism's faults, too. One heckler on August 26 put it pungently, accusing Giuliani of preaching war and castigating President Wilson as a pig.[18] The heckler drew supporting huzzahs from some in the crowd.

All in all, much of Bay View was in no mood for Giuliani's religious and patriotic tub-thumping. So far as most of the Italian Colony was concerned, Giuliani was a Sunday afternoon spoiled.

But the good minister was unfazed. God had called him to this work. In spite of the catcalls and tense moments that first afternoon, the evangelists returned to the Third Ward on the streetcar satisfied with the day's modest progress. About one hundred people had gathered to watch the rally—many of them approvingly, thought Giuliani.[19] He would come again.

Sunday, September 2, threatened rain.[20] Giuliani and his followers returned to Bay View, perhaps after notifying the police just in case.[21] As the assemblage gathered in the street at the intersection of Bishop and Potter Avenues, in the heart of the Italian Colony, Giuliani and Richter led the evangelists in a rousing chorus of "O Columbia, the Gem of the Ocean."[22] Perfect: an ode to America so compatible with an Italian point of view that even Christopher Columbus might have blushed. But some in the crowd answered with "a bad song, an anarchistic song."[23] Later, some in the crowd sounded a threat to throw Giuliani and his followers in the lake if they came again.[24]

Nothing if not persistent, the following Sunday, September 9, Giuliani and his flock did come again. That day there was serious trouble, as we will see. The police later in the day and throughout the night arrested dozens of Italians. Eventually, they winnowed the arrested group to twelve, one of whom died within days. Eleven remained.

It was these eleven who sat in the city jail on November 24 when the bomb exploded, awaiting a trial scheduled to begin in just four days—a trial that, until then, really had concerned only the trouble on September 9. With no clear suspects at hand and but little imagination, the police and everyone else in the city could conjure the motive for sympathizers of the Bay View eleven to blow up Giuliani's church. As it happened, the eleven accused might have perished in the bomb blast themselves, because the city jail sat on the second floor of the central police station.

But the eleven did not die. On the second floor, only Edward Spindler succumbed. After the dead, dying, and injured had been carried out of the ruined first floor, the first order of business was to round up Italians. This the police did with zeal. Chief Janssen set the tone. "I have lost nine good men and nothing can be said by anyone to mitigate this bloodthirsty murder," he thundered on Saturday night.[25] Hours after the blast, that very night, Captain John T. Sullivan, Jack to those who knew him,[26] boasted, "I have ordered wholesale arrests and we are going to get at the bottom of this thing if it takes every man in my Department the rest of his natural days."[27] That the police had no reason to suspect most of those they arrested was a nicety lost on Jack Sullivan. Italians would be taken in if they could not explain themselves to the satisfaction of patrolmen or detectives.[28] Initially, Sullivan detailed fifty officers to the task—a large number for a department its size.[29]

On Saturday night and Sunday alone, police officers dragooned twenty-five Italians for questioning but soon released all of them. By Monday, the police already held another six Italians suspected of involvement. These six were "being put through a vigorous third degree."[30] That number had swelled to twelve by early Tuesday, all getting the "third degree."[31]

A day later, Wednesday, November 28, the *Milwaukee Sentinel* reported, "The city and county jails are crowded with prisoners, but the police department says it has not learned anything tangible."[32] One woman, a new follower of Reverend Giuliani, reportedly had "implicated many." All of those soon were in jail, "and all of them are resisting the 'third degree.' But the inquisition continues and there is hope for its success," the *Sentinel* assured its readers.[33]

Customarily the newspapers referred without adornment to "Italians." That broad term, of course, cast a pall of suspicion on an entire group. In the press, the subjects of the third degree were not more abstractly men or women; they were "Italians." But neither were they more concretely Italian immigrants newly arrived in Bay View, second-generation Sicilians from the Third Ward, or of any described trade, age, street, or past activity. To reporters, they simply were "Italians," one and all.

The police often acted on a similar view. After more than forty years of significant migration to the city from Italy, Corsica, and Sicily, the Milwaukee Police Department in November 1917 seemed to employ not a single detective who spoke Italian. The department evidently had made some efforts to develop an Italian detective detail, but to no avail.[34]

To compensate for this gap in investigative capability within the neighborhoods of the Third Ward and Bay View, the Milwaukee Police Department telephoned for help from Chicago. Three detectives from that city's police department, all of Italian heritage, took the train to Milwaukee on Sunday. Sullivan called the three, Julian Bernacchi, Gabriel Longobardi, and Michael Devito, "the best of their kind in the country" and praised their cooperation. But the Chicago detectives returned home on Wednesday after less than three full days in Milwaukee.[35] Short-term strangers, they likely served most usefully in the functionary's role of translator during interrogations. They could not have offered much help on the streets, in the butcher shops, or in the taverns, where they would not have known a soul. New and unknown, they could not have enjoyed any reputation for keeping their word—or keeping a secret—among Milwaukee's Italian immigrants.

The plea for help from three detectives for three days revealed a great deal, though, about the Milwaukee Police Department, if not about the bombing. The local police faced a crime that had killed ten and destroyed much of the central police station. It could have killed many more had the bomb exploded in or near the Italian Evangelical Mission Church, as intended. Police detectives suspected strongly that the outrage emanated from an entrenched immigrant group clustered in two wards of the city. Some original members of that immigrant group had not just children born in Milwaukee as American citizens but also grandchildren born in the city. The city as a whole approached half a million inhabitants. Yet the Milwaukee police had no one in its detective ranks with sufficient ties to the Italian population to provide meaningful help. The call to Chicago was a confession more revealing than any the police would gain by trick or truncheon in the jail.

In short, the department had to police the Italian neighborhoods from the outside in. Presumably, for decades it had been doing exactly that. The police could rely upon housing patterns that isolated and concentrated immigrant groups. Loathing and distrust imposed these patterns externally, and affinities of language, food, family, or culture more broadly maintained them internally. The police did not segregate Milwaukee, but they benefited from and, more subtly, bore a burden because of it. Rather than assimilate within the immigrant bloc or at least thread working ties into it, the police could contain it only from without. They could cordon. In a pinch, for a short time they could occupy. Day to day, if they could not solve or prevent a crime within these neighborhoods, at least in the main the police could confine crime to these neighborhoods. In this way, they might make both crime and the need to stop it seem less pressing. Why, it was "dago" on "dago," a Sicilian or Italian thing. Sixteen murders, eleven unsolved; ten bombings. Make it eleven.

The police peered in from the outside. There was little urgency to do more, until now.

And so the call went out to Chicago. Locally, it also went out to a shadowy man named Frank J. Carchidi. When he first arrived from Italy, Carchidi was a tailor and musician. But after seventeen years in Milwaukee, he was a sometime ambulance chaser and hustler for local lawyers, an insurance agent, and an occasional real estate man (by his description, anyway).[36] He also was a minor crook. One way or another, Carchidi had scraped together enough to move out to the city's genteel west side. Although he moved his family ever further to the west, the Carchidis lived for a while on 49th Street near Story Park, in a better neighborhood of brick homes and boulevards with elegant elms standing like giant sprays of flowers. During that time, Carchidi lived just a few doors from Win Zabel, the district attorney.[37]

Hoping perhaps to win the favor of the city's moneyed and influential, Carchidi affected disdain for the Italian-born—which he was.[38] These he conspicuously referred to as "Dagoes" at least once while testifying under oath.[39] Carchidi extended that show of disdain to serving at the behest of the police as a jailhouse informer. The police would place him in a cell adjacent to those of arrested Italians. Carchidi later would report what he overheard or claimed to overhear. At other times, Carchidi served in court as an interpreter for Italian witnesses and defendants.[40] With his penchant for bad checks and shady financial dealings, Carchidi was a man who volunteered to do favors of this sort for the police and the courts, ingratiating himself and knowing the time would come when he needed to call in a chit.[41]

This time, though, Carchidi evidently overheard nothing of import in the city jail. The men and women arrested either knew nothing or said nothing. But Carchidi's time would come. His absence in the weeks before Christmas would be significant, too.

Some of the Italians the police treated well and cleared quickly. Sam Mazzone, for one, survived the blast shaken but unscathed in the entry hall. Understandably, the police quizzed him immediately. But he was foolhardy at most, not malicious.

His role was that of trusting delivery boy. Maud Richter vouched for him and his errand. "He is a splendid Christian gentleman," she assured the police and public.[42] Detectives soon released Mazzone.

Other Italians were less fortunate. Repeatedly, and with unruffled tone, Milwaukee's newspapers wrote of the police applying "the third degree" to Italians in stationhouse and jail. The general public and the mainstream media had not begun to question police brutality. Even Victor Berger's *Milwaukee Leader* reported gingerly. A headline three days after the blast captured that paper's muted tone: "Possible Confession Seen in Drag-Net Use by Police Officials."[43] Yet the mistrust of the police among vulnerable groups carried an overlooked cost. That cost was silence. It was information withheld in icy defiance, in fear, or in pervasive resentment.

Not by design, the *Milwaukee Sentinel* had illustrated the problem of Italian distrust of the police a few weeks earlier. "As is the case in all Italian outbursts of disorder, quiet reigned Sunday night in the vicinity of the riot," the newspaper reported in September. "The Italians kept to their homes and darkened the houses. Late into the night practically the entire detective force followed clews and rumors that led them through the heart of the Bay View Italian settlement, but everywhere they went there was silence. Men and women routed out of bed professed to know nothing of the battle or of any one connected with it."[44]

On Wednesday, November 28, the scheduled start of the trial of the eleven accused Bay View rioters, the lead defense counsel, William Benjamin Rubin, still was in Buffalo, New York, at an American Federation of Labor meeting. Judge Backus adjourned the case for two days but warned that he would not brook further delay.[45] Back to the city jail went the eleven until Friday. Not one faced any charge related to the November 24 bomb disaster. All the same, long after the smoke cleared over the central police station, that pall would remain over the trial of the eleven Italians arrested for the September riot.

The intervening day was Thanksgiving. Convicts at the Milwaukee County Jail, men and women adjudged guilty and already serving sentences, dined that day on roast stuffed turkey, baked potatoes, cranberry sauce, pumpkin pie, and coffee (the county House of Corrections additionally offered chicken or goose with gravy). But presumptively innocent men and women awaiting trial in the city jail got by on bologna sausage, bread, and coffee.[46] The Bay View eleven ate their bologna sandwiches and awaited court the next morning.

3

American Anarchists

The eleven Italian immigrants arrested in the aftermath of the Bay View riot each faced up to thirty years in prison. Formally accused of assault with intent to murder, the ten men and one woman also faced a less formal accusation that would affect their treatment at every step of their journey through the American legal system. In part because of the literature discovered in the clubroom where some of them had gathered to hear a political lecture hours before the Bay View melee and in part because of that neighborhood's reputation for radicalism, the mainstream press and the public viewed the Bay View eleven not merely as Italians but as Italian anarchists—an accusation that gained still greater momentum after the bomb turned up at August Giuliani's church two months later. Fellow anarchists, the theory went, had planted the device there in support of their comrades in the city jail.

Later, at their trial, a few of the Bay View eleven would admit, more or less, to muddled anarchist leanings. But a belief in anarchism did not in and of itself constitute a crime. Moreover, if some or all of the accused in fact adhered to anarchism, that label hid a rich spectrum of hues. It was a term no more illuminating than "terrorism" is today.

At the most general level, the common thread in all anarchist theory at the time was its dissimilarity to the chaos and lawlessness, the image of an atomized society run amok, that the term "anarchism" suggests to us today—just as it did to the uninitiated or skeptical then. This association of "anarchism" with "anarchy" never has been quite accurate. Instead of chaos, anarchists envisioned the replacement of a coercive state, with its repressive institutions (sometimes including economic institutions, plutocracies, or even capitalism generally), by voluntary collections of autonomous individuals or of their small, organic affiliations in harmonious and free association. If anarchists presented a utopian vision, still theirs was an ordered utopia. Rather than an order imposed externally by a paternal state or industrial barons, though, anarchists advocated an order imposed internally by the informed and free human mind, collaborating for both individual and mutual benefit in associations that all constituent members deemed useful. At that most general level, anarchist doctrine echoed faintly the thinking of Sir Thomas More.[1] Philosophical anarchism no more envisioned chaos than More did in 1516, when he penned his humanist hopes for religious men and women, bound only by shared beliefs and choice, in *Utopia*. Some anarchists viewed social upheaval, even armed rebellion, as a necessary passage to a peaceful society without authoritarian institutions. But constant cacophony and conflict, a Hobbesian state of nature, was not the expected end. Anarchists were not determinists. Instead, they believed in free will and the peaceable perfectibility of humankind. Naive, perhaps, but anarchists in the decades around the turn of the twentieth century were optimists. They believed tomorrow could hold something better.

Still, anarchists differed greatly in their tolerance or encouragement of violence as a means to achieve the ultimate stability they sought. And many who did not propose violence nonetheless were quick to apologize for it when it served the cause. They often described violence as inevitable and understandable, a form of self-defense or defense of others, given the much grander violence and injustice that the capitalist system and the government inflicted, protecting wealth and privilege by arms and by law. Other anarchists favored violent revolution openly, as necessary to work social change.

To the extent that many Italian immigrants were suspicious of or hostile to America's entry into the world war, some anarchists delivered a message that resonated with many in the Bay View community. Anarchists addressed the riddle of war just as many other Americans did. Americans in general might say they opposed violence and favored peace, but patriotism, national economic interest, and the biases of press and government all contributed to wide support for a war that killed millions. Patriotism and economic interests were notorious pillars of war; press biases were less open. The press gave regular play to German U-boat attacks on merchant ships, with loss of innocent life.[2] It paid almost no attention, though, to Great Britain's slow starvation of the civilian populations of Germany and Austria-Hungary by imposition of a naval blockade of the North Sea ports.[3] Neither did America's political leaders. A selective attention to violence fed war fever.

Alexander Berkman, a leading exponent of anarchism, spoke slyly of both anarchists and Americans generally when he explained, "We all believe in violence and we all disbelieve in violence; it all depends upon the circumstances."[4] Opposing the war on simple grounds of pacifism was not a plausible posture for most anarchists, whatever their stripe.

Emma Goldman struck her balance by opposing not war generally but "Capitalist wars" specifically.[5] She, like many on the left, readily perceived that America's extension of billions of dollars in credit to Allied nations that purchased American-manufactured arms and the country's many trade links to England and France provided an economic incentive to enter the war on the Allies' side. Public claims of the rectitude of the Allied cause were but a cover for the real motivation, in Goldman's view: preserving the capitalist economy.[6]

Anarchism's font is Pierre-Joseph Proudhon, the French philosopher and economist who wrote in the middle years of the nineteenth century and first called himself an anarchist.[7] With indistinct lines of separation, by the twentieth century the ranks of anarchists included subgroups of syndicalists, humanists, socialists, feminists, individualists, communists, and various hyphenated hybrids. Then there were shades of difference that crept in with ethnicity and language. The historian Paul Avrich describes these as "ethnic anarchists."[8] German anarchists, like Johann Most, offered ideas that varied from those of, say, Russian anarchists. These notably included Peter Kropotkin and Mikhail Bakunin, who split early from Proudhon. Bakunin and, later, Kropotkin controversially favored communal ownership over private, and Kropotkin called himself an anarchist communist. New York's bohemian community had its own variations in German and Yiddish and English.

Avrich traces the origins of Italian anarchism in the United States to the 1880s, with the first wave of Italian immigration.[9] Errico Malatesta, the great Neapolitan anarchist thinker who, like Bakunin and Most, tilted toward armed insurrection, influenced many who read Italian newspapers and pamphlets. Italian-born Carlo Tresca did the same. Another Italian anarchist, Luigi Galleani, for fifteen years published the Italian anarchist journal *Cronaca Sovversiva*. Avrich makes the case that Galleani was the most important of all Italian anarchists in the United States,[10] imbued with a "magnetic personality" and an "ultramilitant" attitude.[11] Trained in Italy as a lawyer, Galleani used both "fiery oratory and [a] brilliant pen."[12] His *Cronaca Sovversiva* was widely distributed, as was another Italian anarchist journal, *La Questione Sociale* (which Galleani earlier had edited during the period 1901–2, following Errico Malatesta's similarly short stint).[13] These newspapers made their way to Milwaukee. At least one of the eleven accused, Vincenzo Fratesi, referred to reading one or the other when interviewed on September 12.[14] The police also found a copy of *La Questione Sociale* in the Bay View clubroom where some of the eleven had gathered on September 9.[15]

To the extent that some of the Bay View Italians were admirers of Galleani or Malatesta, they consumed a militant brand of anarchism. Galleani believed in—more, he advocated—violence as a legitimate means of effecting social transformation. Malatesta also justified violence. Dynamite and guns were acceptable tools for workers to take up, Galleani and Malatesta preached. Like Bakunin and Most, these men were at the violent edge of anarchism.[16]

Apart from the differing perspectives of adherents on the question of violence, anarchism also encompassed a jumble of political and philosophical views. Some anarchists were materialist, in the philosophical sense that Karl Marx and Friedrich Engels were, and subscribed to one or another permutation of their creed. Others were much more interested in liberty than economics and, contrary to Marxist theory, viewed the individual as the indispensable basic constituent of society. Even these believers differed in their tolerance (or encouragement) of violent revolution and in their views on the proper sphere of the individual, including in property ownership. Some anarchists aligned with other contemporary movements, particularly socialism and labor activism. Others, such as the Czech-born anarchist Hippolyte Havel, took pains while living in Greenwich Village to distinguish anarchism from these causes: "Disruption [of Anarchists] is imminent with the Socialists, who have sacrificed the idea of liberty and embraced the State and politics. The struggle is bitter, the factions irreconcilable. This struggle is not merely between Anarchists and Socialists; it also finds its echo within the Anarchist groups. Theoretic differences and personal controversies lead to strife and acrimonious enmities."[17]

In every variation, much of anarchist theory was thick stuff. Some of it was the work of educated writers for a relatively small group of educated readers. Other writings were so bombastic and exclamatory that they could appeal only to the converted; they were very unlikely to convert. In that sense, some anarchist writing had a quality of a closed conversation among enthusiasts.

Yet anarchists of the late nineteenth and early twentieth centuries sought to reach the masses, who were their great concern and hope. The problem was that most anarchist theory decidedly was not for mass consumption. Neither were many of the arcane reasons for the dissension among anarchists. Theory and its finer distinctions had to be expressed in writings, which achieved meager distribution. Only the broad generalities lent themselves to soaring oratory at the lectern before large audiences. Emma Goldman, America's most famous anarchist, understood this in time. "Gradually, and with no small struggle against this realization," she wrote, "I came to see that oral propaganda is at best but a means of shaking people from their lethargy: it leaves no lasting impression. The very fact that most people attend meetings only if aroused by newspaper sensations, or because they expect to be amused, is proof that they really have no inner urge to learn. It is altogether different with the written mode of human expression. No one, unless intensely interested in progressive ideas, will bother with serious books."[18]

Because the appeal of their various causes was so similar and many of the initial goals the same, the ranks of labor activists, socialists, and anarchists at the grass roots in large part overlapped. Permutations of doctrine were innumerable, in part due to fuzziness of understanding. Here at ground level, passion arose more from dispossession (or empathy with the dispossessed) than from doctrinal precision. That is not to gainsay the existence of real disagreements. Many labor activists were not of a socialist bent; some labor activists with socialist leanings nonetheless fervently supported the war effort; and so on.[19] But the very fact that these disagreements arose illustrated the linkage and the support of many workers who took an interest in socialism, syndicalism, communism, or anarchism. All of these doctrines shared at least a basic resentment of the existing economic and class structure. Although the socialist *Milwaukee Leader* decidedly was not an anarchist newspaper, for instance, it gave alleged anarchists a more sympathetic portrayal than the conservative press.[20]

So while purists of any radical persuasion might disagree with other radicals' ideas in part or abjure their methods, at ground level their views and actions often overlapped considerably. And when any one of them struck a blow at a common enemy—the government, capitalists, the police—others might set aside quibbles and rally at least temporarily to the side of the rebel who had acted. Even more would that phenomenon hold when a common enemy set upon a rebel without apparent cause. If the other dissidents did not always know exactly on whose side they were, they certainly knew on whose side they were *not*. Socialists, anarchists, and labor activists generally did not side with the state or its coercive institutions and wished to make that clear, so perforce they stood when necessary with those against whom the state and the police sided.

When the Milwaukee press identified the Bay View eleven as anarchists, as reporters did immediately, it was America's best-known anarchist who eventually would come to their defense. Although the Department of Labor's Bureau of Immigration eventually rejected her claim of naturalization, Emma Goldman was the quintessentially American anarchist. Born in Kovno, Russia (now Lithuania), in 1869, she came to the United States to join an older sister at age seventeen. Goldman arrived in the very early days of 1886, after leaving Russia in December 1885.[21] She settled just in time to watch the newspapers chronicle the bombing in Chicago's Haymarket Square on May 4, 1886, and the trial that summer of eight anarchists accused of provoking the bomb thrower. Even then, Goldman reported years later, "My sister Helena and I became interested in the fate of the men during the period of their trial."[22] When, two or three years later, she learned more about the men (four of whom the state of Illinois hanged on November 11, 1887), Goldman "saw a new world opening before me."[23] Politically, she was born at the odd intersection that formed Haymarket.

Goldman became more polemicist than philosopher, although her ideas had a principled grounding. Simply, she was a staunch individualist and a believer in liberty. And a remarkable polemicist she turned out to be. Short but straight-backed, plain but pleasant in appearance, she would stand erect on podium or platform in her starched and carefully pleated shirtwaist, tucked into a dark skirt, and with self-assurance shout her hopes and warnings to the world. With her pince-nez glasses and her hair pulled up, she could look ferociously severe or, with a flicker in her expression, appear but a mischievous schoolmarm. Most of Emma Goldman's admirers thought of her warmly and treated her as a familiar figure, not as an unapproachable icon. They called her simply "E.G." She referred to herself that way, too, in the pages of her magazine, *Mother Earth*—a demanding creation that was her only child.

A leading Goldman scholar, Professor Candace Falk, quotes the journalist William Reedy, who knew and liked Goldman:

> She's a little woman, somewhat stout, with neatly wavy hair, a clear blue eye, a mouth sensitive if not of classic lines. She is not pretty, but when her face lights up with the glow and color of her inner enthusiasm she is remarkably attractive. She has a fine manner, easy without swagger, free without trace of coarseness, and her smile is positively winsome. Conversationally, she is a delight. Her information is broad, her experience comprehensive, her reading in at least three languages almost limitless. She has wit and humor, too, and a compelling sincerity. What does she talk? Art, letters, science, economics, travel, philosophy, men and women. Pictures, poetry, the drama, personalities—the best substance for talk, and all from the standpoint of one who looks forward to the revolution. She has the eye for character and the gift of succinct expression. She is simple and not violent. She is positive without truculence. She is gentle and even at times tender. Her whole personality pulsates with a fervor that is infectious.[24]

If her physical appearance was every bit the sweatshop seamstress that she had been for a time after coming to the United States, Emma had a quick mind undulled by repetitive and monotonous work. She not only mastered English rapidly but within fewer than ten years was speaking eloquently in that second language to audiences of hundreds or thousands, with only the trace of an accent. And she was doing all this as a woman leading men, years before American women could vote and decades before they sat regularly on juries.

Lecturing, conferring, carrying on a heavy correspondence, and scaring up $46.50 here or $73 there for the cause, she criss-crossed America by train and sailed abroad many times. Throughout, in her public persona, Goldman challenged every convention, conceit, and call to conformity that she could. Anything, from childbirth to war, that squelched individual freedom or smothered human potential she railed against. Often, as with her campaign for birth control to free women sexually and economically, she was decades ahead of her day. Not infrequently, as when she came suddenly and fervently to the defense of the odd young man, Leon Czolgosz, who assassinated President William McKinley in 1901, Goldman angered her allies. The government and establishment press painted Czolgosz as an anarchist, when in truth he was a cloying hanger-on whom anarchists generally distrusted and suspected of spying for the police. But Emma Goldman would not tolerate radicals who condemned Czolgosz, including those, like Alexander Berkman, who were dearest to her; the more they reviled Czolgosz, the closer she hugged him.[25] The police and government feared and despised her. She went to prison when necessary. That violent inhumanity was government's usual and cynical remedy for those it claimed preached violence. Goldman was among this number.

Goldman never exalted violence, but she often excused it. Answering vigorously the objection that anarchism "stands for violence and destruction," Goldman revealed the tension inherent in a dream both populist and philosophical: "Destruction and violence! How is the ordinary man to know that the most violent element in society is ignorance; that its power of destruction is the very thing Anarchism is combating? Nor is he aware that Anarchism, whose roots, as it were, are part of nature's forces, destroys not healthful tissue, but parasitic growths that feed on the life's essence of society. It is merely clearing the soil from weeds and sagebrush, that it may eventually bear healthy fruit."[26]

Implicitly here, the masses needed a vanguard—maybe an occasionally violent one—but the vanguard eventually would blend into the peaceful masses. In the same way, destruction would become creation or, more accurately, re-creation. But the transformation initially would require destruction, of course, and Goldman clearly accepted the anarchist idea of the *Attentat*. English does not capture exactly the nuances of the German term. Roughly, an *Attentat* is a violent act or attack, typically an assassination, designed to shock and to serve as a catalyst or at least to draw the attention and support of the masses more effectively than mere spoken propaganda might do.[27] Alexander Berkman's 1892 shooting of the industrialist Henry Clay Frick (who survived; Berkman went to prison on a twenty-two-year sentence and served fourteen) was an *Attentat*.[28] Goldman offered not even mild reproach—unsurprisingly, for in her autobiography she later confessed her involvement in Berkman's plans.[29] Czolgosz, the assassin whom Goldman defended so controversially, she viewed as a classic *Attentater*.[30] Her acceptance of the *Attentat* stopped just shy of outright advocacy.

Goldman was brave and immodest in her goals but realistic in her recognition that others could not follow fearlessly. For example, after rejecting state, society, and God with gusto in just a few pages, she lectured:

> Anarchism, then, really stands for the liberation of the human mind from the dominion of religion; the liberation of the human body from the dominion of property; liberation from the shackles and restraints of government. Anarchism stands for a social order based on the free grouping of individuals for the purpose of producing real social wealth; an order that will guarantee to every human being free access to the earth and full enjoyment of the necessities of life, according to individual desires, tastes, and inclinations.
>
> This is not a wild fancy or an aberration of the mind. It is the conclusion arrived at by hosts of intellectual men and women the world over; a conclusion resulting from the close and studious observation of the tendencies of modern society: individual liberty and economic equality, the twin forces for the birth of what is fine and true in man.[31]

Whatever her failure to persuade the greater public that it could do without the four walls, the ceiling, and the very floor in an existential sense, this was as tight a summation of Goldman's anarchism as she could offer. Her fierce individualism and a stinging rejection of Marxian socialism shone in her essay "Minorities versus Majorities." The essay is a polemic against popular majorities: "Without ambition or initiative, the compact mass hates nothing so much as innovation. It has always opposed, condemned, and hounded the innovator, the pioneer of a new truth."[32] An apologia follows. "Not because I do not feel with the oppressed, the disinherited of the earth; not because I do not know the shame, the horror, the indignity of the lives the people lead, do I repudiate the majority as a creative force for good. Oh, no, no! But because I know so well that as a compact mass it has never stood for justice or equality. It has suppressed the human voice, subdued the human spirit, chained the human body. As a mass its aim has always been to make life uniform, gray, and monotonous as the desert."[33]

In differing details, Goldman's thinking reflected something of Proudhon, Bakunin, Most, and others before her, but became a composition distinctly her own. She tolerated some variance in viewpoint, though. *Mother Earth* magazine, which Goldman founded in March 1906 and published and edited until the postmaster general revoked its second-class mailing permit in September 1917, sponsored a range of anarchist thought. Its May 1917 issue advertised for sale at the magazine's Harlem office the works of Peter Kropotkin, Alexander Berkman, Mikhail Bakunin, Voltairine de Cleyre (an American anarchist whom Goldman greatly admired and who had died in Chicago in 1912), Goldman herself, and others.[34]

Emma Goldman characteristically drew on thinkers in all fields of humane endeavor, for she understood the anarchist cause to speak to the full human spirit. Not surprisingly for that reason, Goldman echoed Henry David Thoreau and Ralph Waldo Emerson in places. She evidently admired both writers.[35] When the shorter *Mother Earth Bulletin* replaced *Mother Earth* in October 1917, it quoted Walt Whitman near the beginning of the first issue.[36] Emma Goldman was a sensualist. Although she never said, "If I can't dance, I don't want to be in your revolution," the epigram most often attributed to her, she offered exactly that sentiment in her 1931 autobiography, *Living My Life*, and took a lifetime's joy in the arts and every expression of humanity.[37] She not only reveled in freedom; she demanded it. Of necessity, Goldman was a feminist. She could not be otherwise.

Goldman's real talent as a social critic lay in description, not in prescription. For example, her succinct assessment of the United States of America is as penetrating today as it was in 1910, if not more: "If I were to give a summary of the tendency of our times, I would say, Quantity."[38] Perhaps she had neither remedy nor even practical palliative for the ills she saw in the young nation to which she had emigrated, but still she was fully American—although at last the nation would not have her. The Justice Department deported her and 248 others to the new Soviet Union on the *Buford* on December 21, 1919; with the exception of one three-month visit,[39] the U.S. government permitted her return only after her death, in 1940. She lies in Chicago's Waldheim Cemetery, near Voltairine de Cleyre and those condemned and executed for the bombing at Haymarket Square.[40]

Emma Goldman is a touchstone for the Bay View eleven. Within a few months of the September melee and arrests, it probably was she who would extend herself by reaching out to a casual acquaintance—at a time when she herself faced prison—on behalf of the eleven Italian immigrants in Wisconsin, then almost bereft of other hope. She did not know or owe them, but she cared. Her intercession, along with the help of her acquaintance Clarence Seward Darrow, eventually would change their lives.[41]

Until September 9, 1917, those lives had gone unnoticed. The eleven had not been arrested in the years of the Great War for anything that attracted the attention of law enforcement officials interested in political radicals. For all the record shows, they may not have been arrested previously for anything. Their mere presence in Milwaukee on September 9 or 10 suggests that they had no recent arrests: all were aliens, not citizens, and by 1917 they might have faced deportation if the government had pegged them as radicals and they had fallen into official grasp. In decades past, radical immigrants had traveled out of the United States and back with relative ease, lack of citizenship no obstacle. Goldman, for example, had gone several times to Europe and elsewhere to lecture and confer. She returned each time.

No more by 1917, though. The Bolshevik revolution in Russia, rising intolerance of radicals at home, heightened fear and national security anxiety attending the unprecedented war raging in Europe, the Immigration Act of February 5, 1917, and the Espionage Act that Woodrow Wilson signed into law just a few months later all combined to make a noncitizen's hold on American soil much more tenuous if he or she was unsympathetic to American institutions and to the capitalist economy.[42] A nativist and authoritarian wave, swelled by fear of foreigners seen as out of step with dominant political norms, would reach its crest in 1919 and early 1920 under Wilson's attorney general A. Mitchell Palmer and his preening young special assistant, John Edgar Hoover. In a span of months that fall and winter, Palmer and Hoover arrested as many as sixteen thousand suspected communists and anarchists, deporting en masse some who were not citizens. Emma Goldman herself was one.

Already in 1917, key federal government movers were in no mood for troublemakers. If the government could not crush them, it at least would harass them or shoo them away. All over the United States, the federal government and local police were cracking down on perceived anarchists at the very time that events were unfolding in Milwaukee.

Sometimes government acted directly; sometimes it acted indirectly, tolerating or abetting vigilantes and thugs. In Butte, Montana, six vigilantes dragged a strike leader, Frank Little, from bed and lynched him. No less than Vice President Thomas Riley Marshall evidently thought this officially tolerated murder hilarious: he punned, "[A] Little hanging goes a long way" toward labor peace.[43] Authorities made no serious effort to arrest anyone. Seventeen members and supporters of the Industrial Workers of the World, or IWW (also known as Wobblies), were "beaten, tarred and feathered in Tulsa, Okla., and driven half-naked and bleeding into the brush."[44] In Seattle, seventy-four members of the IWW faced trial on murder charges arising from the Everett lumber strike, after the sheriff and management strikebreakers shot to death five IWW members and two deputies were wounded fatally.[45] Just four days before the Bay View riot, the Justice Department raided IWW headquarters in Chicago and local halls across the nation. Agents seized "tons" of documents, literature, and office equipment.[46] A federal indictment against 166 IWW members (later trimmed by dozens for trial), including Carlo Tresca and IWW leader Elizabeth Gurley Flynn, followed in September 1917, in Chicago. "Big Bill" Haywood, an IWW officer and a leader of western miners, was the principal defendant in that case. Emma Goldman kept a close eye on pretrial proceedings before Judge Kenesaw Mountain Landis.[47] Three days after the bomb blew up in Milwaukee's central police station, police arrested another one hundred suspected Italian anarchists in Seattle. They also seized literature and books in Spokane, Tacoma, and Portland, Oregon.[48] At the same time, the government mustered federal troops to Topeka, Kansas, to protect corporate property from "agitators" in the IWW.[49] On November 30 the U.S. Immigration Commissioner in Seattle linked the Milwaukee bomb "and others that have appeared from time to time throughout the country" to the scattered chapters of the anarchist Circolo di Studi Sociali. The *Milwaukee Sentinel*'s article on the events that followed the bomb explosion in Milwaukee referred to the federal government's "recent roundup" of anarchists "throughout the entire northwest."[50] The same day, Detroit police reported finding a bomb on a window ledge at the police station.[51] In part on false evidence, by that autumn the labor activist Tom Mooney was under sentence to hang for a bombing in San Francisco. Other labor leaders faced trial there in the same case.[52]

The season that followed saw continued mass arrests of suspected anarchists and other perceived radicals.[53] In February 1918 a federal grand jury indicted fifty-five IWW followers in Sacramento, California.[54] By April 1918 *Mother Earth Bulletin* counted about two thousand IWW members then in jail.[55] Likely reporting only the part of the story that furthered the cause, *Mother Earth* in August 1917 even described thirteen persons arrested in Philadelphia "and charged with treason for distributing a leaflet entitled 'Long Live the Constitution of the United States.'"[56]

The government did not always act against large masses of suspected malcontents. Sometimes the effort to dissuade opposition to the war and dissent from mainstream political norms was tightly focused. In New York City, Assistant District Attorney Minton undertook a campaign to investigate and stiffen punishment of the "seditious and treasonable utterances of certain soap-box orators"; to that end, he met with Chief Magistrate McAdoo to hector the courts about lenient sentences.[57] In Toledo, Ohio, federal agents searched the home of Professor Scott Nearing, a socialist who opposed conscription and the war, and also searched the local IWW headquarters.[58] Again in New York, a federal judge declined to enjoin the postmaster general from refusing second-class mailing privileges to *The Masses*, an important socialist literary magazine under Max Eastman's editorial control with a national readership. The journal's offense? It "continues to 'hold up violators of the Conscription act to admiration,'" the *New York Times* quoted Judge Augustus N. Hand as saying. The judge added to the journal's sins that it said "what the editor thought he could safely say to promote opposition to the war."[59] Even in the small paper-mill town of Appleton, Wisconsin, where the Fox River connects the north end of Lake Winnebago to Green Bay, a local German-language newspaper, the *Appleton Volks Freund*, reluctantly converted to English. It switched languages "on account of the stringent law compelling publishers of German papers to submit a correct translation of all war news, editorials or comments on the war to the postmaster before publishing."[60]

Emma Goldman herself and her longtime friend and colleague Alexander Berkman faced prosecution in federal court in New York in June 1917. The case was related to their short-lived No-Conscription League. Nominally about conspiring to cause young men to refuse draft registration, the prosecution was a transparent attempt simply to silence Goldman and Berkman.[61] Eventually, it worked, in part. Convicted promptly and sentenced to two years in prison, Goldman secured release on bail (after a few weeks in the Missouri State Prison) only until the U.S. Supreme Court affirmed her conviction, in January 1918.[62] Her deportation in December 1919 followed the prison term.

In short, the Wilson administration in 1917 was taking no chances with radicals or with those whose language, ethnicity, or opinions raised suspicion. It would arrest, imprison, and deport if it could. If it could not do all three, then it would settle reluctantly for two of those outcomes, or one if necessary.

For all that appears now, the Bay View eleven probably did not make anarchism their constant work or cause in any devoted way. "The cause," as professional anarchists called it, seems not to have shaped their daily lives. More probably, the need to eat shaped their daily lives. Some, maybe most, of these eleven who sat in jail with their bologna sandwiches were not anarchists, at least not as the newspapers and public believed.

If the term today conjures images of itchy ideologues in owlish round eyeglasses or bearded speechmakers sputtering incessantly to small audiences about big evils, these eleven banish such images quickly. To a person, they had left Italy with at best the equivalent of a fifth- or sixth-grade education in the United States.[63] Each bore the mien of a laborer. Photographs show faces hardened and lined by physical work. Impassive eyes dot expressions flat with resignation. These were plain folk. Almost all either had worked in the rolling mill at some point or still did at the time of arrest.

Milwaukee's newspapers, including even Victor Berger's socialist *Milwaukee Leader*, made no effort to portray the eleven as individuals. Readers knew them only as an indistinguishable clump of Italians or anarchists. Today, it is difficult to learn much about them as people. But, among them, Pietro Bianchi was the oldest, at something more than thirty-five. He had lost an eye while working in the rolling mill and now was a clerk at a sundries co-op in the Italian Colony. Bianchi thought of himself as a "socialist-anarchist" rather than as a "socialist-democrat."[64] But even Bianchi claimed no active role in advancing anarchist thought, and the court reporter's summary of his testimony about his own political views at trial suggests, charitably put, something a bit muddled.[65]

Vincenzo Fratesi, probably the hottest-tempered of the group, was thirty-two. He had a pronounced scar on his face, which he attributed unconvincingly to a bicycle accident in France. He had little schooling but had belonged to a socialist party in Italy. In the United States, he had joined the IWW in 1916. In a loose way, he could explain anarchist and socialist ideas, both of which he described approvingly.[66]

Both Vincenzo and his brother, Adolfo Fratesi, lived with Maria and Pasquale Nardini as boarders in the Nardinis' house. Maria was their sister. Adolfo said that he had completed only two months of formal schooling when he left school for good at age twelve. He, too, had a brief flirtation with the IWW, which he claimed to have quit in June 1916.[67]

The Nardinis were the only married members of the group. Maria was a year older than Pasquale: she was thirty-six to his thirty-five. Together they had a four-year-old son, Areno. The family had come to Milwaukee just about the time war broke out in Europe, in 1914. Pasquale, at least, had no formal education at all. Maria also could not read or write. Not active Catholics, Maria and Pasquale even so had married in the Catholic Church (in France, for some reason, not in their native Italy). They supplemented Pasquale's income from the mill, where he had worked since they came to Milwaukee, by renting out space in their small, two-story home to as many as ten boarders.[68] In whatever free time she had, Maria dabbled in local political theater.[69] She had been slated to play a lead role in a "recital" planned by the Dramatic Lovers' Social Circle "for benefit of the victims of capitalistic reaction" and set for Saturday, September 15. The Dramatic Lovers' Social Circle had booked the hall at the dead end of Potter Street, two short blocks west of the site of the September 9 disturbance.[70] Bowing to the week's tumult and his star's arrest, the director canceled the performance. From this remove, the intended show sounds earnest but tiresome; what "recital" is not? Maybe in the day the neighborhood anticipated the spectacle differently, though. One fan, a local barber, bubbled that Maria Nardini "is one of the leading emotional actresses of the city."[71] In any event, the fragmentary evidence available intimates that Maria Nardini confined her efforts to occasional local theater, playing roles and mouthing words that others authored. Emma Goldman later would assert that Maria had no political ideas at all.[72]

Gavino Denurra, twenty years old, was one of the two youngest among the accused. He had gotten no formal education back home in Italy, where he was raised on the Sardinian islands. Like the Fratesi brothers, he roomed upstairs at the Nardinis' house. Denurra was the one member of the group whom Pasquale Nardini had never seen at the Circolo di Studi Sociali's little clubhouse. He also was the one man who had accepted Giuliani's offer to shake hands after the confrontation the first Sunday that the church group rallied in Bay View.[73] The other twenty-year-old, Angelo Pantaleone, lived upstairs at the Nardinis' house, too. Although Pantaleone pitched in a nickel or a dime occasionally to help with the rent at the clubhouse, he was a construction worker and may well have been out of town on a construction site at the time of the melee in Bay View. Pantaleone had two years of formal schooling, ending when he was eleven, before he left Italy.[74]

Amedeo Lilli was twenty-three and a regular visitor to the clubhouse every Saturday and Sunday afternoon. Unlike the Nardinis and their boarders, who lived a block and a half north of the clubhouse, he lived a few blocks south. By his own account, Lilli had been at all three of Giuliani's gatherings in his neighborhood. He had completed two full years of school before quitting at age twelve and going to work in Switzerland with his father, both as stone masons. He traveled to the United States at age nineteen and had been in Milwaukee barely one year when he was arrested. Lilli admitted owning a revolver.[75]

Daniele Belucci, twenty-six, and Luigi Serafini, twenty-eight, were friends. Serafini was the most educated of the group: he had completed three years of formal schooling. He was rooming at Steve Zawec's saloon, above the clubhouse. Although Serafini had been a stonecutter in Italy, by August 1917 he was working at the rolling mill.[76] Belucci's grueling job at the rolling mill had him working nights one week, days the next. He had been a miller in northern Italy, where he was born, before coming to the United States three years earlier.[77]

Finally, Bartolo Testolin, at age thirty-two, was the most itinerant of the eleven. He was a farmer by birth and had come to America four years earlier, after spending time in Switzerland. Before leaving Italy, he had two full years of schooling and part of a third. To fit in, Testolin invited English speakers to call him "Bert." He specifically denied that he was an anarchist or a socialist. Testolin had worked for three months in Milwaukee in 1916, then wandered to Chicago for work. From there he went north again to tiny Belgium, Wisconsin, on Lake Michigan's shore about thirty miles north of Milwaukee, and then back to Bay View. He took his meals at the Nardinis' and shared a bed with another worker in this sense: when on the day shift at the rolling mill, he paired with a night-shift worker so that each could have the bed when the other was at work.[78] A bullet struck Testolin in the back as he fled the fracas on September 9.[79]

Several of these eleven found some appeal in anarchist ideas. Some indeed thought of themselves as "anarchists" (Reverend Giuliani claimed that a half dozen admitted that they were, but he may have exaggerated).[80] At most, though, they were members of the crowd, not leaders on the podium. These eleven were followers if they were anything. They were neither the effete nor the elite.

They also, of course, personally planted no bomb at Giuliani's church. All were in jail at the time and had been for more than two months when Erminia Spicciatti's little girl found the bomb in its package.

But if the eleven Bay View workers did not make anarchism actively theirs, the lively possibility remains that anarchists may have made the eleven, and millions like them, theirs. These eleven represented a most desirable audience for activists. The distinction between how the eleven were influenced by anarchism and how anarchism influenced events through them is important. It reveals why, if the Bay View eleven were not well-shaped anarchists, anarchism still played a role in the neighborhood responses that late summer and autumn to Reverend Giuliani's admixture of preaching and patriotism and to the police who were protecting his group.

The first decades of the twentieth century saw disaffected masses of laborers—whether in sweltering forges and factories or in fetid shops clacking with the deafening noise of looms or sewing machines—drawn to radical arguments of many stripes. Some of those radical arguments were broadly socialist; some were built on the belief that laborers could be organized to act collectively; and some were based on anarchism of one shade or another. Neither the commercial press of the day nor the general public tended to trouble themselves with close distinctions.

Workers of all kinds, and immigrants in particular, were attractive to anarchists. Mass production then depended intensively on human labor. Hours were long, often half again an eight-hour day, with the work week running to six or even seven days. Wages were paltry, with no legal recognition of the right to bargain collectively. On that score, courts, federal and state, were ever sure to side with management or capital. Millions of workers lived in poverty, cramming into tenement rooms or paying exorbitant rents back to their employer for company housing. These included workers at the Illinois Steel Company's rolling mill in Bay View, which owned much of the housing in the Italian Colony. Working conditions commonly were dangerous, depending on the industry. Miners died regularly in numbers, crushed by falling rocks or by cave-ins as men "firing shot" dynamited the face of the vein to move forward or deeper within the mines.[81] Workers in foundries and in heavy manufacturing died, although not as often in large groups. The physical toll elsewhere was also pernicious, if less obvious. The needle trades, for example, eventually dimmed eyesight, and the crowded, hot, stuffy working conditions invited the rampage of communicable disease, whether tuberculosis, influenza, or the common cold. Fire was not an uncommon threat in factories. The disastrous March 25, 1911, fire at the Triangle Shirtwaist Company in Greenwich Village became a symbol of that risk.

Living in these conditions and confronting daily their essential expendability, millions of laborers in America's festering big cities were disillusioned and desperate. They could not hope to prosper, as the American myth teased cruelly they should. They could not even hope rationally that their children would fare better. After all, their children often worked in the selfsame mines and factories and sweatshops by midteen years or earlier. Immigrants faced all of this despair and more. They were isolated by language barriers and faced racial hatred or distrust. Many had come with dreams that far exceeded what early twentieth-century America provided. Further, because they had not grown up in the United States, they did not necessarily share the cultural norms of native-born Americans. Although they or their children might in time become more fervently American than many born in the United States, new arrivals did not always immediately have the same sense of patriotism, were not inculcated from birth with loyalty to the American way. They might acquire some of these traits, but they did not arrive with them.

Or so those who sought to induct them into progressive and radical movements reasonably could conclude. America's laborers and immigrants constituted a vast potential column of supporters, if only they could be convinced to volunteer their voices, carry placards, or raise their fists to fill the ranks for speeches, labor strikes, and marches. If mustered in this way, immigrant laborers might allow a show of deep support for an eight-hour day, women's suffrage, union membership, pacific opposition to America's entry into World War I, communal ownership of capital and the means of production, or any of a host of other progressive, socialist, communist, or anarchist proposals.

Building this popular base was the challenge that faced radicals and progressives in the first decades of the twentieth century. Famed radicals or agitators like Emma Goldman, Alexander Berkman, or Eugene V. Debs most often drew the government's attention and prison terms. They made headlines. Occasionally, their names captioned U.S. Supreme Court decisions. But in some ways, the efforts of forgotten men like John LaDuca were more important to understanding the work of mobilizing immigrants and laborers. Lesser figures like LaDuca made no headlines but worked near the front lines and the bread lines.

At age thirty-one, LaDuca was secretary of the Italian Department of the Socialist Party of the United States.[82] Not a lofty position, but it was an important one for a committed socialist. He was a native speaker of Italian and his post allowed him to work among Italians. Probably it provided a small but sufficient salary. Outside the circle of party functionaries and regional pockets of interested Italian immigrants, few knew of John LaDuca. He was not a household name. But when he sent word of plans to travel from his Chicago office to speak in Milwaukee, his name could be printed on a few broadbills, and at least his position within the party would attract a small crowd. Maybe a dozen workers, maybe a score or even two or three score might show up on a good day. Most would listen laconically out of mild curiosity or for want of something more interesting to do and then drift off. A few, though, might linger afterward or find inspiration to pitch in: to join a march, to spread the message to neighbors or fellow workers, to distribute literature. To the people like LaDuca within the socialist, labor, and anarchist movements fell the hard, unglamorous work of grassroots organizing.

John LaDuca was the scheduled speaker on Sunday afternoon, September 9, 1917, in the little clubroom behind Zawec's tavern. If the Circolo di Studi Sociali was not exactly his sponsor, if he was not exactly an anarchist, and if the Circolo was not exactly a club or a recognizable organization, none of it much mattered. Under the loose auspices of the Circolo, LaDuca could find a modest hall and the prospect of sympathetic listeners to fill it. He later estimated his audience, optimistically, at about four dozen that day.[83] Hazily he explained that he spoke for about an hour "on evolution and revolution, social revolution."[84] His was not an anarchist message, according to LaDuca, and he was not an anarchist.[85] Socialism and anarchy "are opposed to one another," LaDuca insisted without nuance.[86] He spoke therefore on his "own subject, even to anarchists and [to] try to convince them, to change them from being anarchists." But whatever the title of a speaker's address, the basic message to these potential recruits, drawn from the ranks of puddlers and furnacemen and railroad yard workers and mechanic's assistants, would be similar whether a socialist, anarchist, or labor organizer delivered it: it's you against them, against the bosses, the owners, the people who oppress you.

That message might come by mouth, as in LaDuca's speech, or by written word in cheap pamphlets and penny books meant for uneducated audiences. Either way, the idea was to shake the class of workers out of what intellectuals and ideologues viewed as torpor, with some condescension diluting their compassion. To the anarchist or socialist thinker, to the Wobbly leader or the union firebrand, the question was not whether workers had reason to resent the owners and managers of the factories and shops that employed them or to resent the economic system that consigned them always to the hindmost. The question was how to rouse these workers to act on resentment, rather than to trudge on as ever for fear of change or an empty stomach.

Anarchists both sought to reach people like the Bay View eleven, then, and to adopt them in times of trouble. If workers served as foot soldiers behind the ideologue's banner, fine; if they did not but became a useful cause célèbre later, that was second best or sometimes better. These twin recruiting efforts carried an element of using workers as instruments or means, rather than as ends in themselves. But that hardly was new to workers. Factory bosses put them daily in physical peril for nickels an hour to enhance their own profits. Police and prosecutors arrested and charged them upon light suspicion or for the common charges (bad checks, disorderly conduct, abandonment) that always have filled American jails with the unmoneyed. The Army used them to kill and be killed. Although harm might come from them, too, radicals were the least of the workers' risks.

Yet we cannot know how deeply committed the Bay View Italians were to anarchism, whether to Luigi Galleani's incendiary views or some other brand, or even how well versed they were in those views. The distribution of Italian anarchist publications may have been spotty in Bay View, far away from the East Coast centers of Italian anarchist thought in the United States. For all the trial evidence later showed, the police found only the single copy of *La Questione Sociale* in the raids following the September 9 melee. That journal was influential, to be sure. Its home had been Paterson, New Jersey, a place of symbolic importance for anarchists of the day and for Italian anarchists in particular. Alexander Hamilton had conceived Paterson in 1791 as the first planned industrial city in America. He chose the site for its perch at the Great Falls on the Passaic River, where the energy of water rushing to a seventy-seven-foot drop could power the textile mills that Hamilton envisioned. Better still, Paterson was a mere thirty miles west northwest of New York City. By the late 1800s, thousands of immigrants, including Italians, toiled there in the mills. Silk was the special, although not the exclusive, product. Paterson became "Silk City."

But to anarchists of the day, earlier Italian immigrants had made the place special. Malatesta and Galleani had lived there. And among the Italians who settled in Paterson in the late nineteenth century was Gaetano Bresci. A quiet man and a weaver by trade, he had helped to found *La Questione Sociale*, if only by offering a modest loan. That did not make his name at the time. He earned his place in the anarchist pantheon by returning to Italy in 1900 and assassinating King Umberto I at Monza. Less than a year later, Bresci died, strangled in his cell. The Italian Ministry of the Interior ruled it suicide, but that conclusion is open to fair doubt; guards may have murdered him.[87] Anarchists elevated Bresci to a martyr's place. Paterson had been his home in America, as well as the home of the anarchist journal once associated with him. No city resonated more strongly with radical Italians.

Still, *La Questione Sociale* had ceased publication in 1916, about a year before Milwaukee police found the lone copy of the paper in the Bay View clubroom. Obviously, by then it was a dated curiosity for whoever kept it.

What the police did not find in the little clubhouse or in the homes of those they arrested reveals much more. The police did not find (at least judging by the evidence at trial) a copy of the *Cronaca Sovversiva*. The charismatic Galleani was still publishing that journal in September 1917 (although it had lost its second-class mailing permit in June 1917, at the same time the federal government arrested Goldman and Berkman for their antidraft organizing), and it would have been likely reading material for any committed anarchist who preferred his texts in Italian.[88] Indeed, Avrich ranks it "one of the most important and ably edited periodicals in the history of the anarchist movement."[89] Whatever the leanings of the working men who frequented the room behind Zawec's tavern, then, and however appealing they may have been to anarchists as potential supporters, the absence of this critical dogmatic source suggests that anarchist organizers had much work yet to do in Bay View.

Those anarchists who opposed World War I also would have appealed to many Bay View Italians, even if they had different reasons for reaching the same antiwar stand. The Bay View Italians could find common cause with this strain of anarchism, for instance, even if they were not especially hostile to capitalists. Many Italians resented Italy's break with Austria when it joined the side of England, France, and the United States in the war. That Milwaukee also was home to a large population of expatriates from the Austro-Hungarian empire—including

Bay View's Steve Zawec, who owned the tavern that housed the Italian clubhouse, and, more famously, Victor Berger—only would have broadened the appeal of an antiwar message.

In yet one more way, anarchism may have affected some in Bay View. Anarchists generally had no use for organized religion. Goldman, for one, saw religion as confining the human mind.[90] She devoted a full essay to an attack on "Puritanism," which she understood as the Calvinist form of Protestant faith that underlay much of American culture.[91] Those who left Italy disaffected with the Roman Catholic Church well may have shared the sense that religion, and the Church's hierarchy especially, worked in concert with government and the owners of capital to preserve an unjust social order. The Church urged millions to seek their reward in an after-life, while a wealthy few insiders unabashedly enjoyed the rewards of this life. Bishops, dressed in elaborate raiment, well fed in famine, and ensconced in opulent cathedrals, appeared always part of that privileged class.

How many of Bay View's Italians were disenchanted with the Church or actively opposed to it no one knows today. But anarchists found at least a potential audience in that group.

Anarchism had something to do with Bay View in 1917, then, even if most in Bay View did not know exactly what they had to do with anarchism. Into that neighborhood marched August Giuliani and his small band of followers behind two cornets and a bleating accordion in late summer. This conservative, prowar, Protestant preacher—an apostate Catholic priest to boot—may not have known just what and whom he was facing. Or perhaps he did. Giuliani was a purposeful man. In any event, he courted trouble, and it was about to court him.

4

Doffed Hats and Honored Flags; Buttoned Coats, Pigs, and Rags

America's most prominent historian of anarchism, Paul Avrich, has argued that the disturbance in Bay View on September 9, 1917, was the "opening battle" in a war "in which anarchists with bombs stood on one side and the authorities on the other."[1] He linked the events in Milwaukee that autumn, especially the bomb blast, to Mario Buda and Carlo Valdinoci, followers of Luigi Galleani and companions of Nicola Sacco and Bartolomeo Vanzetti. All four helped to publish and distribute *Cronaca Sovversiva*—the newspaper so conspicuously absent from the haunts and homes of Bay View's malcontents that September. Buda and Valdinoci went to Mexico with Sacco and Vanzetti in the spring of 1917. There, dozens of Italian anarchists, committed Galleanists, re-grouped to oppose the world war.[2] They trickled back into the United States in autumn 1917. Buda later would be with Sacco and Vanzetti the night of their arrest on May 5, 1920, but would escape.[3] Valdinoci met a gruesome fate on June 2, 1919, blowing himself to bits when he set a bomb at Attorney General A. Mitchell Palmer's home in Washington, D.C.[4]

But if only the explosion at the central police station later that autumn drew national attention to Milwaukee, it was the events in Bay View more than two months earlier that established the context for the November bombing. The eleven who would face trial before Christmas stood charged not with the bombing, for which jail provided their airtight alibi. They faced trial for the September 9 melee.

Unlike before his first two rallies in the Italian Colony, this time Giuliani spoke in advance to the chief of police and to the U.S. Department of Justice.[5] Forewarned, the Milwaukee police stationed two or three detectives in plain clothes at the rally site and sent another two on the street car with the group.[6]

Giuliani again brought his group to a halt at the intersection of Potter and Bishop Avenues.

Trouble simmered quietly a block south. An Austrian immigrant, Steve Zawec, ran a tavern there in a larger frame building at 300 Bishop Avenue.[7] At the front on the ground floor, the tavern did its essential work, quenching the thirst left by a day in close companionship with the rolling mill's furnaces. The bar accommodated a pool table and tables for card games.[8] Upstairs were living quarters for rent. At the very back of the building, to the east, a cobbler kept a small shop. In between tavern and shoemaker, the building included a windowless hall. This Zawec rented for $3 a month to a ragtag bunch of local Italians who participated in a small chapter of the Circolo di Studi Sociali.[9] The Circolo was a loose organization that promoted anarchist ideas and appealed to working Italians. According to Avrich, dozens of these small groups dotted America; their dimes and quarters later would keep alive the Sacco-Vanzetti Defense Committee until Massachusetts executed the two men.[10] Today, facts are murky; whether Bay View had a functioning chapter of the Circolo or just a casual group who came into possession of anarchistic pamphlets, photographs, and leaflets is a question lost to time.

The Bay View confrontation was a local affair on September 9. With the exception of John LaDuca, the socialist speaker invited from Chicago to address the group, the people gathered on the street corner lived in the neighborhood within a block or two. Or they came with Giuliani from the Third Ward, just two or three miles to the north as the crow flies but a generation of assimilation removed. True, some in Bay View's Italian Colony had been there only days or weeks, drifting from farm or quarry to find work in the rolling mill.[11] But others had been in the neighborhood for years, working either in the mill or in the shops that supported the colony.

That Sunday was bright and clear in the way that Wisconsin is on a good day in September. Rain had pushed summer out a few days earlier. With the humidity gone, even in midafternoon the crisp air and the unfiltered blue sky whisked in the first chill of autumn.[12] A day before, the temperature had reached 70 degrees at noon. This Sunday, it would top out at 52 degrees and fall to 46 by nightfall. Frost would threaten the following night.[13]

LaDuca's speaking engagement at the clubhouse was at 2:30 p.m. Thirty-five or forty people gathered there to hear him (LaDuca puffed the number to forty or fifty), although some retreated from the rhetoric to Zawec's bar after a few minutes for the simpler pleasure of beer.[14] LaDuca had a second booking to speak in the Third Ward to the Socialist club at 4 p.m., so he would have to make his way toward the trolley by 3:30 p.m. if he was to stay reasonably close to schedule. But he fell behind as he warmed to his topic of "evolution and revolution, social revolution."[15] He lectured for an hour or more.[16]

At half past three or possibly closer to 4 p.m., Giuliani's contingent arrived for the third Bay View rally.[17] They numbered perhaps twenty.[18] Maud Richter had her accordion. Sam Mazzone and another opened the meeting with a cornet duet.[19] As the group gathered at the corner of Bishop and Potter Streets, they would sing an Italian version of "O Columbia, the Gem of the Ocean." Several people in the neighborhood recalled its theme as "Jesus came to save the Italian people,"[20] and Giuliani's later translation of the lyrics was close to that.[21] At age nineteen, Joe Famolaro had the honor of carrying a large American flag for the evangelical group, which he would unfurl at the proper moment.[22] This was to be, in Detective Albert H. Templin's words at the preliminary hearing before trial, a "patriotic meeting."[23]

One block south, LaDuca had finished speaking and his meeting was breaking up. Some drifted out of the back clubhouse into Steve Zawec's saloon toward the front of the building. Others made their way to the street. The brassy blare of the cornets carried in the dry, cool air, and men coming into the bar may have brought word that the church group was back for the third Sunday in a row. If the two previous Sundays had brought only escalating unpleasantries, today LaDuca's audience had social revolution fresh in mind. Several men walked out together to confront the former priest and his group of interlopers. They walked a block north, up a gentle incline, on the east side of Bishop Street. The group included thirty-two-year-old Vincenzo Fratesi, a quarrelsome sort with a scar on his face from (he said) a bicycle accident in France.[24] His brother Adolfo Fratesi tagged along. Amedeo Lilli walked with them. Gavino Denurra likely did, too. An impetuous Tony Formaceo came, his gray suit concealing a pistol.[25] And, by Giuliani's melodramatic account, Maria Nardini led the group: a working man's Marianne, that iconic French symbol of liberty, if a more stolid and modest example than Delacroix's classic rendering in oil paints. She strode from the south with her husband, Pasquale Nardini, and their four-year-old son, Areno, between them.[26] As Giuliani later would portray it, the group marched in near-military ranks, two by two—almost surely a colorful overstatement.[27]

This small group of a half dozen or more people passed the clapboard workers' cottages and the two-story frame houses that sat a few feet off the street, some up a tiny, steeply mounded front yard with scruffy grass and a few steps leading to the stoop from the sidewalk. Houses stood barely an arm-span apart from each other, with dingy walkways squeezed between them. The two-story homes, like the cottages, were cheaply constructed and plain, in an unadorned Victorian style. This block boasted none of Milwaukee's distinctive bungalows and none of the city's more durable and expensive homes of brick. Most of the houses with two floors took in boarders. Six, eight, or even more adults lived cheek-by-jowl in their small rooms between shifts at the mill. Some of the eleven who later stood trial roomed in the very block that the ragtag collection traveled to reach Potter Street.

At Potter Street, they crossed to the north and gathered at the northeast corner of the small intersection. The evangelical group now was singing on the northwest corner, directly across. Strains of the modified "O Columbia, the Gem of the Ocean"[28] met the clubhouse crew. Some in that group were ornery. A respectful rendition of "America" would follow. Then, in the ensuing hush, Giuliani would speak.

The clubhouse crowd would have none of it. They broke boisterously into labor songs on the opposing corner to drown out the evangelists. Possibly these were IWW songs; that union had a repertoire, and singing was a strong aspect of its identity.[29] The Fratesi brothers in particular may have known workers' songs from which to draw on in marches or strikes, for they each had belonged briefly to the IWW in 1916 and had small booklets from the IWW to show for it.[30] A bit disingenuously, the Italians arrested would say later that they sang workers' songs not to provoke but only to compete, claiming, "I sang for my own account."[31] Hearing the commotion, a crowd of curious onlookers from the colony gathered.

The two opposing camps on their corners stood but one block south of the end of Bishop Street where St. Clair Street cut it off, slicing perpendicularly to the northwest. Sunday idlers began to crowd the short block as they drifted off stoops and out of kitchens. Children skittered around adult legs and spindly trees. The Third Ward and downtown, visible between the smokestacks, lay not three miles distant to the north.

As Giuliani waved "Columbia" to a close with a maestro's gesture, Famolaro, in the center of the cluster, began to spread the national colors before this melange of new immigrants. Musicians paused before starting solemnly into "America."[32] To a person, the men in the evangelical group by habit respectfully doffed their caps and hats and held them hand to breast or obediently behind them with both hands silently fingering bill or brim.[33] Not so the other group. Their hats and workman's caps sat as before atop their heads, suddenly conspicuous and defiant.[34] Even casual observers noted the symbolic insult.[35] Whatever emotions this flag stirred, if any, it would not have a ritual honor from the Italian working men and women on the northeast corner. God might shed His grace on thee; they would not. Tension sharpened the air still further.

Giuliani noticed Gavino Denurra, barely twenty years old, across the way.[36] Denurra was the same young man who, two weeks earlier at Giuliani's first foray into the Italian Colony, had stepped forward to shout, "I don't believe in God, I don't believe in Priests, I don't believe in Government, I don't believe what you are saying!" to general acclaim from the clubhouse crowd.[37] Giuliani that Sunday had been speaking about the war, the draft, and registering Italians for about ten minutes. On that occasion, Denurra and his group then quieted until after the evangelicals' meeting. Afterward, Giuliani approached them to talk. Amedeo Lilli spoke up first, explaining, "We don't believe in this war." Another man chimed in more pointedly, accusing Giuliani, "You came here because you want to preach about the war. We don't believe in any Government, Wilson is a pig, the American flag is a rag and this country is a jail!"[38] According to Giuliani, Vincenzo Fratesi hissed that those in the group were "more than socialists, we are anarchists."[39] Giuliani allowed as how he was sorry to hear that and advised them not to speak such things in English, as a policeman was near.[40] Then, ever the innate politician and evangelist, Giuliani offered in a conciliatory way to shake hands. All refused but one. That one was Gavino Denurra.[41]

Denurra remembered the incident much the same way, although he cast himself in a slightly more diplomatic role. As Denurra would explain his first encounter with Giuliani, he had been dumbstruck to hear an Italian deride the Roman Catholic Church and had taken offense. But when Giuliani approached him with polite conversation, including small talk about Denurra's birthplace in the Sardinian Islands, Denurra accepted his handshake. He offered (in the stilted language of a marginally proficient interpreter), "With great pleasure, if you come I will receive you" in response to Giuliani's promise to return the following Sunday for another rally and to visit Denurra at his home.[42]

This day, two weeks later, Giuliani not only saw Denurra again; he claimed to see Denurra buttoning his coat—an Italian gesture of preparation for a fight.[43] Cap on and coat buttoned, Denurra stepped out into the street toward Giuliani's throng. An animated Vincenzo Fratesi came with him, as did Amedeo Lilli and Bartolo Testolin.[44] Fratesi quickly became the primary antagonist. He crossed to Giuliani's side, went back to his group, and then crossed again, back and forth perhaps three times,[45] hectoring others as he became more agitated.[46] "Coward for such a rag!" he bellowed at Giuliani.

The confrontation was on. Raised fists shook. Back again on the northeast corner, Bartolo Testolin was "howling worse than the devil."[47]

After the minor confrontations of the two preceding Sundays, Giuliani this time had arranged for police protection. In his vaguely self-important way, he had gone "personally" earlier that week to see Chief Janssen of the Milwaukee Police Department and to the U.S. Department of Justice for protection.[48] This third Sunday, before leading his flock to Bay View, Giuliani and the congregation met at City Hall after 2:30 p.m. with Detectives Albert H. Templin and Paul J. Weiler. The two detectives accompanied the group on the streetcar to Bay View. At the corner of Bishop and Potter, Detectives John F. Wesolowski and Joseph H. Rydlewicz joined them.[49] All of the detectives were in plain clothes. They stood by unobtrusively as the two contingents on their opposite street corners gathered, each singing to overcome the other. As tension mounted palpably, the detectives became edgy. Their sympathies lay entirely with Giuliani's crowd, who had come for "patriotic" purposes.[50] Now, with Fratesi and others crossing the street back and forth, advancing uncertainly toward Giuliani's congregation and rousing others to an increasing show of hostility, the detectives moved in.

The corner itself was small. This was not a commercial area, although it hosted small shops that served the neighborhood. The streets were not wide. It was a close-packed residential outpost of company housing and boarding houses near the rolling mill. Houses abutted the sidewalks or enjoyed a separation of four or five feet of grass at most. To this day, the lightly traveled intersection is uncontrolled, without so much as a yield sign at any corner.

Detective Weiler posted himself on the northeast corner. He saw Amedeo Lilli standing with Vincenzo Fratesi and August Marinelli. The latter was very excited.[51] Perhaps after consulting Giuliani midstreet about what Fratesi was saying, Weiler strode up to Fratesi directly.[52] He told Fratesi to move along and barked that Fratesi had no right to disrupt the evangelical group. Then Weiler, with a proprietary air, grabbed Fratesi's coat to search him.[53] Before Weiler got his hands into Fratesi's coat pockets, Tony Formaceo, standing just behind Fratesi, produced his revolver. He pointed it directly at Weiler and fired. Although no doubt Weiler pawed Fratesi rudely (a seemingly disinterested observer, E. N. Reynolds, later testified that Weiler "pushed [Fratesi] along"),[54] by all accounts Formaceo fired the first shot.[55] At the ear-splitting report of the pistol, cornet and accordion stopped raggedly at midbar.

Weiler understandably thought that Formaceo had aimed at him "point blank," but the shot missed all the same.[56] Weiler dropped down and back, opening his coat to reveal his police badge and drawing his gun.[57] Templin, just behind Weiler and "a very large man,"[58] now was in the line of fire. He was occupied, though, with Amedeo Lilli, who he claimed also pulled a gun and shot "point blank" at him before jumping back into the crowd.[59] Templin wheeled to see Formaceo still shooting at Weiler. Templin fired. At the same time, a shot hit him.[60] The bullet nicked his left forehead and pierced the rim of his derby hat.[61] Templin wiped blood from his eyes with one hand and kept firing.[62] Wesolowski

Doffed Hats and Honored Flags; Buttoned Coats, Pigs, and Rags ran over to Fratesi, threw over his lapel to reveal his badge, and tried to grab Fratesi before he plunged back into the scattering crowd.[63]

For a short time, the frantic gun battle beat a deafening staccato against macadam streets and clapboard walls. All four police officers were firing. Wesolowski emptied his gun.[64] The gun smoke hung so dense, even in the cool, dry air, that one could not see from a few feet away on the northwest corner who was firing.[65] The acrid smell of half-consumed gunpowder, reeking of nitrate and sulfur like burnt fertilizer, assaulted mouths and noses. Men and women fled in all directions, some yanking at the arms of children, others ducking behind trees or the corner of the nearest house.

At least two Italians in the neighborhood had guns, Formaceo and Marinelli.[66] By Templin's and Joe Famolaro's accounts, Lilli also fired a gun and Vincenzo Fratesi was armed.[67] That would have made four. Detective Rydlewicz claimed that he had seen "at least five revolvers" among the colony Italians.[68] Setting aside reasons to embellish, he hardly would have had much time to count. For his part, Weiler did not see Fratesi with a gun, and even Templin acknowledged that Lilli's gun had disappeared by the time of his arrest shortly after the shooting ended.[69] When asked just five days later, Weiler and Wesolowski counted only two guns among the Italians: Formaceo's and Marinelli's.[70]

As the shooting exploded, Templin hauled Lilli over to Wesolowski to hold while he turned back to the fray. With his free hand, Wesolowski beckoned an approaching bystander (and non-Italian), Robert Blackwood. Wesolowski trustingly passed Blackwood his revolver to reload, and accepted the gun back.[71] Just then, the shooting abruptly stopped. Saltpeter smoke dispersed. Brass and free-reed, horn and accordion were silent, the musicians in headlong retreat. Quiet claimed the void.

The rage had lasted one minute, two at the most.[72] E. N. Reynolds heard fifteen or twenty shots, maybe more.[73]

Of the police, only Templin and Rydlewicz suffered injuries. Blood streamed down Templin's face and neck, although the bullet had just grazed his forehead.[74] Blackwood daubed Templin's face with his handkerchief until it was soaked through and then tied Templin's own handkerchief over his head.[75] Like Templin, Rydlewicz was comparatively lucky: a bullet skimmed his finger.[76] The *Milwaukee Sentinel* reported that this was the second shooting in a few months involving Rydlewicz and Wesolowski. Both times, according to the newspaper, Rydlewicz saved Wesolowski's life by promptly returning fire.[77] On the first occasion, two bullets had hit Wesolowski and "for nearly a month he hovered between life and death."[78] This time, Wesolowski escaped injury. As for Templin, depending upon which of the *Milwaukee Sentinel*'s two versions deserves credit, he returned to work either the next day or the next week.[79]

Not so lucky were the Italians and at least one bystander. Bartolo Testolin claimed that he had been searched just before the shooting started, then saw a detective with gun in hand after Formaceo fired. Testolin pleaded, "Please don't shoot," and turned to run.[80] He flopped facedown with a shot in the back as soon as he dashed away.[81] The newspapers reported that he had a "good chance for recovery."[82] In fact he would live, with only a scar to show. A shot also hit Amedeo Lilli in the left shoulder through his coat.[83] He claimed that he had been singing with Denurra;[84] true or not, he put himself near the center of the outburst. A gawker from the neighborhood, Michael Magunik, whom the newspapers usually described only as "an Austrian," also was hit but hobbled away. Wesolowski found him a few minutes later lying in the kitchen of Zawec's saloon, writhing with a wound in his leg.[85] The police later showed little interest in Magunik. They thought him a casual observer caught in the shooting.[86] Perhaps his ethnicity, un-Italian, helped his cause.

In the street, Tony Formaceo sprawled dead in his gray suit.[87] One shot had caught him straight in the face, piercing the left front of his mouth and splintering his teeth and jaw. Two other bullets had crossed through his chest and heart, one from the left armpit and one from the right; both lodged in his chest. Either would have killed him almost instantly.[88] A fourth bullet from the right had passed through him entirely. Formaceo also had suffered two wounds to his hands, one grazing his left middle finger and the other his right thumb.[89] These might have been defensive wounds; perhaps he had raised his hands in front of him, imploring a shooter to stop. He had not fallen immediately but had stood momentarily. In all, four shots had hit him in the torso or face and two more had hit his hands. The crossing paths of the bullets to his chest did not necessarily mean that two men had fired at him from opposing sides, for he could have twisted in firing, flinching, or falling. But the three bullets that the pathologist, Dr. Daniel Hopkinson, recovered all were .32 caliber—from police pistols, although which officer fired which shots no one ever resolved.[90]

August Marinelli also lay in the street, with a shiny revolver next to him.[91] He was the unluckiest of all. According to both Wesolowski and the *Milwaukee Sentinel*'s account of the coroner's inquest on Friday, September 14, Marinelli had fired only once before crumpling to the pavement, the first Italian to drop.[92] Only one police bullet hit him, but that one tore into his upper right front chest, deflected off his breast bone, found the right lung and the heart, and then cleanly clipped his spinal cord as it punched through a vertebra.[93] He was paralyzed immediately, although able to call vainly to Lilli for help.[94] The doctors and nurses at Emergency Hospital could do little more than watch him lie inert and bleed to death internally, very slowly at that. On Monday night he remained "hovering between life and death."[95] Not until early Saturday morning, almost six full days after he fell, did Marinelli finally succumb, drowning in his own blood as it filled his right lung and the surrounding chest cavity.[96] He was twenty-three years old.[97]

Within five minutes after the shooting stopped, a horse-drawn patrol wagon arrived. The police loaded—possibly "threw"—Formaceo's body and Marinelli, limp and unable to move, into the wagon.[98] In went the wounded Testolin and Lilli as well.[99] Early arrestees like Adolfo Fratesi, Angelo Pantaleone, and Pietro Bianchi piled into the same wagon.[100] Old Officer Miles, like a sordid Saint Peter with his gold-capped teeth and white beard, stood by the wagon and received the dead, the dying, and the prisoners.[101] Off they went to the police station a few blocks away on Kinnickinnic Avenue, the main commercial street in Bay View where the trolleys traveled.[102] Marinelli, Testolin, Lilli, and Magunik the Austrian went from there to Emergency Hospital. Formaceo's stop was the morgue.

After collaring those within immediate reach, the police awaited reinforcements. These came quickly from the Kinnickinnic Station. When the shooting started, Blackwood had gone immediately to a little store on the southeast corner of the intersection to telephone for help. Frightened, presumably, the people in the store had slammed the door in his face. He yelled to them to call for help before he returned to aid the police.[103] Officers arrived in the patrol wagon, in automobiles, and on foot. Many more patrol wagons appeared to help cart off those detained.[104] With adequate numbers, the police began to swarm through the neighborhood, going door to door. In the hours that followed, being Italian was almost reason enough for arrest.

The first pack of police officers, numbering up to twenty, burst into Zawec's saloon about fifteen or twenty minutes after the shooting stopped.[105] Angelo Pantaleone, Daniele Belucci, and Luigi Serafini were standing at the bar drinking beer. Even if these three had been at the corner when the shooting erupted, they had not participated actively. Two witnesses placed Pantaleone at the corner, but neither said he had done anything more than stand in the crowd.[106] Identifications of Belucci and Serafini at the corner were just as thin, resting primarily on Maud Richter's observations. Again, even she did not attribute to them any active role.[107] Zawec later would testify that Belucci and Serafini both were in his bar drinking beer during the shooting.[108] Serafini, for that matter, lived in a small room at Zawec's saloon.[109] The police may have had no good reason to believe that Pantaleone, Belucci, and Serafini had done anything worse than gather as Italians and drink a beer together a block from the melee. But perhaps the picture of these three sipping beer at the bar a few minutes and one short block from the shooting seemed too studied in its indifference to the police. This very saloon, after all, housed the club that had contributed the core group of dissidents who had tried to hoot and sing over Giuliani's group on the opposing corner and with whom Formaceo and Marinelli had stood. Further, Gavino Denurra may have been in the saloon too; Pantaleone put him there, although Denurra placed his arrest at the Nardinis' home and Detective Wesolowski waffled (eventually agreeing with Denurra that the arrest occurred at the Nardinis' house).[110] If Denurra was in the saloon, that would have cast a different light on the others. Denurra clearly had been an antagonist, albeit not a violent one, at the corner confrontation. In any event, together this scene was enough for the police to cast them all into the patrol wagon with Formaceo's oozing corpse and the other arrested unfortunates. The police thus set a pattern immediately: arrest now, worry about fault later.

Not long after arresting the patrons of Zawec's saloon and possibly even before, the police went en masse to 239 Bishop Avenue.[111] Pasquale and Maria Nardini lived there. Although available records do not explain why the police targeted that house so quickly, several reasons seem possible. For one, Maria Nardini would have been conspicuous as the only woman actively engaged in challenging Giuliani's group, and with little Areno accompanying her at that. Her home also was just a few houses north of the shooting, on the west side of the street, so both police officers and others may have noticed her retreat there. For that matter, her brothers Vincenzo and Adolfo Fratesi lived in the same house, as did Denurra. Several of the Italians probably ran for that house, then. Finally, the police almost surely accosted people in the neighborhood, questioning everyone they met. Even without enthusiastic cooperation, someone in the colony may have pointed the police to the Nardinis' home. When the police came to the door, Wesolowski said they found it "barricaded." They promptly broke down the door and rushed the Nardinis, Vincenzo Fratesi, and perhaps the wounded Amedeo Lilli; all were in the first room with their hands up, saying something in Italian.[112] The police snatched young Areno with the adults. Keen for an anarchist queen, the *Milwaukee Sentinel* described Maria Nardini as saying nothing and asking for nothing. According to that newspaper, even her stoic little boy "never whimpered."[113]

The mainstream press, not always with the *Sentinel*'s vivid color, shared an eagerness to paint the conflict in Bay View as a clash between two groups: new, eager patriots; and un-American, ungrateful troublemakers. One group consisted of iconic newcomers, struggling to assimilate, to be "American." These immigrants were proud of their adopted country and optimistic about their children's prospects. The other group was composed of the disillusioned, factory fodder who had fled oppression for repression—of their language, their habits, their hopes. This latter group found the wider culture largely impermeable. They responded to the felt rejection by rejecting those who rejected them and thus became isolated, not just by neighborhood and wages but also by attitude. Little but disdain, disregard, or worse wafted back to them from the native-born and even from assimilated immigrants. If they had jobs at all, theirs carried the greatest danger, drudgery, or just plain dirt for the least pay. The camps at the northwest and northeast corners of Bishop and Potter in tiny Bay View neatly reflected in miniature this fracture that Sunday afternoon in September.

In the establishment newspapers, then, the Bay View melee was due to malcontents who ungratefully or even seditiously opposed America's war effort. They had dishonored the flag and resisted the game appeal of their countrymen to join the purposes of the American government. Worse, the troublemakers were anarchists, an all-purpose condemnation of the day. "Anarchy alone was the cause of the rioting," Detective Captain Dennis Sullivan told the *Milwaukee Sentinel*. The *Milwaukee Journal* agreed. While it called Giuliani's group a "religious revival meeting," a lead paragraph flatly named the conflict "the Anarchistic riot Sunday afternoon."[114] The "gang" on the northeast corner had "cursed the country" before shooting.[115] "I can see no other reason for the attack than that the patriotic touches of the meeting angered these anarchists," Giuliani remonstrated to the *Journal*.[116] That newspaper entertained no competing explanation or hypothesis. Farther away, the *New York Times*, virulently antilabor at the time, wrote that Giuliani had been "making patriotic speeches to his countrymen" when "I.W.W. anarchists" started the deadly battle.[117]

Victor Berger's socialist *Milwaukee Leader* offered an alternate view. In part, Berger probably wished to deflect heat from anarchist ideas; he had no specific sympathy for anarchist theory but did share anarchists' opposition to the war and other capitalist ills. The day following the melee, the *Leader* explained, "The primary cause of the riot Sunday is supposed to have been the holding of evangelistic meetings which have been conducted by the Rev. A. Giuliani, pastor of the Italian Evangelical church, . . . and his assistant, Miss Maude [*sic*] Richter, at Potter and Bishop Aves. for the last few weeks." Even offering a competing hypothesis like this remained outside the editorial sensibilities of the *Sentinel*. And the *Milwaukee Journal* offered one only disparagingly, near the bottom of its first story. "While the police, according to Capt. Sullivan, believe that the anarchistic teachings of the rioters was the sole cause of the riot," the *Journal* allowed, "others, acquainted with the Italian temperament, believe that religious prejudice had something to do with it."[118] By comparison, Berger's *Leader* only winked at the role of the locals in noting that the gunfight "followed an attempt to break up a religious meeting."[119] The *Leader* dressed up the clubhouse group. It wrote, for example, that Formaceo was "an intelligent, modest" young man, adding grudgingly, "but quick-tempered."[120]

The following day, after its reporter spoke with denizens of the colony, the *Leader* was more emphatic still in asserting that Giuliani's religious provocation had led to the shooting: "The meeting Sunday was not primarily a patriotic one all insist, but a religious one and the trouble was started, they say, when several bystanders who were voicing their disapproval of the speaker were roughly handled by detectives. They also claim that no flags were torn down by any members of the society and that no disloyal demonstrations were made."[121] Giuliani's "stubbornness" was to blame, the local Italian barber contended, for he insisted on holding his meetings in the colony "in face of repeated and politely expressed protests."[122] In part, the reporter was right: Giuliani was stubborn and the colony locals tore down no flags. But "polite" was a graciously indulgent description of the protests. "The Italians of Bay View are for the greater part 'irreligious,'" the reporter went on to lecture, "in the sense that they do not profess affiliation with any creed and do not believe in an organized religious institution."[123] That qualification made it harder to portray the outburst as a product of pure religious insult, of course, unless the colony residents were not just indifferent to religion but hostile to it. The *Leader*'s apparent purpose, though, was not so much to explain the fight in a wholly coherent way as it was to exonerate the local Italians of the charge that they were anarchists. To that end, it offered a laughably prim argument that the clubhouse behind Zawec's saloon "was nothing more than an organized group of students of literature and social problems."[124] By their own assessment, unfortunately, most of the "students of literature" barely could read. Probably only Bianchi and Vincenzo Fratesi had any serious interest in reading.[125]

Three months later, after the bomb explosion at the police station, matters were not as clear to Berger's newspaper, and greater objectivity emerged. The *Leader* explained that Giuliani, an "Evangelical revivalist and pastor," "had invaded the Italian district of Bay View with gospel intentions." But maybe it was not just that. "One version," the *Leader* suggested, "has it that he preached political salvation by obedience to the government, the other that he lauded Evangelism at the expense of Catholicism."[126] In an editorial the day after the November 24 bomb explosion, Berger attributed the attack to "fanatics, apparently excited by religious controversy";

this was an obvious, although unstated, nod to the assumed linkage between the September melee in Bay View and the bomb at Giuliani's church.[127] In another implicit acknowledgment of the tie between the September events and the November bomb, the *Leader* also took pains the next day to acquit the IWW of the *New York Times*'s charge that the Wobblies were behind the Bay View disturbance. The *Leader* quoted police captain John T. Sullivan as saying, "It never entered my mind to link up the IWW with this [the November 24 bomb] affair." According to the *Leader*, Jack Sullivan denied ever suggesting that the IWW had any connection to the bomb.[128] If the IWW had no connection to the November bombing, logically it also had no organizational stake in the September confrontation. Setting aside some casual overlap in sympathies and membership between the Italians on that corner and the IWW, the IWW played no discernible role in either the September or the November events.

For their part, several of the eleven who would stand trial for the September incident did suggest plausibly some discomfort with Giuliani's religious message. Most spoke of their Catholic roots—although they were hazy about any present connection to the Church[129]—and both Gavino Denurra and Maria Nardini claimed umbrage at Giuliani's comments about their religion.[130] The defense also elicited testimony that Giuliani's group offered the New Testament for sale, apparently to suggest that the church group's real aim was to spread evangelical Protestantism.[131] In and of itself, peddling the Christian Testament obviously should have given no affront to Catholics, so this defense evidence carried a tacit admission that antipathy to all organized religion held greater sway in the colony than the Pope.

Writing with the advantage of greater distance from the September affair and also with benefit of a trial transcript, the Wisconsin Supreme Court two years later acknowledged the competing theories of the melee's cause, patriotism versus either anarchism or religious insult. The court tentatively sided with the theological cause: "It appears clearly enough that most of the defendants were angry at Guliani [*sic*] and his party. Whether it was because he spoke about the war and the citizen's duty to the state, or whether it was because he was not a Catholic and spoke slightingly about that religion, is not clear. Probably because of both, but perhaps chiefly for the latter reason."[132]

The commercial press favored only one theory, though, and not the one toward which the Wisconsin Supreme Court tilted. Certainly the first theory, patriotism clashing with anarchism, fit better with a thematic narrative of a pernicious national threat from a shadowy network of anarchists, labor radicals, and socialists. In this narrative, not even Milwaukee was immune from the conspiracies and attacks of the menacing leftists, often either foreign-born or influenced by foreigners and foreign ideas. Indeed, places like Milwaukee were key fronts in the war against America that the mainstream media and government portrayed. The lines between combatants, between good and evil, were clean. True Americans were good; their antagonists, whether they wreaked their destruction with bombs, guns, mass marches, or mere dissent, were bad. The black hats also were easy to distinguish because usually they were foreign-born.

The second theory, religious competition, presented several problems and thwarted easy narrative classifications. Perhaps foremost, fomenting religious conflict ill becomes a hero, and Giuliani was an emblematic immigrant hero to the establishment newspapers. Further, religious competition did not lend itself to a local or even a national description. Religion crosses borders and defies easy ethnic and political stereotypes. People of faith—and good faith—are found on each side and all sides, not just on one. Religious conflict can be prosaic and petty at the individual level, but again too complex for easy answers in a broader setting. In the messy clash of faiths that the second theory suggested, neither encamped army could be amassed behind one banner, good over here and evil over there. In both armies, mercenaries would mix with believers, cynics with clerics, and profiteers with prophets. Finally, not to be overlooked, both sides of this conflict featured self-described Christians. While Protestant evangelicals and Roman Catholics each viewed the other as misappropriating it, they both claimed Christ's mantle. Milwaukee's commercial newspapers would not have sided overtly with one group or the other: their readers came in significant share from both groups. At the time, according to reports of religious organizations, roughly 62.7 percent of Christians in all of America were Protestant, and 37.3 percent were Roman Catholic.[133] But with its heavy complement of Poles, Germans (not a few of whom were *Deutsche katholischers*, rather than Lutherans), and Italians, Milwaukee's Roman Catholic community was proportionately much larger than that.[134] Little wonder that the corporate newspapers chose simple, clear narratives that avoided religious dispute but fostered a sense of social order (or fear of social disorder) and a stable consumer market in which to sell newspapers and their advertisers' soaps and sundries. The commercial press had every reason to prefer the first thematic narrative, that of an America imperiled without and within by an ominous other.

Might the melee have played out according to deliberate anarchist plans? Perhaps. Two from the clubhouse group were armed, maybe more. When the police moved in, Formaceo may have intended his effort to shoot a policeman point blank as an *Attentat*, of the kind that Emma Goldman understood and never condemned. But some obstinate facts weaken this theory. The police had not attended the two earlier gatherings that Giuliani led, at least not visibly.[135] Even on September 9, the four officers were in plain clothes. So Formaceo may not have expected the police at all when he came to the corner. Further, by Detective Paul Weiler's own testimony, he first revealed himself as a police officer only after Formaceo's errant shot.[136] Quite possibly, Formaceo unknowingly took aim at a police officer when he overreacted impulsively to the plainclothesman's rough approach to Vincenzo Fratesi.

Whatever its causes, the September shooting was partly an accident of the few dozen people who gathered that Sunday afternoon—their individual notions, moods of the moment, and passions. Some were long-time residents of the colony, working a block or two away from the scene of the shooting. Others essentially were passing through the neighborhood, nothing more. No one, including the newest arrival, Testolin, seems to have come specifically for a confrontation with Giuliani.[137] The small evangelical group had held its first meeting only two Sundays earlier. Only one other meeting had occurred in the meantime. In 1917 that hardly allowed time to collect a group with a national call to comrades. Most of the eleven people eventually charged were at two or all three of those meetings. That repeated attendance corroborates the absence of an influx of more committed or sophisticated anarchists who pursued politics as their first priority. The numbers at the corner also never swelled significantly over the course of the three evangelical meetings. And, regardless of his pretensions, Giuliani was not a figure who attracted much attention outside his Italian ministries in the Third Ward and in West Allis, on Milwaukee's west side.

The police still were in the neighborhood late that Sunday evening, long after dark. As they broke open doors or gained entry by banging and yelling, they met neither assistance nor active resistance. From the perspective of the anti-Italian *Milwaukee Sentinel*, which drew its version from the police, the neighborhood simply fell silent. "Late into the night practically the entire detective force followed clews and rumors that led them through the heart of the Bay View Italian settlement, but everywhere they went there was silence. Men and women routed out of bed professed to know nothing of the battle or of any one connected with it," the newspaper told its readers.[138] The entire police department again had not a single Italian speaker in its ranks, which surely contributed to the sense of silence. Other than in broken phrases, colony residents and the police generally could not speak to each other. But the Italians also were closing ranks. Isolated they may have been, and probably not altogether in sympathy with those among them who had started the shooting. Still, the habitués of the colony deflected police questioning with shrugged shoulders and helpless expressions. For the police, they knew nothing.

Now, when a reporter from the more sympathetic *Milwaukee Leader* approached the following day, many were happy to speak to him, and they seemed then to know a good deal about the principals in the shooting. The reporter found only one—John Travis, the Italian barber with an anglicized name—who was willing to be named, but he encountered many "others who were eager to give their version of the happenings Sunday."[139] To a person, these laid the blame for the disturbance entirely on Giuliani. Speaking to an outsider, as even the *Leader*'s sympathetic reporter was, they did not blame those in the neighborhood or anyone who frequented the Circolo di Studi Sociali clubhouse. Adroitly, they also did not blame the police. A "heavy police guard" remained in the Italian Colony "to avoid further disturbances."[140]

The lack of information and cooperation did not stop the police from arresting perhaps seventeen Italians on Sunday and another dozen or more on Monday.[141] Presumably, the police applied the same criterion that they would apply a little more than two months later, after the bomb tragedy: Italians who could not explain themselves to the satisfaction of a patrolman went to jail.[142] The Monday arrests included John Formaceo and two others whom the police seized at the morgue when John came to identify his brother Tony's body.[143] The police would not disclose the names of most of those arrested.[144] That was an important step in holding arrestees incommunicado because it discouraged inquiries from family members or, worse, lawyers; police officers could answer with the same unhelpful shrug of the shoulders they had gotten from the colony residents on Sunday night. By Wednesday, September 12, the police probably released most of those they arrested. District Attorney Winfred C. Zabel charged twelve people—eleven men and Maria Nardini—that day, and the police released three more who still remained in jail.[145] Releases went as unexplained as arrests.

During the searches, the police seized a tin sheet that hung on the door of the clubhouse, shot full of holes and surrounded by plastered wall and wood also well pocked with bullets.[146] Less ominously, detectives also "confiscated bundles of literature and posters which, according to the police, contain inflammatory and seditious sentiments" from the Circolo clubhouse.[147] Searching house to house, they seized guns, newspapers, IWW cards, letters, pamphlets, bullets, buttons, and even a "black robe" from trunks in bedrooms and kitchen tables.[148] These filled boxes.[149] The state introduced 129 seized books and pamphlets alone at trial (which the judge speedily received "for the purpose of throwing light, if any, on the subject of conspiracy").[150]

Throughout, the police had nary a search warrant, let alone a warrant for arrest.

While the police searched, confiscated, and arrested on Sunday evening, Giuliani reported to the central police station downtown to speak with Captain Jack Sullivan. That went well. Chief Janssen vouched for the reverend the next day, proclaiming, "So far as our information goes he is a good, courageous man and he has been doing much work where it was badly needed."[151]

For Giuliani, it had been a hard fourteen months. On July 23, 1916, Katherine gave birth at age forty-one to their first child, Waldo August Giuliani. It killed her. In an economical acknowledgment of her calling, her headstone read, "Ital. Missionary."[152] The former priest whose love of Katherine had caused him to renounce his vocation, his faith, and his country now was left alone to raise Waldo. This was a son he might have supposed just six years earlier he never would have. In an October 13, 1916, postcard thanking a member of his congregation, Giuliani added plaintively, "pray for us."[153]

In the year that followed, Giuliani buried his grief in work. In 1917 he still was just thirty-six years old. He had an intense sincerity that accompanied and fed his self-importance. Giuliani believed that people mattered. His mission in the Third Ward fed and clothed the needy. It offered English classes in the evenings for eager immigrants in his church and branch missions.[154] There is some irony in the fact that he and John LaDuca or, for that matter, the anarchists all were in the Italian Colony for the same basic reason: to reach and lift up an isolated and struggling group of new immigrants. All wanted their commitment, their voices and feet. The zeal of both Giuliani and his competitors was undeniable.

So was the gulf between a LaDuca and a Giuliani, though. LaDuca relied on his listeners' disaffection for the America they found, which differed dramatically from the America they had imagined. Giuliani relied on a showy display of American patriotism and pride as a means of defeating the suspicion and prejudice he faced as an Italian immigrant. Like many immigrants, he was eager to prove himself more American than an American—thus hoping to win acceptance. His belief that he could reach and teach even those of his newly arrived countrymen who led the most hardscrabble lives there in the shadows of the rolling mill drove Giuliani to return to Bay View those three Sundays in a row. There was self-importance, too. While his assistant, Maud Richter, estimated the crowd at the first gathering on August 26 at twenty or twenty-five, Giuliani grandiosely put it at about a hundred.[155]

Zabel, the district attorney, took charge personally of the investigation and prosecution. The politician in him sniffed immediately the publicity that a trial of Italian "anarchists" would bring that fall, as the war effort expanded sharply and as the establishment newspapers each week carried stories of new outrages linked to

Wobblies and anarchists or of their mass arrest. Zabel could not have known it, but the Russian revolution, too, was just more than one month away when the police and the district attorney set out to punish the bumptious Italians for the shooting in Bay View. He would have his publicity.

First, the police would have their way. The *Milwaukee Sentinel* spoke euphemistically of a "rigid"[156] investigation the evening after the shooting: for the first time that autumn, police were applying the third degree to the three dozen or so they held after the mass arrests. A few federal agents joined too, as the police "grilled" thirty-five witnesses on Monday. Expansively, and with a suggestion of the aggressiveness of police techniques, Captain Jack Sullivan puffed, "All of the men we are now holding admit being anarchists and several of them openly boasted of not having registered."[157] Monday passed into Tuesday. Those under arrest remained incommunicado. The police released no names, so family members or friends could only wonder about the wellbeing of the missing men from the Italian Colony. Most were not foolhardy enough to make inquiry at the police department. After all, Formaceo's brother had done no more than appear at the county morgue to identify Tony's body; the police needed no better reason to arrest him and his two companions as well. Word of that should have passed quickly through the colony, and it is unlikely that many others tempted fate by presenting themselves to the police with demands to know what had become of a husband or brother.

By Wednesday morning, up to fifteen were ready for the district attorney's personal examination. The police marched them one short block west on Oneida Street, down a gentle hill to the district attorney's office in City Hall. Zabel had summoned the willing Giuliani to play his second role in the affair (in addition to victim). He would serve as interpreter during Zabel's interviews.[158] This invitation fed again Giuliani's belief in his critical importance in the course of local events. As someone eager to prove his patriotic devotion and love of lawfulness too, Giuliani seized the chance to interpret on behalf of the district attorney. For his part, Zabel was a wily and aggressive prosecutor. He could rely on Giuliani's sympathies and on his personal stake in the events at issue to produce translations that tilted toward what Zabel wanted to hear. Giuliani naively may not have thought about the conflict of interests in his roles as victim and interpreter, which robbed him of neutrality. He had been asked to help, he wanted to help, and he was an important personage: he alone could understand both the English and the Italian speakers and ensure that each understood the other. Zabel exploited all of this personal interest and pride.

Once the fifteen exhausted arrestees had shuffled into the offices of the district attorney, Zabel and Detective Wesolowski took at least six of them, one at a time, into Zabel's private office. There they met Zabel, Giuliani, and a shorthand reporter. With a show of officious authority, Zabel administered an oath to each man and began questioning him, with no warning of the privilege against self-incrimination. This was a sham. Although Zabel as a lawyer also was a notary public and had statutory authority to administer an oath, he could do so only in proceedings for which a statute allowed or required an oath. Wisconsin statutes made no provision for questioning suspects under oath in the chambers of a prosecutor, outside proceedings under judicial control and without an opportunity to secure a lawyer. Albeit gently, the Wisconsin Supreme Court later would chide Zabel for this gambit and its "idle ceremony" of an oath.[159] The local bar also remembered the episode, to Zabel's discredit. One lawyer and political opponent of Zabel six years later derided Zabel's questioning as "star chamber proceedings" and recalled that the Wisconsin Supreme Court had held against the practice.[160]

The nearly illiterate Italians subjected to this procedure of course had no idea that it was lawless.[161] They had been in custody for two, possibly almost three, days without any charge. They had appeared before no judge, seen no lawyer, and heard from no family or friend. They had no way to know how long their detention would continue. Sleep surely had been difficult and brief, if the police had allowed it at all. Officers had applied the third degree. Now an elected official, a high one for all the prisoners knew, stared at them with his piercing eyes, his sharp, almost effeminate, features, and his thick hair combed backward in a fussy pompadour. Zabel questioned them peremptorily at best; he liked to bully by yelling.[162] They had only their principal accuser, Giuliani, through whom to make themselves heard. Not surprisingly, Bianchi, Lilli, Pantaleoni, Pasquale Nardini, and the Fratesi brothers later disputed much of what Giuliani attributed to them in that September 12 session in Zabel's office.[163]

Today we cannot know how fairly Giuliani translated. Even then, Zabel coyly avoided that question, pleading, "I do not understand Italian."[164] But another man's absence from the trial may tell something. That man was Frank Carchidi, the self-loathing wheedler who had gained favors from the police by volunteering to sit in city jail cells next to other Italians for the purpose of repeating to the police—or claiming to repeat—their unguarded words. Although the evidence is not at all clear, he probably served that undercover informant's role during the days immediately following the September 9 shooting.[165] Assuming that he did, the state's decision not to call him as a witness at trial meant one of two things.

Either his secret role was ongoing at the time of trial and too important to sacrifice by revealing it to the defendants and the public, or he had heard nothing from the eleven on trial so incriminating that it was worth repeating to a jury. The first possibility is real. The trial of the eleven Bay View defendants began days after the November 24 bombing while the police still were fervently seeking the culprit or culprits in that disaster and arresting Italians willy-nilly.

But the second possibility also is real. And Zabel, at the time he prosecuted the eleven, had no reason to believe that he ever would have a chance to charge the November 24 bomber. Instead, he sought convictions of the eleven he had in hand. Yet Carchidi made no appearance in the roughly two weeks of trial during the advent season. He would appear in the Italians' case only much later, after the trial.

Zabel filed his criminal complaint against twelve of the Italians the afternoon of September 12, "after a morning spent in questioning all of the men taken in the police drag net following the riot."[166] Marinelli's death not three days later would reduce the number to eleven.

A close reader of the newspapers the day Zabel filed the complaint would have spied an omen. A Milwaukee jury had convicted a young Italian in another murder case after twenty minutes of deliberation and a trial that took less than seven hours in total, lunch included. The man would go to prison for life. It was "one of the shortest murder trials in the history of Milwaukee County."[167]

So the case of eleven accused Italians began as another Italian's ended.

5

Chaos

From the start, the mainstream newspapers labeled the eleven Italian defendants "anarchists," mostly as if there were no question about it.[1] The local judiciary probably viewed them the same way. When these eleven made their initial appearances in district court, which handled preliminary matters in felony cases before shifting defendants to municipal court for trial, the judge set extraordinarily high bail. Bianchi, Lilli, and Vincenzo Fratesi all faced the impossible task of raising $3,000. The judge imposed $2,000 bail on each of the eight others.[2] In today's dollars, that would be more than $35,750. For immigrant wage laborers, the number might as well have been $1 million. All eleven would sit in jail awaiting trial, unable to make bail. That plainly is what the judge intended.

After setting bail, the court adjourned the cases for two weeks, until September 28.[3] Nothing much would happen that day in the cases of the eleven; the court would delay their preliminary hearings again for about two weeks, until October 15.[4] But just ninety miles south, in Chicago, something big happened the day of that late-September court appearance that would prove an unfortunate coincidence for the eleven Milwaukee Italians.

On September 28, 1917, the federal government announced the indictment of 166 leaders and members of the IWW in Chicago.[5] The indictment inspired banner headlines. "U.S. HURLS TON OF EVIDENCE AT I.W.W.," Milwaukee's most widely circulated morning paper screamed. In type not much smaller, the sub-headline explained, "*Charge 150 with U.S. Conspiracy.*"[6] The defendants included the famous, or infamous, former chief of the Western Federation of Miners, William D. "Big Bill" Haywood. The indictment also named another trophy defendant: the prominent Elizabeth Gurley Flynn—"known as 'Princess of the Reds,'" the *Milwaukee Daily News* added breathlessly about the only woman indicted.[7] And of course, the IWW indictment included Italians. Carlo Tresca (Gurley Flynn's lover and a well-known anarchist), Arturo Giovannitti, and John Baldazza merited mention in Milwaukee.[8] The *New York Times* called Tresca "the

Italian leader" of the IWW and "one of the most rabid of the I.W.W. trouble makers."[9] Giovannitti ("another Italian I.W.W. agitator of almost equal prominence") was the IWW leader whom the *Times* had on September 10 linked—speculatively—to Milwaukee's Tony Formaceo and August Marinelli.[10] He was a poet of sorts and cut an interesting figure—a smooth-skinned, rotund little man with jet-black hair brushed straight back, given to windsor knots for his ties.[11] In all, perhaps more than half of the Chicago defendants were foreign-born, and most of those were not citizens. Most of the IWW members the government viewed, interchangeably, as anarchists.[12]

This confluence of events made the case of the eleven Bay View Italians seem of a piece with the massive IWW federal indictment, although that appearance was both accidental and misleading. A coordinated series of federal raids across the nation on September 5, in as many as fifty cities and towns (including Milwaukee) just four days before the Bay View disturbance, had led to the Chicago indictment.[13] The *New York Times* supposed that the documentary mass presented to the grand jury "was of such a volume as actually to weigh a ton or more,"[14] although the same newspaper wrote the very next day without a hint of irony that "the indictments were returned before half the evidence seized in recent raids on I.W.W. headquarters had been examined."[15] Whatever the precise volume and however haphazardly the evidence was considered before the indictments were handed down, federal agents had seized vast quantities of literature and propaganda from local IWW headquarters across the country.[16] Agents searched not just IWW offices. They raided the homes of Big Bill Haywood and others in Chicago and the shared Chicago headquarters of the Socialist Party and the *American Socialist* newspaper.[17] The Milwaukee newspapers provided an echo of these raids just days later when they recounted the police seizures from the Circolo clubhouse and colony homes in Bay View.

There was at least one other apparent similarity between the federal raids on September 5 and the Bay View searches four days later: official contempt for the search-and-seizure limitations of the Fourth Amendment. A federal appellate court later would find that the affidavits supporting the nationwide IWW search warrants failed to describe specifically the property subject to seizure, offering instead only "reference to its general character."[18] The Fourth Amendment expressly requires that search warrants particularly describe places to be searched and things to be seized so that law enforcers are not left to rummage where they will and take whatever seems to them interesting. Lax limits on police searches leave the citizenry's privacy to a government official's whim and smacks of the general warrants and writs of assistance that England used against the colonists. The experience with those writs of assistance helped shape the protections of the Fourth Amendment.[19] But the September 5 raids were just one example of the judicial temptation to allow the government's agents ample room to snoop. More striking still, the September 5 warrant applications "failed to state any facts from which the magistrates could determine the existence of probable cause," the U.S. Court of Appeals in Chicago eventually conceded.[20] The federal appellate court concluded that the searches were grossly illegal, unconstitutional. But that transgression would prove no obstacle to the government's efforts.

The September 5 national raids received wide publicity, so regular readers of the newspapers in Milwaukee were well aware of the raids in their hometown and across the Midwest and the West. When the next morning broke, the banner headline on the major newspaper marched the width of the page in type twice the height of the newspaper's name in the masthead. "NATION-WIDE RAID MADE ON I.W.W.," it bellowed.[21] The *Milwaukee Sentinel*'s editors gave much of the front page to the general topic, with four separate stories headlined there. After all, three of the raids happened right in Milwaukee. At 3 p.m. on Wednesday, September 5, federal agents searched three separate IWW offices in the city on search warrants that the local federal judge had issued as part of the national sweep.[22] The *Sentinel* reported darkly that "extremist literature" had been collected in the Milwaukee IWW offices and gave examples covering an eye-popping range: politics ("Sabotage," by Elizabeth Gurley Flynn and Emily Pouget); religion ("Anti-Catholic works and pamphlets," a particularly volatile accusation in heavily Roman Catholic Milwaukee); titillation ("Sex Science," a series of pamphlets); and even the unintentionally comedic ("a number of books marked 'Discarded from the public library'").[23] Worse, at least one Milwaukee IWW office reportedly contained the butt ends of billiard and pool cues, wrapped with tape "for better grip."[24] The newspaper also tantalized readers with the story that the lowlifes and labor agitators who "lounged" in the IWW offices had received a tip-off an hour before the raids, although the article hastened to assure readers that any such tip did not come from government ranks (from where else might it have come?). A local federal agent promised an investigation into the suspected leak or tip.[25]

Then the charges in Chicago followed later that month: seditious conspiracy and four other conspiracy counts.[26] So, too, in Milwaukee. Conspiracy eventually would be Zabel's theory in binding together the eleven Italians he charged during the course of the unfolding IWW events. However inaccurately, the *New York Times* forged the final supposed link between the federal IWW raids and the Bay View uprising. It called the September 9 shooting incident an "I.W.W. Riot" and suggested (fancifully, for all that appears) the connection to Giovannitti.[27]

This sharp reminder of anarchists in Chicago, Milwaukee, and several western cities added to the dominant worry that autumn, the war engulfing Europe. Day after day, as Christmas 1917 approached, the newspapers brought fretful news. "President Can End War, Says German Socialist Leader"; "Germans Are Held in Verdun Attack"; "*War Reports*" (a regular front-page feature); "Sixty-Three of U.S. Ship Crew Missing"; "Italians in Drive Smash Enemy Lines"; "Enemy Kills Women, Say Rome Cables"; "U.S. Wants 800 Navy Men from Milwaukee"; "BARE NEW GERMAN PLOT AGAINST U.S."; and so on, ceaselessly.[28]

In the nineteen months of its involvement in World War I, the United States lost 116,500 men in combat and noncombat deaths. By comparison, it took more than eleven years in Vietnam for just about half that number, roughly 58,000 American soldiers, to die. The first three years of the Iraq War—a period almost twice America's total involvement in World War I—resulted in fewer than 2,500 American military deaths.[29] The numbers are all the more dramatic in the context of the population of the United States: about 103 million on July 1, 1917, and nearly 300 million by March 2006, three years after the start of the Iraq War.[30] As a percentage of population, then, an equivalent loss would have been 348,000 American deaths in the first year and a half of the Iraq War. In part because of World War I, the population of the United States actually fell by about sixty thousand persons between July 1, 1917, and June 30, 1918.[31]

Faced with this staggering carnage, Americans in the main rallied patriotically. Politicians' behavior offers one imprecise but interesting measure of the public mood. On October 4, 1917, the *Milwaukee Daily News* reported that the U.S. Senate had approved an urgent appropriation of $7 billion to bolster the war fund. "The measure is said to be the greatest of the kind in the history of any government," the paper reported. That was no exaggeration: the equivalent today would be $125.1 billion. How thoughtful were the deliberations for such a huge expenditure? The *Daily News* claimed that the Senate approved the conference report in three minutes.[32] If any significant portion of the American electorate objected, the newspapers later offered no hint.

Rather, when a lone U.S. senator, Wisconsin's own Robert Marion La Follette, dared to oppose the American war effort, it was he who endured intense public outrage and the scorn of other politicians. On the very day that the eleven Italians in Milwaukee appeared again in court for a preliminary hearing, former president Theodore Roosevelt spoke at Lakeside Auditorium in Racine, little more than thirty miles south of Milwaukee on Lake Michigan. He spoke about the war, and the cause was personal. Roosevelt himself was a warrior, having served famously in the Spanish-American War. And three of his sons would serve in World

War I—the youngest, Quentin, giving his life the following year. With Roosevelt whipping them on, a crowd of four thousand people noisily demanded Senator La Follette's resignation. "Col. Roosevelt did not mince words in speaking of Senator La Follette," the *Milwaukee Free Press* reported. "He declared that any American who upholds Germany in any manner on the sinking of the Lusitania is a traitor to this country and that La Follette occupies the same position in this war as did the copperhead in the civil war [referring here to northern Democrats who, between 1860 and 1864, sought to appease the South or make peace with the Confederacy]. He said that La Follette and his allies in the I.W.W. were the most sinister foes of democracy in the United States and he denounced La Follette in the name of liberty loving people of the United States."[33] For good measure, Roosevelt added that he wished he could send La Follette and other copperheads to Germany where the senator might enter the Reichstag, as he was out of place in the U.S. Senate.[34] This was a former president of the United States speaking of a sitting U.S. senator—and both men had their roots in the progressive wing of the Republican Party.[35]

Just five years earlier in Milwaukee, a crackpot had shot Teddy Roosevelt as he arrived to give a speech there. But no one shot at Roosevelt in Racine in 1917. Quite the contrary. He had the crowd with his searing denunciation of La Follette.

To the great mass of Americans living with the dread of the war and the threat of its personal toll on their families, anarchists and antiwar voices indeed seemed disloyal if not dangerous, an insult added to the war's horrific injuries. Americans reacted resentfully, even angrily. Citizens were sacrificing, often in very personal ways. Dissenters and self-described pacifists not only resisted personal sacrifice, it seemed to most Americans, but attacked the very causes that most thought noble and worthy of their sacrifice.

That autumn brought other reminders to feed the anger and resentment. Facing a desperate threat from the central powers in Europe and Asia, the country also seemed under attack from within by determined radicals and agitators, generally foreign-born, who often tossed bombs if the newspapers had it right. With the benefit of thirty years' hindsight, one reporter much later distilled the situation calmly. In 1914 "war had broken out in Europe and Milwaukee, with its large German population, was tense," he conceded. Then he added, "There also was a determined opposition to the draft by a segment of the Italian population."[36]

Then it got worse. The three months between summer and year-end 1917 also saw the revolution in Russia. Bolsheviks overthrew the tsar's government that autumn. Events in Petrograd and elsewhere moved very quickly in the last week of October and the first week of November. These were "ten days that shook the world," as the sympathetic American journalist John Reed named his book on the revolution two years later. Tsar Nicholas II had agreed earlier to a provisional government, in the hope of avoiding the complete collapse of his family's dynasty. But that October ended his hope. The Bolsheviks would murder the tsar and his family the following July. Communists now led a vast country.

The burghers of Milwaukee, like other Americans in thousands of cities, villages, and farmsteads, could have been forgiven for believing that the whole world was collapsing in chaos, their genuine personal sacrifice notwithstanding. At home, from the Midwest to the Pacific Northwest, police and federal agents were arresting dozens or even hundreds of radicals at a time. Many of them were disloyal foreigners. To native-born Americans, it seemed the country suddenly was awash in them, drowning. They were Wobblies or anarchists or socialists — whatever the fuzzy lines that separated those groups, most Americans knew little of these and cared less. The police were not perceptibly winning the fight, either, for bomb blasts were frequent in the nation's cities. Still other bombs were discovered in the nick of time.

And there Milwaukee sat, near the center of domestic radicalism, Chicago. A generation later, one of that city's wary lovers would call Chicago the "most radical of all American cities: Gene Debs' town, Big Bill Haywood's town, the One-Big-Union town."[37] But, to the writer Nelson Algren, it also was a city of "bone-deep grudges," including the "big deep grudge cast by the four standing in white muslin robes, hands cuffed behind, at the gallows' head. For the hope of the eight-hour day."[38] Algren wrote, of course, of Haymarket Square.

Now, in 1917, Chicago's grudge was against the 166 indicted IWW members, many of them anarchists like their forebears at Haymarket a generation earlier. With the arrest of more than 150 of the indicted IWW members and sympathizers, Assistant Attorney General William C. Fitts, the ambitious, young John E. Hoover (or J. Edgar, as he preferred), and the U.S. district attorney in Chicago got down to the business of trial preparation.[39]

In the assigned branch of the U.S. District Court sat one of America's most colorful federal judges, Kenesaw Mountain Landis.[40] With a face as craggy as his name, under a thick, weedy outcropping of white hair, Judge Landis came straight out of central casting for the role of no-nonsense judge. In fact, he had played a judge in an early federal government movie, *The Immigrant* (not to be confused with the Charlie Chaplin movie of the same name that followed in 1917).[41] His parents had named him for the place at which his father was wounded in the Civil War. As the story went, his wounded father, Dr. Abraham Landis, arrived home from the war on the very day of his son's birth, November 20, 1863.[42]

If Americans see the iconic figure of Justice as a blindfolded woman holding carefully aloft in her left hand a delicately balanced scale, Judge Landis evinced throughout his judicial career as much interest in the less noticed large sword that the serene woman usually holds in her right hand. Judge Landis coincidentally would be the one to sentence Victor Berger in 1919 for violation of the Espionage Act. Later, in a speech to an American Legion post, the judge railed, "It was my great disappointment to give Berger only 20 years in Leavenworth. . . . I believe the law should have enabled me to have him lined up against the wall and shot."[43]

Not one to miss an opportunity for public acclaim, Landis seized the IWW case with gusto. As the late months of 1917 yielded to the new year, Judge Landis made preparations for the nation's first mass trial in civilian courts.

More than 110 defendants initially would be packed into one courtroom in Chicago's grand old federal courthouse. Even the arraignment, normally a dry affair at which defendants enter simple not-guilty pleas after learning formally of the charges against them, got interesting: one of the defense lawyers, George F. Vanderveer of New York, was carrying a revolver in his hip pocket as he entered the courtroom. When Judge Landis's bailiff accosted him about it, Vanderveer blustered, "Certainly I have a gun. I'm George Vanderveer, one of the attorneys for the defense," as if that ought to settle the matter. Visibly unmoved, the bailiff relieved Vanderveer of the gun and remarked tartly, "Well, you can't carry a gun into the courtroom, no matter who you are."[44]

The trial itself would run four full months and more, from April to mid-August 1918.[45] The *New York Times* called it "one of the longest criminal cases on record in this country" and did not suggest any case that might have run longer.[46] In the end, the IWW trial produced thirty thousand pages of transcript.[47] Landis submitted four separate conspiracy charges in the indictment to the jury.[48]

After four months of evidence against ninety-seven remaining defendants,[49] the jurors deliberated for all of sixty-five minutes. Then they convicted everyone of everything.[50] Their efforts had amounted to about forty seconds of deliberation for each defendant. They were done and home comfortably for dinner the day they heard closing arguments.

The IWW had predicted the outcome. During the trial, *The Industrial Worker* printed an article addressed to the "gentlemen of the prosecution":

> Every morning now our boys file into your court to listen to the droning mockery of your justice. In a few more weeks—perhaps in a few more days—the farce will be over and we shall hear the verdict. What will it be?

It is a bitter thought that the fate of our superb organization now lies in the hands of one Judge and twelve jurymen and a bitter and vindictive prosecutor in a courtroom in Chicago.

It is one of the ironical twists of the insane present, but it is true. And we of the I.W.W. have no illusions about that court. We have no faith in the wisdom of its verdict.

We do not expect justice.[51]

The much smaller group of suspected anarchists in Milwaukee likely did not expect it, either, even before November 24, 1917. That day, of course, brought young Sam Mazzone and his package to Milwaukee's central police station.

With that package, violent anarchism on a national scale had blown into town. Foreigners in general, and Italians specifically, were to blame. After months of war abroad and chaos at home, fear, anger, and plain hatred were a combustible mixture, and Milwaukee was ready to explode. As the city awoke at this volatile moment on Sunday morning, November 25, the trial of the eleven Bay View "anarchists" was but three days away.

Even apart from the police funerals, grief, and tumult in Milwaukee, those three days were eventful elsewhere. Another one hundred suspected Italian anarchists were arrested in Seattle, and authorities simultaneously seized more anarchist literature in Spokane, Portland, and Tacoma on November 28. That was the very day the Milwaukee eleven were to face trial.[52]

6

Of Counsel

The most flamboyant and possibly the most self-important of the lawyers in the trial of the eleven accused Milwaukee anarchists was pressed for time and distracted. William Benjamin Rubin still was in Buffalo, New York, on Wednesday, November 28.[1] The judge was impatient and insistent that the trial move forward. Indeed, Bill Rubin in a sense was AWOL: he was not in court the day trial was to begin and had not arranged an adjournment in advance.

But the American Federation of Labor was holding a convention in Buffalo. Rubin hardly could miss it. An assiduous pursuer of AFL leader Samuel Gompers, Rubin in the end would serve twenty-five years as outside counsel for the AFL.[2] Understanding the trial that Rubin was about to undertake, and the cracks and flaws in American justice that it would reveal at a microscopic level, means knowing something of Rubin himself and of his principal antagonist, District Attorney Winfred Zabel. The defendants, like the countless others before and after them, in the end were not true players in the contest that concerned them. They were the objects with which the contestants played—the ball, not the ballplayers. The players were unmistakable: the competing lawyers and the judge.

Each of the principal lawyers had less colorful colleagues at his side. At the defense table, Tom Leahy represented one of the eleven defendants, Pietro Bianchi. Leahy was a competent and curmudgeonly Irish lawyer,[3] obstinate enough never to drive again after his first experience behind the wheel of an automobile led to an unhappy few moments of lurching and careening around the block.[4]

Zabel's second at the prosecution table, Assistant District Attorney Frederick F. Groelle, was an itinerant practitioner whose stint in the Milwaukee County District Attorney's office was short. He would have something shocking to say almost five years later, but his role at trial was limited to supporting his boss and shepherding the lesser witnesses through their stories.

Rubin and Zabel claimed the spotlight. As 1917 drew to a close, Rubin was nearing the top of his game professionally. He was forty-four years old. With his wavy brown hair and his soft face, corners of his mouth upturned, he retained a boyish, mischievous look. He was putty-sculpted about right to be a criminal defense lawyer. Always clean-shaven under the crest of unruly hair, he appeared an imp trying to sneak in as a cherub. Six feet tall and pudgy, Rubin's extra weight enlarged his physical appearance. He had courtroom presence. That presence he amplified frequently with bombast and self-aggrandizement. He was not exactly a natty dresser but not rumpled, either. Rubin wore a vest with his business suits and kept his black dress shoes polished. In the summer, he favored a straw boater's hat. Photographs in later years show him with a pocket square peeking neatly from his suit coat breast pocket.

Bill Rubin was an intemperate, emotional man. In late October, he had dashed off a letter to the judge who was presiding over the case of the Bay View Italians. He dictated the letter in a fit over a goading comment that Win Zabel had made in court. Zabel—who made an art of getting Rubin's goat—had dropped an aside that Rubin took as calling into question his son Abner's courage and patriotism as America was entering World War I. Rubin exploded:

My dear Judge:—

Mr. Zabel, in open court this morning, to feed an imaginary grudge, endeavored, by improper remarks, to slander my son, although the boy's age is well known to him.

As it happened, just before I went to you in Court this morning, I received a letter from my boy, and I have had a copy of it stricken off so that you may read it. I am also sending you a copy of my reply, which had been written prior to my leaving for court this morning. These letters speak for themselves.

I regret that it is necessary for me thus to disclose my private correspondence to refute remarks which were made in court this morning, but in justice to my son, I am sending these copies to you.

Respectfully yours,
W. B. Rubin

P.S. The only son of my brother, J. H. Rubin, has enlisted, holds a lieutenancy, and is now at Waco, Texas. Charles Rubin, who is the son of my other brother and within the age limit for service, volunteered, but was rejected because of his eyesight.

W.B.R.[5]

The letter was quintessential Rubin. Pompous and sputtering with self-righteous anger, which Rubin sought to mask as mere desire to defend his son, the letter made the necessary assumption that Rubin (and his son) were of sufficient importance that it would be appropriate and edifying for the judge to have copies of letters exchanged between father and young Abner, studying at Cornell University.

November then had been hectic for Bill Rubin. An important client, the International Molders Union, had run into some potential trouble with the U.S. Department of Justice. By November 2, Rubin had enlisted the help of his friend John P. Frey, the editor of the *International Molders' Journal* who eventually would head the AFL Metal Trades department, in begging off court dates before Judge Backus early that month.[6] Rubin traveled to New York City on a "wild chase" and then back home.[7] He hoped to be able to board a train again for the Buffalo convention by Friday, November 23.[8] As late as the day before, though, his plans remained in flux. But he would go. On Friday he dashed a hurried note to his nephew in Chicago canceling tentative plans there for Sunday; it was "all aboard" to Buffalo.[9] For all his correspondence and travels reveal in the very month the defendants were to go to trial, Rubin seems to have directed little of his energy to what he described as "the Italian Case."[10]

Had they any expectations or means by which to gauge a lawyer's efforts, his clients well might have been disappointed. Rubin represented no fewer than ten of the jailed Italians whose liberty was in peril for thirty years. Today, representing ten people in a criminal case would be unthinkable for an American lawyer. Indeed, representing two usually would. With two or more clients, the lawyer would find that the duty of loyalty to one client almost surely would clash with the same duty to another client. One client might have an opportunity to gain advantage by testifying for the prosecution against another. Or one might intend to accuse another in the defense case. At a minimum, the defense of one might require assigning some blame to another at trial, through cross-examination, defense witnesses, or both. But until the middle or late decades of the twentieth century, courts and bar associations generally left clients and lawyers to assess and accept those potential or actual conflicts of interest if they wished.

And if in 1917 ten defendants in the same case wanted Rubin, that was no surprise. At the time, a criminal defendant in Milwaukee likely would find his way to Rubin's office. Born in September 1873 in Borispol, Russia, Rubin had come to America at age nine, a Russian Jewish émigré like Emma Goldman and at about the same time. Unlike Goldman, though, Rubin was the son of prosperous merchants.[11] The Rubin family settled in Milwaukee, where young Bill did well in school. He breezed through old East High School (later Riverside High School) in just two years.[12] By age twenty-two, he had graduated from the University of Michigan with a law degree after abandoning civil engineering at the University of Wisconsin on the suggestion of an engineering professor who noted Rubin's talent at debate.[13] Beginning a law practice at twenty-two was not bad for a young man who had arrived thirteen years earlier speaking only Russian. Rubin returned from Ann Arbor to set up shop in Milwaukee in 1896.

He married Sonia Mesirow of Chicago in 1897, not long after opening his law office.[14] She would bring him his only child, the future Cornell student Abner Joseph Rubin, on October 27, 1898.[15] But Sonia would die young in April 1915. Rubin seems to have felt her death deeply. Writing more than two years later to Abner and to Sonia's niece, Rubin sounded lovelorn.[16] A short, failed marriage followed in 1925.[17] Ten years after that, Rubin married for the third time at age sixty-two, to Josephine Geraghty, a Milwaukee French teacher. That marriage lasted until his death.

From the beginning, Rubin's law practice thrived. His first and dearest professional love was labor. Rubin's core sympathies were with working people, and he sought to establish himself not only as a union lawyer but as a strategist and public advocate for the labor cause. Just ten years into law practice, a significant case on behalf of the Iron Molders Union helped him gain a national reputation in organized-labor circles. The union and four locals took on a huge nearby manufacturer, the Allis-Chalmers Company. As employers usually did, the company sought an injunction against the strikers that would have gutted the union's ability to urge replacement workers to honor the strike. Although Rubin lost in the federal district court in Milwaukee, the federal court of appeals in Chicago trimmed the injunction to allow some room for speech and persuasion by striking workers.[18] A lawful noisy picket line—for that matter, a lawful picket line at all—was a rarity then, and Rubin won that liberty for the strikers. His star was on the rise. He would go on to represent the Michigan, Wisconsin, Illinois, and Chicago Federations of Labor, steelworkers in the big strike in Pennsylvania in 1919, and Actors' Equity during its 1919 New York strike, among others.[19]

Along the way, Rubin became impressed with his own importance to the labor movement. Others may not have ranked him quite as highly as he esteemed himself. Even by conventions of polite correspondence at the time, his letters to Samuel Gompers were fawning and often puffed with unsolicited advice. They were melodramatically conspiratorial at times. "My dear Mr. Gompers," Rubin began unfailingly, and he always ended, "yours respectfully" after flowery assurances of his regards for Gompers's family. In between, the busy Gompers might find two, three, or even more typewritten pages of detailed reporting on Rubin's interactions with those in the labor movement's ranks, always with a self-serving slant and usually with tactical suggestions that Rubin plainly regarded as sage. Sometimes Rubin urged confidentiality or even designated his words superfluously as "not for publication."[20] At least once, Rubin managed in a single parenthetical comment to sound both pathetic and peevish: "(I told Nockels to convey certain information to you in Minneapolis, showing you that I am on the job all the time, but which was disregarded by you at that time)."[21]

When Gompers replied in writing at all, his responses usually were brief—all business, even curt. One unusually long letter from Gompers in February 1913 upbraided Rubin like a schoolchild for misunderstanding the merits of an English worker's-compensation law.[22] Undeterred, Rubin regularly sought the intervention of Gompers and John Frey on behalf of Abner during his son's time at Cornell and urged Abner to curry the favor of such powerful men on his own.[23] His correspondence as a whole suggests someone enamored of power, convinced that the world worked by pulling strings, swelled with his own station in life, and a bit sycophantic with those he perceived as above his station.

While Rubin viewed "unionism" as his principal devotion, to a very large extent it was the defense of small-time thieves, grafters, brawlers, and the occasional murderer—in general, the scruffy raw material of Milwaukee's criminal courts— that allowed him to prosper.[24] Civil cases for personal injury supplemented the firm's income as well, and would increase over the years. But in 1917 Rubin's criminal defense business was staggering. A former district attorney estimated that summer, before the events in Bay View, that Rubin's firm commanded more than 95 percent of the criminal defense work in the county.[25] Even allowing for exaggeration (that percentage surely reflects some), unquestionably Rubin's criminal practice was busy. At the time of the eleven Italians' trial, the firm of Rubin, Fawcett & Dutcher had a letterhead listing seven lawyers—sizable for its day.[26] Although the letterhead suggested that he had two other nominal partners, Rubin's own financial statement in October 1918 revealed himself as "sole owner and proprietor" of the firm.[27] So, if Rubin had a burgeoning national reputation in labor circles, he also had a profitable reputation locally as a criminal defense lawyer. The labor movement was his passion. Criminal defense paid the bills.

Much later in life, he disclosed perhaps more than he knew in a quip at his eighty-first birthday party. "The biggest thing in my life has been that I loved my fellow men," he proposed with his usual self-flattery. "And I could see virtue in every client—and the greater the fee, the greater the virtue."[28] Whether intended or not, Rubin's quip revealed one conception of the practice of law: a way to make a living, not a calling. Much of Rubin's legal correspondence betrays the same limited inspiration, although his correspondence on labor issues was much more spirited.

As a midwestern lawyer bracketing the end of the nineteenth century, vitally interested in the struggles of organized labor but banking money mostly with criminal defense work, Rubin calls to mind a much more widely known lawyer, Clarence Darrow. With a practice based in Chicago, not in smaller Milwaukee, and an established range across the country when defending the accused, Darrow linked his passions to his courtroom battles much more coherently than did Rubin. He integrated his life's work with his day's work more successfully. Although Darrow, too, took clients to pay the bills from time to time, he made his cases his causes. Rubin himself showed real insight into Darrow years later, when he observed that the great Chicago lawyer did not argue to a jury for a client; he argued to a jury for something much bigger than one human being, with the hope that the jury's acceptance of that greater purpose would spare the man on trial. Darrow "never pleaded for an individual. His plea always was for a cause. Juries acquit men when they believe in their cause," Rubin wrote.[29]

Darrow and Rubin knew each other. In his usual grandiose way, Rubin spoke of Darrow as a "friend," for more than thirty years at that.[30] Privately, Darrow likely considered Rubin more an acquaintance. But the interests they shared and the similarity of their professional paths meant little surprise that Rubin had the honor of introducing Darrow as the speaker at a labor meeting in Milwaukee shortly after Darrow's acquittal in his first jury bribery trial in Los Angeles in 1912. In his windy way, Rubin toasted the evening's speaker:

> The man of tonight is a strong type of . . . brainy man. He, in defiance of all that has meant respect and honor and happiness and wealth, has dedicated his whole life, his glittering genius, his matchless eloquence to the cause of the down-trodden. . . .
>
> Let you and I do our share of honor to the living now. It cheers the heart on to battle for the great cause. It quickens the blood into golden deeds.
>
> Ladies and Gentlemen, it is our honor to listen to Clarence S. Darrow.[31]

Rather than the "down-trodden," Rubin's typed remarks that night originally were to assert only that Darrow had given his matchless eloquence and the rest "to the cause of organized labor." However, in a hurried change, Rubin scribbled in the broader—and still accurate—description of Darrow's work. Possibly the change came in recognition that Darrow's star was setting at that very moment with organized labor. The indictment of Darrow in Los Angeles followed the trial of the McNamara brothers, James B. and John J., two labor activists who had been charged with capital murder for the bombing of the *Los Angeles Times* building. Darrow had pled the men guilty during jury selection, saving their lives but costing him the trust and affection of organized labor.[32] He never fully regained either.

Given the sweep of Rubin's practice in the 1910s, it would have been almost odd had the poor Bay View Italians and their supporters not found him. Locally, he was to Darrow as his Milwaukee was to Darrow's Chicago—similar up to a point, but not so outsized or spectacular.

Perhaps it was no surprise, too, that Rubin found scant time for the Italians. He was elbowing his way into the senior ranks of the Milwaukee bar during the second decade of the twentieth century. As his law practice prospered and his reputation spread beyond the state, he faced the mixed blessing that successful lawyers eventually face: too many clients, all in need of too much. Rubin had six other lawyers in his office to share the load, but it was his reputation that drew the clients there. Criminal defense was then and is now a very personal business. Clients did not come to his firm; clients came to Rubin. It was in him that they invested their hope to avoid jail or prison. When it was time to pick a jury, or give an opening statement, or cross-examine a witness, or cap a closing argument with frothy oratory that would make the blood rise in a prosecutor's face, no lesser-known lawyer in the firm would do. Rubin had to be there, on his feet.

At the same time that his growing reputation as a lawyer required more of him than a day's work, that reputation also caused him to bend his mind to causes larger than a single client's case. Part of this was no more than Rubin's increasingly grand sense of self. If unions as far away as Pennsylvania and New York sought his services and most of the criminal defendants in his home city insisted on him, then surely his ideas on social issues or political questions of the day must be of similarly broad interest to the public. Rubin began to see himself as a man of many talents with much to say. The year before the Bay View trial, he authored a book, *The Toiler in Europe*, that purported to explore the psychology of working conditions in Europe. In 1921, he wrote a play (a "comedy drama"), *The Bolshevists*, attacking the new regime in Russia.[33] He appeared in debates, opposing capital punishment. Among many articles Rubin published, one, "The Kansas Anti-Strike Law," captures again something of his grandiosity: "I would rather suffer a lifelong perturbedness of freedom than have one day of peace in slavery. God forbid the oncoming of a dictatorship whether by a state of compulsory abstention or compulsory labor. I would rather face in mortal combat a thousand foes in life's struggle for freedom than have at my side a single aide of the modern bobbed haired, pantalooned peregrinator of 'thou shalt not' for the exercise of my own rational free will."[34]

As he grew older, Rubin's strongest interests would merge with politics. Although progressive, he avoided the extremes of American political thought. He supported America's entry into World War I. All in favor of unions, still Rubin swam in or near the mainstream; he had nothing but scorn for the IWW.[35] In private letters, he was critical of Victor Berger, both personally and politically.[36] Publicly, he moved stunningly from beatifying to vilifying Berger. Rubin spoke up for Berger when the postmaster general tried to silence him by revoking the second-class mailing permit of the *Leader*; then Rubin all but spat upon Berger after the socialist editor's federal conviction in Chicago for sedition.[37] He bragged when it suited him that Clarence Darrow was a friend, but he also viewed Darrow as having "spoken rather hastily and foolishly" in a Labor Day speech and told Gompers so.[38] In later years, Rubin would break from the ACLU, claiming that it was "giving comfort" to Nazis, Fascists, and Communists in the guise of protecting the Bill of Rights.[39]

By 1932 Rubin would find a man he could support wholeheartedly: Franklin Delano Roosevelt. He served as a Wisconsin delegate for Roosevelt at the 1932 and 1936 Democratic conventions. True to form, though, Rubin wanted something in return. Three times he maneuvered for an appointment to the federal bench, twice trying to reach Roosevelt in 1936 and 1939 and once President Harry S. Truman in 1949 (at the improbable age of seventy-six). All three times he was disappointed.[40]

There always was something of the outsider in Rubin. Subtly but unmistakably, polite society and Wisconsin's powerful excluded him time and again. His law practice was not the accepted stuff of advising corporations on issues of common stock, helping to organize new banks or civic associations, or counseling the city's business and political leaders in sundry other weighty affairs. It was grubbier. In criminal cases, he defended the guilty, the friendless, and, perhaps worst of all, the ridiculous. In civil cases, it was not much better. When a careless streetcar driver ran over an urchin scrambling across the tracks or a tired factory worker hopping off the car, Rubin represented the penniless parents or the newly crippled worker, not the streetcar company. The respectable corporate lawyers had that work sewed up, with the luxury of sending monthly statements that the streetcar company and other corporations paid promptly. As often as not, the urchin's parents or the crippled worker might learn of Rubin at the hospital from one of the hustlers who wandered in and out of his office daily, almost literally chasing ambulances when not loitering around his firm, and others that subsisted in part on personal-injury cases.[41]

Then there was the fact that Rubin, although intellectually agnostic and a free thinker, was Jewish as a matter of heritage and birth.[42] As a rule, corporate law and leadership positions in the Milwaukee and Wisconsin bar associations were the domain of Protestants. These men were Episcopalians or Presbyterians or Lutherans from the city's affluent areas or from its new, prosperous suburbs to the north on the bluffs along Lake Michigan. Criminal defense, plaintiffs' personal-injury work, and the law's other grubby pursuits the Brahmins left for the occasional Jewish or Roman Catholic lawyer. In his day, Bill Rubin was the best example in Milwaukee of the Jewish criminal defense lawyer.

Rubin's chief adversary in the Bay View Italians' case was another man not quite seated among the social elite, District Attorney Winfred C. Zabel. Like Rubin, Zabel had immigrated to the United States as a boy with his family, but from Dresden, Germany, rather than from Russia.[43] With his older brother, William, but otherwise traveling alone, Winfred came to the United States at the age of seven, in 1884. The boys' father, a silversmith, had died in Winfred's infancy. Their mother had left for America a few years after her husband's death with hopes of furthering her career as an opera singer. That dream withered. Clothilde Zabel then settled in Milwaukee and arranged for her sons to cross the Atlantic to join her.[44] So, after a significant period of separation for a young boy, he rejoined the only parent he ever had known.

Soon, though, Clothilde married a cold, stern pharmacist who had little use for Winfred and William.[45] Under the spur of this indifferent stepfather, Winfred sold newspapers on the street as a boy and later worked for two years in the offices of the *Milwaukee Sentinel*. He went through the city's public schools and then on to Spencerian Business College. From there, Winfred went off to Ohio Northern University in Ada, Ohio, to study law. Admitted to the Tennessee bar after graduation in the summer of 1900, he taught law for one semester in Tennessee before returning to practice in Milwaukee.[46] For ten years he worked in the private practice of law, gaining no great distinction.

Now, at age forty, Win Zabel still had his thick, light-brown pompadour atop delicate, bird-like features. Everything about Zabel's face looked sharp—not hard, but intricately carved, with fine edges along the ridge of his nose, pronounced cheekbones, thin but defined lips, and a gracefully pointed chin. His eyes added to the effect; they had an icy blue glint. His dress was dapper, if not downright dandy. The overall effect was arresting. Zabel was made for political life.

And that is what he craved. The year of his marriage, 1905, Zabel joined the Social Democratic Party.[47] After five more restless years edging toward politics, he announced his intentions in 1910. He would run for district attorney. Consistent with the progressive ideals of the Social Democrats, he seized upon two issues that Milwaukeeans of the day rightly understood as a clean-government platform. He wanted to crack down on loan-sharking (which the police had condoned unofficially). Most of all, he wanted to close the city's red-light district, which also enjoyed the wink of police and politicians alike.[48]

That district was a great financial boon. Much of the business community celebrated it and Milwaukee's wide-open image.[49] Following the lead of prosperous businessmen, the police and local officials not just tolerated the city's bawdy houses on and near River Street; they all but bumped hips with the denizens of those houses. As the sun rose each day over Lake Michigan, the houses of prostitution lay almost literally in the shadow of City Hall, which housed some of the county's criminal courts and the district attorney's office. Just a half block separated City Hall from the tawdriest saloons, flophouses, and brothels imaginable. And the central police station was only one more full block away from the moral muck along the east bank of the Milwaukee River. Politicians, police officers, and prostitutes—about one block apart physically, and closer than that in every other way. As one of his eulogists put it, Zabel "saw women, cadets, corrupt politicians, and crooked policemen plying nefarious harlotry under the very shadows of the temple of justice."[50] Zabel told Milwaukee voters in the autumn of 1910 that he would clean out all of it.

They believed him. Zabel took the district attorney's oath of office for the first time in January 1911. He did crack down on loan-sharking. Then, rejecting a written petition by "one thousand business men and merchants" to spare it, in the summer of 1912 Zabel "practically" wiped out the red-light district.[51]

The term "practically" is an important qualifier, for in truth, sex continued to sell as always. The prostitutes simply moved a few blocks to new quarters west across the river. But now, with the houses of ill repute clustered in or near the city's black neighborhoods, no one outside that powerless population much minded. The party had moved, but most of the revelers adjusted. Those in the know whispered that prominent police officials and a particular assistant district attorney continued to cavort drunkenly over card games with women whose virtue was as flimsy as their clothing, at this safe remove on the other side of the river.[52] According to a young man's sworn account, one memorable evening at an upstairs brothel at 12th and State Streets began with two police detectives and the assistant district attorney downing great quantities of "Dago Red," a basement wine from the Third Ward, while playing cards. The evening ended with the detectives— guns drawn—merrily scampering from room to room after giggling prostitutes. For his part, the prosecutor shouted profanely as he tried to rut with a tart named Edna on the same table lately laid for poker and lowball glasses of Dago Red.[53]

On the surface, though, it all looked a pretty good start for perhaps the first socialist ever elected district attorney in the United States.[54] The shenanigans were conveniently beyond sight of City Hall.

The fall of 1912 brought Zabel a flash of national attention. That October, small, chunky John Flammang Schrank shot Theodore Roosevelt outside the Hotel Gilpatrick in downtown Milwaukee, just west of the river. When the loopy Schrank tried to plead guilty without a lawyer, Zabel was the one who suggested instead a sanity examination.[55] Doctors decided that Schrank was insane, and he went to the state hospital, rather than to prison. In that day, this caused no great stir. Indeed, a Wisconsin Supreme Court justice years later commended Zabel's "efficient manner" in resolving the case without "the needless expense and newspaper publicity which often is so disparaging to the parties involved in such cases."[56] Zabel's actual motives are lost, but for a newly elected public official in the most visible case of his career, rejecting an easy guilty plea that would have made him a hero in favor of a methodical exploration of the accused's mental health was undeniably remarkable. After all, Schrank had meant to kill a popular former president of the United States (who then was running again for president as the Progressive Party candidate) and very nearly had succeeded.

Zabel's position was especially precarious because Wisconsin district attorneys served just two-year terms. He was running to keep his job at the same time he was contending with Schrank's attempted assassination of Roosevelt. Some of the business community likely remained sore over the relocation of the red-light district. In any event, Zabel lost his first bid for re-election in 1912 and returned to private practice.[57]

Five years later, though, as the Italians' trial approached in November 1917, Zabel not only had reclaimed his job as district attorney but had kept the office through a re-election campaign. Itchy to return to the prosecutor's office after his defeat, Zabel had run again at the first opportunity, in 1914. He regained the office. Zabel continued to improve his political agility and won again in 1916 and in 1918, avoiding the embarrassment of repeating as a short-time officeholder.

Along the way, Win Zabel had a falling out with the socialists. He blamed his disenchantment on the party's antiwar platform in the months before and after President Wilson led the nation into the thick of World War I. Perhaps. But Zabel did not resign from the Social Democratic Party until 1919, after the war was over.[58] Just possibly the rumors of corruption, overly aggressive tactics with witnesses and citizens, and unethical conduct with other lawyers that by then swirled in Zabel's wake left the party more disaffected with him than he with it. Whatever the reasons, Zabel the socialist nimbly declared himself a Republican not later than 1919.[59] The new Republican again won the 1920 election for district attorney.

This stint would last until 1922, when Zabel lost once more.[60] By that time, he had squandered the support of many in the bar and the business community by his unethical—maybe downright illegal—and arrogant behavior.

Already in 1914, the young reformer of 1910 was not who he had been. In this second stretch in office, Zabel made a hiring decision that looked initially no worse than common nepotism: he employed his older brother, William, as his chief deputy. If that seemed a reversion to the grimy government that the sanctimonious socialist usually railed against, it drew no great criticism. Soon, though, both Zabel brothers became connected with two slick local businessmen, Oscar Adler and Charles J. Fox, owner of the Gayety Theater burlesque house, in an enterprise called the Theatrical Curtain Advertising Association. The firm's ostensible purpose was to sell advertising for display on theater curtains, drawn before a show and during intermissions.

The Zabels were shareholders—and they took their shares for free, a "gift" from Adler.[61] Each received $1,000 in stock, a not insubstantial amount at the time. Indeed, according to the company bookkeeper, Will Zabel helped to set up the company,[62] keeping Win one step removed from potentially awkward questions for a self-styled reformer. Will would play the role of go-between repeatedly for his younger brother as time went on. For his part, Charlie Fox, the theater owner, would become a regular social visitor to the district attorney's office. Win Zabel in turn became a frequent visitor to the Gayety Theater, where he was welcome backstage.[63]

The district attorney also accepted at least $1,000 in free stock, possibly more, in a mineral water company west of Milwaukee.[64] That gift again came from the ever-generous Adler, through his lawyer.[65]

Evidently, the Zabel brothers appreciated gifts. Each drove about town in expensive automobiles that a local car dealer gave first to Charlie Fox, partly in exchange for more stock in the Theatrical Curtain Advertising Association. Fox then passed the cars immediately to the Zabels. William got a shiny 1916 six-cylinder Lexington worth $1,200 (at a time when Henry Ford's Model T was selling for about $850). The auto dealer valued Win's car at even more, $1,884. But the best was yet to come. In 1920, when Win Zabel tired of the first car, Fox obtained another for him from the compliant car dealer. This one was worth $2,935, or about $35,000 today.[66]

Soon a familiar lurker appeared again in connection with the Theatrical Curtain Advertising Association. He was none other than Frank Carchidi, the petty crook, police informer, and jailhouse plant.[67] Carchidi later would claim under oath that he had met with Win Zabel, Charlie Fox, and another man at the

Gayety Theater. There, Zabel told Carchidi that he would dismiss a pending criminal case against Carchidi if the latter would pledge his $5,000 bail for stock in the Theatrical Curtain Advertising Association.[68] Carchidi could raise only $1,500, though, which Fox was to pass to Win Zabel at a remote crossroads restaurant far west of town. The deal fell through. Zabel did not dismiss Carchidi's case.[69]

Others, from retired policemen to current members of the Sheriff's Department to lawyers, eventually offered tidbits, rumors, or secondhand information along the same lines. Two of those witnesses were a lawyer and a former "investigator" (his actual role was ambulance chaser, in all likelihood) in another prominent lawyer's office.[70] The lawyer recounted a colleague's boasts that he had influence with the district attorney's office, Judge A. C. Backus, and the police station.[71] The investigator was more specific. He had the impression that the prominent lawyer's relationship with Win Zabel was "very crooked." In part, that impression traced back to the occasion on which he claimed that the prominent lawyer told him point-blank that District Attorney Zabel would get $1,500 of a proposed $3,200 fee from a criminal client.[72]

No one ever proved conclusively that Win Zabel took bribes. In 1923 a state grand jury indicted the same prominent lawyer and Zabel over a $100 case of Christmas champagne—a fairly petty charge, suggesting that the more serious claims had little credibility.[73] And that case against both came to naught.[74] Many (but not all) of the other bribery allegations were secondhand.

Accounts of Zabel's high-handed bullying were something else again. As to that, many people later came forward to offer sworn statements from firsthand knowledge. Often, although not always, Zabel's bullying involved women. He had an uneasy relationship with women generally. Even an obituary writer, in an otherwise predictably glowing piece, noted of Zabel: "One of his particular aversions was women lawyers, and his associates often recalled that Mr. Zabel even disliked women on juries. That, it was said, might be traced to his fears that women's sympathies might color their conclusions regarding evidence. Nevertheless," the writer added, "Mr. Zabel won a number of his most important cases when women were on the jury."[75]

He would not have won with Jane Borstad on his jury, though. She became the most unfortunate pawn in Zabel's effort to destroy a well-known local businessman whom Zabel despised as a "son-of-a-bitch" and a "degenerate."[76]

Jane and her husband were going through a rough patch in their marriage. Evidently, her husband was a man of some means. When he and Jane decided upon a trial separation, he installed her in a hotel in Milwaukee.[77]

She then embarked on what her doctor later would call a course of "diversion and amusement."[78] One August evening, she, a girlfriend, and two businessmen visited a number of roadhouses and drank themselves into a stupor. One businessman escorted her home. Some amorous episode, consensual or not, followed. Eventually she decided that, whatever happened, she bore equal responsibility. She did not want unhappy publicity.[79]

But the incident and the threat of public notoriety weighed heavily on her. Jane became "greatly depressed, crying frequently, and sleeping poorly." Within a few days, her physician diagnosed a "nervous condition" and referred her to a sanitarium in Shorewood, along Lake Michigan just north of Milwaukee.[80] She arrived "depressed and slightly agitated," in a "poorly developed state, and poorly nourished."[81] The doctor put her on bed rest at the sanitarium. Meanwhile, word leaked out of the ambiguous and unpleasant episode in her room, probably because the other young woman in the roadhouse merriment that evening told someone after Jane confided in her.[82]

As rumors about the evening leaked out, a lawyer and his shill, a newspaper reporter, smelled money. They sought to convince Jane to file suit against the businessman, but she was having none of it.[83] The lawyer hit upon a swell idea: go to Winfred Zabel. Soon Zabel was aboard.

Rather than charge the man with rape or some other crime, Zabel took a different tack. He joined with the lawyer and his shill. During this time, frustrated in their efforts to sign up a willing client, the two simply went ahead and drafted a lawsuit in the names of Mr. and Mrs. Borstad. They proposed to ask $50,000 in damages from the businessman.[84] But they needed the signature of the intended complainant, Jane Borstad. Now Zabel would have his role to play.

At 10:00 a.m. the next day, in walked Zabel with a stenographer from his office, the lawyer, and the shill, as Jane Borstad lay still in her bed hoping for some recuperative peace and quiet. They strode into her room without a knock on the door.[85] Not bothering with an introduction either, Zabel opened the conversation.

"I understand you are in a very bad condition."

"I am ill," Borstad agreed.

"Dr. Studley tells me that you are in a bruised condition," Zabel followed.

"Yes," Borstad replied cautiously.

"He tells me that you are badly bruised; I would like to see some of your bruises," Zabel pressed. As yet, he had not even told the convalescing Borstad who he was or why a stenographer and two men she twice had sent away were in her hospital room, now with this impertinent stranger.

Jane Borstad declined to display any bruises.

At that point, Zabel announced that he wanted to ask a few questions and said, "We are here to help you." He told her that she ought to retain the lawyer. It now dawned on Borstad that the three men "weren't there for any good purpose." So she demurred. "I am ill, I am here to be let alone, and I don't want to be bothered."

That did not sit well with the prosecutor.

"Well, I think you will have to answer my questions, young woman, I am Mr. Zabel!," he barked. "I am the District Attorney, and things like this cannot go on in Milwaukee. It will be much to your benefit if you talk plainly to me and tell me things."

Up to this point, Zabel had been "commanding, but he had also taken the attitude that he was there to help me," Borstad explained. But when he found out that she did not wish to be "helped," Zabel's tone changed.

"You are living in an apartment by yourself on Van Buren Street?"

"Yes."

"How long have you been there?" Zabel continued the interrogation. She answered.

Isn't it true that the businessman had been paying her rent?

"Absolutely not, I never saw him—only once in my life!"

"He has been buying your clothing?"

"He has not, I have an ample allowance to clothe myself."

"You have been entertaining callers in your apartment?" Yes, she had.

"You have had men callers there?!"

"I have," Mrs. Borstad conceded.

"I can't permit this!"

With that, Zabel paused dramatically, quieted, and again became cloying. We all are here to help you, he assured Jane. "We have a paper here that we would like to have you sign"—the civil complaint.

Why should she do that, Borstad asked.

"You are in this hospital in a very bad condition, you will be—lay here for years—or months, more probably, you will be here for a year, probably, and haven't the finances to pay it with. The people who are responsible for this had better pay it. You better let me see to it that you get help," Zabel cooed. "And the best thing you can do is sign this paper" suing the man for $50,000.

She refused.

"You better start a civil action against him," Zabel retorted, raising his voice a bit.

When Borstad remained steadfast, Zabel became "very angry." If she did not sign this paper suing the man for $50,000, "I will haul you in the criminal court tomorrow morning!"[86]

By this time, Borstad had rung twice for the nurse to ask her to summon the doctor in charge. No one came.

Borstad ventured that the doctor "wouldn't permit my being taken to the criminal court."

The doctor "hasn't a thing to say about it, not a thing!," Zabel snarled.

Now Borstad was frantic and ringing again for the nurse. The three men huddled briefly by the window, then abruptly ushered their stenographer out of the room and followed her. Zabel wheeled in the doorway as he left.

"You will hear from me in the morning!" He turned as if to leave again. Then, once more, he spun toward the bed and shook his finger at her.

"I will have you in criminal court tomorrow, young lady!"[87]

The door banged and they were gone. Borstad slumped back in her hospital bed, sobbing.

Zabel's threat was empty. She never heard from him again.

Usually Zabel's heavyhanded official misconduct was not so sensational. A landlady who owned Milwaukee rooming houses lost only $100 to him, for example. One of her tenants had asked to keep some Liberty Bonds and other papers in the office safe. The landlady obliged. When the tenant appeared three or four months later to reclaim the bonds, the landlady gave her the sealed envelope from the safe. Thirty minutes later, the tenant returned, claiming that a $100 bond was missing. The landlady denied knowing what might have happened to it. The tenant then complained to the district attorney. Zabel summoned the landlady to his office.[88]

She had the sense to retain a lawyer before reporting to Zabel's office. Together they went to see Zabel. The meeting started poorly.

"Zabel lit into her; I wouldn't treat a streetwalker the way he treated her," the landlady's lawyer recounted angrily.

"He said 'why don't you take that paint off of your face, yes, you go around with silk dresses on you. No wonder you wear silk dresses when you steal the money from your clients!'"

The bottom line? "I want that $100 returned here before 5 o'clock. If it isn't, I am going to issue a warrant for you," spat Zabel.[89]

The landlady and her cowed lawyer complied. What Zabel did with the $100, no one knows.

Sometimes citizens did not face Zabel's wrath directly; instead, it was just a matter of Zabel pushing his weight around with other lawyers or flat-out deceiving them. He was nothing if not a bully. An assessment of Zabel by one who knew him well rings true, at least of his temperament and courtroom antics. Zabel was "a good scrapper," yes, "but he over-awed Judge Backus; it was impossible for the average fellow that wasn't a fighter to the last ditch to get a fair shake in that court, because Zabel would just simply yell down, and it would resolve itself into practically no orderly proceeding at all."[90] So said Bill Rubin.

The most intriguing aspect of Zabel's intermittent life in private practice was the man he chose as his law partner, every time: that same Bill Rubin. During his first ten years practicing in Milwaukee, from 1901 through 1911, Zabel learned at Rubin's side. Although just a few years Zabel's senior, Rubin bristled at the notion that Zabel was his equal during that first decade. No, he snapped when asked years later if he had been Zabel's partner, "I was formerly an *employer* of Mr. Zabel."[91] At the time, though, the two men were close enough that Zabel served as a pallbearer when Rubin's wife Sonia died, in 1915.[92]

Whatever Rubin's initial feelings about Zabel's ascendancy to the district attorney's job, their relationship as professional foes quickly became acidic. The ferocity of their court battles went well beyond the needs or ordinary strains of an adversary system. They feuded at a deep, personal level. Rubin elliptically described a "breach" between the two men, followed by a "make-up" and then yet another "breach."[93]

What to make of Zabel repeatedly rejoining Rubin when out of the district attorney's office, then? One possibility is kindness; at bottom, passing quibbles aside, Rubin may have liked Zabel, and vice versa. Another possibility is Rubin's loyalty. Certainly loyalty was among the traits that polite people recalled about Rubin.[94] Yet another possibility is that Rubin thought of Zabel's salary as an investment, a modest price to pay for future influence in the event that Zabel regained the district attorney's office—as he did. Still one more possibility is that one man, or both, chose to keep his enemy closer even than his friends. Each man could do the other less harm, presumably, from an adjoining office than from separate quarters located some few city blocks away.

A final possibility is more subtle. After Zabel left office the second (and last) time, in 1923, brother Will remained in the district attorney's office, where he had been since 1916. Eventually, Will himself ran successfully for the top prosecutor's job and served as Milwaukee County district attorney from 1933 to 1936.[95] With Will in the prosecutor's office, any existing collusion with the Zabel brothers might continue. Only by taking in Winfred could Rubin ensure that hanky-panky would inure to his financial benefit, directly or indirectly.

But when they were professional adversaries because Zabel was in the district attorney's office, the rivalry between Rubin and Zabel was savage, disturbing. Rubin schemed to destroy Zabel. Whether Zabel attempted to return the favor is uncertain, but he surely spoke venomously of Rubin.

The most striking incident culminated in a clandestine confrontation between the two in the frigid blackness of Milwaukee's Lake Park late on a Sunday night one December. Only a fragment of that episode is clear: shortly before election time, Rubin had threatened through intermediaries to go to the editor of the *Wisconsin Evening News* with *something* about Zabel. Rubin's account of the information he threatened to make public on the eve of the election was plausible but predictably self-serving, too. As Rubin had it, he had called the meeting in Lake Park to tell Zabel that the district attorney's office "was not on the square" and that he ought to fire everyone but two assistant prosecutors.[96]

What this tidy story does not explain, though, is why Rubin would have had to resort to the snowy, desolate reaches of an abandoned park on a December night to deliver that message. Although it was delicate, Rubin could have broached the subject sotto voce in a quiet restaurant booth over brandy and cigars after roast beef or duck à l'orange. Anyone who might have noted such an intimate dinner between the district attorney and a leading criminal defense lawyer also would have known that Rubin and Zabel long had been law partners too. No great suspicion would have arisen had Rubin addressed the subject in such a meeting. And if implicit blackmail with an impending newspaper story was not part of Rubin's plot, then there was no special urgency to his warning of corruption that warranted cold feet and frozen fingers on a wintry Sunday night in Lake Park.

Whatever the role of a possible story in the *Wisconsin Evening News*, the timing of Rubin's version, if not of the secretive meeting itself, matters. Rubin gave this recounting of the episode after Zabel had lost the district attorney's office but before he rejoined Rubin's firm. It was while Zabel was preparing to leave office for his second brief spell as a law professor, this time at Milwaukee's Marquette University. Rubin and Zabel's tortured relationship was in another period of flux. They no longer would be adversaries on opposite sides in the criminal courtrooms. But they had not yet made amends for the professional damage they had done each other either. Rubin's version, then (even if true), was the tale of a man not yet sure whether he should administer a professional coup de grâce to Zabel or whether he yet might profit from that relationship.

Oscar Adler, Zabel's old crony from the Theatrical Curtain Advertising Association, offered a different story about Rubin's sizzling scoop for the *Wisconsin Evening News* that was more tawdry and earthbound than Rubin's version. As Adler told it, the *Evening News* had fired a warning shot on a Saturday evening: a caricature of Zabel, blindfolded, had appeared in the newspaper.[97] Both Rubin and Adler were friends of the editor. Zabel learned, somehow, that Monday's edition of the newspaper would carry a story with "a lot of notoriety" from "some former trouble Zabel had."[98] Rubin was behind that story, obviously: he told Adler to watch for the *Evening News* on Monday night.[99]

This threat and the Saturday night caricature were enough to propel Zabel into near nervous collapse. Zabel called Adler in such a panic that he convinced Adler to skip his own brother's wedding the following day. Instead of attending the nuptials, Adler shuttled back and forth among Zabel, Rubin, and the editor of the *Evening News*. He arrived at Zabel's house late on Sunday to report what he knew. Zabel shooed his wife upstairs and then paced back and forth with Adler, every avian feature—face, eyes, hands—aflutter. He implored Adler, "Go down to Rubin and see what you can do with him. Try your best and everything that I can do for you I will gladly do. I will give you a chance to make some money, but for God's sake do everything you can but get it out of the paper, for that thing will ruin me!"[100] Zabel's icy blue eyes flitted around the room, at once terrified and insistent.

Adler went back to Rubin and pleaded with him, saying that Zabel "wanted to make up with him." Rubin kept Zabel on tenterhooks, telling Adler that Zabel should go to the editor of the *Evening News* himself.[101] Zabel did exactly that. On Monday morning, Rubin and the editor met. The story did not run.[102]

Zabel then tried to arrange an appointment with Rubin, again through Adler. Will Zabel apparently was to accompany Win, but the brothers spooked and called off the initial appointment because they feared a "leak." They rescheduled— this time under cover of darkness, far from snooping eyes and ears, in Lake Park.[103] There, in the frozen jewel that Frederick Law Olmsted conceived for Milwaukee before dementia overcame him, Zabel and Rubin reached some accord after the immediate threat of the newspaper story had passed.[104] What that accord was, they never hinted.

According to Adler, though, Zabel had averted publication of a scandalous story indeed. Years earlier, the district attorney had met a young woman from Indiana. He had fathered a child, a boy, who was born an "invalid." On the sly, Zabel traveled to Indiana, married the woman to make the child legitimate, and then promptly divorced her.[105] Doubtless there was a financial arrangement. All the while, of course, he was married in Milwaukee and raising a daughter and a son.[106] The story would have ended his career in public office, all right.

This Indiana episode also was the sort of jam that a younger man in trouble well might have confided to his older law partner and reluctant mentor when it happened, perhaps out of panic or necessity. A loan, a salary advance, time un-expectedly away from the office, a cover story, even reassurance—there would have been some need to talk with the senior partner. Rubin, then, likely would have known about the incident. With this knowledge, he would have acquired something valuable. Here, at least in Adler's version, the older lawyer threatened to play his trump card in a betrayal that would have made Zabel's own betrayals of other lawyers look amateurish. But then Adler himself hardly was a virtuous man or a reliable reporter of facts.

In the end, the late-night Lake Park meeting remains obscured, just as its participants intended. Whatever it was, though, a collegial chat between two fast friends on a starlit stroll does not make the list of possibilities. These men were bitter foes. As exactly that, they resumed a law partnership in 1926.

It continued another twenty years and more. On New Year's Day 1948, the wind howled incessantly and more than nine inches of snow fell on Milwaukee, drifting high.[107] The next morning, shortly before noon, Win Zabel died of heart failure at Mount Sinai Hospital. His health had been failing for months.[108] Then and only then, safe at last with Zabel's ashes entombed at Forest Home Cemetery, did Rubin offer a flowery tribute.[109] Obligatory kind words in the end, not before.

For now, though, November 1917 was about to give way to dark December. Rubin and Zabel were the main antagonists in the hotly anticipated trial. They would bring and act on all their enmity for each other. Eleven supposed anarchists were in the dock. Newspapers and the public both wanted revenge for the previous weekend's bloodbath in the central police station. None of the people on trial had anything directly to do with the bomb blast, but that little detail mattered not. Someone would pay, and these eleven Italians were as good as anyone.

Rubin was stuck in Buffalo at the AFL convention, while Judge Backus drummed his fingers impatiently back in Milwaukee. The trial would start, and start soon. Judge Backus adjourned it just forty-eight hours, from Wednesday, November 28, to Friday. With or without the lead defense lawyer, he would permit no further delays, Backus warned tersely.[110]

Cursing roundly, Bill Rubin made his way to the train station in blustery Buffalo that Wednesday evening to return home. He would be somewhere between Lake Erie's eastern tip and Lake Michigan's western shore on Thanksgiving Day. His wife was two and a half years dead and his son was studying at Cornell, so Rubin would have had a lonely holiday no matter where. The next morning would find him in court.

Looking southeast from the intersection of Broadway and Oneida Streets. Milwaukee's central police station sits on the corner, with the larger, castlelike armory immediately east of it. The November 24, 1917, bomb blast destroyed much of the first floor, especially the room to the right of the front door in this photograph. Neither building stands today, and Oneida Street now is Wells Street. (photograph courtesy Wisconsin Historical Society, WHi-8047)

Sgt. Robert Flood of the Milwaukee Police Department, far left, accompanies former president Theodore Roosevelt, hatless in the center, as he strides out of the train station in Milwaukee. Hours later, a mentally ill gunman would shoot and injure Roosevelt outside the Hotel Gilpatrick. Prosecuting the assailant, Milwaukee District Attorney Winfred C. Zabel took his first turn on a national stage. (photograph courtesy Wisconsin Historical Society, WHi-2096)

These two undated photographs of portions of the Illinois Steel Company's Bay View rolling mill suggest the size of the plant. It sat on Milwaukee's lakefront just down a small hill from the "Italian Colony" to the south. (photographs courtesy Wisconsin Historical Society, WHi-7015 and WHi-7451)

Rev. August Giuliani, the Methodist minister whose evangelical efforts among Bay View's Catholics put him at the center of the September 9, 1917, shootout. Here he cradles his first child, Waldo, in 1916. (photograph courtesy Milwaukee County Historical Society)

Milwaukee's young district attorney, Winfred C. Zabel, at about the time of the 1917 trial. (photograph courtesy Wisconsin Historical Society, WHi-34394)

Judge August C. Backus presided over the 1917 trial of the suspected anarchists. This portrait was a thank-you gift to supporters in his 1919 re-election bid. (photograph courtesy Milwaukee County Historical Society)

William Benjamin Rubin, two years before he represented ten of the eleven immigrants from the Italian Colony. (photograph courtesy Wisconsin Historical Society, WHi-62491)

Atlantic City June 4 1921

Two Americans who are thoroughgoing in
their defense of human rights and liberties.
Left to right—W. B. Rubin and Sam'l Gompers.

Rubin (*front row at far left*) poses in March 1918 on a platform at Milwaukee's railroad depot with members of the British Labor Commission. (photograph courtesy Wisconsin Historical Society, WHi-34397)

Left: Bill Rubin (*on the left*) marked Flag Day 1919 with the diminutive Samuel Gompers, leader of the American Federation of Labor, on the boardwalk in Atlantic City, New Jersey. This was about eighteen months after Rubin finished the trial of the Bay View eleven. (photograph courtesy Wisconsin Historical Society, WHi-34396)

Milwaukee's City Hall about one year after the trial of the eleven Italian immigrants, as the city welcomed home troops following the armistice in November 1918. The view is from the south. (photograph courtesy Milwaukee County Historical Society)

Another view of City Hall, shot from atop the armory and looking west down Oneida Street. The central police station was just below the lower left corner of the photograph. Undated, this photograph appears to have been taken in the years immediately preceding the December 1917 trial. (photograph courtesy Milwaukee County Historical Society)

A 1924 photograph of Milwaukee's municipal courtroom depicts the scene of the trial on the fourth floor of City Hall but shows none of the 1917 trial's participants. (photograph courtesy Milwaukee County Historical Society)

Clarence S. Darrow was America's most famous lawyer by 1917, when he posed for this photograph—the same year his eleven future clients in Milwaukee stood trial. Darrow autographed this copy and gave it "To my friend," William B. Rubin. (photograph courtesy Wisconsin Historical Society, WHi-3220)

Top right: This aerial view of the Wisconsin State Capitol in 1919 shows the East Wing in the foreground. That wing houses the state supreme court, directly above the governor's office. (photograph courtesy Wisconsin Historical Society, WHi-31330)

Bottom right: Rev. August Giuliani, a few years after the 1917 trial. (photograph courtesy Milwaukee County Historical Society)

Bill Rubin was a stalwart of the Democratic Party in Wisconsin for decades. Here, center of the front row, he sits for a portrait of the Wisconsin delegation to the Electoral College that in January 1933 formally elected Franklin Delano Roosevelt to his first term as president of the United States. (photograph courtesy Wisconsin Historical Society, WHi-17501)

Bill Rubin beams from the second row, in a formal black bow tie and holding flowers, at his son Abner's wedding reception. The elder Rubin's longtime law partner (and frequent nemesis), Winfred Zabel, stands to the far right in the third row. (photograph courtesy Wisconsin Historical Society, WHi-34395)

In his later years, Bill Rubin confers with another delegate before the July 1944 Democratic Party convention in Chicago. The photograph, incidentally, is the work of Arthur M. Vinje, longtime photographer for the Wisconsin State Journal and nephew of Judge Aad J. Vinje, who wrote the Wisconsin Supreme Court's opinion in the appeal of the eleven Italians. (photograph courtesy Wisconsin Historical Society, WHi-40260)

In 1934, fifteen years after deporting her, the U.S. government allowed Emma Goldman to return for a speaking tour. She spoke in Madison at the University of Wisconsin, where she is pictured here. Goldman had been an ardent supporter of the eleven Bay View Italians. (photograph courtesy Wisconsin Historical Society, WHi-16746)

7

"The Public Mind Has Become Violently Inflamed against All Italians"

Come Friday morning, the last day of November, Rubin was in court and on time. Zabel was too, dressed nattily and preening. Frederick F. Groelle, assisting Zabel in his first and only case of note, busied himself near Zabel's side. Arthur H. Bartelt, another assistant district attorney, also was at the prosecution table that day. He would assist Zabel with the trial too, but mostly out of court. At the defense table, Tom Leahy sat watching Rubin and scanning the courtroom, which was filling rapidly. Already, at Judge Backus's direction, sheriff's deputies were frisking thoroughly any spectators whom the deputies did not recognize. Members of the bar were excepted.[1] The judge's order had the effect, perhaps intended, of discouraging any few friends, family members, or supporters of the eleven accused from attending the trial. By experience, they would have been the most apprehensive about any contact with police officers. The random house-to-house searches in Bay View all night after the September 9 shooting still were fresh in mind.

Soon the police would march the eleven defendants as a group from the city jail, in the badly damaged central police station, to Judge Backus's courtroom on the fourth floor of City Hall. Because City Hall was not connected to the jail by tunnel, newspaper photographers would have a time-honored opportunity to snap pictures of the defendants under the proud dominion of the police. If necessary, the police would tell the newspapers in advance when the walk would begin and delay it until photographers were in place. No single tradition better illustrates the role of the commercial press in exalting the power of the state: photographs of the "perp walk," snapped every time the police offer the chance, show the superior position of law enforcers, suggest the obvious guilt of those who nominally are presumed innocent, and taint the jury pool to the prosecution's benefit.

Here, the photographs would remind Milwaukeeans and prospective jurors that the defendants already languished in jail before trial began. All but a statistical sliver of the citizenry heartily approved of that custodial status. The mainstream newspapers had done their part at every step to bend any doubters toward the state's theory by text and images suggesting the defendants' certain guilt. These efforts would continue throughout the trial. The presumption of innocence sold (and sells) no newspapers. Worse, it sells no advertising space.

Two days earlier, before Judge Backus reluctantly adjourned the trial until Friday because of Rubin's absence, the eleven Italians all comported themselves well when the police paraded them for newspaper photographers. They even paused to do something utterly ambiguous from this remove: they saluted the American flag as they walked by it.[2] At the time, though, even the mainstream press took the gesture at face value.[3] The *Milwaukee Journal* noted that only Maria Nardini failed to salute the flag as she walked by but excused her failure because she alone had no hat to remove and tip.[4]

Perp walk and all, somehow in the next few hours, Rubin and Leahy would have to sift out twelve men, if they could, who might offer at least the hope of impartial judgment to the eleven immigrants. Even now, the longtime clerk of the court, John W. Woller, was assembling a jury panel on the floor below the courtroom.[5] Prospective jurors were milling about nervously, well aware of the case set for trial that day.

The twelve men who eventually would serve—by law, women could not sit on Wisconsin juries until 1921—would be citizens one and all and would come predominantly, although not exclusively, from the business class.[6] Wage laborers would be few. Still, the jurors all would have the essential virtue of coming fresh to the prospect of judging their fellow human beings. They would be inhabitants of a broader world in which good and bad, right and wrong, fair and unfair exist and matter. They would be unlike judges, those laborers in a grim criminal justice mill in which a noxious fog of bad and worse, wrong and dead wrong, is all there is to breathe. In that stupefying haze, differences between guilt and its absence often go unseen and hardly matter even when perceived dimly. The overconditioned judge sees only sooty shades of guilt. Whatever their own prejudices and weaknesses, jurors would bring the fresh air of life outside the courts and the will to seek justice to the closed, fetid atmosphere of the courthouse mill.

So the Italians and their advocates, if Rubin and Leahy's hearts were in it, could hope, anyway. In the jury alone, the idea of justice might keep hold.

The English did not invent the jury, or at least not alone. Danes, Franks, and Normans all had early variants of juries. But the English embraced and sustained it when others on the continent turned to Roman civil law. Today, the jury is the English-speaking world's great contribution to the project of popular justice. It appeared fitfully, in limited roles, in England as early as the eleventh and twelfth centuries, both in private and in royal proceedings after the Norman Conquest. But the jury began to flourish in the thirteenth century.[7]

The jury's spread did not flow entirely or even mainly from the source many assume, Magna Carta. For direct impact on the future of English trials, Magna Carta arguably was the second-most important event of 1215, not the first. As restive nobles pressed a reluctant King John in negotiations at Runnymede, the powerful Pope Innocent III convened the meeting, many hundreds of miles southeast, that perhaps topped Magna Carta in lasting effect on fact-finding in trials: the Fourth Lateran Council.[8] That gathering in Rome confounded trials in England when it barred clerical participation in proof by torture or physical contest.[9] Suddenly England found itself without the customary methods of determining guilt or innocence, right or wrong—trial by ordeal and trial by combat. So, following the Church's edict, crown justices turned to innovative and expanded uses of an idea that had seen only limited application until then. That idea was the trial jury. Very gradually after the Fourth Lateran Council, as the common-law historian R. C. Van Caenegem put it elegantly, "*vox populi* had simply taken the place of the final and inscrutable *vox Dei.*"[10]

While a jury was a splendid idea in general and surely a better bet for the eleven Italians than the tender mercies of Judge Backus, a jury from Milwaukee hardly would do.[11] The last of the police officers' funerals from the bomb blast had occurred just two days earlier. Mourners were still red eyed. The rest of the city was roiling with news of the investigation, for the bombing was unsolved. Or maybe partially unsolved: Italians were responsible, the press and public already had concluded. Which specific Italians was all that remained unclear. Because the bomber had intended Reverend Giuliani's church as the target and the eleven jailed Italians also had confronted Giuliani, those linked to them obviously were the culprits. About to stand trial for conspiring to shoot four police officers in Bay View in September, the eleven defendants already stood convicted in print and in the public mind for a role in murdering nine more officers the Saturday night immediately past. This was the wrong moment in the wrong place. No, a Milwaukee jury would not do.

With officers now leading the eleven into the nearly full courtroom, the murmurs rose sharply and then subsided expectantly. A hush descended. Soon, all stood as Judge A. C. Backus strode out of chambers and took the bench. He was disarmingly young (just forty years old), still brown haired, clean shaven, and handsome.[12] Backus parted his hair meticulously on the left side; pomade kept it plastered down neatly above his forehead. After the bailiff called court to order, Judge Backus invited all to sit down. He then called the case. "Court calls Case No. A 1338, State of Wisconsin versus Adolph Fratesse *et al.*"[13] It was just after 10:00 a.m.[14]

As matters stood at that moment, there were three separate charging documents against assortments of the accused. Pietro Bianchi was charged alone as an accessory both before and after the fact to an assault with intent to murder. Vincenzo Fratesi and Amedeo Lilli were charged together in a second document alleging assault with intent to murder while armed. The remaining eight defendants were charged in a third document alleging that they, like Bianchi, were accessories both before and after the fact to Fratesi and Lilli's assault with intent to murder. These documents dated back more than one month, to October 19, 1917.[15] Now, on the morning of trial, Zabel wanted to join all defendants for one trial.[16] Further, he wanted to file a new set of charges that would increase the stakes for nine of them. Rather than mere accessories to Vincenzo Fratesi and Amedeo Lilli, the other nine now would be co-conspirators. In other words, all eleven would become principals in the crime.

To that end, he asked leave to file an Amended Information naming all eleven defendants in two counts. The first count charged that the eleven made an assault on four police officers with intent to murder them, while armed with dangerous weapons, "to-wit, loaded revolvers." Although not alleged expressly, this was a conspiracy charge, for the state had no intention or hope of proving that all eleven assaulted anyone or that all eleven were armed. The conspiracy notion seemed simple: all schemed that some would shoot. Similarly, the second count charged that nine were accessories before the fact, because they "did unlawfully, feloniously counsel, aid, abet and procure" Vincenzo Fratesi and Amedeo Lilli to commit the assault with intent to murder. This, too, implicitly rested on a conspiracy theory, for the nine could not have procured the other two without some agreement amongst themselves, in which Vincenzo Fratesi and Lilli then also supposedly joined.

In short, the state intended to proceed on two murky conspiracy theories. Moreover, the state sought two chances to convict on what amounted to the same conspiracy. The fact that most or all of the defendants had left the clubhouse in Bay View together the morning of September 9 and walked as a group the block north up the gentle slope to Giuliani's gathering now would take on the legal significance of a conspiracy. All could go to prison for the agreement that Zabel claimed these acts portended, no matter whether they actually did anything at the street corner. He would ask the jury to infer an elaborate agreement among the eleven from their clubhouse departure as a group and from the pamphlets (some years old) that the police later had seized in the clubhouse and in the defendants' rooming houses.

In the first of many favorable rulings the state would enjoy during the trial, Judge Backus agreed to consolidate all defendants for one trial. He also granted leave to file the Amended Information.[17] On the morning of trial, the state successfully had shuffled the specific offenses, changed its entire theory of prosecution, and enhanced the seriousness of the charges. In the process, it turned what presumptively would have been three trials into one. If that surprised the defense unfairly, Judge Backus showed little interest.

Rubin and Leahy spoke next. They had a short "plea in abatement" to file. Just five sentences long, the plea in abatement sought dismissal of the charges on conclusory grounds that the "entire proceeding" violated unspecified "laws of this state." Additionally, the arrests were without due process, the complaints stated no crime, and the preliminary examination demonstrated no probable cause.[18] Zabel asked to enter a general denial to that plea in abatement. After much argument, some of it becoming heated between Zabel and Rubin right at the outset, the court took both the plea and the state's denial under advisement.

Already the noon hour approached. Backus adjourned court until 2:00 p.m.[19] Spectators, antsy to see the pretrial legal maneuvering end and testimony begin, shuffled to the door in a crescendo of hubbub as thoughts turned to a midday meal at home or at a lunch counter or perhaps to the cold liverwurst sandwich wrapped that morning in waxed paper and stuffed in a coat pocket. In Milwaukee, the liverwurst likely was *braunschweiger*, the spicy smoked variety that the city's Germans favored.[20] The Catholics would have fish or vegetable soup instead. It was Friday.

Before 2:00, they were back, *braunschweiger* and mustard wiped from mustaches. A general din prevailed until the retinue of police officers marched the defendants back in to take their seats. Counsel stood, anticipating Judge Backus's entry. The gallery quieted slowly.

After the judge again took the bench, Rubin had a surprise. On behalf of his clients, he asked for a change of venue. Still shaking off the effects of the long train ride from Buffalo, Rubin stepped a few feet forward to tender his petition to the deputy clerk, with a supporting affidavit of Vincenzo Fratesi. Nine of the defendants wanted to move the trial out of Milwaukee. (For reasons entirely unclear, Maria Nardini was not listed as joining the motion. Thomas Leahy's sole client, Pietro Bianchi, also did not join.) The petition itself was dry. But setting aside the tedious writing style—typical of the day and not atypical now—of the lawyer who drafted it, Fratesi's affidavit was anything but dry. He swore:

> That on Saturday, November 24, 1917, a bomb was delivered to the central police station in the city of Milwaukee by one or more Italians and that the delivery of said bomb resulted in a terrible catastrophe and death of ten or eleven persons. That it is the general belief throughout the county that said bomb was made by Italians and was intended as an instrument of murder and was intended to cause the death either of witnesses and persons concerned in this trial or of police officials concerned in the prosecution of this case.
>
> That among the victims of the said bomb were a number of well-known police officials of long terms of service well liked throughout the county and that by reason of said catastrophe, and its terrible result, the public mind has become violently inflamed against all Italians and especially against all of the defendants in this action and that frequent statements have appeared in the public press that the defendants in this action were concerned in or had knowledge of the making and sending of the said bomb. That the funerals of some of the victims of said bomb catastrophe created extremely widespread public sentiment against all Italians and especially against the defendants in this case, and that public sentiment at the present time is still at such a pitch of excitement that a fair and impartial judicial proceeding in an action against these defendants or against any Italians concerned in riots or bloodshed is an impossibility in the county of Milwaukee.
>
> That the public is inflamed with a desire for vengeance against the perpetrators of the bomb catastrophe and that it will be impossible to secure a jury in the present action which is not actuated by feelings of revenge and a desire to punish someone who may have had knowledge or who may have been concerned in the said bomb outrage, and that, as the court knows, it will be impossible to secure a fair and impartial jury to try this action.[21]

The affidavit attached a few newspaper clippings. It also cited Zabel's bellowings in the newspapers "to the effect that the trial of these defendants will be hastened and that any attempt to postpone the trial will be vehemently resisted, implying thereby that it is intended to secure a prompt conviction of these defendants and satisfy the public clamor for punishment of someone on account of the catastrophe."[22]

The basic recitations about the public mood after the police station bombing all were true, of course. And the last inference about Zabel's intentions, drawn here by a lawyer who knew Zabel well, also rang true. Zabel would have done the calculation quickly. The bomber or bombers had eluded arrest so far. The public was seething and soon might turn on the police or the district attorney for their failure to find the culprit. Here, close at hand, were eleven Italians. They probably were of the same ilk as the bomber. These eleven already were in jail and due for trial. Quite obviously they were guilty of something, disloyalty if nothing else. Who cared that they risked conviction indirectly for a crime that no one had charged? Convictions might sate the public for a time until Zabel and the police could bring the bomber to justice. These or any Italians, guilty by sheer ethnicity and ideology, were a convenient sacrifice to the populace. Better them than Zabel.

Privately, Rubin was blunter in his assessment of the public mood than he put it in Fratesi's affidavit. In a letter to a Milwaukee businessman twelve days after the trial, Rubin wrote, "The whole city was up in arms and everybody talked against these Italians, and the common expression was even if they are not guilty, let's convict them. Maybe by convicting them, the problem will be solved."[23]

Vincenzo Fratesi's affidavit included near the end some comments, cagily buried to provide possible grounds for appeal that Judge Backus might overlook, about the first stages of the trial itself. The affidavit swore that "the extreme suspicion which the public feels against all Italians at the present time was manifested by this court when in the presence of the jury and while these defendants were present in court, it ordered all spectators in the room to be searched for dangerous weapons and ordered that no person be permitted to enter the room with bundles and ordered that the number of spectators permitted in the court room be restricted."[24]

Here Rubin, using Vincenzo Fratesi as his proxy, jabbed a sharp elbow at the judge. Possibly Rubin intended generally to set Backus's teeth on edge, to signal that this would not be a genteel trial. Or possibly he meant specifically to call Backus on a lack of impartiality and judgment, with just a hint of indirection in his jargon. Whatever Rubin's core purpose, the affidavit reveals the stature that Rubin enjoyed among members of Milwaukee's bar in 1917. He could speak bluntly to a judge, calling things as he saw them. Additionally, the affidavit gives a glimpse of just how edgy Judge Backus seemed to be.

Backus had reason to be uptight. Although he had handled big cases before—most notably the prosecution of John Flammang Schrank for shooting Teddy

Roosevelt outside the Hotel Gilpatrick—still, the Italian case well could prove his most notorious trial.[25] Indeed, it could be one of the nation's most notorious. True, Judge Landis soon would preside over a much larger trial, that of the IWW leaders and sympathizers in federal court in Chicago, involving the more than 160 defendants indicted in September. But Landis's trial would not begin for another four months.[26] For now, Backus might expect a national spotlight as he rode eleven foreign radicals to justice at a time when many Americans thought the world was collapsing. With the national press watching, Backus would have to appear absolutely in control, both of his courtroom and of the defendants. If nothing else, Backus held an elected office and was young enough that he had to worry about keeping the job at election time. Law and order would prevail, and all who followed the case must know that.

With that imperative never far from mind, Backus took up the request for a change of venue. The facts were undeniable. Just six days earlier, someone had planted a bomb at the church of the Reverend August Giuliani, who of course just happened to be the protagonist and star prosecution witness in the case Backus now was prepared to try. Every regular reader of a newspaper knew that. The minister, his congregation, and the defendants all were Italian. Through misadventure, the bomb had traveled to the central police station. There, it killed nine police officers and a civilian in one awful instant. The city had interred the last of the slain officers just two days earlier. Every newspaper in the county blazed with banner headlines and pictures of the police station carnage on the front page. Italians in general were to blame. And, given Giuliani's connection, Italians who supported these eleven Italians were to blame in specific.

That was a lot to blink away. Backus was up to it. Motion denied.[27] The trial would proceed—today. It would proceed here in Milwaukee. It would proceed less than two blocks from a ruined police station almost smoldering still.

In such a closely watched trial, Judge Backus faced another more subtle but conflicting imperative. While he must appear a vigorous enforcer of order and safety, he also must not appear too clumsily biased. Obvious antipathy to one side would be vulgar, common; as a learned man, a member of a robed elite, he had to pass as impartial, at least to the casual observer. Plus, defense counsel was a lawyer of some influence. One way to strike this difficult balance was to throw the defendants—and their lawyer—a sop. He could deny the change-of-venue motion "without prejudice."[28] Legal jargon aside, such a ruling really would mean this: if the judge actually failed to find twelve prospective jurors who either were unaware of recent events or could lie convincingly that they would keep an open mind, the defense could renew its motion for a change of venue. In theory, the court then could cut the trial short during jury selection and reschedule it in a different county after passions had cooled. Backus picked exactly this course, possibly fooling the more credulous members of the public but not the lawyers. The lawyers surely knew from the outset what to expect from Backus in this case. He would steer the trial decisively to convictions.

Zabel was not content to rely on the judge's preference for the prosecution, however. Or perhaps he sensed a need to provide the judge some cover. Whatever his reason, by late morning of that first day, Zabel and Rubin already were taking every opportunity to goad each other. Zabel knew exactly how to make his former partner's cheeks redden and was impulsive and cocky enough himself to rankle Rubin just for sport. For his part, Rubin was an easy mark: self-important, windy, and aware deep down before trial even began that he was fighting a cause he could not win—yet with an ego that would not suffer the loss easily. The impatient judge had haled him back from the AFL convention early for this, to boot. All of that combined to make Rubin more short-tempered than usual, frustrated, and in very ill humor. Perhaps for those reasons, Rubin fired the first shot.

Immediately after the judge called the case that morning and even before Zabel filed the amended charges, Rubin rose with a motion calculated to enrage the chief prosecutor. He asked the court to cite Zabel for contempt because the jail had turned away a notary and an interpreter from Rubin's office when they had attempted to interview Maria Nardini as they prepared for the case.[29] That motion drew a classic Zabel response. Why, he would have permitted the interview between defense lawyer's staff and their client, he said, if only they had permitted the district attorney's office to have a representative present for it.[30] Zabel, in his zeal, apparently saw no reason why a criminal defendant should be allowed any confidential discussion with people sent by her own lawyer for the purpose of gathering information in preparing a defense.

Backus's reaction was delphic. Unwilling to chide the district attorney, let alone to take any concrete step, but also concerned that he appear to give Rubin his due, the judge spoke so cryptically that no casual observer would be able to make any sense of him. On the one hand, the judge observed, the sheriff had the right to control who spoke to prisoners; on the other hand, "members of the bar must be allowed to interview their clients."[31] With those awkwardly juxtaposed platitudes announced, Backus refused to take any further action.[32] The lawyers should have heard something that the audience and newspaper reporters did not: "you boys work this out between yourselves and leave me out of it."

There was little chance of that. The coded message did nothing to promote civility between Rubin and Zabel. They were in no mood to work out anything together. As the court's attention turned to Rubin's plea in abatement, Zabel fired back. During the course of his argument opposing the plea in abatement, Zabel referred to the defendants as "a bunch of anarchists."[33] Surely Rubin would take that bait.

He did. Leaping to his feet, Rubin insisted that the court bar Zabel from any further role in the trial. Zabel's statement, Rubin howled, was made "to inflame the public mind and was unwarranted and prejudicial."[34]

Again, Backus ducked. He simply said and did nothing at all.[35]

The day wore on in this fashion. "Proceedings were halted many times by clashes between Mr. Zabel and Mr. Rubin," the *Milwaukee Sentinel* reported that evening. "Judge Backus finally told them he would have to take definite action unless they stopped wrangling."[36]

At the end of Friday, Backus adjourned until Monday, ostensibly to consider the part of the defense plea in abatement that challenged the sufficiency of evidence at the preliminary examination. When court reconvened on Monday morning, Backus announced that the new charges could stand. But that did not dispose of the plea in abatement entirely. There remained the propriety of the arrest warrants. Judge Backus would take testimony on that and adjourn again until Wednesday. Then he would rule.[37]

When court opened once more on Wednesday, December 5, Backus promptly and predictably disposed of the last issue in the plea in abatement. The warrants were proper; the plea in abatement was denied.[38] Jury selection would proceed. Backus now had stalled the trial itself for a week from the last of the police detectives' funerals, which he could hope would reduce the prospects of the state supreme court overturning on appeal his refusal to change venue.

With the same concern in mind, Backus proceeded cautiously in jury selection. He started with a large panel of fifty-two men. Shortly after 10 a.m., he asked the jurors if any wished to be excused on grounds of work obligations or for other reasons. Seventeen hands went up. This provided an excellent opportunity for the judge to cull the panel of daily wage earners, in the guise of demonstrating concern for their well-being.[39] Laborers would not be paid the day's wages if they served on a jury rather than reported to work. They might not have a job at all at day's end with such an absence. This trial could run three weeks, and laborers certainly would be out of a job after that extended absence. Salaried men or those who owned their own enterprise faced no equivalent problem. Feigning concern for them, Judge Backus excused nine wage laborers immediately, retaining for the moment the other eight men who wished not to serve.[40]

Of the forty-three who remained, two answered early that yes, they were prejudiced against the Italians on trial. The judge promptly excused them, too.

These may have been honest "talesmen"—the state still retained the old term for prospective jurors—or they simply may have been smart enough to know how to avoid the inconvenience of a December cooped up in a courtroom. Possibly fear of a verdict's consequences lurked in their minds as well. If the defendants' supporters were capable of planting a bomb, as the public supposed, imagine what they might do to jurors following a conviction. In any event, by 11 a.m. only two men had passed muster for final consideration as jurors.[41] Backus had ten to go.

By the time court adjourned in the early darkness of a December afternoon, only eight more men had passed through Backus's and Zabel's questioning and taken seats in the jury box to await the defense lawyers' questions. One of those, Lawrence P. Deuster, admitted that he had formed an opinion about the case but said that he would set it aside. Rubin was unconvinced. He asked the judge to excuse Deuster for cause. Backus refused.[42]

One signal of just how many such prospective jurors Rubin faced shines even today. Deuster eventually served as one of the twelve jurors.[43] How did that happen, when both defense and prosecution get a final chance to remove jurors for any reason they like or for no clear reason at all? Rubin and Leahy simply did not have enough so-called peremptory challenges to weed out all of those who already had decided that the defendants were guilty. For that matter, some prospective jurors may not have shown even Deuster's minimal candor in admitting that they arrived before trial with a fixed opinion on guilt. A prospect who wanted to serve could lie, and no one would be the wiser.

After twenty-one years trying criminal cases, Rubin knew all of this. But his possible remedies were dwindling. Given the massive publicity about the bombing and the widely assumed linkage to the defendants, Rubin asked Judge Backus on Wednesday to allow the defense nine peremptory challenges, rather than the usual four. No, Backus responded. Each side would get just four.[44] Zabel, of course, hardly needed one, let alone four. Jury selection ground on.

Before the court broke for lunch on Thursday, both sides had accepted twelve men—the defense only because Rubin and Leahy had exhausted the four strikes they shared. It had taken just more than one day to pick the jury. Although now nearly a week had passed since the trial process started, and jury selection hardly was riveting, the *Milwaukee Sentinel* noted that "every seat was occupied during the greater part of the day."[45]

Rubin made one last-ditch attempt to avert trial by a Milwaukee jury still in the throes of grief and anger. He chose his words carefully and spoke in the formal manner of lawyers, addressing the court impersonally. "In view of the fact that the court granted the defendants but four challenges; in view of the fact that 44 percent of the talesmen examined had to be excused because they were prejudiced; and in view of the fact that the court denied the motion of counsel for the defense for a change of venue, I challenge the array of the jury." Without a word from the prosecution, Backus overruled Rubin's request and ordered the jury sworn.[46] Opening statements would begin at 2 p.m. sharp. After obligatory comments from Judge Backus on their solemn duties, the newly sworn jurors rose and filed out. Spectators followed, scuffling and murmuring in anticipation. The real show was about to begin.

The jurors who occupied the choice seats for that show were exactly as expected. All twelve men were white, of course. Most had German surnames. Two had Polish surnames and the rest either Scandinavian or names suggesting origins in the British Isles. Not one was Italian. They were middle-aged or older. Their home addresses and smart attire, including neat white collars, neckties, and snappy homburgs (only one wore a workman's cap in the group photograph), marked the men as shopkeepers, salaried office clerks, supervisors, or other members of the solid middle class.[47]

The afternoon session started with Zabel's opening statement. Immediately, Zabel began to enjoy the benefits of his new conspiracy theory. The formal charges alleged only that the eleven defendants had committed their assault with intent to murder on September 9, 1917. The persons they had supposedly sought to murder were four police officers, not anyone else.[48] But Zabel would offer much more in the name of proving the agreement that is conspiracy's essence. He would prove, he said, that some of the same defendants had also tried to disrupt Reverend Giuliani's street meetings on August 26 and September 2. Some had "cursed the president and the American flag." Others had admitted being anarchists. Worse, "The state intends to prove the defendants belonged to an anarchistic club opposed to the government and that similar organizations exist in many of the large cities throughout the country," Zabel promised. So the defendants were to be tried not just for an assault on September 9. They were to be tried for their catcalling and singing one and two weeks before, for slandering President Wilson and the flag, for their ideology, for their politics and associations, and indeed for the activities of others "in many of the large cities throughout the country."[49] By setting for himself the goal of proving an agreement among at least eleven people to kill four police officers on September 9—plainclothes police officers the eleven realistically could not have been certain would be there that day—Zabel now opened wide the other, uncharged activities that he could offer in his attempt to prove that conspiracy. He would trust in the end that the inference the jury might draw from the overall stench of the defendants' political views, insulting words, and milling about together on three successive Sundays would prove greater than the sum of its evidentiary parts.

Rubin interrupted the prosecutor's opening statement once to object, to no avail. Backus ruled that all of the events of the two weeks preceding September 9 could come in to show intent.[50]

Having spun his tale of "a concerted effort" by the defendants, including their "intent to kill if necessary to carry out their purpose," Zabel sat down.[51] Kill whom? When? Minor details, unworthy of discussion. A conspiracy theory was beautiful for its vagueness and thus its expansiveness. The broader the tar brush, the less precision anyone would demand of the person wielding it.

Judge Backus then invited Zabel to call his first witness. There was just a moment's dead quiet as Zabel rose again and spectators craned in anticipation. "State calls the Reverend August Giuliani."

In the black of his clerical garb and collar, with an inch of starched white just below his Adam's apple, the fastidious minister strode forward, past the bar and toward the witness stand, where he stood erect awaiting the oath. He had trimmed his neat mustache meticulously that day. In his heavily accented English, rich with Italian roll, he affirmed that he would tell the truth and nothing but. Giuliani mounted the low podium on which the wooden witness chair sat and took his place. He surveyed the courtroom from his perch, which was second only to the judge's in elevation.

Zabel started with a brief bit of background, allowing Giuliani to explain, "I am a preacher by profession," connected with the Methodist Church. He described his main church and two branch missions.[52] Then it was on to the first rally in Bay View, on Sunday, August 26. Very quickly, Zabel built the pattern for his entire case: asking witnesses to identify whom of the Italians on trial they could recall seeing at the three successive street meetings and what (if anything) they recalled particular defendants saying or doing. Zabel moved methodically in chronological order through the three meetings. Giuliani, like almost all of the nineteen state witnesses who followed him, pointed out defendants in the courtroom and named them as he could. Having identified a defendant, Giuliani would offer a fragment or two of that defendant's words or actions. On August 26 he recalled Gavino Denurra saying, "I don't believe in God, I don't believe in priests, I don't believe in government, I don't believe what you are saying."[53] The following Sunday, he saw one of the Fratesi brothers, Amedeo Lilli, and Bartolo Testolin with others on the same corner, "and they were looking at us very friendly."[54] Not so Maria Nardini, apparently. She said to her group, which numbered about fifteen that day, "Coward, take a gun and shoot them, who is the first?" She called Giuliani "a coward, a man paid by the government, we do not want to listen about the war because we have our brothers in the war in Italy, and we will smash your face, we destroy you and will throw you in the lake if you come again."[55] Giuliani responded that he was not a coward, that he would come again, and that he would bring the police to protect his group. No matter—he claimed that Maria Nardini replied, "We kill you and the police, too."[56]

Mostly, though, Giuliani could do little or nothing more than place a given defendant at the scene on one or another of the three Sundays. As to some, he could not do that much. In the end, only one state witness would identify each of the eleven defendants as present on the critical third Sunday, September 9. That was Maud Richter, the young settlement worker who had dithered with the bomb at Giuliani's church on November 24. And even she did not claim that most of the accused had done anything other than appear at the September 9 gathering.

Rubin objected loudly and often to testimony about the two Sundays preceding the September 9 events at issue. His objections reflected the common imprecision of the day but often had an alliterative flourish. "Incompetent!" he would stand and interject when stirred only mildly. But when he was more agitated, it was a full-throated, "Incompetent, irrelevant and immaterial!"[57] The difference mattered not to Backus, whose response almost invariably was the same: overruled.

A subtle theme of Zabel's direct examination of Giuliani was that the minister's meetings in Bay View were patriotic, not religious. Milwaukee had a large number of Catholics, even if Protestants dominated the city's elites. The possibility of an apostate priest simply baiting people over their religion might not have sat well with jurors. A religious purpose would have cast Giuliani in a decidedly less flattering light, making him a petty sectarian engaged in a dangerous game. It also would have left the impression that the whole Bay View disturbance was an internal affair among Italians, although police officers in the end were slightly wounded by gunfire. Zabel was much smarter to lay emphasis on Giuliani's secular purposes of urging support for President Wilson's war effort and for the draft specifically. With the nation at war, those purposes had almost universal support among the middle and upper classes. They also put Giuliani in the flattering role of a well-intentioned immigrant acting on love for and loyalty to his adopted nation.

Rubin understood the importance of these competing themes. He sought to portray Giuliani's motives just the opposite, as primarily religious. His cross-examination of Giuliani opened with innuendo and a rapid assault. He suggested that Giuliani had taken a different name after leaving Italy and that he had been defrocked as a Catholic priest. Rubin then intimated that Giuliani had left the priesthood after raping a parishioner.[58] If Rubin had evidence to support that inflammatory (and potentially very unfair) accusation, the record is barren of any hint of what that evidence might have been. At best, the leading question was a cheap shot; what bearing really would sexual misconduct years earlier in Italy have had on Giuliani's credibility in this trial? At worst, if Rubin had nothing to support a good-faith belief that the question's implication was true, it was a grotesquely unethical assertion. Interestingly, though, a very similar allegation against Giuliani arose in his congregation several years after the trial.[59]

In objecting to Rubin's questions, Zabel used the same ritual formula that Rubin himself had employed: incompetent, irrelevant, and immaterial. But Backus seemed to like it better coming from the prosecutor. He sustained the district attorney's objections almost as consistently as he overruled Rubin's.[60]

Giuliani testified for nearly a full day in total, leaving the stand finally at noon on Friday. One reporter thought Rubin's cross-examination "severe."[61] The minister came through well, however. He held his ground. Specifically, Giuliani never wavered in his claim that his speeches were intended to inform the neighborhood about the draft and an immigrant's duty to America, not to proselytize.[62]

Later on Friday, the police station bombing that provided the backdrop of the entire trial entered the proceedings overtly and breathtakingly. In effect, two police detectives testified from beyond the grave. Detectives Albert H. Templin and Paul J. Weiler had accompanied Giuliani's retinue on the street car down to Bay View for the September 9 rally. Weiler's rough effort to search Vincenzo Fratesi instigated the first shots from Tony Formaceo, and Templin was the first officer hurt, when a bullet nicked his left forehead. They had testified, including on cross-examination, at the preliminary hearing for some of the defendants in October.[63] Then, on November 24, both perished in the bomb blast at the central police station. Because they now were unavailable, an exception to the rule against hearsay permitted the introduction of their former testimony at trial. Zabel could read their preliminary hearing testimony for the jury.[64] Done deftly, this would have enormous emotional impact.

Zabel did it well. Before reading their testimony, he called Detective John F. Wesolowski to testify that both men died in the explosion.[65] The witness chair was eerily empty when the two dead detectives should have settled into it. But their words, accusing the eleven Italians, lived and resounded in the hushed courtroom. By artful lawyering, with aid of a judge who would not tell him no, Zabel managed to create the appearance of a direct linkage between the defendants and the bomb that killed nine police officers.

Rubin and Leahy objected vociferously. Backus would have none of it. He thought the testimony admissible against at least some of the defendants and ruled disingenuously that he would consider its admissibility against the others later—as if jurors truly could apply the words of the martyred detectives, who all assumed had died at the hands of the Italians' supporters, against some defendants and not others.[66] Before resuming his seat at counsel table, Rubin said finally with exaggerated formality, "I desire at this time to say of record that the admission of the evidence would be prejudicial so that no reversal of the ruling would cure the error." Backus shot back, "I didn't know that you were the Supreme Court, Mr. Rubin. You have made your objections and you have taken your exceptions and those arguments do not help you any. Read the testimony."[67]

The prosecution's case continued six days in all, including Saturday because Judge Backus was pressing to finish before Christmas.[68] Most of the state's witnesses identified some of the defendants as present at one or more of the three Sunday rallies that Giuliani led. Few of them could attribute specific words to any of the eleven Italians. How exactly Maud Richter could have taken note of eleven specific strangers in a crowd that she put at twelve or fifteen, in addition to many more bystanders, while occupied with her own group of twenty and playing the concertina herself was anything but clear.[69] Her identifications of one and all apparently came as a surprise to the defense.[70] However, she stuck fast to her story on cross-examination.[71]

By Monday, December 10, the jurors had grown sufficiently bored during long periods in the jury room while the lawyers and judge clashed that they formed a small orchestra. One tooted the saxophone, another played the concertina, and a third plunked at a piano that the bailiff compliantly wheeled over from the jail. The long, terrazzo hallways of City Hall now echoed periodically with the strains of their amateur musical efforts.[72] It all hardly could get any odder.

There was a reason for the jurors' long idle stretches. Things were not going well between Zabel and Rubin.

If their early confrontations had done nothing to elevate the proceedings, the two lawyers now demonstrated intently that they could push the trial into a still steeper descent. By Tuesday of the trial's second week, the newspapers reported almost daily "sallies" between Zabel and Rubin that delayed the proceedings. Judge Backus was ineffectual. "I wanted to try and finish this case by the end of the week," he whined, "and to do so, you will have to eliminate side remarks. Stick to the facts."[73] The lawyers paid no heed. That very day, Assistant District Attorney Groelle stood up during testimony and accused one of the defendants, Bartolo Testolin, of making a silent threat against a witness who then was pointing out Testolin for the jury. According to Groelle, Testolin had put his fingers between his teeth. Groelle took that as an Italian threat. He wanted the court to order Testolin to stand and repeat the gesture, just in case jurors had missed it. Rubin leapt to his feet, shouting, "In view of the remarks made by the Assistant District Attorney in the presence of the jury with the intent and sole purpose of prejudicing the jury against these defendants, I now ask for a mistrial. I had no idea that anything like that means anything at all, there has been no testimony in this case as to that. For the prosecution to pick on a defendant, make him stand up and do these things is outrageously prejudicial."

Backus, continuing a sly tack to blur the record of the proceedings and make an appellate reversal less likely, simply ignored Rubin. Instead of ruling on the mistrial motion, the judge affirmed that he too had seen Testolin put his fingers between his teeth but told the jury to draw no inference from it.[74]

Rubin, who resorted to occasional cheap tricks like his insinuation about Giuliani's sexual morals, faced daily a prosecution team that made accusations like Groelle's in the jury's presence and that repeatedly called the defendants "a bunch of anarchists."[75] He faced a judge who indulged the district attorney's every barb and insult against the accused. The same judge had sought to foreordain guilty verdicts by trying the case in Milwaukee near the rubble of the police station. The trial in its entirety was slanted sharply against the woman and the ten working men from Bay View. But Rubin invited only wrath when he stooped to meet judge and prosecutor on their level. He and Zabel fired sarcastic remarks at each other all day until Backus resorted to banging his gavel.[76]

One exchange shortly before the rhubarb over Testolin's supposed gesture typifies many. Rubin was cross-examining a nineteen-year-old who was a member of Giuliani's church and had been at the third Sunday meeting. He was pressing the young man, probably pointlessly, on some small detail of one defendant's movement. Suddenly Zabel was on his feet.

"Let's try this case like lawyers; I object to this cheap comedy."

"I object to any of this cheap criticism from a cheap District Attorney," Rubin responded.

"I think your remark was improper, Mr. Rubin," interjected the judge, predictably siding with Zabel.

"So was the remark made by the District Attorney. He invited it," Rubin protested.

"I shall put in an objection every time there is an attempt made to turn this case into a travesty or a burlesque, and my objection was addressed to the court, not to anybody at the rear table. As long as he continues with his comedy and travesty I shall object," Zabel retorted.[77] The exchange confirms Zabel as a bully of extraordinary talent: he could flip reality on its head with such speed and audacity that he disarmed both opponent and judge. Here, in a sham trial before a judge and a jury who probably had decided on the eleven Italians' guilt before proceedings even began—all after mass arrests, third-degree tactics, Zabel's illegal sworn interrogations, perp walks, and searches of spectators in the courtroom—it was Zabel who accused Rubin of a travesty.

The next day Zabel brought the state's case to a close by reading aloud to the jury excerpts from pamphlets, newspapers, and circulars that the police had found in the little clubhouse room behind Zawec's saloon. "Gentlemen of the jury," Judge Backus instructed after overruling every defense objection to the admission of these writings, "all these pamphlets and papers are received for the purpose of throwing light, if any, on the subject of conspiracy." The court allowed 129 books and pamphlets in all.[78] Perhaps stewing over the absurdity of reading selected parts of tracts that the defendants never might have seen and that the several illiterates among them could not have read, Rubin boiled over again. As Zabel finished reading one excerpt that slandered President Wilson, Rubin barked at him, "You said worse things about Wilson when you ran for office!"

"I take exception to the remark," Zabel snapped back. "Were this remark made anywhere but in a courtroom I would take charge of you!"

"Well, I'm ready," retorted Rubin, rising again to his feet and looking menacingly at Zabel.

"You're a contemptible pup!" Zabel howled back.

Backus tried to reclaim control and order. "Both remarks are improper," he said wanly, in an attempt to appear judicial. He ordered the two lawyers to proceed, allowing Zabel to continue in the vein of trying the eleven defendants on the unpopular opinions of anarchist writers found in loose papers lying about the Circolo di Studi Sociali clubhouse. Rubin could not resist one last gibe. "I'll take care of the man who said that in due time," he muttered darkly as he took his seat.[79]

Three days later, Rubin nearly did exactly that. Following a two-day break, the defense case had begun. Now the prosecutors and police, no longer content with scathing aspersions in the jury's presence and the subtle dissuasion of the defendants' supporters that the courtroom searches produced, stepped up their harassment. When John LaDuca, the Socialist Party speaker from Chicago who had lectured at the clubhouse on September 9, left the courtroom after appearing as a defense witness, the police arrested him as he stepped from the elevator to walk out of City Hall.[80] There were no charges. Instead, the police said initially that they would question LaDuca indefinitely. Later, they instead claimed vaguely that they had acted at the request of federal authorities.[81] LaDuca simply would remain in custody; why and for how long no one would say. Eventually, federal authorities claimed that immigration officers were holding him for deportation.[82]

When his partner, Frank Fawcett, told Rubin of the arrest, Rubin acted immediately. While questioning another witness, he announced, "I want to make a motion that our witnesses be protected. Mr. LaDuca, who just left the stand, was arrested as he left the courtroom. The action was taken with the purpose of intimidating our witnesses. Many of them have been scared and we could not subpoena them, because they feared being arrested." Rubin wanted Judge Backus to hold the arresting police officers in contempt of court.[83] Posturing for the onlookers, Zabel trilled that he was incensed that Rubin would say such things in front of the jury and added that he now wanted the jury excused. He betrayed not a hint of shame at his hypocrisy. Backus sent the jurors out. They could resume efforts with their impromptu orchestra.

Against the backdrop of Christmas cacophony on a bleating saxophone and accordion, punctuated by the plinking piano, the lawyers slid into black rage. Implausibly, Zabel insisted, "I know nothing of this affair, and furthermore, it is none of counsel's business what the police do with any of his witnesses after they have been excused." Ignoring the little matter of false arrest, Zabel added, "When this man left the courtroom he was through with this case and the police had a right to take him to the station for interrogation." Rubin protested in response that LaDuca also had a subpoena for an Illinois proceeding and should have free passage back home to comply with that subpoena. Zabel labeled Rubin a liar. "Counsel knows that it is impossible to subpoena a man across the state line, and the statement is untrue." He sought to call Rubin's bluff. "The best way counsel can prove his remarks is by coming across with the subpoena which would show where the man was subpoenaed."

"I'll come across with a punch on the nose!" Rubin shrieked.

Zabel jumped from his chair. "I take exception to that remark and think it is about time that the court invoke certain powers which it has!"[84]

Possibly genuinely dismayed at the depths to which two of the city's most prominent lawyers, former partners at that, had sunk, Judge Backus at last said something sensible and honest. He addressed both men. "These side remarks have been carried too far. There is no reason for it and they only hurt your case and your professional standing. When the court once invokes an order under contempt proceedings, it will be a severe one."[85]

But would he take any action to prevent the state from blatant intimidation of defense witnesses? No, he would revert to his feigned impartiality and ignorance. "I have no right to pass upon anything that occurs outside the courtroom. There is nothing before the court. The witness was excused and this court has nothing to do with this matter. I cannot invoke contempt proceedings," Backus demurred.[86] In so many words, he issued the police and Zabel a blank check to harass defense witnesses.

They would use it. In all, the police arrested four defense witnesses.[87] There were no charges against any of them.

Several years later, those days remained seared in Rubin's memory. He recalled the combination of Zabel and Backus as resulting in a "scandalous" trial and recounted how he had "openly threatened to knock [Zabel's] head off."[88] For now, though, what he could do was seethe—that and demonstrate his own poor judgment when goaded.

Occasionally, Judge Backus himself would step in to belittle the defense when Zabel missed a chance. Unsurprisingly, though, Backus tended to pick on the weaker members of the defense team when he did so. Rubin was a man of stature, like it or not. It was easier for Backus to push around Rubin's younger partner, Frank Fawcett. Cross-examining another member of Giuliani's congregation, the younger lawyer asked a clumsy, sarcastic question: did the witness even know where the Tiber River is in Italy?

"Unless you confine yourself to proper cross-examination I shall excuse this witness from the stand," Backus upbraided him spontaneously.

"If Your Honor please—"

"Sit down, Mr. Fawcett; take your seat now, proceed in a lawyer-like way."

"May I ask the court in what way I have been un-lawyer like?"

"The court has ruled," Backus replied imperiously. "Will you take your seat, Mr. Fawcett."

"Yes, certainly, if the court commands me to. I would like to know if I may inquire considerately and courteously of this court why the court makes such a ruling?"

"I don't care to hear from you." Backus closed the subject.[89]

Rubin and his clients had not just Zabel's tactics and Backus's complicity to worry about. They also had Giuliani. With so few Italian speakers who enjoyed the trust of Milwaukee's law enforcement officials, Giuliani appeared not just as a witness in the anarchist trial but also played a crucial role as translator. The seized articles and pamphlets from the clubhouse of course were in Italian. Yet Zabel read them to the jury in English. The translator of most of the documents? The Reverend August Giuliani.[90] There is no evidence that Giuliani translated unscrupulously. His competency as a translator is unknowable too. But by his own admission, Giuliani did not read everything. He just looked over the material "superficially" and "when I found something strong in an article I read the whole of it and then translated excerpts from some of them."[91] At best, then, Giuliani was a selective translator who picked and chose the most inflammatory passages that he thought would best assist the prosecution, whose star witness he was.

This was not the last of Giuliani's role as a translator. It was one thing to offer bits and pieces of anarchist literature that any given defendant might not have seen or could not have read. It was another thing to serve, as Giuliani did, as Zabel's translator for the sworn interrogations that the prosecutor had conducted shortly after the defendants' arrests. Zabel offered many of the defendants' supposed statements at trial, rendered into English by the man who was their chief antagonist. According to those translations, six of the eleven defendants had admitted that they were anarchists.[92]

Here the historical record reveals that the accuracy of Giuliani's translations was in dispute.[93] After Giuliani resumed the witness stand (as he did several times throughout the trial) to affirm the accuracy of his translations, Rubin rose to cross-examine him. "Is it not a fact that you did not interpret the questions right and lied?" Betraying the fact that he did not need an interpreter for everything, the hotheaded Vincenzo Fratesi sprang up, jabbed his finger at Giuliani, and shouted, "Yes, sir. Yes, sir!" A deputy sheriff quickly shoved Fratesi back into his seat. Giuliani glowered and said only, "No."[94]

In all, it was an uncomfortable duality of roles for the evangelical minister. He testified to his own observations on the three successive Sunday gatherings in Bay View, just as any witness might. But then he also took up an active role assisting the prosecution in building its case against his countrymen by translating selected materials. Finally, Giuliani quickly accepted the opportunity to manipulate or recast, if he wished, the factual versions of the same events that the defendants gave when the district attorney questioned them in custody and without counsel. At the time, that meant most of the defendants could speak to the district attorney only through their principal accuser. Later, the defendants could cross-examine him or testify themselves; at trial they could challenge the accuracy of Giuliani's work both ways. That did not make his role as translator-advocate any more savory.

For his part at trial, Zabel (like most of the other lawyers) took a turn on the witness stand that legal ethics today would forbid.[95] He and the others acted as both advocates and sworn, objective truth-tellers at trial. Under questioning by Groelle, Zabel testified piously that the defendants' "statements were entirely voluntary, free, without any promises or suggestion, or without any threat or intimidation at all."[96] If the fawning mainstream press was even close to accurate in its reports of third-degree tactics and "rigid"[97] interrogations, Zabel likely perjured himself, or at least kept himself deliberately ignorant of events in the police station.

Unseen, building pressures on him during the trial may offer at least a partial explanation, although not an excuse, if Zabel did lie. Some of the pressures were obvious and manageable. Three-week trials are arduous, even without the incessant bickering and personal attacks that marked relations between Zabel and Rubin. The watchful eyes of a corps of newspaper reporters also contribute to a lawyer's tension. But Zabel and Groelle bore another burden secretly.

As the trial wore on, the two prosecutors accumulated a "wastebasket full of threatening letters."[98] Sometime during or just after the trial, the Milwaukee Police Department became concerned enough to assign plainclothes officers to follow Judge Backus, Zabel, and Groelle wherever they went and to watch their homes at night.[99] These mounting threats were real. The most serious threats came from those who followed the trial only from afar, so they took time to become manifest. After the trial, Groelle's wife and daughters drove to a play at the Pabst Theater one Friday or Saturday evening, hosting a couple who were friends of the Groelles. When the party of five returned from the play between 11 p.m. and midnight, a man who appeared Italian, wearing a slouch cap, walked out of the pitch black and stepped up to the car as it approached the garage. He held a pistol and approached the back seat, in which Groelle usually sat. One of Groelle's daughters was driving. She and the other women began screaming when the gunman appeared in the dark. Then the car lurched into a corner of the garage. The gunman fled. He fired no shots, but then he had not found Groelle in the car as he probably expected, either.[100]

A more elaborate plot unraveled one month after the trial. A young woman, Ella Antolini, not yet eighteen years old and enthralled with the anarchist leaders she had met, rode the train from Ohio to Chicago with thirty-six sticks of dynamite in her black leather grip. She was to deliver the dynamite to a "Mario Rusca" there, whom Paul Avrich surmised was none other than Mario Buda, bombmaker extraordinaire.[101] From Chicago, the dynamite would go to Milwaukee.[102] It would be a loud and deadly answer to the trial of the eleven Italians. Thanks to an alert porter who devised a clever trick that allowed him a peek inside her grip, the police were waiting in force for Ella Antolini at the platform in Chicago on January 18, 1918.[103] In the ensuing months, Antolini stoutly resisted every attempt to pry the names of her confederates from her.[104] She eventually pled guilty in federal court, where the familiar Judge Landis gave her eighteen months in prison—every day the law allowed him to impose. The Pullman porter in a starched white smock, T. W. Johnson,[105] who had a keen eye for suspicious passengers, quite possibly had saved Zabel's life. They would never meet or even know of each other.

Zabel's experience later got even more harrowing. On April 15, 1918, police officers discovered two unexploded bombs planted outside his house, one on either side.[106] Each contained about twenty pounds of dynamite and shrapnel, enough to destroy the home and everyone in it.[107] Quite plausibly, Zabel asserted at the time that the failed bombs were "nothing more than an attempt at retaliation" for the trial of the eleven Italians.[108] He maintained public bravado, even joking to a reporter, "Oh, they paid me a visit last night."[109] But privately Zabel was "practically a nervous wreck."[110] He considered resignation and told others in the district attorney's office that he had sought an additional life insurance policy but was turned down.[111] One of the bombs was a duplicate of the bomb that had destroyed the central police station, according to Captain Sullivan, who had examined both of them.[112]

During trial, though, the menace to the lives of the prosecutors and judge reached only the stage of the dozens of mailed death threats. Still, the tension was unrelenting. Even the end of the state's case-in-chief did not allow Zabel to relax. He had to prepare to cross-examine the defense witnesses, who eventually would far outnumber the prosecution's.[113] Zabel spoke only figuratively on Wednesday morning, December 12, when he rose shortly before noon to announce, "The state rests."[114]

The defense case focused on either rendering innocuous various actions at the three Sunday rallies or demonstrating that some defendants were not present at all. Rubin first tried valiantly, if vainly, to erase Zabel's violent caricature of anarchism. In a full day of reading translated passages of the seized papers less incendiary than those that Zabel shared with the jury, he sought to place anarchism in its philosophical context or reduce it to a benign strain of socialism.[115] In Rubin's own brief turn on the witness stand, he boasted that he was something of a student of literature and then explained to the jury who Voltaire was. The police had recovered an extract of the French thinker's writing in their raids.[116]

Mostly, though, the defense case wore on with witnesses from the neighborhood who had seen nothing improper in the defendants' actions if they had seen the defendants at all. Many of these witnesses testified for no more than a few minutes. One critical distinction between the state witnesses and the defense witnesses emerged slowly as Rubin sought to counter Zabel's subtle strategy. Defense witnesses often perceived Giuliani's purposes as evangelical, not predominantly patriotic. For example, Pietro Bianchi's sister-in-law, Appolonya Bianchi, recalled Giuliani's group singing a tune with the line "Jesus has come to save the Italians."[117] That line stuck with other Italians as well.[118] The emphasis on an evangelistic purpose, as opposed to a purely patriotic one, was consistent with the theme that Rubin had struggled to develop since his first cross-examination of Reverend Giuliani.[119]

For his part, Zabel used his cross-examinations, when he could, to tar defense witnesses with their political views, their support for the IWW, and their lack of citizenship.[120] Responding to Rubin's objection, Zabel explained, "It shows the attitude of certain of these people towards the government." He did not elaborate on why support for a radical labor-rights organization necessarily equated with bias against the government in this case. Then again, he hardly had to explain. Backus overruled Rubin's objection.[121]

The only real excitement during the defense case occurred just outside the courtroom door, with the arrests of the four defense witnesses who never got as far as the street after they left the witness stand. On the third day of the defense case, though, someone very small offered a genuine, if fleeting, glimpse of humanity.

It came on Monday, December 17. Little Areno Nardini, Pasquale and Maria's four-year-old son, had been in the county's custody since his parents' arrest, lodged at the home for dependent children on the Milwaukee County grounds in the still rural community of Wauwatosa near the county's western edge. The superintendent of the home, August Kringel, on a kindly impulse brought Areno downtown to see his parents, if only from the courtroom gallery. As soon as Areno spied his mother, he broke away from Kringel and bolted for Maria. She gasped in joy as she saw him, got up, and rushed toward Areno to embrace him. Maria was sobbing by the time she hurried back to her chair, with Areno wrapped around her. The confused witness broke off in midsentence, and now the jury gaped at Maria and Areno. Pasquale, seated right behind Maria, reached out to hug and kiss his son. Tears streaked his cheeks. Unlike Maria, who had been permitted occasional brief visits in jail with Areno, Pasquale had not seen his child since his arrest. Judge Backus by this time was rapping his gavel and Zabel was protesting furiously this intrusion of unscripted human kindness into his trial. The judge ordered the jury out of the courtroom, gruffly agreeing that he disfavored such a display. But, after some inquiry and for reasons unknown, Backus melted just a bit. When trial resumed, he allowed Areno to remain on Pasquale's lap until the next break, if the child would sit quietly. The little boy did.[122]

As the defense case wound down that week, all eleven accused took the witness stand themselves. The nearly overlooked Daniele Belucci went first. Others followed, roughly in ascending order of their prominence in the testimony and arguments at trial. Dramatically, Maria Nardini, who quietly wore the taunting label "queen of the anarchists" that the *Milwaukee Sentinel* pasted on her, went last. They all told their simple stories. None had much education. Quitting school at age twelve or earlier to work in Italy, after maybe two or three years of education, was the norm. Yes, they were Catholic by upbringing, although most denied any active interest in religion now. No, they were not citizens. No, they had not behaved violently at Giuliani's rally, nor carried a gun, nor made any plan with anyone to disrupt or shoot. Most said that they belonged to no anarchist club. They could not read much.[123] Their English? Not good or nonexistent. Pasquale and Maria Nardini confessed that they had never attended any school at all; they were utterly illiterate.[124] With the possible exception of Pietro Bianchi's, Maria's testimony was the longest.[125]

The six defendants whose purported statements to Zabel the state had introduced found themselves with some further explaining to do. Bianchi admitted, "I am a socialist anarchist." But he deflected Zabel's cross-examination with some skill. "I don't hope for the revolution—I hope for the education of the people."[126] The others denied making the more inflammatory statements that Giuliani and Zabel had attributed to them. Vincenzo Fratesi, ever the most intemperate, insisted that the entirety of his statement was untrue; it was Giuliani's and Zabel's invention.[127] His own testimony, though, was inconsistent and often self-contradictory. He had very little schooling, could barely read, but did manage to read *The Moral of Anarchy* and *Workmen's Organization*. He also acknowledged reading two newspapers at home, *La Parola* and *Progresso*.[128] He was neither for government nor against it: he claimed indifference.[129] In all, Vincenzo's words rang of dissembling and deceit.

When at last the defense rested, on Wednesday morning, December 19, the state offered a brief but biting rebuttal.[130] Louisa Ferraro worked for Associated Charities as an interpreter for Italians. On Monday morning, she was in the first row of the gallery on the defense side, awaiting the start of proceedings. She claimed that Rubin leaned toward Gavino Denurra and another of the defendants, summoned the rest over to him, and instructed them, "You say that he spoke against the pope." The defendants bowed, shook their heads, and smiled. "You say that," Rubin repeated.[131]

Rubin contested her claim on cross-examination, of course. But he did not take the witness stand again to deny it. Instead, he recalled all eleven defendants. All denied that Rubin had coached them to say that Giuliani had insulted the pope. In fact, they denied that Rubin had spoken to them in English at all.[132]

One, Luigi Serafini, dropped a passing comment that revealed much. Other than in court, he said, he had seen Rubin on only one occasion in his life.[133] The trial had included almost no testimony about Serafini, who by the time he testified in surrebuttal had been in jail for more than three months, convicted of nothing.

Evidently, he was a client as insignificant to Rubin as he was a defendant insignificant to Zabel.

With all evidence closed on Wednesday, December 19, lawyers from both sides could have considered the net effect of the proof. As to many of the defendants, it was not much. Only Maud Richter placed Daniele Belucci at the corner on September 9, and even she no more than noted his presence. The same with Luigi Serafini; although he was there, according to both Richter and Louis Sgajalio, neither had seen him do anything or say anything whatsoever.[134] As to Pietro Bianchi, Adolfo Fratesi, Pasquale Nardini, and Angelo Pantaleone, more than one person identified them as present. But no witness attributed the slightest wrongful action or comment to them. They merely had been present, for all the evidence showed. As to Bartolo Testolin, Gavino Denurra, and Maria Nardini, there was a bit more: Testolin was "howling worse than the devil"; Denurra had buttoned his coat as an Italian might do if preparing to fight and had crossed to Giuliani's side of the street; and Maria Nardini had marched in the lead from the little clubhouse, talked excitedly with several of the men in her group, and called Giuliani a pig.[135]

The state made its strongest showing against Vincenzo Fratesi and Amedeo Lilli. Most important, at least one prosecution witness claimed that each had been armed and had displayed a pistol on September 9.[136] Several witnesses described the dead men, Tony Formaceo and Augusto Marinelli, as firing guns. But Vincenzo Fratesi and Amedeo Lilli were the only two people on trial whom any prosecution witness recounted as armed. Several witnesses also testified to aggressive comments and behavior by Vincenzo Fratesi and Lilli, including crossing over to Giuliani's side of the street. According to Reverend Giuliani, for example, Vincenzo pointed to the American flag and shouted at Giuliani, "Coward for such a rag!"[137] But even this evidence made a much stronger case for assault or attempted murder as to those two men than it did for reaching an agreement with others to achieve those ends. That agreement is what the state's conspiracy charges required, in theory.

Zabel and his prosecution team were not about to get bogged down in legal niceties, though, or lost in the minutiae of evidence. Frederick Groelle gave the initial summation for the state. Acquit these defendants, he warned the jury, and they might place a bomb under your window. Rubin protested immediately. Well, what he had meant, Groelle explained, was that the defendants were teaching a doctrine of anarchy, which was to say they were teaching the making of bombs. Backus predictably blessed it as fair argument.[138]

In his fiery rebuttal argument for the prosecution, the last words that jurors would hear from the lawyers, Zabel was even less oblique. Purporting to explain conspiracy, Zabel urged, "If I place a bomb loaded with high explosives in a church hoping thereby that the bomb will explode and kill human beings, and if someone takes that bomb to the police station and the bomb there explodes and kills ten or twelve human beings, I am responsible!"[139] Objection, objection, Rubin bellowed. The eleven defendants were not on trial for placing a bomb, were not charged with placing a bomb, and could not have placed a bomb; they were in jail at the time. Backus paused just a moment before excusing Zabel's argument as "the personal illustration of the District Attorney." Zabel could proceed.[140] It may have been Backus's most disingenuous moment, although there were many others in close contention.

Emboldened, Zabel whipped the jurors to convict, "Lest they forget Czolgosz, the fiend who killed McKinley. The teachings which might prompt a diabolical deed, to place a bomb which might kill a police officer!" A tired Rubin objected again. Overruled; Zabel could go on.[141]

When Zabel at last neared the end and reminded the jurors of the seized papers from the clubhouse and the defendants' rooming houses, selected excerpts of which he had read them, he exclaimed, "These letters blow up their defense far worse than the bomb blew up the police station!" If only for form, Rubin objected hoarsely yet again. Judge Backus once more covered for Zabel. "If any of you gentlemen of the jury understood the District Attorney as referring to the bomb incident at the police station, you will understand he has said nothing about the defendants as being connected with that incident. You must not consider anything that was said as to that, as against these defendants."[142]

With arguments completed at about 5:30 p.m., Backus instructed the jury. He dropped the second count of the Amended Information. That left the first charge, assault with intent to commit first-degree murder while armed, on the state's conspiracy theory. On that same theory, he also invited the jurors to consider the lesser included offenses of assault with intent to cause great bodily harm and simple assault.[143] To aid the jurors in considering the conspiracy theory of culpability, Backus read them the state's criminal anarchy statutes. Those statutes forbade advocacy of violent overthrow of the government or assassination of executive officials or incitement to do such things.[144] They dovetailed neatly with the state's arguments as to the papers the police had seized. The trouble was that the defendants were not charged with criminal anarchy and had been afforded no warning that they would be tried for it. By the end of the trial then, two new charges announced on the first day had dwindled to one, but lesser included offenses had appeared and criminal anarchy, never charged, also tempted the jurors to convict on a patchwork theory of their own creation.

At 5:55 p.m. Backus adjourned court until 8 p.m. so that the jurors might have dinner before beginning their deliberations.[145] He need not have bothered.

After this three-week trial, with fully twelve days of testimony and exhibits, the jurors deliberated for just seventeen minutes. They voted only once. The verdicts: guilty of the most serious charge, assault with intent to commit first-degree murder, all eleven defendants.[146] Those seventeen minutes of deliberations allowed about ninety seconds to consider the evidence bearing on the individual guilt of each one of the eleven defendants. Less, actually, because the jurors also elected their foreman in that time.[147] The defendants took the verdict with their "accustomed stoicism."[148] All the same, that night the sheriff beefed up security at the jail after bailiffs led the defendants back to their cells, in train.[149]

Rubin made a perfunctory motion for a new trial before he even packed his briefcase slowly and trudged out into the dark of an icy, desolate December night, after 8:30 p.m. Judge Backus set that motion for a hearing the following Thursday,[150] two days after Christmas. But the motion would receive only cursory consideration, obviously, for Backus set sentencing at the same time. Each of the defendants faced up to thirty years in prison.[151]

The morning after the verdicts, Zabel took time with reporters to deliver an encomium. He addressed it nominally to the police, Giuliani, and jury but meant it also for his own glory. "The conviction strikes at the root of this hotbed of anarchy. This gang, dangerous as it was, would in time become more violent. For years they gathered in their anarchist hall . . . and filled their brain with the contents of anarchist books," he said with a flourish.[152] He thanked the Reverend August Giuliani. Then Zabel went on to inflate his case and, in the process, himself. "This gang is but one of the links of a long chain of such organizations whose main purpose is to overthrow the government, with violence if necessary. Bomb plotting is going on on a large scale and one can imagine just what these defendants would have done had they been allowed to go on uninterrupted. There are similar organizations in most of the large cities throughout the country and I am glad to say that the Milwaukee officials have succeeded in uprooting the one here. The conviction will have a wholesome effect in stamping out these organizations."[153] The eleven working Italians hardly would have recognized that portrait of themselves, if they had been able to read a newspaper—or read at all—the day after the verdicts as they sat in their cells and awaited a bitter fate.

Christmas passed in jail. Areno spent it with the orphans and other sad urchins who filled the sleeping hall of the county home for dependent children.

As expected, Judge Backus summarily denied the motion for a new trial on December 27. If the Wisconsin Supreme Court thought the convictions unfair, its seven members collectively could bear the public outrage over an order reversing the verdicts and directing a new trial. Plus, that higher court would have benefit of the passage of a year or two as the appellate process meandered to its conclusion. The public's attention span was short. Meanwhile, Backus himself would be seen as having avenged the deaths in the police station and rid the public of eleven immigrants whose assumed beliefs seemed a festering sore to most Americans. That the bomb and the defendants' beliefs were not the crimes charged was beside the point.

Now came the matter of sentences for the eleven convicts. The judge had before him eleven different human beings. There was some range in ages. One was a woman. At least the Nardinis had a child. Bianchi was blind in one eye. The proof at trial suggested widely varying roles and participation, even assuming that it sufficed to prove all guilty. In short, the eleven were scattered across a spectrum of culpability, to say nothing of other individual considerations that might have borne on an appropriate sentence.

In the view of the jury and Judge Backus, though, they also all were conspirators. The consequence of conspiracy was that anyone who joined an illegal agreement both implicitly ratified the steps that others took before he joined and accepted joint responsibility for every foreseeable future step in pursuit of the agreement's ends by the others. In for a penny, in for a pound. "You acted in concert. It was a conspiracy, well calculated and well planned, and you must answer to the law for your inexcusable conduct," Backus lectured.[154]

Moreover, the ten men and one woman before him all were foreign. They spoke only babel, to Backus's ears. The eleven seemed from his vantage point to have much in common with one another but almost nothing in common with him and those he knew. "All of you are aliens," he sneered. "In this country but a few years. You have cast aside all of the American institutions which have offered you advancement. This is the greatest country in the world. By your anarchistic teachings and doings you sought to destroy by violence. You are not a creative or constructive force. Your purposes are destructive and ruinous and the court must measure out such punishment as is commensurate with the crime which all of you have committed."[155]

Even that was not the worst of it. Playing directly to the newspapers, Backus became purple, in oratory if not in complexion:

> You have banded yourselves together and have worshiped before
> the shrine of criminal anarchy. You have been drinking from the
> bitter cup, the poison of which has led to your destruction. Cain

hurled defiance at his Creator, "Am I my brother's keeper," and the blood of his brother Abel cried out aloud from the ground and branded him with an awful murder. Cain became an outcast, branded and a fugitive. . . . Here we find men in our own community worshiping pictures of their so-called martyrs who have murdered officers of the law, and there at your meeting place you defied your God with your so-called prayer, "Cursed be God." No court record has ever been so stained or branded with anything so vile.[156]

On and on he howled.

Most of the eleven Italians could not understand a word. The court had neglected to retain an interpreter that day. So Backus pressed Pietro Bianchi into the demeaning service of assisting him in sentencing Bianchi himself and his ten fellow prisoners. Bianchi translated for the others.[157]

When at last Backus finished his harangue, he imposed sentence. The terms of imprisonment would be twenty-five years at hard labor, for one and for all.[158] Backus made no attempt to differentiate the people standing before him—not their roles in the crime, not their prospects for future obedience to law, not their families' interests, not their character. He treated them as one. And as one, the entire group would go to the state's only prison, in the small town of Waupun, one hour north and west of Milwaukee by train. Maria Nardini would spend her time confined in the small women's wing when not at menial labor. The men would join the state's other prisoners in the larger facilities, caged behind an oddly handsome sandstone and iron pike wall that rose to twenty feet or more.

The train for Waupun left that very afternoon at 2 p.m. Sheriff McManus, eight deputies, and four detectives took the eleven to the Milwaukee depot.[159]

Only two of the eleven showed any emotion as they boarded the train. Pasquale and Maria Nardini wept inconsolably. They cried for Areno. At age four, he "would have to make the rest of his way through life to manhood parentless," as the *Milwaukee Sentinel* put it. Although the Nardinis had relatives eager to take in the little boy, Judge Backus declared him a ward of the county.[160] This time, no one brought Areno to see his parents.[161]

8

Darrow

Late the day of sentencing, after he had returned to the office from court, Bill Rubin dictated a short note to a friend in New York City. "As you know, I lost the Italian Case," he admitted. "With no chance on earth to get justice, we did not get it. The bomb explosion excited so much hatred and prejudice, and to be compelled to go to trial a couple of days after the burial of eleven [*sic*; the correct number was nine] policemen, made the whole thing a fore-gone conclusion. However, I expect to take the case to the Supreme Court, and hope for better results."[1] His letter included not a word about the sentences. Rubin was looking forward. And he was not alone in thinking immediately about an appeal to the Wisconsin Supreme Court.

By Emma Goldman's reckoning, the Milwaukee jury had convicted only two real anarchists. "The others are radicals of different shades," she reported, "whose main offense consisted in fighting the Catholic Church." Maria Nardini and her son drew Goldman's special sympathy. Maria "is a woman without any ideas whatever, but evidently a fine brave spirit." After the state wrested Areno from the Nardini relatives, "the whole situation seems too terrible to contemplate and will need competent hands to handle."[2]

Goldman was America's most prominent anarchist at the time, so her assess-ment carries some weight. But she also was sentimental and demonstrably wrong about some of her facts (she thought, for example, that the jury had convicted twelve defendants).[3] As with so much else about the individual defendants, their true politics remained obscure even after their convictions.

Locked away in the state prison in Waupun, the eleven had lost what little ability they ever had to seek a lawyer or pursue freedom. They could not help themselves. Their days passed in the tedium of manual labor and standing in line for food or head counts. They were lost to the world, and it was lost to them.

At a distance, though, Goldman and others remained keenly interested in their plight. Before trial, a sympathetic few had taken up the practical task of raising funds for a legal defense. As early as October 14, a man in Chicago wrote to Goldman's *Mother Earth Bulletin* to alert readers to the plight of the eleven Italians in Milwaukee. After urging the unjustness of the arrests, the writer came to his pitch. "There is another big job on hand. The lawyer wants $3,000 to take up their defense, $1,500 before the trial and the remainder afterwards. To tell the truth I have lost faith even in the lawyer, for I have found out it is just as bad to trust him as it is to trust bankers, in fact the lawyers are nothing but blood-suckers."[4] Sincere, but otherwise a clumsy appeal for contributions to the defense fund. Then as now, even the most charitably minded may not donate willingly to benefit a lawyer, let alone one portrayed as a human wood tick.

The effort to raise money for the defense took on a more polished look only after the trial. Not a week after sentencing, Emma Goldman penned a letter to her own lawyer, the eminent Harry Weinberger of New York City, from a train en route to Chicago. She had met with William Judin, "one of our most active fellows," who was arranging a Sunday meeting to take up the means of paying for an appeal for the Milwaukee eleven. Judin was to call on Weinberger in his office on Monday, January 7. Although Goldman clearly hoped that Weinberger would take the appeal, she assured Weinberger that she understood that he would need at least $200 for his time just to look into the case and that he then would assess what further fee he might require. "You can be blunt about it" with Judin, she closed.[5]

Just more than two weeks after she wrote to Weinberger, Goldman published a scathing article titled "The Milwaukee Frame-Up" in the January 1918 edition of *Mother Earth Bulletin*. She accused the police of framing the eleven and called the scheme "so cruel, deliberate and revolting as to arouse even the sluggish minds and hearts of those who never care what happens to others just so they are allowed to exist."[6] Continuing the gentle handling of lawyers' egos that she had demonstrated in her letter to Weinberger, Goldman did not attack Bill Rubin as a "blood-sucker" or anything of the sort. Instead, she curried his good will and quoted liberally from a letter Rubin had provided that described the trial and its circumstances. Her article finished with a deft fund-raising plea that invited the reader to take part in something really grand. "It goes without saying that such a terrible crime cannot go unchallenged," Goldman implored. "Already an International Defense League has been organized in Chicago to begin a campaign of publicity so that the people may learn of this latest outrage in Milwaukee. For that and the appeal money is most urgently needed." Contributions were to be addressed to Judin.[7] This would be a worldwide effort, the inspired donor might believe.

But the reality was something less. Judin had missed connections with Weinberger in New York. Weinberger had waited in the office until 6:50 p.m. on the appointed Monday, but Judin never came. Later, Weinberger learned that Judin had left for Chicago. Still, Weinberger was gracious in offering to help. "I would consider a reasonable fee, $1,000, and my expenses which would probably be going to Milwaukee not more than once or twice," Weinberger suggested.[8] He even offered to take up the cause of getting Areno transferred back to the custody of relatives.[9] That was a smaller cause dear to Goldman: her comments about the case never failed to note the little boy's plight.[10]

Goldman continued her efforts to secure appellate counsel. She evidently met with Rubin in Milwaukee, although the meeting may have been brief; soon she could not exactly recall his name. But she wrote to Rubin's longtime secretary, Leola Hirschman, who on January 10, 1918, provided her a copy of the letter that Goldman excerpted later that month in the article in the *Mother Earth Bulletin*.[11] Rubin also made a trip to Chicago on New Year's Day to discuss the appeal but did not name the "friends" of the eleven defendants with whom he met.[12]

Between the time that Rubin's secretary replied to Goldman and the time the January issue of the *Bulletin* went to press, Goldman's life became emphatically more difficult. On January 14, 1918, the U.S. Supreme Court affirmed her federal conviction in New York City for conspiring to cause resistance to the draft.[13] That prosecution was the government's response to the No-Conscription League that Goldman and Alexander Berkman had organized. It ended the league and forced Goldman to mute her direct opposition to the war. She had posted bail pending appeal, but now the stay of her prison sentence was at an end. Harry Weinberger's best efforts on her behalf and Berkman's had failed. Goldman accepted her own fate cheerily, joking to her friend Kitty Beck that she would keep all posted on how she was "faring at Jefferson University," meaning the Missouri State Prison at Jefferson City. Yet she felt deeply sad for Weinberger, who she knew would be "bitterly disappointed because he has worked so hard and given his very soul to getting us free."[14] It was not to be.

For the time, Goldman was staying in Chicago at the New Southern Hotel. She was receiving mail there in her own name.[15] As it had been since before the Haymarket bombing, Chicago was the center of American anarchism. The New Southern may have been a small hotel, but sitting on Michigan Avenue at 13th Street, two blocks west of the current site of the Field Museum of Natural History between downtown and Hyde Park to the south, it was not exactly inconspicuous.[16]

And Goldman was not hiding. Anticipating imprisonment, she returned to New York City shortly after Sunday, January 13.[17] The sentencing judge ordered her surrender in New York on February 2, 1918.[18] In Harry Weinberger's company, she and Berkman surrendered that morning.[19] By February 6 a deputy U.S. marshal had escorted Goldman back to Jefferson City. The *New York Times* gloated that Goldman was "again in stripes."[20]

The prison soon would assign her to sew clothes for other inmates. So she would end her days in America precisely as she had started them: a seamstress at slave wages.[21]

With a sense of urgency, Goldman spent her last three weeks of freedom in Chicago and New York City working to secure appellate counsel for the eleven Milwaukee Italians. Rubin remained interested in pursuing the appeal, as did Weinberger. First and foremost, though, Rubin was interested in being paid. While he was out of town in Detroit on a "labor case," Leola Hirschman was handling his correspondence on the Italian case. Responding to a Chicago Italian who claimed he was acting for the defendants, Hirschman explained that Rubin's younger partner, Guy Dutcher, was appearing at a hearing at Waupun on the deportation of the Italians. But she declined to send a copy of the record of the case—something that an appellate lawyer would want as a first step in considering whether to take the appeal. She demurred that Rubin's office "would have to incur considerable expense" to get the record. True, but sending the record also would have meant easing the task of anyone who wanted to shop the appeal to other lawyers. Then she assured the writer, "Mr. Rubin is anxious to prosecute the appeal, but there will have to be some guaranteed fund before the same can be successfully taken."[22] Rubin had in mind $2,000 to $3,000 for the appeal, which he had begun efforts to raise on the day of sentencing.[23]

Goldman's letter to Rubin's office on January 8 requested that Rubin come to Chicago for a second meeting.[24] With Rubin in Detroit, Hirschman's polite reply on January 10, enclosing Rubin's description of the trial, was all she would get. An idea well may have occurred to Goldman then to look both higher and closer than Rubin or even Weinberger. Here she was in Chicago for a last few days, staying not far from Hyde Park and the University of Chicago. Just a matter of some forty blocks to the south, close to the lakefront, lived America's preeminent lawyer and defender of the damned. She was all but in Clarence Darrow's neighborhood.

There is no ironclad proof that Goldman convinced Darrow to take up the cause of the eleven Milwaukee Italians. Darrow certainly had other ties to radicals in Chicago and elsewhere, one of whom might have come to him directly on behalf of the eleven. But given Goldman's own stature, motivation, active involvement, and proximity, the confluence raises the strong suspicion that she was the direct link to Darrow.

Goldman had known of Darrow for years. By 1901 she already knew his reputation well but had never met him personally.[25] Her first indirect contact with him was not good. It came in the form of a visit from an unnamed lawyer in Darrow's office after Leon Czolgosz assassinated President McKinley. The lawyer's effort to dissuade her from speaking out on Czolgosz's behalf did not sit well with her. Possessed of an accurate sense of her own place in the hierarchy of the left at the century's turn, Goldman "demanded to know why Mr. Darrow himself did not come if he was concerned, but his representative was evasive."[26] Surely Darrow and Goldman met at some point in the ensuing years, although he appears only twice—briefly both times—in her autobiography.[27] Still, she credited him as "a brilliant lawyer, a man of broad social views, an able writer and lecturer."[28] Given her interest in the Milwaukee Italians' case and her role in coordinating efforts to mount an appeal, it would be odd if Goldman had not reached out to Darrow, directly or indirectly, or at very least orchestrated another's overture to him.

In any event, Clarence Darrow entered his appearance on behalf of the eleven prisoners. His bookish and most loyal partner, Peter Sissman, joined him. Although in theory this change in lawyers required the approval of the eleven clients, in fact they seem to have relied entirely on the judgment of others.

Rubin was dumped. He did not even know it at first. On January 19 Rubin wrote to the Italian contact for the defendants in Chicago that he was receiving "daily inquiries relative to what is being done in the matter of the appeal of the Italian cases." He upbraided the recipient: "Things are at a standstill, and time is running fast. You said that you would have the money necessary to defray the expense of a transcript of the testimony and printing bills, etc., within four or five days after you saw me, to-wit, on New Year's Day. Now it is already the 19th of January, and I have heard nothing from you."[29]

Four days later, the Italian contact informed Rubin that he would not be the lawyer on appeal. Rubin's reply was peevish, unsurprisingly. "I have your letter," he wrote. "Thank you for at least answering my last letter. I am glad to be relieved of the burden. I have given my best efforts and time, at a tremendous loss to myself, to fight against the injustice to your fellowmen."[30] With that, Rubin was out. In a separate letter that day to a woman who had assisted at trial as an interpreter, Rubin tacitly acknowledged his dismissal and asked, "Is ingratitude becoming a common vice?"[31]

His papers do not disclose whether those paying for the appeal offered Rubin the small consolation of serving as Darrow's local counsel. Professional pride, though, probably would have led him to decline any offer to serve only as Darrow's helpmate. Rubin had tried the case. A lawyer of his standing would not accept that demotion on appeal, even for the chance to work with Clarence Darrow. His correspondence on the case ends with an ambiguous comment that may or may not have been a swipe at Darrow. "If publicity is your sole object in fighting that case," Rubin huffed, "I am not the lawyer you want on the job."[32]

Another Milwaukee lawyer of purely local repute, A. C. Umbreit, instead would serve in the minor role of Wisconsin counsel for Darrow and Sissman.[33] Umbreit was scholarly. He had a master's degree in Greek and had taught for twenty years at Marquette University Law School while maintaining a private practice. A staunch Republican, he had married a distant relative of Edwin M. Stanton, President Lincoln's secretary of war. That shirt-tail association was a matter of family pride: the Umbreits named their eldest son Stanton.[34] Umbreit's station in Milwaukee and his pretenses would matter little if at all, though. The appeal was Darrow's.

The United States has produced many lawyers famed as presidents, framers of the Constitution, and politicians in every public office. Clarence Seward Darrow, though, remains the nation's most famous lawyer known principally as a lawyer.

Nothing about his origins suggested that arc. Outside "the obscure village" of Kinsman, in northeast Ohio near Pennsylvania Dutch country, Emily Eddy Darrow gave birth to her fifth child on April 18, 1857.[35] Eventually, she would have eight. A toddler would die shortly after the fifth child's birth, leaving this one exactly in the middle: he had three surviving older siblings and three younger.[36] His parents named him Clarence Seward.

The boy's father, Ammirus, moved the family into town when Clarence was seven. From then on, Ammirus was the town coffin maker, furniture maker, atheist, and crank. Others in Kinsman erected the modest clapboard Victorian houses that were the mode. Ammirus Darrow bought his family an octagonal house covered in stucco.[37] Although "the village infidel," as Clarence called him, Ammirus also was the graduate of a Unitarian theological seminary.[38] The contrarian Ammirus was a staunch Democrat in stoutly Republican Ohio, but he also was zealous in his antislavery views and assisted slaves in passage through the Underground Railroad.[39] Neither prosperous nor much interested in prospering, he had ample time for books and little time for convention. Clarence admired his father as a lifelong "visionary and dreamer."[40]

Into early adulthood, the son's trajectory seemed much like his father's: quirky, layered with seeming contradictions, intellectually curious but limited in expression of his values through work.[41] Clarence loved books and baseball.[42] He did not love school but did well enough there. "I was none too industrious, and I have never loved to work," Darrow confessed, tongue in cheek. "I always preferred diversions to duties, and this strange taste has clung to me all through life."[43]

Clarence's opportunity to attend Allegheny College ended after one year when the economy skidded into recession with the Panic of 1873.[44] He returned home. During the next few summers, Clarence helped his father make furniture. While school was in session, he taught for three years. The young school teacher, not yet twenty-one, already displayed traits that endured all his life. He flatly rejected corporal punishment, lengthened recess periods during the school day, joined his pupils at play during recess, and broadened the topics of classroom discussion to anything that interested him. As his biographers Lila and Arthur Weinberg commented, whether the students learned more "is open to question, but that they were a happy group is obvious."[45]

During this time back in Kinsman, Darrow also began to study law. He studied alone with borrowed books.[46] Studying solo suited Darrow. His intellect was unstructured and dreamy, like his father's. He picked up his father's knack for assembling an identity from a jumble of contradictions that, taken together, resulted somehow in an integrated whole. Eventually, his father and two siblings insisted that Clarence go to the University of Michigan Law School. That structured setting lasted only one year too.[47] In 1878 he returned to the only city of any size near Kinsman, Youngstown, and read law in a lawyer's office.[48] After a long night with bar examiners and about a dozen other aspiring advocates in a Youngstown tavern, the examiners admitted him to practice. Quite fittingly, Darrow was called to the bar in a bar.[49] The coffin maker's middle son now was a lawyer.

But, like his father's, his mind still wandered farther than his feet. Clarence Darrow remained then a very local young man. He married local, to Jessie Ohl, a family friend.[50] Although he considered hanging a shingle in Youngstown, at twenty thousand people the town's size overawed him.[51] So he opened his practice in the little village of Andover, ten miles from Kinsman.[52]

In part, the influence of Darrow's father was a result of the death of his mother when Clarence was but fourteen. He later recalled Emily Darrow in distinctly general terms but with deep sentiment and all his life found it too hard to visit her marble headstone when he returned to Kinsman.[53] With the exception of one occasion, he passed the cemetery gate rather than enter.[54]

That marked a rare setting in which Darrow permitted a fence between him and his emotions. "I had a strongly emotional nature which has caused me boundless joy and infinite pain," he explained late in life. "I had a vivid imagination. Not only could I put myself in the other person's place, but I could not avoid doing so. My sympathies always went out to the weak, the suffering, and the poor."[55]

At some point, those sympathies began to stir Darrow, the small-town lawyer, to pursue something more. Initially, his moves were modest. After about two years in Andover, Darrow moved his practice to Ashtabula, twenty-five miles away and appreciably bigger, with a population of about five thousand. That city "furnished a somewhat broader field, but was not especially exciting."[56]

His next move was the one that changed his life. In 1888 Darrow moved to Chicago. He would be long forgotten today and probably would have remained unknown in his own day had he not made that move. It changed everything.

Darrow later attributed the move, unconvincingly, to a mere fit of pique over a home purchase gone sour.[57] Whatever role that episode played, the fact that Darrow's older brother, Everett, then was teaching in Chicago also played a part in the move.[58] But there was something more too. He began very quickly to live a life that expressed through his work the precarious assemblage of ideas, values, and sentiments that made him Darrow. Ammirus labored with his hands, a craftsman but not an artist, and never linked his work to his ideas. His fifth child, Clarence, suddenly did. Almost from the month he arrived in Chicago at age thirty-one, the younger Darrow began to use his labor and his voice to make tangible the ideas and ideals he held.

In some ways, his first efforts were no nobler than those of many ambitious young lawyers, then and now. He wanted to get his name in the newspapers, to acquire a clientele through publicity and notoriety. To that end, Darrow assiduously pursued speaking opportunities with political clubs. He joined the Single Tax Club first and became an adherent of the political economist Henry George, the leading advocate of the idea that government should fund all its undertakings through a single tax on the unimproved value of land. The single-taxers were at once both progressive and libertarian: they would have treated land, valued in its natural state, as the common inheritance of all; the titleholder's tax essentially would be a rent payment to the public as a whole. But their tax would not discourage productivity or achievement, as taxes on income and on improvements to land arguably do.[59] After several speeches went unnoticed, Darrow finally drew the attention of the press (and of Henry George himself, who preceded Darrow at the lectern that night) in a striking address at a "free trade convention" in Chicago's Central Music Hall.[60]

Up to that time, Darrow had used the formal style of oratory in which he had learned to recite as a schoolboy and that he had heard in stump speeches of politicians. He now was about to reject that florid style completely. Eventually, he came to despise it. "I hope people have outlived oratory," he wrote in his waning years. "Almost none of that is sincere. The structure, the pattern, the delivery are artificial."[61]

When he eschewed the orator's devices, Darrow developed instead a habit of using "simpler words and shorter sentences, to make my statements plain and direct and, for me, at least, I find this the better manner of expression."[62] That distinctive, plainspoken style, which gave the impression of a genial armchair lecturer or even just a learned companion, became Darrow's power. He used it when standing, thumbs hooked under galluses, before a jury; he used it before throngs in stuffy halls or amid fluttering moths under the electric lighting of vast summer Chautauqua tents; he used it in his writing. Coupled with his dry sense of humor, the speaking style he cultivated was soft, elliptical, and effective. It persuaded gently. He never shoved; he nudged. A scowl always had a twinkle. Stiff words came with a smile, and he consistently chose jests over jeers. He was unafraid of sentiment and could verge on the maudlin, although his wit usually rescued him at the last moment. Darrow's thoughts on poker (which he greatly enjoyed) offer a glimpse of his mature style:

> I don't know whether I would recommend the sport or not; I doubt if I would recommend anything if I thought my advice was to be followed. Everything depends on one's point of view of life. I am inclined to believe that the most satisfactory part of life is the time spent in sleep, when one is utterly oblivious to existence; the next best is when one is so absorbed in activities that one is altogether unmindful of self. Poker is able to supply this for many, in all ranks of life; yet I would not advise anyone to play, or not play, but do most emphatically advise them to keep the limit down.[63]

Although Darrow's new publicity did not result in a flood of clients, it did lead to a lucky break. A man named DeWitt Cregier, whom Darrow did not know, sat in the audience the night Darrow gave his rousing talk after Henry George. Cregier, also a Democrat, soon became the mayor of Chicago. Out of the blue, Cregier then invited Darrow to become the special assessment attorney in the Chicago corporation counsel's office. With no legal work to keep him busy, Darrow jumped at the salaried position of $3,000 a year, which he conceded was "fabulous sum" at the time.[64]

In quick succession, through serendipity, Darrow became the assistant corporation counsel and then acting corporation counsel. The Chicago corporation counsel remains a powerful position today, and it was then. These jobs gave Darrow access to all of Chicago's aldermen and other officeholders, as well as to the city's corporate leaders.[65]

After about two years, this key position led to a real plum: a chance to become the general attorney for the Chicago & Northwestern Railway Company. Again, Darrow leapt.[66] He now was the chief counsel for one of the nation's major corporations. Not bad for an unknown lawyer from Ashtabula, Ohio, who had arrived in town with little more than suitcases, a wife, and a young son barely three years earlier. He was highly paid. Daily, he advised the railway's president and top officers. He had casual, first-name relationships with the city's principal politicians. Darrow had risen to the top of a corporate legal world that still was small and elite. While he later claimed some discomfort in taking "the side of the railroad company against one who had been injured in their service or against a passenger,"[67] Darrow had kind words for the executives he served, and he seemed to flourish.

Then came 1894, the American Railway Union; its leader, Eugene V. Debs; and the strike that Debs organized against the Pullman Company (and against all trains that included Pullman cars).[68] Both the Pullman Company and the Chicago & Northwestern Railway were based in Chicago, and Darrow's railway regularly entrained Pullman sleeper cars. The strike directly affected his employer. Railroad cars were going up in flames in the yards, each side blaming the other.[69] His employer, with the other large railway companies, planned to seek injunctions against the strikers from compliant federal courts, which invariably sided with capital on the stated concern that rail stoppages might affect delivery of the U.S. mails.[70] Here, the Justice Department made no attempt even to conceal the cozy collaboration between the corporations and the federal government: it appointed the lawyer who represented a committee of the railroads in the strike as special attorney for the federal government.[71] Darrow now had to confront squarely the conflict between his will and his wallet. Or rather, the conflict confronted him.

Then and there, the Clarence Darrow whom the world remembers came to be. In a sense, it happened literally overnight. Darrow decided that, faced with a conflict between the great corporate interests of the railroads and the interests of the hundreds of thousands of workers who built the cars in the vast factories, assembled trains in the yards, operated the trains, and served as porters in the parlor cars and the stations, he must side with labor. That meant siding against his employer, his professional associates, his new class. He walked into the railway president's office and resigned his position with the Chicago & Northwestern.

Having done that, he did not quail or stop at moral support. Rather, he took up the defense of Eugene Debs, who soon was indicted in federal court for conspiracy to violate the vague, broad injunction that the employers had obtained under name of the United States government. Darrow was thirty-seven.

In effect, a member of senior management had joined labor's picket line. Just that quickly, Darrow had left a life of passive sympathy for the underclasses that he secured with a paycheck from the upper classes. He had taken leave of comfort, convention, and acclaim by the powerful for confrontation, contempt, and the occasional inarticulate affection of the powerless.

When he easily might have remained seated, he had stood.

If Darrow sought self-respect at cost of respectability by acting on principle, it cost him something of his own sense of self too. He gave up his marriage, or perhaps gave up on it, within three years after he broke from the life of a corporate lawyer. Jessie understood him but did not share his new life.[72] She had married a small-town lawyer and craved the unexceptional and quiet life she rightly had anticipated with that union. Darrow no longer was the man she thought she had married. She had not changed, but he had. In doing so, he simply had moved on from her. His claim that the divorce was "without contest or disagreement and without any bitterness on either side" was true in the main, if only because Jessie forgave the man who left her.[73] He had lost—no, actively abandoned—the woman who had loved the man he used to be. Darrow's correspondence for the rest of his life reveals a warm cordiality for Jessie.[74]

What he gained in the divorce was the chance finally to integrate his values fully with his work and his life, the chance to make his causes also his cases. In this sense, he became a fortunate lawyer, although not necessarily one destined to make a fortune.

In 1894, about the time he embarked upon the defense of Debs, Darrow hired a young man just admitted to the bar. Peter Sissman was a Russian Jewish émigré whom Darrow had met at a socialist gathering while Sissman was a law student. Sissman's talent and humanity had impressed him. Although Sissman left Darrow's firm only two years later when, now established, he opened his own firm, he remained loyal to Darrow.[75] He would reappear later at a critical juncture in Darrow's life to return the favor that Darrow, his mentor, had done him when Sissman embarked upon his law practice.

Even as Darrow set out to defend Debs in the injunction case against separate charges of conspiracy and criminal contempt of court, he still harbored the common disdain for defending those accused of crimes. Abstractly, he understood the problems the accused faced. "Every advantage in the world goes with power. The city, the State, the county, the nation can scarcely be wrong. Behind them is organized society, and the individual who is obliged to contest for his rights against these forces in either civil or criminal courts is fighting against dreadful odds."[76] But in concrete practice, he confessed, "I had never had anything to do with criminal cases and, like most other lawyers, did not want to take them."[77] But take them he did. "By no effort of mine, more and more of the distressed and harassed and pursued came fleeing to my office door." In time, "Strange as it may seem, I grew to like to defend men and women charged with crime. It soon came to be something more than winning or losing a case. I sought to learn why one man goes one way and another takes an entirely different road. I became vitally interested in the causes of human conduct. This meant more than the quibbling with lawyers and juries, to get or keep money for a client so that I could take part of what I won or saved for him: I was dealing with life, with its hopes and fears, its aspirations and despairs. With me it was going to the foundation of motive and conduct and adjustments for human beings, instead of blindly talking of hatred and vengeance, and that subtle, indefinable quality that men call 'justice' and of which nothing really is known."[78]

Darrow won the criminal conspiracy case for Debs, in the ragged sense that criminal defendants and their lawyers learn to count victories. The jury leaned 11–1 for acquittal when a juror's illness required a mistrial. After some posturing, the government dismissed the case rather than retry it.[79] Debs was free of the conspiracy indictment. In the contempt-of-court case, though, he had no right to a jury. A federal judge, on essentially the same evidence, found Debs guilty and sent him to jail for six months. The U.S. Supreme Court let that sentence stand. But if, as Darrow noted, "The imprisonment of Eugene Victor Debs in the Woodstock jail made him a world-wide figure,"[80] his own efforts also went a long way toward making Debs's lawyer a national figure.

After Debs, Darrow's next case of significance was in Wisconsin. The town of Oshkosh, on the west shore of Lake Winnebago, was a lumber and paper mill town just like the communities dotting Lake Winnebago north of it, up to Appleton at the lake's northern edge. The Paine Lumber Company, then the nation's largest sash and door manufacturer, faced an effort to organize its workers. Thomas I. Kidd was general secretary in Chicago of the union that led the organization effort. Bending obsequiously to the company owner, George Paine, one of the wealthiest men in town, the district attorney charged Kidd and two other union officials with criminal collaboration.[81] Darrow got the case. After a three-week trial, the jury was out less than an hour. Not guilty.[82] Again Darrow's renown as both labor lawyer and criminal defense lawyer—the two often overlapping considerably in that day—grew.

Like the Debs case, the Kidd prosecution rested on a conspiracy charge. Of course, that was exactly the state's theory in the case of the eleven Milwaukee Italians too. As he slogged through the Debs and Kidd cases, Darrow was developing strong opinions about the Anglo-American tolerance for loose conspiracy theories and the waterfall of hearsay that flooded courtrooms in those cases. "Whenever a king wanted to get rid of somebody, whenever a political disturber was in someone's way," he argued to Kidd's jury, "then they brought a charge of conspiracy, and they not only proved everything he said, but everything everyone else said and everyone else did."[83]

More than a decade after the Milwaukee Italians' appeal, he reflected on the effects of the evidentiary flood and the imaginary greater evil that a claim of conspiracy summoned:

> If there are still any citizens interested in protecting human liberty, let them study the conspiracy laws of the United States. They have grown apace in the last forty years until to-day no one's liberty is safe. The conspiracy laws magnify misdemeanors into serious felonies. If a boy should steal a dime a small fine would cover the offense; he could not be sent to the penitentiary. But if two boys by agreement steal a dime then both of them could be sent to the penitentiary as conspirators.
>
> If A is indicted and a conspiracy is charged, or even if it is not charged, the state's attorney is allowed to prove what A said to B and what B said to C while the defendant was not present. Then he can prove what C said to D and what D said to E, and so on, to the end of the alphabet. . . . To make this hearsay or gossip competent, the state's attorney informs the court that later he will connect it up by showing that the defendant was informed of the various conversations, or that he otherwise had knowledge of them. Thereupon the complaisant judge holds the evidence is admissible, but if it is not connected up it will be stricken out. A week or a month may go by, and then a motion is made to strike it out. By that time it is of no consequence whether it is stricken out or not; it has entered the jurors' consciousness with a mass of other matter, and altogether has made an impression on his mind. What particular thing made the impression, neither the juror nor any one else can know.[84]

Setting aside minor adjustments that cinch a bit more tightly the necessary proof that a defendant actually joined a conspiracy, Darrow's critique is solid today just as it was then.

A string of national roles followed the Kidd win. Darrow represented Pennsylvania's anthracite coal miners, labor organizers in cities large and small, and, most spectacularly, Big Bill Haywood and other leaders of the Western Federation of Miners in a series of Idaho prosecutions for the assassination of former governor Frank Steunenberg. He became the unrivaled favorite of the labor movement over the first decade of the twentieth century.[85]

Then in 1911 he lost the trust of AFL president Samuel Gompers and many other labor leaders because of his actions in a case involving two brothers, John and James McNamara, who were accused of bombing the printing plant of the anti-union *Los Angeles Times*. The bomb killed twenty employees. After accepting a staggering fee for his services, Darrow became convinced that his clients were guilty. He opened up back-channel discussions with the Los Angeles County District Attorney about guilty pleas that would save the lives of the McNamaras.

Meanwhile, as the trial was about to begin and just before the surprise guilty pleas, the Los Angeles police arrested a member of Darrow's defense team for bribing a juror. That arrest led two months later to Darrow's own indictment on two counts of bribery. In the end, after two arduous years, he was acquitted on one count. In a separate trial, the second count resulted in a hung jury. Although the prosecution decided not to pursue the case through a third trial, disillusioned supporters of organized labor fled Darrow in droves.[86] Gompers did not forgive him.[87]

In the following years, Darrow won back only fragments of the trust and loyalty of organized labor, and slowly at that.[88] He never again served as counsel in a significant labor case. Labor neither fully abandoned nor fully embraced him again for the rest of his life.

By the time he took the train home from Los Angeles at the conclusion of the bribery cases in 1913, his tenuous law partnership with Edgar Lee Masters, the unhappy lawyer whom the world remembers instead as a poet and the author of *Spoon River Anthology*, was over.[89] So Darrow returned to Chicago with no law partner, no law practice, and no spirit for resuming the practice of law after months in the defendant's chair himself. The expense of retaining lawyers to defend him through two lengthy trials, in addition to his own living expenses in Los Angeles, had consumed his fee from the McNamara case and most of his savings.[90]

Worse, he had left Chicago as its leading lawyer but returned as a presumed criminal, only half-exonerated. The taint scared away clients and acquaintances alike. Darrow had to learn the lesson that every person first accused of a crime learns. "One who has serious trouble always has two surprises," he explained accurately. "One over the friends who drop away, and another at the supposed strangers who stand by him in his hour of need. Perhaps this is due to the fact that we exalt our seeming friends, and do not justly estimate those who have looked askance, and whom we have not really known."[91]

In short, Darrow came back to Chicago both broke and broken. At fifty-six, he wanted to quit the law. He imagined that lecturing, debating, and writing would restore somehow both his name and his finances.[92] At that moment, one friend who did not drop away, or perhaps a near-stranger long overlooked, re-appeared: Peter Sissman, the bookish and sincere lawyer whom Darrow had given his start almost twenty years earlier. Sissman insisted that Darrow not leave the law and offered him a new partnership. His own firm was well established by then. Demonstrating both his modesty and his esteem for Darrow, Sissman named the new firm "Darrow & Sissman," not the other way around. Sissman necessarily undertook to carry Darrow financially until the older man's practice slowly grew again.[93]

And grow it did during the five years that separated the trials in Los Angeles from his agreement to represent the eleven Milwaukee Italians on appeal in the Wisconsin Supreme Court. These were unglamorous years for Darrow, during which he returned to the basic work of trial lawyers in early twentieth-century America: perhaps a personal injury case for a passenger injured by one of Chicago's elevated trains this week, a theft or murder case next week, a pardon hearing the week after that.[94] "It is hell," he groused gently to his longtime friend and short-time lover Mary Field, "to be the General Counsel to the poor."[95]

In fact, some of the cases for which Darrow is best remembered lay ahead of him in the 1920s. In late 1925 and 1926 there would be the African American physician in Detroit, Ossian Sweet, and his family, who faced murder charges for firing into a white mob to defend their home in a previously white neighborhood. Darrow would speak with remarkable honesty about race and would convince twelve white men to acquit a black man who was party to killing a white one.[96] In the hot summer of 1925 there would be the orchestrated face-off with William Jennings Bryan over the teaching of evolution in public schools that came with the state of Tennessee's contrived prosecution of John T. Scopes, a high school teacher in Dayton, Tennessee. Darrow would speak for science and progress, losing a case but winning a large share of public opinion.[97]

The summer before that, Darrow would offer much expert testimony and argument in an attempt to save the lives of Nathan Leopold and Richard Loeb, the nineteen-year-old sons of two of Chicago's wealthiest families. They had killed twelve-year-old Bobby Franks in exercising their notion of Nietzsche.[98] As he had in the McNamara brothers' case, Darrow would plead Leopold and Loeb guilty and argue only over punishment. The judge eventually would spare them the gallows. Darrow's final argument remains a stirring, sentimental standard in opposition to the death penalty.

Of course, in the five years between his Los Angeles trials and the Milwaukee Italians' appeals, Darrow could not know that any of these cases lay ahead of him. For the most part, he was just trying to pay the bills in those years straddling the first world war.

After spreading out in detail Darrow's probable guilt in the Los Angeles cases, biographer Geoffrey Cowan credits him in the years following 1913 with much good. "Darrow had changed; he was fundamentally chastened by his experience in Los Angeles," Cowan writes.[99] He notes too that Darrow's friends and allies thought the great lawyer humbled and worthy of forgiveness, as well.[100] In 1922 an obscure prosecutor in Milwaukee would make some striking statements, unnoticed then and since, that would have called those assessments into doubt had they emerged publicly. But for now Darrow sought during the five years following his Los Angeles trials to regain his law practice and his reputation. He prevailed.

He also won back his place at the speaker's dais and on the Chautauqua circuit. Ever the amalgam of contradictions, Darrow used his gentle sense of humor, plain speech, and untamed spirit to entertain and provoke audiences. In debates, he almost invariably took the negative. Lila and Arthur Weinberg recount a story from one debate in which Darrow had not read the document that underlay the debate. "Trust me," Darrow whispered to the worried moderator, "I can debate any question in the negative."[101]

Debate he did. Somehow offering nihilism with a twinkle, he argued the negative of the question "Is life worth living?" against the eminent anthropologist and ethnologist Frederick Starr. He argued against prohibition when the country was considering the Eighteenth Amendment and the Volstead Act. Facing the Reverend John Haynes Holmes, who supported prohibition, Darrow made clear his libertarian sentiments. "I am one of those," he admitted, whom Reverend Holmes had defined as doubtful and suspicious of authority. "I don't like it. I think the less we have, the better. [Reverend Holmes] describes that as bordering on the philosophical anarchist view. I would speak for that as against the extreme socialist view, which says that everything on earth should be regulated or controlled."[102] Addressing then the specific topic of strong drink, he finished with a bit of classic Darrow: "Take out of this world the men who have drunk, down through the past, and you would take away all the poetry and literature and practically all the works of genius that the world has produced. What kind of a poem do you suppose you would get out of a glass of ice-water?"[103]

Darrow's determinist bent was always pronounced, perhaps even more so after his Los Angeles trials. A rare run for Darrow at the lectern on the affirmative side of a question occurred during a series of debates with a leading historian, Will

Durant, on this proposition, variously posed: "Is man a machine?" or "Are we machines? Is life mechanical . . . ?"[104] Now there was an idea Darrow could get behind. But he softened with humor, often self-deprecating, even this dark vision of humankind utterly without free will. When, at the invitation of a progressive sheriff, he addressed the inmates of Chicago's vast Cook County Jail in 1902 on the subject of the causes of crime and recidivism, he argued, "There are people who are born with the tendency to break into jail every chance they get, and they can not avoid it."[105] He prefaced that wry comment, though, with this argument: "There is no such thing as a crime as the word is generally understood. I do not believe there is any sort of distinction between the real moral condition of the people in and out of jail. One is just as good as the other. The people here can no more help being here than the people outside can avoid being outside. I do not believe that people are in jail because they deserve to be. They are in jail simply because they cannot avoid it on account of circumstances which are entirely beyond their control and for which they are in no way responsible."[106]

Returning to this theme much later in life, Darrow clarified, "People talk of criminals as though they were utterly different from 'good' people; as though specially created in order that a large class of the community should have the pleasure of hating them." He refuted that idea, arguing that the same instincts and emotions drive all people. Carrying his argument to its end, he lectured, "All men have an emotion to kill; when they strongly dislike someone they involuntarily wish he was dead." Then, his saving wit: "I have never killed any one, but I have read some obituary notices with great satisfaction."[107]

Like their new lawyer in 1918, none of the eleven Italians in Wisconsin had killed anyone. Still, notwithstanding that modest shared quality, some distance more than geographical separated clients from lawyer. Prior to taking up the case of the eleven, Darrow had not had much direct experience with anarchists or with Italians. He revered John Peter Altgeld for his pardon of the surviving Haymarket Square defendants after Altgeld became governor of Illinois in 1892, but he showed only general sympathy for the executed and imprisoned defendants themselves.[108] For Darrow, the Haymarket case was more about the courageous example of forgiveness and justice that the governor set—an example that cost him his political career. Altgeld was a formative figure in Darrow's life and, for a time, his law partner.[109] Indeed, Altgeld is the only law partner in Darrow's long career who gained so much as a bare mention in his autobiography. Altgeld got more than a mention: he got two chapters and an appendix. Not even Sissman, who lifted Darrow and showed him great kindness at his lowest hour, won a word in Darrow's final accounting of his life.

With one exception, Darrow seemed to have no close affinity with anarchists after the Haymarket disaster either, although he teased that the philosophy of anarchism was close to his own anti-authoritarian leanings. The exception was John Turner, an English-born anarchist facing deportation from the United States whom Darrow represented (unsuccessfully) in his first case in the U.S. Supreme Court.[110]

Darrow's only other memorable case involving Italian defendants came in New York almost a decade after the Milwaukee appeal. In 1927 he went to the Bronx to represent a pair of Italian Americans charged with murdering two fascists who were on their way to march in a parade. At trial, an eyewitness faltered in his identification of the two defendants and Darrow won a not-guilty verdict. Notably, the Italian anarchist Carlo Tresca played a personal role in securing Darrow to represent the two accused.[111] Darrow likely continued some connection to Tresca. As late as 1931, Helen Keller felt compelled to explain at length to Darrow her absence from a dinner honoring the Italian.[112]

Milwaukee's own Victor Berger, the first Socialist Party member elected to the U.S. House of Representatives and publisher of the *Milwaukee Leader*, described Darrow as a "'philosophic anarchist' and so considered by everybody, including himself." So it was not just Unitarian ministers, like the good Reverend Holmes, who had the notion that Darrow was intrinsically an anarchist. Berger's description followed an anecdote that revealed something else of the true Darrow: the contrarian. He reported that Darrow caused much hissing in 1907 when, while dining in the elegant Silver Grill restaurant in Spokane, Washington, not long after the Haywood trial, he had refused to rise as the house orchestra struck up "The Star-Spangled Banner" and a young woman sang it. Darrow alone among the restaurant's patrons remained seated in a silent protest against idle patriotism.[113]

In all, though, whatever a Milwaukee congressman's opinion or an East Coast minister's, the Milwaukee case was a departure for Darrow, and not just because it involved Italian immigrants or accused anarchists.[114] It was an appeal. Much as he enjoyed writing generally, Darrow was not an appellate lawyer by preference.[115]

Appeals primarily require writing, which grounds a lawyer to his office while he prepares detailed briefs to an appellate court after a thorough review of the pleadings, exhibits, and transcripts or court reporter's notes that compose a trial record. While appellate courts almost invariably entertained oral argument in Darrow's day and still do in many cases, that argument was and is a relatively formal, dry affair. Lawyers from each side have an allotted time (at least today they do; some courts were more flexible in Darrow's day) to frame the strongest arguments in their briefs and to answer questions that a good appellate lawyer hopes will come from the appellate court's three, five, seven, or nine judges.

However it might engage the intellect, oral argument in an ornate supreme court chamber has none of the earthiness and opportunity for theatrics and the common touch that a jury trial afforded Darrow. Men who came from other walks of life and entered a courthouse for jury duty uninitiated in the mechanics, jargon, and callousness of criminal justice administration were Darrow's preferred audience. Appellate judges decidedly were not. Besides, appellate practice required an attention to minute detail—exact wording of testimony, fine distinctions between the present case and the facts in earlier published decisions, precise page citations to lengthy transcripts—that did not suit Darrow's bent to think and speak on the broadest questions of humanity.

But Sissman was good at the tedious office work of preparing an appeal. He was willing to labor at his desk in the shadow that Darrow cast when he stood at a lectern or counsel table. They complemented one another. Sissman would play a crucial, if uncelebrated, role in the eleven Italians' appeal.

In one sense, the Milwaukee appeal was partly an act of atonement for Darrow. After much thought, Darrow, who was more pacifist than patriot, had supported America's entry into World War I. In 1917 and early 1918 he traveled the country giving speeches to rally support for President Wilson's war effort. This alienated him from Debs, importantly, and from other friends on the left.[116] After the war, and perhaps having second thoughts about his role, Darrow rebelled against the harshness of the government's treatment of objectors to the war. He decried the Espionage Act of 1917.[117] And he took up the defense of communists and others facing criminal charges for their opposition to the war. He lost the biggest of these cases, a 1920 prosecution of William Bross Lloyd and more than a dozen other communists in Chicago for an alleged plot to overthrow the U.S. government. Within two years of that trial, though, he obtained pardons from the Illinois governor.[118] The case of Lloyd and the communists would prove to be at least the third time that Darrow was instrumental in attaining pardons for radicals. The first was his effort with Altgeld in 1892, before the Haymarket pardons. The second would come in Wisconsin.

So Darrow began in winter 1918 what Lila and Arthur Weinberg call the most active decade of his career.[119] He began it with the Milwaukee Italians' appeal.

For some reason, that April, Darrow's friends gave him an unusually extravagant party for his sixty-first birthday. In the glow of the evening's tributes, which came from Carl Sandburg, Sissman, and many others, Darrow rose to thank the 135 in attendance at the Auditorium Hotel.[120] The lawyer "with his young, old heart," as Edgar Lee Masters described Darrow poetically during an approving phase in their oscillating relationship, gathered his thoughts and spoke.[121] Darrow waxed of the consolation that true friends bring, adding, "I have often told young men starting out in business not to make acquaintances, but to make friends. Acquaintances are of little value unless you want to run for office, and I know that each of you have an ambition higher than that." He mused, "Most of life is hard for those who think." Yes, "for those mortals who must look life in the face and cannot dream, there is nothing left but a sense of humor and hard work. Hard work is good. It is good because it brings a loss of consciousness. It makes man live an intuitive, automatic life, where he forgets that he is living. Hard work, like sleep, is an interruption of life; it is unconsciousness and death and is, therefore, peace." He bemoaned the fact that "I have always yearned for peace, but have lived a life of war. I do not know why, excepting that it is the law of my being." But this was not his chief objection. "The one thing that gets me, perhaps more than anything else, is the terrible cruelty of man. . . . Men torturing animals, regardless of the suffering of the weak. Men torturing each other, simply for the joy of doing it."[122]

Darrow may not have had in mind his eleven new clients, awaiting appeal in the prison in Waupun, Wisconsin, that festive night. But those eleven likely were on the mind of Winfred Zabel. Darrow's birthday bash came just three days after someone planted the two bombs at Zabel's house.[123] The famed defense lawyer soon would go about trying to end the State of Wisconsin's cruelty to his eleven clients. The district attorney would go about thinking how to stop his faceless enemies from torturing him over the convictions of the eleven. The appeal was under way.

9

May It Please the Court

Superficially, appeals in 1918 were not much different than they are now. If he wishes to appeal, the losing party was and is responsible for two main tasks: seeing that the history of the case in the trial court—the written pleadings, testimony, and exhibits that together are the "record"—is assembled for transfer to the appellate court and writing a paper for the appellate court—the "brief"—that explains the facts of the case and how the trial court erred. The losing side also sends that brief to the winning side. The winning side then has its chance to file a brief, defending the result in the trial court. The losing side next may file a reply brief. Often, the appellate court then will hear oral arguments from lawyers for both sides. Finally, in due course, the appellate court issues a written opinion explaining its reasons for either affirming the result in the trial court or reversing the result there because of some error or errors.

Depending upon the reasons, a reversal may mean the end of the case (the former loser now is the winner and the case is over) or just a do-over in the trial court, with instructions from the appellate court on how to avoid repeating the mistake. Most of the time, the loser in the trial court also is the loser in the appellate court. Appellate judges tend to favor finality, dislike the perceived waste of ordering a mulligan, and bend to cover for a fellow judge in the trial court. But the appellate process allows courts to correct at least glaring errors.

In general, this was the process that Darrow and Zabel undertook in the spring and summer of 1918, as eleven Italians labored behind prison walls in Waupun. Then as now, an appeal from a trial verdict might take a year or more to run its course.

Beneath the broad similarities, though, appellate procedure also was different in important ways in 1918. The differences start in the technology of the times. Until the modern stenotype machine caught on in the 1930s and later,[1] so-called court reporters—the stenographers who record what everyone says in court—had no mechanical aid. They had to rely on pencil and shorthand. As a practical matter, that meant trials were not always transcribed verbatim in full as they are today.

With or without today's complete verbatim transcriptions, the parties had to confront the question of what issues the losing side could appeal. Then as now, the usual rule was that a lawyer had to object contemporaneously, if he thought that the trial judge was making a significant mistake. The reason for that rule is straightforward: if one calls a mistake to the attention of the trial judge, he has the chance to correct himself then and there, which may spare everyone the time, expense, and nuisance of an appeal later. Also, on occasion when there was no verbatim transcript, the parties later might dispute exactly what the witnesses or the lawyers and the judge actually said. Those disputes could become critical if one side or the other appealed the trial court's judgment.[2]

The solution to both problems was to prepare a "bill of exceptions" listing all of the rulings at trial that the losing party might wish the state supreme court to review on appeal. So typically, a lawyer in trial might stand and interrupt proceedings with "Objection . . . ," after which he would state his grounds. The opposing party might respond with argument about why the objection was not right. The judge then would rule: "Sustained" or "Overruled," perhaps with a short explanation of the ruling. If the objection was overruled, the objecting lawyer then would close the discussion with "Exception." By that, he signaled to the judge and the court reporter that he wished to save the point for appeal, if the case did not go his way.

Whether the lawyer noted an exception at the time or did not, part of the process of pursuing the appeal and readying the record for the supreme court's review was preparing a bill of exceptions. The bill was a comprehensive list of all exceptions to the trial judge's rulings that might serve as bases for claims of error that the losing side wanted the supreme court to consider. If it chose, the supreme court could review mistakes that appeared clearly in the record, even if the losing side did not take exception. But the bill of exceptions was important for errors that were not clear from the face of the trial transcript or from other documents in the trial court's file.[3] For such alleged errors, inclusion in the bill of exceptions was essential. If they did not appear there and were not apparent on the face of the record elsewhere, they could not serve as a basis of appeal. If not preserved in the record in good time, they were beyond the supreme court's notice.

In constructing the bill of exceptions, the losing side's lawyer would compile the bill or list. The bill was in writing but "in summary mode."[4] The lawyer then would present his proposed bill of exceptions to the trial judge. Of course, the opposing party would see the proposed bill too, because one lawyer could not give something to the judge without also providing a copy at the same time to the other side; that was and is a basic tenet of the adversary system. So the opposing lawyer might quibble with the bill of exceptions if he thought it inaccurate. But in the end it was the trial judge's call. If he deemed the proposed bill of exceptions "conformable to the truth of the case," he would allow and sign the bill of exceptions.[5] Doing so did not mean the judge agreed with the merits of the exceptions. It meant only that he agreed that the bill of exceptions accurately recited the points that the parties had disputed and on which the judge had ruled at trial.

Once signed, the bill of exceptions supplemented significantly the court reporter's transcript or notes of the testimony and rulings at trial. The bill itself became an agreed list of possible errors, including the objections made and the trial court's rulings on them. In the eleven Italians' appeal, later events would give reason to pay attention to these otherwise tedious details of lawyering at trial and on appeal.

Early in the appeal process, then, Darrow and Peter Sissman had to pick through the trial record and write their bill of exceptions. This was the last essential step in the trial court, before preparing a brief that they would submit to the Wisconsin Supreme Court in the state capital, Madison, eighty miles west of Milwaukee. The clerk of the Milwaukee Municipal Court would submit the trial record, including the bill of exceptions, after collecting and indexing all of it.

Sissman was the office lawyer who attended to tedious tasks like reviewing the entire trial court record, which here ran to thousands of pages, and writing down the exceptions. He also did the legal research necessary for the appellate brief, handwriting notes about prior cases that other courts had decided on points similar to those in dispute in the case of the eleven Italians. Ideally, those prior cases would come from the Wisconsin Supreme Court itself, for every appellate court is most enamored of its own prior rulings—and most concerned about consistency with its own precedent. But reported cases from other states' supreme courts also would do in the absence of Wisconsin cases that were a close fit. Even older English cases would serve in a pinch, to demonstrate that the proper rule long was clear in the legal tradition of English-speaking people.

Darrow, more often in court on his feet or out drumming up new business than in the office, would review Sissman's work along the way and play the role of the elder lawyer, making changes or suggestions to improve a draft. In the end, Darrow's would be the principal signature at the bottom of the brief to the state supreme court. Sissman's reputation was local to Chicago. Darrow's decidedly was not. Hardly a lawyer or judge in the nation failed to recognize him as the most famous lawyer of that day. No other lawyer, with the possible exceptions of Los Angeles's Earl Rogers and some of the nine justices of the U.S. Supreme Court (which at that time included both Louis Dembitz Brandeis and Oliver Wendell Holmes Jr.), even came close to Darrow's notoriety.[6]

When Sissman finished a bill of exceptions that had Darrow's approval and a secretary clacked it out on a typewriter, the lawyer mailed it to Zabel and to Judge Backus. Zabel agreed with it. Judge Backus signed it. The bill was "conformable to the truth of the case," Backus's signature certified. It was done. Off to the supreme court in Madison it went.

Presumably, none of the three men who bore principal responsibility for it—Darrow, Zabel, and Backus—at that time anticipated the scrutiny that their bill of exceptions might get almost five years later. But that scrutiny would come. This bill of exceptions, dull and clerical though it seemed, would have potential importance well after the appeal of the eleven Italians was over.

For the present, with the bill done, Sissman and Darrow set about the time-consuming process of preparing their appellate brief. Starting with Sissman's scraps of paper and notes protruding from the pages of "reports"—bound books collecting the decisions of state supreme courts or federal courts—the briefing process turned to long sheets of handwritten argument and to passages dictated to a secretary taking shorthand. Typed drafts on onionskin followed, with penciled interlineations, changes, and comments. New drafts came rolling off the typewriter. In the end, the brief would have to be typeset and bound.

And it was. The typeset portions of the record that defense counsel submitted with their brief filled 261 pages. Darrow and Sissman's brief ran to nearly seventy-six pages more, typeset and separately bound. It raised nine main arguments, most with subpoints. The arguments, which filled fifty-six of the brief's pages, were droning and technical in the main. Passive voice prevailed, which made them all the more soporific.

The writing bore little resemblance to Darrow's style in articles and books. It offered only the occasional glimpse of his rhetorical ability to square himself to the world, punch its ugly underbelly in plain but emotional terms, and then finish with just enough wit to make his jab feel like no more than a nudge. One fleeting example of Darrow's style came in the brief's objection to the anarchist newspapers and pamphlets that the police had gathered by the box in the clubhouse and that the state later shoveled into evidence at trial:

> None of these exhibits have the slightest tendency to establish a
> conspiracy to commit murder or an assault with intent to commit

murder. Some of the exhibits may tend to prove that some of the defendants read anarchist literature, and that some of them have regard for anarchists and anarchism. Of the exhibits introduced, portions were translated and read, by what justification is difficult to understand. There was no attempt to show that any of the defendants were in agreement with the sentiments or ideas expressed in the particular portions read. The witness August Guliani [*sic*], who made some of the translations and read some of the exhibits, said that he cannot say that he looked over all of the papers and books that were taken by the police. Did not read over one of them, just looked over superficially and took a statement, marked it here and there where it was "strong and the language forcible"; that the portions read must have left a powerful impression on the minds of the jury cannot be doubted.[7]

Darrow's attitude toward courts and criminal justice also emerged, even if cloaked by the writing style, in the discussion of Judge Backus's lopsided treatment of defense counsel at trial. "Counsel for defendants were constantly interfered with and limited in the cross examination of witnesses for the State. Reprimands by the court were very frequent. . . . We admit that some of the remarks of counsel were not free from criticism, but in most cases were called out by remarks from the District Attorney," Darrow remonstrated. "In reading the record, one cannot help feeling that the defendants through their counsel must have suffered, in view of the frequent reprimands by the court."[8]

As the defendants' brief drew to a close, its peroration at last rang fully of Darrow:

> The verdict of the jury in itself shows that it was the result of passion and prejudice. Eleven persons were brought to trial. The evidence as to each one individually differs with reference to the culpability of each defendant. Take the case of Mary Nardini, what else does it show excepting that she was seen at the scene of trouble with her child at her side, and that previously she was seen reading a book? No evidence even that she came from the hall. Or what evidence is there connecting Peter Bianchi with any conspiracy? There certainly were differences in the degree of proof as to each of the defendants. If the jury had paid any regard to the instructions of the court that the evidence against each of the defendants is to be weighed by them separately, the result would have been that some of the defendants would have been acquitted,

others under proper instructions would have been found guilty of less heinous offenses and some might have been found guilty as charged in the information. The fact that there was a uniform verdict as to all, shows how little regard the jury paid to the evidence, and that it was a verdict of inflamed minds, the result of passion and prejudice.

And we submit that the sentence of the court suggests that the court itself was not free from the feeling prevailing in the community. To impose a uniform sentence of twenty-five years! Practically the extreme penalty, against all the eleven defendants, not one of whom is a hardened criminal—one a woman, a mother of babies—without any attempt to vary the sentence, according to the degree of participation, without any regard for the circumstances of the parties, and of those they are leaving behind, fairly indicates that the judgment of sentence was not free from prejudice.[9]

The Chicago defense lawyers asked then not just that the state supreme court reverse the convictions but that it bar a new trial and set the defendants free.

The state's brief in opposition outdid the defense, if anything. Its statement of facts alone filled nearly sixty-seven typeset pages. It then met every argument that Sissman and Darrow made, conceding nothing. The state further graced the supreme court with eighty pages of translated excerpts from those pamphlets and newspapers that the police had scooped up from the clubhouse and the Nardinis' home.

That brief in opposition bore three names. First came the state attorney general, usually charged with principal responsibility for the prosecution's appellate work in Wisconsin (and in many other states). Next followed Zabel's signature. Third was the man who actually had authored most of the state's brief: Arthur H. Bartelt, the assistant district attorney who had played the smallest role at trial. Frederick Groelle, Zabel's principal assistant at trial, had left the district attorney's office well before the state filed its brief and played no role in writing it.[10] Bartelt remained and did the lion's share of the work.

After a reply brief from the defense, parrying the state's responses, the case was ready for oral argument. It took months for the Wisconsin Supreme Court to schedule the argument. Finally, in late winter as the snow shrank to sooty and sparse, exposing patches of mud and matted, brown grass, the day for oral argument came. It was March 7, 1919. Darrow and Sissman had traveled from Chicago to Madison, some 120 miles to the northwest. Zabel and Bartelt came from Milwaukee.

The Wisconsin Supreme Court occupied the second floor of the east wing of the new state capitol building, atop the highest point of a narrow isthmus between Lake Mendota to the north and west and Lake Monona to the south and east. Four wings pointed out in the cardinal directions from a central rotunda, capped with a dome and a gilt statue of a woman pointing "Forward," the state's motto. The capitol building was just more than one year old, having been under construction for eleven years after the state's second capitol building, on the same site, burned in February 1904. By far the most ornate and grand, this third capitol had cost $7.25 million to build.[11] Surrounding the capitol was a lovely grassy square, planted with circular gardens at its corners and with oak saplings. Because the isthmus ran northeast to southwest and the streets lay in a similar diagonal grid, while the four wings of the capitol pointed due north, east, south, and west, the visual effect was of a building set as an "X" on the square. With a Beaux-Arts exterior executed in gleaming white Vermont granite, its dome rising sixteen feet higher than the U.S. Capitol dome, the Wisconsin capitol made a magnificent impression.

Inside the East Wing, the supreme court's hearing room was distinct from many of the nation's finest courtrooms, but no less impressive. While many appellate courtrooms are paneled in rich, carved wood from floor to ceiling, lending them the hush and warmth of a magnificent library lit in subdued yellow incandescence, Wisconsin's highest court sat in a room struck in German and Italian marble with an ornate skylight in the center of a ceiling that soared fully thirty feet above a gold-carpeted floor. Natural light bathed the room. Four large murals, the work of the artist Albert Herter of New York, filled central places on each of the walls. Herter painted the murals in light shades that accentuated the room's airy feel. The walls were only forty-two feet long, which gave the hearing room a nearly cubical feel because of its height. The massive, straight mahogany bench and chairs of the seven justices of the court and the long mahogany table that counsel shared, separated by the lectern, were the only significant wood complements to the room other than the sturdy upholstered wooden chairs arrayed in rows for visitors in the court's gallery. No bar separated the lawyers from the gallery. That added a bit of intimacy to the otherwise imposing space. If there was a notable architectural failing to the room, it was (and is) this: appearances exceeded acoustics.

After the supreme court marshal brought the gallery to order and the five participating justices—two justices had recused themselves—entered through two doors, one at each end of the long bench, Darrow rose and argued the cause for the eleven Italians. As appellants' counsel, he and Sissman occupied the seats to the right side of counsel table, as a spectator in the gallery behind would view that table. Zabel, rather than the attorney general, spoke for the state. He and Bartelt sat to the left side of the lectern on counsel table from the spectators' perspective.

In his long career, Darrow tried several cases in Wisconsin courtrooms, including the famed 1898 trial of Thomas I. Kidd in Oshkosh.[12] But this was the first of only two appearances that Darrow ever made in the Wisconsin Supreme Court.[13]

No official record remains of the lawyers' words or the justices' questions that early March day. But both Darrow and Zabel surely opened their arguments with "May it please the court," the formal introduction that American lawyers long have used to greet an appellate tribunal.[14] Each side then had a period within which to argue. Then as now, justices frequently interrupted arguments to ask questions, sometimes pointed and sometimes more genuinely inquisitive. Questions could come fast and furious.

One possible fragment remains of Darrow's argument that day. It comes from Darrow's most noted biographer, Irving Stone. He wrote soon after Darrow's death, with benefit of the approval and cooperation of Darrow's wife, son, and close friends. Although he cited only the paper record in the Wisconsin Supreme Court, Stone included a lengthy purported quotation of Darrow's argument that is not in the defense briefs and sounds oral:

> These people have a right to believe in the philosophic idea that they can free themselves by force * * *. It is only when it can be proved that they have used force to injure people, when they have run counter to the criminal code, that they can be prosecuted. There is no such crime as a crime of thought; there are only crimes of action. It is bad taste for guests in a country to call that country a jail; it is bad taste to call its President a pig, but these are errors of judgment rather than transgressions against the legal structure. If we wish to keep speech free, to keep criticism open and alive, we have to tolerate even such criticisms as these, distasteful as they may be to us.[15]

Whether Darrow actually spoke those words as he stood at the lectern in the Wisconsin Supreme Court, as Stone contends, we cannot know now. There is no transcript, and Stone provided no convincing source citation. But it rings true as the kind of expansive, homey argument Darrow favored, whether in court, in a lecture hall, or in his office with newspaper reporters gathered around his desk.

In all events, when the oral arguments ended, the Wisconsin Supreme Court took the case under advisement. The chief justice, in the center chair, announced that the court was recessed and the black-robed justices filed out just as they had entered.

Once off the bench and rid of their robes, the justices gathered in their conference room at the end of the corridor leading from the door at the right end of the bench, from the spectators' perspective. The chief justice would lead the conversation on the morning's docket. He was John B. Winslow, tired and nearing the end of his life at sixty-seven. Winslow had joined the supreme court in 1891 and had served, by virtue of seniority, as its chief justice since 1907.[16] Each of the other four participating justices would have their say on the Italians' case, but the chief justice enjoyed the prerogative of speaking first and last.

After some discussion, the justices announced their tentative votes. Winslow turned to a quiet, intense colleague with a stiff spine, thick gray hair, skeptical eyes, and the trim build of a man raised on a farm who still loved life outdoors. Justice Aad Johannes Vinje would write the opinion.

Vinje, the only member of the court at the time who was not native to the United States, had been born in Norway to Quaker parents. He was not yet twelve when the family immigrated to rural Iowa. The boy spoke no English. Just four years later, astonishingly, he began to take college courses. At age eighteen, he gained a position as a schoolteacher. Six years earlier, he could not speak English; now he was teaching it. In 1878 he enrolled in the literature department at the University of Wisconsin and left Iowa forever. He took his bachelor of arts in 1884 and then obtained work as an assistant in the state law library, adjacent to the supreme court on which he eventually would serve.

Now smitten with law, he re-enrolled in the University of Wisconsin and graduated with his LL.B. in 1887. Vinje opened his law practice in raw, rugged Superior, across the bay from Duluth, Minnesota, in Wisconsin's northwestern corner. Again, he proved unusually able, and after just four years the governor appointed him a judge for that northwestern corner of the state. In 1910 another governor appointed Vinje to fill a vacancy on the Wisconsin Supreme Court. With his wife, Alice, and his four children, he moved to Madison and bought a comfortable but modest house just south of the fashionable Mansion Hill area, an easy walk from the state capitol.

Vinje had matured as a relatively broad-minded man. He was a Republican at a time when Wisconsin Republicans tended to be progressive, even if not fully in the sway of Robert M. La Follette. He also had left the strictures of Quaker life to become a Unitarian.[17] But if his principles were not pinched, they also were firmly planted. He expressed himself concisely, even curtly, and left no doubt about distinctions between right and wrong—although on occasion he also perfumed his writing with the faintest whiff of humor. Nine years after the Italians' case, Vinje answered a letter from Henry Goddard Leach, a prominent New York editor of *The Forum* magazine and a leading scholar of Scandinavian culture. "Dear Sir," he addressed Leach archly, and then got right to the question:

> You ask me whether or not I believe companionate marriage to be moral.
>
> The status to which you refer does not constitute marriage because it lacks not only the sanctions of law and society but also the essential quality of marriage, namely, a union for life—unless dissolved by law. The expression "companionate marriage" is therefore a misnomer and was, no doubt, coined with the hope that it would camouflage into respectability a sexual relation that has always been regarded to be both immoral and unlawful. Now, since neither the quality nor the lawfulness of a relation is affected by a change of its name, I believe the so-called companionate marriage status to be immoral as well as illegal. It has neither legal nor social sanction, and should receive none.
>
> The fact that it may find among its advocates a philosopher or a judge is an odium that I trust philosophy and jurisprudence will survive.
>
> Yours truly,
> *A. J. Vinje*[18]

In all, given his moral rigidity and thin-lipped conversational and emotional reserve, Vinje may have found the garrulous, emotive Darrow personally off-putting, even if he was unaware of Darrow's penchant for "free love." But Vinje also was a disciplined lawyer and, if not compassionate toward the scruffy edges of the working class, at least honest and dispassionate about the prejudices and nativist reflexes of the middle and upper classes. He read the lengthy trial record and sorted through the facts methodically and efficiently. A draft opinion emerged. By April, barely three weeks after oral argument, Vinje had circulated his written opinion and secured the unanimous approval of his colleagues. There would be no dissenters among the five justices who sat on the case.

Just over half of the typeset opinion that the Wisconsin Supreme Court issued on Wednesday morning, April 2, 1919, consisted of a careful factual summary of the three Sunday gatherings in Bay View. This preceded Vinje's legal discussion. While detailed, the factual statement also was unstintingly fair to both sides. Vinje struck no low blows and resorted to none of the demagoguery that the lawyers— especially Zabel—had displayed at trial. The factual story closed with a summary of the evidence as to each defendant, by name. With that, the eleven at last were allowed to rise and stand as individuals, considered on their own merits or flaws rather than as indistinct members of a mass. This was a simple dignity that the trial judge, the prosecutor, and even their own trial lawyers never had afforded the defendants.

When he turned to the legal issues, Vinje did not truck with the technical points that Darrow and Sissman had briefed so minutely. He went straight to the broad panorama of the evidence and framed that big picture. "It will be seen from the foregoing statement of facts," Vinje began, "that as to some of the defendants the only proof of the state as to either offense charged . . . rested solely upon an alleged conspiracy on the part of all the defendants to encompass the assault charged."[19] Vinje conceded that such a conspiracy theory was legally proper. But did the factual proof support it?

No. "It appears clearly enough that most of the defendants were angry at Guliani [*sic*] and his party. Whether it was because he spoke about the war and the citizen's duty to the state, or whether it was because he was not a Catholic and spoke slightingly about that religion, is not clear. Probably because of both, but perhaps chiefly for the latter reason."[20] And that did not make a conspiracy to assault with intent to murder. At most it made out a misdemeanor, an effort to disturb Giuliani's rally. Without the conspiracy, each defendant's actions stood alone. Unless he or she had done something criminal, there could be no conviction.

Justice Vinje then considered again each of the defendants. He turned first to the group against which the proof was thinnest. He was brutally brief in his assessment of the state's case against Pasquale Nardini and Angelo Pantaleone. There was "no evidence whatever" that they had taken part in any crime. In short, for all the proof showed, they were utterly innocent.[21]

Vinje's discussion of the next group was almost as succinct. Even so, it reached with grace toward a greater purpose that makes it striking to readers of more modern appellate decisions, which tend to focus mechanically on technical points and public policy support for a court's interpretation of legal rules. Such modern appellate opinions often feign indifference to the outcome of the case, with judges pretending to busy themselves objectively with process and legal rules rather than with who is right and who is wrong. Vinje's opinion instead proposed unapologetically to dispense justice:

> It is quite probable that Peter Bianchi, Daniel Belucci, and Louis Serafini were not present at the assault. But be that as it may, it is quite certain that as to them and as to Mary Nardini and Adolph

Fratesi the evidence would not warrant the conviction of any graver charge than that of simple assault. While they have not been imprisoned under a conviction of that offense, the fact remains that they have been deprived of their liberty under much harsher conditions and for a much longer time than they could have been had such been their conviction. Therefore, looking at the substance of things rather than at technical exactness in the manner of conviction, and in furtherance of substantial justice, it is held that they have been sufficiently punished under the improper conviction for any offense of which they could have been found guilty. The judgment is therefore reversed as to them, with directions to discharge them from further custody.[22]

With that, six men and a woman who had been in prison at hard labor for fifteen months were soon to leave. Two the court cleared completely. And the other five were done too. They would not face a retrial on a misdemeanor, which in any event could not have led to further punishment. Vinje was clear: the reason the supreme court rejected a retrial for the second group of five was not that the law barred one; it was that justice did.

Four defendants remained. The state's evidence sufficed as to Gavino Denurra and Bartolo Testolin to allow a conviction for the assault with intent to murder that the state had charged. But there was no conspiracy, so the trial court had instructed the jury wrongly on what the state had to prove. At a new trial, properly instructed jurors again could find those two guilty if they chose—but for individual actions, not for the deeds of a group acting on an imagined agreement. So while these convictions could not stand, Denurra and Testolin remained in jeopardy. The state could retry them if it wished. If the state were to convict these two men a second time, though, it would be on the basis of what they had done personally.[23]

That left only Vincenzo Fratesi and Amedeo Lilli. These last two Vinje and the court viewed differently. The evidence against them was strong, albeit lacking proof of any conspiratorial agreement. They had been armed and undeniably present when the shooting erupted. Indeed, there was "credible evidence" that both men actually had used their revolvers during the melee.[24] That evidence warranted their convictions for assault with intent to murder, even in the absence of a conspiracy. What Amedeo Lilli and Vincenzo Fratesi did personally was enough, in other words. But did some other trial error spoil the verdicts as to even these two men and require a new trial all the same?

That question required exploration of the more technical objections that Darrow and Sissman had raised. Most of these Vinje rejected decisively. Although

Vinje was a principled man, here some evidence that he was aware also of the practical and political demands of elected office seeped into his writing.[25] His handling of Judge Backus and the district attorney was diplomatic. As to Backus's injudicious remarks and caustic attitude toward the defense, Vinje wrote, "The trial was necessarily a long and a slow one and was sharply contested. It would be strange, indeed, if both court and counsel did not occasionally, during the fifteen days it lasted, lapse from the desired dignity and precision of language that we all agree should characterize every judicial inquiry. On the whole we feel that the trial court deserves commendation for its impartial discharge of a difficult duty."[26] Vinje had similarly refined words for the competing trial lawyers. He excused and elevated their sniping and bickering, saying, "We realize that counsel are constantly on the firing line and have little time for mature reflection during the progress of the trial, hence it is easy to go too far at times."[27]

Vinje similarly deflected most of the defense's other arguments. A change of venue was unnecessary: after all, the trial judge had secured a jury in less than a day, after questioning only thirty-seven prospective jurors. Here, Vinje conveniently assumed that prospective jurors and the trial judge were faithful to their oaths and truly were unbiased under circumstances that made that assumption very shaky. In the absence of evidence, the competing assumption may have been the more reasonable. But Vinje chose the assumption that ratified the work of the court below. Modern appellate decisions frequently indulge the same shaky assumptions.

Hearsay objections also went nowhere. Vinje rejected even more quickly quibbles about technical compliance with statutes on issuance of arrest warrants and sworn criminal complaints.

In all, the defense landed but one punch in its flurry of tactical legal jabs on behalf of Vincenzo Fratesi and Amedeo Lilli. Zabel's ruse of bringing several of the defendants to his office the day after the Bay View fracas, placing them under oath one at a time, and then questioning them was "in fact but an idle ceremony," utterly lacking legal authority. Vinje rightly acknowledged that the illiterate defendants were vulnerable to the trick. "It is fair to assume they were all ignorant of the illegality of the proceeding," Vinje conceded, "and the district attorney failed to advise them of their constitutional right to refuse to answer any question whose truthful answer they honestly believed would tend to incriminate them." The statements that Zabel obtained that way were "not voluntary."[28] They should not have been evidence at trial.[29] Even so, given the other proof against Fratesi and Lilli, "as to these two defendants the verdict would probably not have been different had their statements been excluded."[30]

No harm, no foul. The convictions and the twenty-five-year sentences would stand in the case of those last two men.[31]

While it visibly sought a just outcome and grappled honestly with the adequacy of the trial evidence, the supreme court opinion addressed no larger questions. It ventured nowhere near the role of dissent in a democracy or the dim prospects for justice that new and unwelcome immigrants faced in a courtroom. The opinion was confined and lawyerly, in the way that disciplined judging often must be.

Yet the state supreme court's decision had one great virtue—one not at all incompatible with proper judicial humility. By the close of the opinion, Vinje had scrupulously separated the mass of eleven poor Italians into its individual constituents. He had insisted that each get a fair look one by one, apart from the others. They were persons, whole in themselves, not just faceless fragments of potter's clay that a skilled lawyer could mold into a menacing clump. In short, Vinje had afforded these immigrants the simple honor of consideration as human beings in full.

Once they stood with individual integrity, rather than together as a malignant mass, the distinct places these eleven occupied on a spectrum running from innocence to guilt became apparent. Some were entirely innocent, at least for all the facts showed. Others had committed only lesser crimes than their convictions represented. Still others might or might not have been guilty of the charged offenses; as to them, the slanted trial left uncertainty, and a new, fairer trial should follow to give them a second look. Finally, two were guilty by any measure. All of them, though, had won at last the basic dignity of being judged alone. No conspiracy theory would conflate them now for the convenience of jurors, judges, and an angry public.

The Wisconsin Supreme Court's decision of course stirred the eleven defendants themselves and their families and supporters. Most could rejoice; two could not. But in a day when densely packed newspapers were the fastest way to tell Americans in one city what had happened in another and when even the eighty miles between Madison and Milwaukee was a distance qualifying as a journey, the supreme court's decision stirred almost no one else. There was no public outcry. Pundits did not foam and fulminate about activist judges. Calls for impeachment of the judges did not come. Cheap squawkers were nowhere heard. Prosecutors seeking political cover did not blame a permissive judiciary or fob off responsibility on the state supreme court for their own failings. Nary a journalist interviewed a miffed juror who wished to edify the world with his distaste for the appellate decision. Not one relative of a victim stepped forward to say "how dare they?" No promises of a prompt and vengeful retrial rang out from the police department or the district attorney's office. Press releases went unwritten.

Both the *Milwaukee Sentinel* and the *Milwaukee Journal* gave the story a place on their front pages the evening of the decision, but the story did not dominate that page or get the banner headline in either newspaper. The reporting was restrained, although the *Sentinel* was loose as ever with details: it offered inventive new misspellings of names and reported seven men freed, overlooking the sex of its former "queen of the anarchists," Maria Nardini.[32] In Madison, the *Capital Times* relegated the story to page three and focused not on the defendants but on the celebrated Darrow.[33] Not one editor of these papers was sufficiently in a huff to offer an editorial on the reversal in the state supreme court.

Zabel too was uncharacteristically reserved. Asked for his reaction to the supreme court's ruling, he remarked only, "While I am surprised at the decision I do not feel that I have any right to make any criticism. The cases were tried and the accused were given every opportunity to defend themselves. In my judgment, I think they had a fair and honest trial. As far as the two men who have been allowed a new trial are concerned, I shall prosecute them according to my judgment and in keeping with my attitude at their first trial and conviction."[34]

Even allowing for the fact that he was reacting within hours after receiving the decision, Zabel's tone was so muted that it raised questions. Had he experienced a change of heart? Had the bombs cowed him? Almost four years later, a possible answer finally would come in secret. But for now, Zabel clearly had no enthusiasm for whipping the public back into a frenzy.

One practical aspect of the decision may have pleased Judge Backus, whether the supreme court intended that or not. The decision came down the day *after* the spring judicial election, in which Backus had to defend his seat against a challenger. He won re-election, scoring what the *Milwaukee Sentinel* called an "easy victory" over his opponent.[35] The supreme court was acutely aware of the election, for one of its own members, Justice Marvin B. Rosenberry, himself survived a challenge from two other candidates the same day.[36] This decision would play no role in the campaign or the election.

After a day or two, in any event, the whole story passed. The commercial press showed no ongoing interest in the eleven Italians on whom they had splattered so much ink and bile barely eighteen months earlier.

The civility with which the media accepted the state supreme court's decision probably is only one reason for the general public's equally calm acceptance. In November 1917 a new draft was whisking troops to European battlefields. But by April 1919 that war was five months over. Johnny was marching home again.[37] Newspapers and the public alike moved on, to new murder trials, the struggling League of Nations, streetcar accidents, soldiers' homecomings, war debt, and the opening weeks of what would end as major league baseball's most infamous season, with eight Chicago White Sox players conspiring to throw the World Series.

As for Darrow, he had little time to savor the victory. By the end of April, he was off to Minneapolis and ensconced in the Hotel Radisson for an extended jury trial.[38]

Of course, at the moment, the ten men and Maria Nardini cared little about other global and local events or their lawyer's next case. For at least seven of them, whatever life now held, it would not unfold behind the tall, plastered stone walls of the prison at Waupun. Two more held at least the hope as they left that they would not return to prison, either.

A final pair would be left behind. To Vincenzo Fratesi and Amedeo Lilli, tomorrow would be just another day at hard work, followed by a long wait with a tin plate for the early evening ladlings of the prison kitchen. To those two men, it seemed then that every tomorrow would offer only that.

10

Infernal Machine

Although the decision on appeal seemed to most observers the end of the story—the last event that newspapers would bother to cover, for example—that decision was not the end for the eleven Italians or for the lawyers and trial judge. The events leading to the trial, the trial itself, and the appeal all would continue to shape and define their lives and reputations. The appeal is not the end of the story either, for anyone interested in its most famous direct participant: Clarence Darrow. A state grand jury investigation, uncovered almost a century after the Italians' appeal and nearly seventy-five years after Darrow's death, raises new questions about the character and methods of the man who remains America's iconic trial lawyer. Maddeningly, the investigation also fails to yield wholly convincing answers to those questions.

The Wisconsin Supreme Court's decision seemed to promise freedom for eight men and a woman, and indeed, it prompted immediate action. Just a day after the court's decision, prison officials loaded the nine Italians whose convictions were overturned on a train back to Milwaukee. After arriving that afternoon, the nine were to stay only briefly in the sheriff's custody until it was clear where they would go next.[1] Perhaps freedom was just a day or two away.

Nothing would be that simple, though. Freedom would prove elusive. The Chicago office of the U.S. Department of Labor's Immigration Service moved just as quickly as the state prison. By the time the train arrived in Milwaukee, the Immigration Service had arrest warrants awaiting all nine on charges that they were deportable as alien anarchists who believed in the violent overthrow of the U.S. government. They went from state to federal custody in the blink of an eye. A Milwaukee journalist, Robert Tanzilo, has traced the fates of some of the nine. Four certainly were deported immediately after their release from prison.[2]

Others escaped the Immigration Service's net, but only for a time. Maria Nardini still remained in Chicago in September 1920, when she corresponded with the Wisconsin Board of Control about the fate of her brother, Vincenzo.[3] There was one essential point of restoration for Maria: she and little Areno at last were reunited. Areno was an orphan at the state's hands no more.[4] But mother and son, too, eventually were deported.[5]

Sooner or later, the remaining few returned involuntarily to the land they had left for America's opportunities.[6] Back in Italy, Bianchi and Lilli remained under the eye of Italian authorities. They lived quietly, Lilli as a tailor and Bianchi as a baker. Even so, the Italian police watched Lilli on and off until 1931 and Bianchi until 1940.[7]

In the United States, despite Zabel's ominous suggestion the day of the state supreme court's opinion, the state never did seek to retry Denurra or Testolin. Referring to the supreme court's rejection of the conspiracy theory, Zabel opined after time that a retrial would have been "an idle ceremony."[8] That was revealing. Without the opportunity to offer wide-ranging evidence of the statements and acts of others and with his proof against Denurra and Testolin limited to what they alone had done and said, Zabel saw little chance of conviction. If to convict them he had to prove that these two had committed crimes themselves, as opposed to proving that others had acted badly in ways that should count against the two on trial, Zabel decided that he would lose.

There was a second reason not to retry the two. Zabel certainly was canny enough to see it. A retrial of these two relatively minor players in the Bay View pageant inevitably would have drawn attention to the police station bombing. That bombing had generated most of the energy that propelled the first prosecution. But renewed attention would have been embarrassing, for the investigation into the bombing had stalled completely in the nearly year and a half since the bomb meant for Giuliani's church had reduced much of the central police station to rubble. Neither local nor federal authorities were any closer to an arrest than they had been the morning after the bomb exploded. A retrial of two minor players only could have reminded the public that the greater outrage—one that Zabel and the newspapers had linked so aggressively to these eleven Italians—had gone unpunished. Zabel and the police did not need that.

In the end, Zabel blinked. Denurra and Testolin would face deportation like the others but not further imprisonment.

The state legal process was not yet over for Vincenzo Fratesi and Amedeo Lilli in 1919. By August 1920 the state Board of Control, sitting as a "Lunacy Commission," concluded that Fratesi had become insane. The state transferred him that month to the Central State Hospital for the Insane, also in Waupun.[9] A healthy Lilli remained in the prison at Waupun.[10]

Their options were limited. The governor's outright pardon or, failing that, the governor's commutation of their sentences was their best hope.

Given those options, Clarence Darrow and Peter Sissman eventually filed a pardon petition for both, after almost two years' delay. The petition went to Governor John J. Blaine on March 1, 1921. It was not an elaborate legal document. Darrow's petition ran to just over three double-spaced pages and bore no sign of careful effort. The petition cited no specific provision of the trial record, delved into no facts in detail, and identified no similar case for the governor's consideration. Instead, it argued vaguely that the immediacy of the trial after the central police station explosion meant that "suspicion was . . . fastened upon your petitioners and your petitioners suffered by reason of the inflamed passions and inevitability of the bias in the minds of the jurors against your petitioners, which was generated by the public sentiment then prevailing." Moreover, "for some reason unknown to your petitioners," the state supreme court had not reversed the convictions of Fratesi and Lilli, so they alone remained in stir.[11] In a word, the petition was cursory. Its only real point was that the state supreme court had been wrong.

Just sometimes, those pleadings are the most likely to succeed. This petition also included, near the end, an interesting paragraph: "And your petitioners are advised and informed by said Honorable A. C. Backus and by said Winfred C. Zabel, the District Attorney, that each of them respectively made their written statements to your Excellency, concerning your petitioners, but that your petitioners are now ignorant of the contents of such statements, or the purport thereof."[12]

That paragraph begged awkward questions. Why would Zabel and Judge Backus make written statements to the governor about a pardon before Lilli and Vincenzo Fratesi even sought one? If the prosecutor and the judge had commented to the governor in advance, why would Darrow and Sissman have to note that conspicuously to the same governor? It is quite possible, of course, that defense counsel would have spoken to the prosecutor and perhaps even to the judge about the prospect of a pardon before filing the petition. Professional courtesy would be reason enough for that. Even better, a savvy defense lawyer might have sought to cajole the prosecutor and the judge either to refrain from opposing the petition or to soften their opposition under the circumstances. In that event, Darrow might have meant that the prosecutor and the judge had prepared but not yet mailed responses. Conceivably, too, Darrow might have taken pains to assure the governor that he was not speaking for the prosecutor or the judge.

But if Darrow really did not know what Zabel and Backus wanted to say about the pardon petition, why wait two years to file it? Darrow easily could have filed his short petition soon after the supreme court's decision in 1919, when the contrasting fates of the last two defendants in prison and the nine released would have been freshest and most compelling. He then could have left the prosecutor and the judge to say what they would, if he was not privy to their views. Possibly Darrow's judgment was that the pardon application would stand little chance of success until Fratesi and Lilli had served more time than the year-plus that had passed between sentencing and the supreme court's decision. That is plausible. But the delay of almost two more years would have been hard to sell to the two imprisoned defendants and to their released friends and relatives.

In fact, Zabel and Backus did not mail anything to the governor before Darrow's pardon petition. They did, however, write just two days after, on March 3, 1921. Darrow's petition would have been mailed from Chicago on March 1. Under the best assumptions of postal service, Zabel and Backus's response went out just one day after they first could have received the pardon petition.

And in sharp contrast to the petition, their response was detailed, running nearly six full pages, single-spaced. Zabel clearly was the author: it was on the district attorney's office letterhead, and the florid tone and crafty structure bespoke his talents and personality. Backus merely endorsed the letter. Theirs was a remarkable document.

The letter outlined the facts in some detail and strove to justify the prosecution and convictions on a conspiracy theory. It then attributed the long sentences to that conspiracy finding: "The court sentenced them each to imprisonment for a term of twenty-five years, not solely because of the assault which was committed by any of the several defendants, but that they were all guilty as having all acted in concert and in furtherance thereof." Zabel continued on the severity of the sentences: "the court undoubtedly realiz[ed] the rule of law that the offense when committed jointly by a number of persons in furtherance of an unlawful conspiracy amounted to a more grievous offense than if the same act were committed by an individual, or by individuals acting independently of each other."[13]

Once he established the importance of the conspiracy as justification for the sentences, Zabel conceded that the supreme court had rejected that conspiracy theory. Without bowing to the correctness of the high court's ruling, Zabel deftly turned it into an opportunity to make himself appear a champion of scrupulous fairness. The case resolved itself, he wrote, "into the individual crimes committed by individuals acting alone," thanks to the supreme court's decision. "It therefore follows that in view of this decision of the Supreme Court that the sentence of twenty-five years now being served by two applicants for executive clemency is more severe than should have been imposed for an act of that kind when committed by an individual or individuals not acting in concert." Fratesi and Lilli should not be required to serve such long sentences and "in my opinion are therefore entitled to executive clemency." He commended those two defendants to the governor's "favorable consideration."[14]

In doing so, Zabel had to overlook the fact that these were the two defendants as to whom the supreme court had found individual actions that entirely warranted conviction. Those actions included possessing and possibly firing guns in a crowd, at policemen, and then lying under oath at trial—or so the jury all but found with its verdict.

Below Zabel's signature, the letter had one last sentence:

> I have read the foregoing letter, and the recommendations therein made, and as trial judge fully adopt the same.
>
> Signed, *A. C. Backus, Judge.*[15]

With that, the prosecutor who had howled himself hoarse in condemning the eleven defendants and the judge who had excoriated them so thoroughly at sentencing invited the governor to undo their work. They offered no concession that they had erred. Instead, they undertook a subtle campaign to blame the supreme court. By inviting the governor to spring the last two Italians from prison, Zabel and Backus painted improbable self-portraits as advocates for parity and justice.

Now the whole matter was on the desk of Governor Blaine. There it sat with defense, prosecution, and trial judge aligned.

Blaine was a progressive Republican lawyer who had risen through a series of political offices. He had graduated with a law degree from Valparaiso University and then served as small-town mayor, member of a county board of supervisors, state senator, state attorney general, and now governor. Ahead of him lay a term in the U.S. Senate.[16]

The governor had at least some prior familiarity with this case, for his term as attorney general had bridged the briefing and oral argument in the state supreme court.[17] In his role as attorney general, he had nominally represented the state on appeal, although Zabel and Arthur Bartelt in fact did the work.[18]

More than six weeks after the pardon petition, Darrow was growing impatient. He wrote again to Blaine. His letter made clear that by then he knew about Zabel and Backus's decision to back the plea for a pardon: "You remember when I saw you a few months ago, I asked for the pardon of Amedeo Lilli and Vincent Fratesi. Letters were received from the District Attorney in Milwaukee and the judge before whom the case was tried. I do not know whether you have yet received them. I feel certain that these men should be pardoned and hope you will see it that way. If you have not received the letters, I will write them about sending letters to you. They both assured me they would do it."[19]

So the whole episode took another twist. Darrow's letter to the governor also had a very personal tone, a sign of his wide reach and prominence; it revealed a cordial acquaintance with Blaine of some standing.[20]

Blaine wrote back promptly, acknowledging that he had "the letters from the district attorney in Milwaukee and the judge before whom Lilli and Fratesi were tried." He hoped "to be able to act upon their application before the next pardon day."[21] This exchange between Darrow and the governor was private. Neither letter reflected copies to Zabel or Backus.

Still the governor dallied with the pardon petition. Months passed. Blaine was willing to grant some relief to Vincenzo Fratesi and Amedeo Lilli, but he also wanted to ensure their deportation upon release.

Finally, in October 1921 Blaine and the chief immigration officer in the Labor Department's Chicago office exchanged a number of letters. If Blaine pardoned the last two defendants outright, the federal government would be unable to deport them on the basis of the 1917 convictions. It would have to fall back on separate deportation grounds that they were alien anarchists who advocated violent overthrow of the U.S. government. However, a commutation of their sentences, leaving intact the convictions and merely truncating the punishment, would not defeat deportation on the basis of the 1917 case. Blaine accepted that advice.

Then a further question arose. Would the state's determination that Fratesi had gone insane in prison thwart his deportation? No, it would not.

On the eve of Blaine's planned commutation, in December 1921, the Labor Department sent a telegram advising that it unexpectedly could not deport the two at that moment as planned. The department asked the governor to wait again. Two more months passed. Upon word in February 1922 that the federal government at last could pick them up, Blaine timed the commutations to coincide with the Labor Department's arrival in Waupun to take Fratesi and Lilli into custody immediately.[22]

So it was that on February 9, 1922, Vincenzo Fratesi and Amedeo Lilli left state custody—in federal irons, bound for Chicago.[23] Their deportation followed within days. Almost a year after the pardon petition, Darrow had won their release but not their freedom.

Eventually, at least three of the eleven Italians returned to the United States. By 1941 Pasquale and Maria Nardini were living in Harlem and running a small grocery store.[24] Maria came with Areno in 1925.[25] Pasquale traveled separately.

Coincidentally, the Nardini family settled no farther than a good stroll from the old offices of Emma Goldman's magazine, *Mother Earth*.[26] But Goldman already was in lasting exile; Areno never would meet the fiery woman, old enough to be his grandmother, who had written so movingly (and skillfully, for fundraising purposes) of his plight. Maria lived in New York the rest of her life, which was long: she died at ninety-five.[27]

Gavino Denurra also returned to the United States in time. He likely did so legally, for he obtained a Social Security card under his real name. A photograph, circa 1960, shows a slight, dapper man, possibly a mite uncomfortable in a suit, next to a stern and proud wife. He died in Santa Clara, California, in 1973.[28]

On the whole, the defendants lived out their lives as obscurely as they had begun them, until the three Sundays in late summer 1917 that led to their prosecution. Whatever their true views or leanings, on one chilly Sunday they happened to be hecklers in a small crowd, caught up in a profoundly local dispute. That dispute's linkage to larger events was accidental. These eleven did not shape the events that engulfed them in the tumultuous autumn of 1917. Rather, they were shaped and controlled by those events. They were nearly anonymous—and unfortunate—extras in the huge cast of an American epic in the years during and after World War I. That epic saw unprecedented death abroad, patriotic fervor and intolerance of dissent at home, and a nativist fear of immigrants and radicals that produced the Espionage Act of 1917, Attorney General A. Mitchell Palmer's raids in 1919 and 1920, and deportations.

Among the giants of American life in that era who touched these eleven laborers in some way, Emma Goldman would find the U.S. government unyielding in excluding her from American shores but for one brief speaking tour in 1934 after her deportation. The speaking tour included a stop at the University of Wisconsin in Madison, site of Darrow's appellate success. In between her deportation and her short trip to Wisconsin, she spent two deeply disillusioning years in the Soviet Union. The United States had forced her out, but she fled the Soviet Union on her own. Goldman died on May 14, 1940. Only after her death did the U.S. government relent and permit her permanent return. She is buried at Chicago's Waldheim Cemetery, not far from the Haymarket Square defendants.[29]

Locally, Judge Backus would leave the bench in 1924 to become the president and publisher of the *Milwaukee Sentinel*, the frothy daily that arguably won the competition among mainstream newspapers for the most sensational, skewed coverage of the events of 1917 that led to the convictions in Backus's courtroom. He later left the *Sentinel* to teach law and died in March 1952 at the age of seventy-four.[30]

Winfred Zabel was seventy-one at his death that snowbound day in early January 1948. Zabel had given up trial work five years earlier and finally resigned from his poisonous partnership with Bill Rubin just a year before he died. In memorial proceedings under auspices of the Milwaukee County Bar Association, Rubin reported heart problems as the reason for Zabel's retreat from the courtroom.[31] The fact that Zabel had destroyed his own good name and good will among the bar by his abuses of power may have had something to do with that retreat too.

Zabel's less flashy older brother, William, who had served as deputy district attorney under Winfred and probably as Winfred's bagman, himself became the district attorney in 1932. Will Zabel ran as a Democrat—a pragmatic (if characteristically unprincipled) choice that year. He died on election night 1936, just as voters returned him to office for a third term.

Both brothers almost surely were deeply corrupt. The newspaper obituaries assured the public instead that they were reformers and corruption fighters.[32]

Bill Rubin's dreams of serving as chief counsel to the American Federation of Labor or as a federal judge never came true. When Samuel Gompers picked Rubin's one-time protégé, Joseph Padway, to serve as AFL chief counsel, it was not because Rubin had adopted the role of *éminence grise* on behalf of the younger man. No, Rubin had actively sought the job and lost out. The same with the federal judgeship: he was not seeking to promote the fortunes of a man with greater politesse who then would owe him gratitude. He had wanted the job himself. Rubin always was long on self-flattery—the Wisconsin Supreme Court even noted this trait in a published opinion—and self-promotion.[33]

Those traits aside, his story remains poignant. He was bumptious and a perennial also-ran. But he also stood consistently with the little guy, and when he lost, he went down with a fight. He lacked polish. But too much polish only makes lawyers slippery. Today, no one stages his ham-handed play denouncing Bolshevism, written in 1921.[34] Perhaps no one ever did. Yet he wrote the play because he, a full-throated liberal, also passionately opposed the totalitarian impulses of the communists. And he wrote that play just four years after the Russian revolution, at a time when many on the American left still were infatuated with Lenin and his cadre.

There was some grace for Rubin in the end. As his thick hair turned gray and then white, he became an avuncular figure in both the Milwaukee bar and the state Democratic Party. Findings of contempt (one with a fine of $25 for quarreling with a judge over rulings during Rubin's cross-examination of a witness) and brushes with disbarment for ambulance chasing in the late 1920s were long forgotten by the time he slowed his pace to "semi-retirement" at the age of eighty-three.[35] He slipped away gently at the age of eighty-five in early February 1959, after nine months in a hospital suffering dementia and the infirmities of old age. Mainline newspapers that had so scorned his Italian clients in 1917, including the *Milwaukee Sentinel*, lauded him lavishly in death.[36]

The Reverend August Giuliani continued the work of an evangelist after the trial and appeal. In 1919, the year that the Wisconsin Supreme Court reversed the convictions of the nine defendants, Giuliani remarried. His two mission churches expanded to three in the 1920s. He resolved to build one grander church in a prosperous neighborhood just north of downtown. On groundbreaking day for the new church in November 1928, Giuliani fell ill. He never recovered fully. Although he rallied sufficiently to attend the cornerstone-laying ceremony, he died just before the church opened. On Thanksgiving Day 1929 the congregation held a double observation: the dedication of the new church and the funeral of the church's founder, Giuliani.[37] Only in that early death did he escape the serial suspicions of sexual impropriety that his first marriage to Katherine Eyerick posed, that Rubin had intimated during the 1917 trial, and that arose again within his congregation in 1922.[38]

The great epilogue to the trial is not the lives and deaths of its participants, though. The most important postscript dates to the years immediately following the trial and appeal, when all of the principals were alive and active in their usual pursuits. None of the principals wrote that postscript. Instead, two of the most obscure participants in the events of autumn 1917 did. Five years after the trial and three years after the appeal, the assistant district attorney who sat at Zabel's side, Frederick F. Groelle, and the lurking Italian informer and manipulator Frank Carchidi appeared once again.

Groelle had something to say. Carchidi backed him on an important point.

In 1922, following a spring primary election in which candidates for district attorney had accused Zabel of graft and corruption, Zabel moved preemptively in the hope of preserving his job in November's general election. He asked Judge Backus to convene a grand jury to investigate the accusations but declared himself too busy to lead the grand jury investigation (which obviously would have been a glorious conflict of interest, anyway). So he suggested that the court appoint a special prosecutor.[39] Zabel now could appear to voters unafraid of an investigation into his conduct. Better yet, he could appear unable to control the outcome of that investigation, for he would not be leading it.

As usual, Backus accommodated Zabel. He appointed two prominent lawyers, George B. Hudnall and Frank T. Boesel, as special prosecutors and empaneled a special grand jury. Both Hudnall and Boesel were corporate lawyers. Hudnall had been president of the State Bar of Wisconsin in 1915–16, and Boesel later would serve in the same position in 1927–28.[40] They interviewed a large number of witnesses and issued subpoenas to some of them to appear before the grand jury.[41]

Beginning in late October 1922 that grand jury, under Hudnall and Boesel's supervision, conducted a wandering inquiry that lasted most of the following year and produced more than four thousand pages of transcribed testimony. At the suggestion of a prominent leader of the local bar who had interviewed Frederick Groelle and heard an interesting tale, the grand jury summoned Groelle as one of its early witnesses.[42]

The nervous man who took the witness stand in October was forty-five years old. He had graduated with a bachelor's degree in law from the University of Wisconsin in 1899. After practicing first in Stevens Point and then in Manitowoc, Groelle joined Zabel's office as an assistant district attorney in June 1917. His stint was short. He resigned effective January 1, 1919.[43] Groelle was in private practice again, still in Milwaukee, when he took the oath before curious grand jurors and George Hudnall and Frank Boesel in late 1922.[44]

Groelle seemed not just nervous but also reluctant. He was testifying under immunity, meaning that he would not face prosecution for any crimes he might admit.[45] All the same, in the first few minutes on the stand, he twice protested that he was unable to hear a question and once asked the court reporter to read back a direct question about Zabel.[46] Asked generally about Zabel's honesty and integrity, he murmured, "I have always found him honest." Had anything occurred during his time in the district attorney's office that led him to believe that undue considerations had ever influenced Zabel? "Oh, no."[47] The evasiveness was palpable.

As Hudnall burrowed in with specific questions, though, try as Groelle might to downplay it, a stunning story emerged in bits and pieces. Yes, he had assisted Zabel at the trial of the Italian anarchists. The two prosecutors had received "a wastebasket full of threatening letters" during the trial.[48] After the trial, in quick succession came two more intimidating incidents: the gunman who confronted Groelle's wife and daughters as they pulled into the garage after a night at the theater and the bombs planted next to Zabel's house.[49] At that point in the early months of 1918, Zabel was "practically a nervous wreck," in Groelle's estimation. Zabel was considering resigning. Groelle himself was badly shaken.[50]

Then Groelle had an idea. Clarence Darrow just had taken up the anarchists' appeal. Groelle recalled Zabel's comment, some time earlier, that Darrow was "a personal friend."[51] Groelle and Zabel had a talk—in fact, more than one.[52] Together, they hatched a simple plan. Slowly, uncomfortably, Groelle dribbled it out under oath with the persistent prodding of the special prosecutors.

Why not meet with Darrow? They could call Darrow and ask to meet with him in Chicago. If Darrow agreed to intercede with Chicago anarchists and persuade them to call off the attempts on the lives of Zabel and Groelle, the prosecutors in turn would agree to fix the record on appeal so that the convictions of the Milwaukee eleven likely would be reversed in the state supreme court. This is what they would propose to Darrow.[53] A straightforward swap: Zabel and Groelle would be left alone; the eleven Italians would go free, thanks to a mutual effort by prosecution and defense to falsify the trial record before it went to the supreme court. Zabel liked the plan. Eventually he passed a telephone to Groelle, who placed a long-distance call to Darrow's office. Yes, Darrow would meet with them. Either later that day or the very next day, Zabel and Groelle would board the train for Chicago.[54]

Before they could go, there was a complication. To alter the record, the judge and possibly the court reporter likely would have to be in on the scheme. It was the judge's job to review the defense's list of exceptions to see whether they were "conformable to the truth of the case"; if so, the judge would sign the bill of exceptions.[55] Judge Backus easily might spot phony entries. And if testimony or lawyers' objections were to be altered, the court reporter's notes would be the source of the changes.

That meant meeting with Backus. Zabel and Groelle did exactly that. They conferred with the judge about the trip before going to Chicago.[56] Groelle at first denied that they actually discussed with Backus the idea of injecting error into the trial record.[57] When pushed, though, Groelle testified that he had talked with Backus even before Darrow called back to confirm the meeting with Groelle and Zabel. After hearing from Darrow, "it was understood that Judge Backus was to go down with us to Chicago," Groelle stammered. But when Groelle called Backus to set the time, Backus summoned Groelle to chambers. The judge had cold feet. According to Groelle, Backus announced, "I have been thinking it over. I don't think it is wise for me to go along. You boys can accomplish just as much without me as to have me go along."[58]

In the end, Backus did not go to Chicago. But Zabel and Groelle did. They went with the express purpose of telling Darrow that the record could be fixed so that his clients would "get off," if necessary.[59] They did not say quite that much to Darrow; in Groelle's opinion, they did not have to put it that bluntly. Groelle thought Darrow a very shrewd man.[60] Taking an indirect approach, Zabel instead told Darrow about the attempts on their lives. Darrow seemed "very much surprised and said he hadn't heard anything or read anything about it in the papers."[61]

Zabel continued. He and Groelle felt that, with the case pending in the state supreme court, if the anarchists attempted to kill them, "it certainly wouldn't help their cause."[62] In short, Zabel told Darrow, "we certainly are worth more to your clients alive than dead."[63]

Darrow's response also was indirect. He turned and asked Peter Sissman to summon an Italian man to the office. "I am glad you boys came down," he assured the prosecutors. "I shall see these parties who are financing this appeal to the supreme court; you can go home and rest in peace from now on; there won't be any more trouble if these parties have anything to do with it." Darrow alluded to the Italian contact. "I shall tell him about it, and he knows the Italian people up there in Milwaukee, and we shall send him up on the next train to see that there won't be anything more."[64]

With that, the meeting in Darrow's office ended. Groelle said nothing more specific about Darrow's response. He and Zabel boarded the train back to Milwaukee. Even for two canny men like Darrow and Zabel, the specifics of an agreement would have required something more, then or later.

But Groelle offered nothing about later contacts between Zabel and Darrow. He also claimed that he did not know whether in fact Zabel and Darrow eventually altered the trial record that went to the Wisconsin Supreme Court. Groelle tendered his resignation from the district attorney's office in late 1918, before final approval of the critical bill of exceptions.[65] Recall that Zabel continued to handle the case on appeal, but with the help of Assistant District Attorney Arthur H. Bartelt, who had played only a minor role at trial. The state's brief and supplemental materials in the supreme court did not bear Groelle's name.

As both Hudnall and J. Gilbert Hardgrove, president of the Milwaukee County Bar Association, acknowledged, Zabel was clever enough to bring in a fresh lawyer, Bartelt, to write the brief on appeal. "The natural thing," Hardgrove opined, "would be to call—after the record was fixed—to call a fellow that didn't know anything about it and put it up to him to write a darn good brief on it. Of course the innocent man could write a more convincing brief."[66] Hardgrove had reason to ponder the scheme. It was to him that Groelle first had told his story.[67] As for Bartelt, even Bill Rubin assessed him as one of only two honest assistants in Zabel's office.[68]

All the while, Groelle insisted that he saw nothing morally wrong with the plan that he and Zabel had concocted. Rather, the only shame he expressed was that the episode had displayed cowardice on his part and Zabel's.[69] They had been willing to trade the convictions for their lives. Asked squarely if there was any impropriety, Groelle answered, "the only impropriety—that is, you would be yellow and cowardly, not wanting the public to know it."[70]

Just before he left the witness stand, two citizens on the grand jury took up the questioning of Groelle and brought it to a still inconclusive end. "If this trip you made to Chicago became public, would there by anything else besides cowardice involved, that is on your part, would there be anything besides cowardice involved, having that become—that known to the public, or do you think the public might become suspicious that the District Attorney's Office is too lenient with the anarchists?"

"I don't know what you mean," Groelle insisted. "Anything else involved except cowardice, I don't know what I quite understand you."

"Is it proper to fix the record in order to—" the juror broke off.

"No, of course it is not," Groelle conceded.

"Then it would be more than cowardice."

"If the record was fixed; I don't know anything about that."

"Well," a second grand juror chimed in, "the intent was there; would you have gone through with it if necessary, without a doubt?"

"Yes, sir." That was Groelle's last word on the subject.[71]

Throughout his grand jury appearance, Groelle obviously was recalcitrant. More than that, his testimony betrayed an odd moral detachment. It left the impression, on the whole, that Groelle either would not or could not grasp the truth: that even if the prosecutors had feared for their lives, intentionally altering the record of what happened at trial so that the Wisconsin Supreme Court likely would perceive an error that never actually occurred and reverse convictions that should stand would be dishonest and a breach of public trust. That strange detachment and amoral evaluation perhaps sapped some of the credibility that otherwise would attach to a lawyer confessing his own involvement in a plan to commit a serious fraud on the state's highest court. A lawyer who understood just how wrong that was and who understood the threat it might pose to his reputation and continued livelihood would not likely admit his role unless it was true and he was seeking to unburden his conscience. But to all appearances, Groelle could have been recounting hesitantly a trifling failure of courage when he had no moral duty at stake. If he had any sense of shame for having planned to throw the appeal in a serious case the prosecution had won, the transcript offers no sure hint of it. By itself, Groelle's story would not warrant a conclusion that Zabel and Darrow had agreed corruptly to fix the appeal or even seriously contemplated it.

His story did not stand alone, though. Another assistant district attorney, Louis Koenig, recalled Zabel's trip to Chicago to confer with Darrow about the anarchist case. Zabel did not suggest to Koenig any improper purpose for the trip, and he evidently did not mention Groelle's role in it.[72] Koenig did remember that the unexploded bombs at Zabel's house had frightened Zabel enough that he had tried to purchase another life insurance policy but was turned down.[73]

Koenig's recollection that Zabel traveled to Chicago to meet Darrow is important corroboration alone. On an appeal, there often is no pressing reason for opposing lawyers to meet at all. If in this case there was some reason, the natural place for a meeting would have been Milwaukee: the case arose there, was tried there, and the files, exhibits, and transcripts were there. As a matter of custom, too, defense lawyers typically come to prosecutors' offices for meetings, not the other way around. Darrow's national stature might have been reason for an exception. But then, Darrow's clients had lost at trial and Zabel had won. While the losing side might want to meet for some reason, the winning side would have little or no reason to meet with the losing side if only the merits of the case were in mind. The winning side would be much less likely to have anything to gain from a meeting. So the mere fact of this meeting is mildly surprising, and its location strongly suggests that Zabel had requested it. The location also suggests that the topic of the meeting did not require access to the trial record. Of course, none of this proves that the meeting was less than innocent. But Koenig's recollection certainly did nothing to disprove Groelle's story, either.

Then there was one more piece of testimony. Frank Carchidi at last reappeared. He told the grand jury that he had gone to a show and had overheard some Italians talking about the appeal.

"One day I was in the Strand Theater," Carchidi testified in his broken English. "And heard somebody talking of the Supreme Court case of these anarchists and one of them said if Mr. Zabel carry his agreement they will be out tomorrow. I went and saw Groelle and told him I heard this conversation and said is it true. He said yes, I went to Chicago with Zabel the same day these bombs were placed and he made a settlement with Darrow, some attorney down in Chicago, that if those anarchists would let him alone, that they wouldn't molest him any more, that he will see to it that when the Supreme Court will take up this case that they be let out."[74] Pressed further, his summary was: "The agreement, I don't know, the agreement was that they were to let Mr. Zabel alone, and he was to see those anarchists, those Dagoes get out of the Supreme Court trial, and they did."[75]

Carchidi also claimed that he and a police officer later put the question directly to Zabel. That caused Groelle soon after to confront Carchidi at Carchidi's office, asking, "Frank, did you squeal?" Carchidi admitted leaking the matter back to Zabel. According to Carchidi, Groelle responded, "God, Zabel called me over and is as sore as hell, raised the devil with me."[76] For good measure, Carchidi lay Zabel's "hatred" of him to the fact that Carchidi had squealed about Zabel's trip to Chicago. Only afterward did Zabel start getting warrants on Carchidi, he complained.[77]

Carchidi's testimony both corroborated and contradicted Groelle's version at places. As Groelle told it, Zabel had called him into the office later and asked him whether he had said anything to Carchidi about the Chicago trip. Groelle testified that he denied talking with Carchidi. Well, Zabel said, he understood that Carchidi had been doing some talking. Again on Groelle's version, he went to Carchidi's office a day or two after that meeting with Zabel and asked Carchidi whether he had said anything to Zabel. No, Carchidi told him. But Carchidi then explained that he had been at a moving picture theater sitting in back of some Italians and that the Italians had remarked "that the men were going to get off, that matters were fixed."[78]

While Carchidi and Groelle each gave self-serving stories about minor details, then, they agreed on the basic outline. Zabel confronted Groelle. Groelle, in turn, met with Carchidi. And Carchidi overheard the discussion among Italians at a movie theater. The theater chatter was consistent with Groelle's recollection that Darrow spoke of sending a Chicago emissary to speak with the Milwaukee Italians.

As to Carchidi's claim that Zabel later retaliated against him, Carchidi had six or seven separate criminal cases pending while the grand jury investigation continued. All involved dishonest financial dealings. Eventually, he was convicted of obtaining $3,000 under false pretenses.[79] That conviction, though, came after Zabel had lost the 1922 election for district attorney and left office.[80] Carchidi appealed. The state supreme court unanimously affirmed his conviction. Carchidi's lawyer, incidentally? Bill Rubin.[81]

Carchidi's testimony and Groelle's partial endorsement of it further support the conclusion that Zabel, Groelle, and Darrow in fact discussed fixing the eleven Italians' appeal, however guardedly or even tacitly. There is no other known explanation for Carchidi's overheard conversation in the theater, assuming that Carchidi really did overhear such talk. More important, there is no other likely explanation for Groelle and Carchidi discussing the issue at all or for Zabel calling Groelle on the carpet over his contacts with Carchidi.

True, Carchidi had reason to dislike Zabel and to wish him ill by the time of Carchidi's grand jury testimony. Zabel had charged Carchidi repeatedly with crimes. Carchidi would have had a motive to lie about the overheard theater conversation and to seek out Groelle or someone else to back his story. But Groelle had the juicier part of the story. This he told only reluctantly. He confessed cowardice but not dishonesty, by his odd moral code. And in part he contradicted

Carchidi on the details of their interactions. So it seems quite improbable that Groelle was lying to the grand jury at Carchidi's behest.

If Groelle told the truth, then, the question of whether the plan to fix the appellate record went forward remains unanswered. The loose, tacit agreement in Darrow's office that a fair reading of Groelle's testimony suggests may not have come to fruition. Perhaps Zabel and Darrow never later agreed on necessary details; perhaps they did but then never followed through. One irony is striking, though. Groelle's testimony, with the partial corroboration of Carchidi and others, well might have supported a public corruption prosecution of Zabel and Darrow on a conspiracy theory even though the underlying crime remained uncompleted. Zabel and Darrow could have been prosecuted on the same pliable theory that Zabel had used or misused so skillfully to prosecute the Italians.

Is it just possible, however, that even though Zabel and Groelle made a corrupt offer, Darrow in fact responded altruistically—that Darrow called off further attacks because it was the right thing to do, without exacting a price? Yes, theoretically. But realistically, that is not likely. First, Darrow would have had to act altruistically without telling Zabel and Groelle he was doing so. Had he told them, Groelle surely would have exonerated himself and Zabel by reporting that detail— if he ever had bothered to relay the story at all. Beyond that, if either the anarchists with whom Darrow was in touch or their friends were violent extremists involved in placing bombs at Zabel's house and menacing Groelle's family at gunpoint, they hardly would have desisted on the mere request of a lawyer, even a lawyer of Darrow's stature. Appeals to their better angels would have been silly: people willing to kill public officials to avenge convictions would have wanted a quid pro quo for giving up.

A search for proof of completed corruption in the appellate process, though, must include the Wisconsin Supreme Court's decision in the case. American appellate courts ordinarily explain their decisions, often at length, and the Wisconsin Supreme Court did. That opinion offers little or no support for the conclusion that Zabel and Darrow actually fixed the appeal, although it necessarily cannot disprove an effort to do so, either. Recall that the supreme court's opinion rested principally on an assessment of the trial evidence as a whole, not on any specific error that the judge may have made on this or that jury instruction or on narrow evidentiary rulings. The supreme court found no evidence of a conspiracy, after reviewing the entire trial.[82] As to two defendants, the state failed to prove any crime. As to five more defendants, the evidence did not warrant conviction for more than misdemeanor assault.[83] So the supreme court reversed the convictions of seven of the eleven without commenting on any possible specific trial error.

The evidence just was too thin on the whole. It then affirmed the convictions of two more, Vincenzo Fratesi and Amedeo Lilli.[84] They certainly did not benefit from any fixed record. That left just two defendants, Gavino Denurra and Bartolo Testolin, for whom the judge's specific mistakes made a difference.

But the error in the jury instructions that the supreme court found was not some mistake in their wording that Zabel and Darrow might have contrived by altering the record. The error lay in giving conspiracy instructions at all. It seems clear that Backus in fact did give conspiracy instructions, for this was the heart of the state's theory of prosecution. The conspiracy theory pervaded the entire trial and arose from the amended charges that Zabel filed on November 30, at the trial's start. The newspapers at the time reported a trial in which conspiracy was a central issue.[85] Even had they tried, Zabel and Darrow could not have rewritten the trial record so completely. And they could not have rewritten the newspapers at all.

The only other defense argument that carried the day on appeal was insufficiency of the evidence. That argument, too, relied not on any slip of the tongue or mistaken ruling; it turned on the entirety of the testimony. Altering the record to create a false impression that the evidence was insufficient, by omitting details or negating the positive assertions of witnesses, again would have been an undertaking so massive and so unlikely to work that it is highly implausible.

Of course, the fact that the supreme court reversed on grounds that corrupt lawyers could not have faked does not prove that Zabel and Darrow never altered parts of the record. They may have done so but, in a sense, unsuccessfully; that is, they may have contrived to create errors that the supreme court later did not recognize. In short, Zabel and Darrow conceivably went to the trouble to fix an appeal that the defense already was destined to win.

In a case corrupted in other ways from its inception, a corrupt prosecutor and his accomplice defense lawyer on appeal may have sought redemption for prosecutors, judge, and defendants alike in, well, what else? Further corruption. And the judicial system, in the richest of ironies, may have found its own redemption only in the supreme court's blindness to the very corruption enveloping it.

Or, perhaps more likely, Zabel and Darrow simply thought about fixing the appeal, even agreed tacitly or explicitly, but never followed through. Both Koenig's and Carchidi's testimony to the grand jury corroborated Groelle's story; the story does not rest on Groelle's word alone. For the plan to fix the record to be wholly fictional, two witnesses would have had to confess falsely to the scheme under oath and an uninvolved third would have had to corroborate their testimony unwittingly. At the very least, then, there is solid evidence that Zabel and Darrow aspired—more, conspired—to corruption.

To this, add the matter of Darrow's history. The evidence of his possible crimes in Los Angeles during the McNamara trial suggests, although not conclusively (especially if the first jury's acquittal and the second's deadlock count to an historian), that he was willing to resort to real cheating to win. Indeed, those trials prove the point if one believes him guilty as many do, notwithstanding the jury trial results. By our lights today, there is little or no doubt that Darrow crossed lines that conventionally honest lawyers do not cross.[86]

Zabel's own character also does nothing to disperse the odor wafting from this appeal. And although it is a small point, an agreement to fix the appeal that never came to completion would explain why Zabel was so remarkably restrained in his comments to the *Milwaukee Journal* the day that the Wisconsin Supreme Court issued its decision. His diplomacy was out of character. While he offered a token defense of his trial performance, he sounded resigned to defeat—and not necessarily unhappy about it. Possibly Zabel just thought graciousness the best approach in discussing the state's highest court publicly. But grace and reticence were not his usual tack.

One last bit of evidence suggests that Zabel and Darrow agreed generally to fix the appeal (and talked again after the initial meeting in Chicago that Groelle described), even if they did not accomplish that end—even if they later quailed and backed out or the defense accidentally won on the merits. That last bit of evidence strongly implicates Judge Backus as well. It supplements Groelle's claim that Backus was in on the plan.

That evidence is the March 3, 1921, letter that Zabel and Backus wrote to Governor Blaine and the circumstances surrounding it. The timing of both the Zabel and Backus letter, mailed just two days after Darrow mailed out the pardon petition, and Darrow's later letter to Governor Blaine demonstrate that Darrow and Zabel had talked earlier and agreed that Zabel and Backus would support executive clemency. Zabel surely did not compose his carefully considered and politically dexterous six-page letter overnight, after receiving Darrow's petition. For his part, Backus must have read the letter or at least considered its possible ramifications on his own career before signing it. Darrow's reference to assurances from both Zabel and Backus that they would write to the governor confirms the existence of an agreement before Zabel and Backus ever sent their joint letter to Governor Blaine.

The content of the Zabel–Backus letter also seems nearly inexplicable without the fix being in, at least among Darrow, Zabel, and Backus. The convictions of the eleven Italians had been the capstone of Zabel's career, garnering him more publicity than even his prosecution of former president Theodore Roosevelt's attempted assassin. The Italian case also had given Backus his longest turn in the spotlight. Barely three years before their letter to Governor Blaine, both Backus and Zabel had insisted that only the harshest punishment would answer the magnitude of the crime. Here were the two prisoners at the very core of the case, Amedeo Lilli and Vincenzo Fratesi, the worst of the eleven. Those two men had lost their appeal entirely. Their twenty-five-year sentences were intact, their day in court over, the state finally triumphant. And now the prosecutor and the judge were muttering awkwardly that they should enjoy clemency? With nary a concession that the convictions were mistaken, that the wrong men were in prison? Almost incomprehensible.

Incomprehensible, that is, unless Zabel and Backus were keeping their end of a secret deal that they thought would spare their lives.

For his part, in just a few years Clarence Darrow would go from the Milwaukee appeal and commutations to some of his most celebrated cases. He died at home in Chicago on March 13, 1938, just shy of his eighty-first birthday. By then, the bribery trials in Los Angeles a quarter century earlier were an asterisk, nothing more. The great defense lawyer never went to jail himself. In a sympathetic obituary, the *New York Times* reported—accurately—that in the hundred or more murder cases he defended, no client of Darrow's ever died on the gallows or in the electric chair. Darrow lived and practiced in a time when the death penalty was common for murderers. If that one achievement were all that he had left, and it decidedly was not, it would inspire lawyers today. "Clarence Seward Darrow spent his life fighting for 'lost' causes," the *Times* eulogist mused, "most of which he won."[87]

Finally, for their part, Zabel and Backus did escape with their lives. After the two bombs at Zabel's house in the spring of 1918, there never was another incident. From the radical supporters of the eleven Italians, there was only silence.

What of the person or persons who actually placed the bomb along the side wall of Giuliani's church? Ten people, including nine police officers, died because of their crime. Many dozens more could have died during Sunday services the next morning had the charwoman's daughter not happened upon the deadly package. Yet in 1918 the investigation into the planting of that bomb—that "infernal machine"—soon stalled. The Milwaukee Police Department, the district attorney, and for that matter the federal government never named a culprit or charged anyone. Zabel in particular was done with it all.

Decades later, Paul Avrich named the famed East Coast anarchists Carlo Valdinoci and Mario Buda as leading suspects.[88] But during their lifetimes, Buda and Valdinoci never faced even the accusation, let alone a Milwaukee jury or the prospect of earthly justice, however flawed. Sometime in the nearly one hundred years since the explosion at the central police station, the violent bomber and his accomplices, whoever they were, went to their graves. They went with an intact secret.

Zabel, Backus, and Darrow all did the same. Whatever the special prosecutors and grand jurors thought of Groelle's and Carchidi's testimony, in the end they charged no crime in connection with the Italians' appeal. Unsurprisingly, because Zabel was a principal target of the grand jury investigation, he never received a subpoena to testify. The district attorney never faced a single question under oath (or otherwise, so far as the historical record shows) about Groelle's allegations. After a year, the grand jury disbanded quietly.

That grand jury left one last mystery, though. Unlike Zabel, Judge Backus did testify in the grand jury. When Backus finally appeared under oath before the grand jury in its waning days, he encountered not one question about the Italians' trial or their appeal. After all the testimony from Groelle, Carchidi, and other minor corroborating witnesses, the two silk-stockinged corporate lawyers serving as special prosecutors held their tongues. Every grand juror did too. Prosecutors and grand jurors alike sat mute rather than ask Backus for the truth. Unlike some of the defendants, unlike Zabel, and unlike Backus, they did not howl. They fell silent. Even more than wrathful noise, the awkward silence as the will to seek justice or the truth failed them—well, it suggested something worse than the devil.

The November 24, 1917, bomb blew apart human beings and brought down part of a brick building. But neither the bomb nor the machinery of criminal justice could blow open secrets or blow out the corruption of weak, ambitious, or frightened people. Infernal machines, both.

Appendix

I did not write this book only, or even primarily, for academics or lawyers. Still, some background on the United States criminal justice system over the past one hundred years or so is important for anyone who wants to delve into the deeper story fully and to understand the parable.

Two areas of legal history and doctrine are especially important. The first is a most durable hand-me-down from English common law to American law: conspiracy. That doctrine of criminal liability played a major, if not always coherent, role in the trial of the eleven Milwaukee Italians and their appeal. It explained in part why both jury and judge found it so easy to overlook the individuality of each person accused and to consider them only en masse.

The second is police interrogation techniques that were in 1917—and much less frequently are today—known as "the third degree." Those techniques were not the only police excesses that this story includes. Long detention without charges, warrantless and nearly random searches, arrests on the flimsiest of suspicions rather than on anything like probable cause—all of these happened too. But those repressive searches and seizures, which will seem so jarring today to many readers, in part had a pretty simple explanation: the U.S. Supreme Court did not hold the states (as opposed to the federal government) to the limitations of the Fourth Amendment until 1949 and, as a matter of Fourth Amendment doctrine, did not require states to exclude most unlawfully gained evidence from trial until 1961.[1]

Conspiracy

American law students encounter in their first-year criminal law course a standard explanation that American law, drawing on English law before it, permits the state to punish not just completed crimes but offenses that are merely budding: crimes in the offing, or "inchoate" offenses. Mainly, there are three such incomplete crimes. They are solicitation to commit an offense, attempt to commit

one, and conspiracy to commit one. The first two are relatively concrete. A solicitation concerns a wrongdoer's effort to coax another, who may be in the know and
thus culpable himself or unknowing and thus innocent, to commit some crime
that the first wishes to see done. A simple example is a jealous husband who offers
a thug $5,000 to kill his wife's lover. The husband is guilty of solicitation to commit
murder.

An attempt is even more straightforward. Someone who wishes to commit a
crime is guilty of an attempt if he takes a substantial step toward completing the
crime, under circumstances that bespeak intent to finish it. The devil is in the
details—what steps are "substantial" and not just preparatory or tentative?—but
the concept is plain enough.

Then there is the third, conspiracy. It is an agreement among two or more to
commit a specific crime or crimes. That sounds magnificently broad and malleable,
and, in many ways today, it is. But the common law history of that offense is both
indistinct, as an idea rooted centuries before the printing press may be, and limited
originally in ways that would surprise many American lawyers.

By the term "common law," today we usually mean a gauzy concept: the law
that English judges developed incrementally over the centuries after the Norman
Conquest in 1066. That is only the most general accepted definition of common
law, though, and it misleads in its generality. For purposes here, the focus on judicial
development of the law masks the fact that some early English law was statutory,
as soon as thirteenth-century Plantagenet kings founded and nurtured Parliament.
Statutes were few and far between, though, and they often addressed broad issues,
like the relationships between English institutions (for example, the proper realms
of the ecclesiastical courts and the civil courts), in a general way. English judges
had much to do in filling gaps.

Even so, conspiracy was born of statute, not purely of judicial invention. And
a modest birth it was. Near the end of the thirteenth century, in the reign of
Edward I, Parliament enacted a statute that established local punishment for
persons who combined together to cause a false indictment and conviction or
otherwise combined to abuse the legal process.[2] There may have been a nascent
concept of conspiracy even before that first statute. Glanvill, the twelfth-century
judicial official who is the earliest reputed writer on the customs that became
consolidated as English law beginning with William the Conqueror (again, the
Normans after the Battle of Hastings), says nothing of any notion recognizable
as conspiracy. But the next great writer who followed, Bracton (first half of the
thirteenth century, roughly 1210–68), does refer to some loose antecedents for
punishing group crimes.[3]

Although a second significant statute came along under Edward III, who reigned for half of the fourteenth century, still the concept of conspiracy reached no further than abuse of the legal process. For centuries, moreover, conspirators faced no liability themselves unless their machinations led to both the indictment and the acquittal of a person wrongly accused.

When exactly judges began to loosen those requirements and to expand the law's reach to plotters whose false accusations did not succeed is unclear. But the case most often credited with the first significant expansion of conspiracy liability from a completed crime to an inchoate one came from a tribunal notorious for its aggressive procedure on other fronts as well, the Star Chamber. The decision was the *Poulterers' Case* of 1611. It arose when a group of poultry dealers agreed to accuse a competitor falsely of robbery. However, the man was so obviously innocent that the grand jury declined to indict him. He later sued his false accusers, and they answered the writ of conspiracy by noting the rule that the absence of an indictment and acquittal defeated a claim of conspiracy. The Court of Star Chamber squarely rejected that argument and held that the gist of the offense simply was confederating for the wrongful purpose.[4] The wrongful purpose now need not have come to pass.

That case led gradually to England's common law abandonment of any requirement that a conspirator engage in a concrete act toward completion of the crime. Again, on the logic of the *Poulterers' Case*, the essence of the crime was the unlawful agreement itself.[5] By 1716 an important English legal treatise writer, Sir William Hawkins, acknowledged this as the rule, although he distinguished a formal action based on a writ of conspiracy from an action "in the nature of such a writ."[6]

While the concept of a conspiracy expanded gradually in England, eventually also reaching beyond abuse of process, it appears not to have become wildly popular among the Crown's prosecutors.[7] Even by the second half of the eighteenth century, the famed writer Sir William Blackstone had little to say about conspiracy. True, American lawyers and judges celebrate too much Blackstone's compendium of English law simply because it happened to be the most contemporary assessment of that field as the American colonies declared and later gained their independence. He was the current best seller. Still, Blackstone, writing between 1765 and 1769, produced a more readable, detailed, and organized survey of the main tenets of English law than had Sir Edward Coke or Sir Matthew Hale, writing in close succession more than a century earlier. Yet Blackstone devoted just one short paragraph to conspiracy, in a four-volume treatise.[8] It was not a frequently used prosecutorial tool.

All the same, the breadth that the *Poulterers' Case* portended in the early 1600s allowed continued expansion over time. That expansion has gone mostly unchecked in this country, which seems always to have relished a good conspiracy theory.

Come the late nineteenth and early twentieth centuries in America, the concept of conspiracy expanded so widely that it outgrew its definition as an incomplete crime. Lawyers and judges came to see distinct dangers in conspiracy itself: principally that the group enterprise enhances the odds that the intended crime will succeed and spawns the risk of ancillary crimes. American law grew to see those risks as elevating the gravity of that crime beyond the mere incompletion of something more concrete. Conspiracy became a familiar charge, alone or in tandem with the completed offense.

By 1925 a well-known and careful American judge, Learned Hand, rightly could call conspiracy "the darling of the modern prosecutor's nursery."[9] Not two decades later, federal conspiracy charges had grown so common and ambitious that the U.S. Supreme Court intervened, deciding a string of conspiracy cases that imposed both some modest limits and some structure on American conspiracy law. That was almost thirty years after the Milwaukee Italians' case, but the modern generalities of conspiracy law already were clear in 1917.

The gist of the offense was and is an agreement among two or more to commit a specific other crime or crimes. Notwithstanding that intangibility—traceable at least back to the *Poulterers' Case*—statutes written in more recent times often (not always) also require proof that one conspirator did some act in furtherance of the conspiracy's objective. But that act is not so much necessary to proving the crime of conspiracy as it is essential to locating the proper place and time to prosecute the crime and to determining who might be liable for the crime. First, the act establishes a proper locale, or venue, for filing the criminal charge. Second, in the nineteenth and early twentieth centuries, the concrete act was necessary to corroborate the existence of the agreement, which of course usually left no obvious trace.[10] Third, the concrete act, a step toward completing the crime that was the object of the conspiracy, also marked the point after which conspirators could not withdraw (or at least not easily).[11] Again, before our age of proliferating statutes, the crime itself remained just an agreement. In all events, neither English law nor American law after it ever has required that an act in furtherance of a conspiracy be illegal in and of itself. That act may be entirely innocent, considered alone.[12]

For its part, the agreement that is the essence of conspiracy can be wholly unspoken and entirely informal, so long as a jury later reasonably can infer that two or more people in fact reached an agreement on what crime or crimes to commit. Moreover, people who merely agree that the intended crime should occur but who take no active role themselves in promoting it are as guilty as those who actively pursue the finished crime.[13] Once in, withdrawal from a conspiracy is hard to accomplish, even for the small fry. A withdrawing conspirator has to get out before any other conspirator takes a substantial, concrete step toward completing the intended crime and in withdrawing has to do more than just walk away or bail out: he has to take some affirmative step either to defeat the ends of the conspiracy or to notify authorities that the criminal agreement is afoot. Plus, at trial, the American rule became by 1912 that the defendant has the burden of satisfying the jury that he withdrew; the prosecution does not have to prove that he remained a conspirator at relevant times after he initially agreed.[14] Of course, notifying authorities likely would result in his own arrest, at least until the police sorted it all out, so once in a criminal conspiracy, even the most tangential player likely remains in it.

Getting out of a conspiracy once in it is not the biggest problem that peripheral players have faced, though. American law applies a sort of "in for a penny, in for a pound" rule to conspiracy. That is, every conspirator is criminally liable not just for the illegal agreement itself and not even just for the additional completed crime if the conspiracy succeeds (for then the prosecution may charge and punish both the conspiracy and the completed offense). Every conspirator also is on the hook for each and every foreseeable *other* crime that any fellow conspirator might commit in pursuit of the conspiracy's core objective.[15] An example: if three people agree to rob a bank—and that's all, so far as their agreement goes—but then one of them shoots a teller who screams and a second rams a car and injures someone while the group is trying to flee, the hapless third conspirator who did neither of those things faces conviction for the conspiracy to rob the bank, the bank robbery itself, and then the murder of the teller and the reckless injury of the innocent person injured in the getaway fiasco. The third man cannot complain about the first two charges, because he did agree to rob the bank. But he did not really bargain for the murder and the injury charges; the law of conspiracy simply imputes those to him on the theory that he took the risks of group criminal activity, in which each participant becomes the agent of the others.

Today, at least the prosecution generally must charge conspiracy expressly if it wishes to prove conspiracy, as a theory of criminal liability.[16] In 1917 and for centuries earlier, the charge itself did not even have to put the defendant on notice that the state would argue conspiracy.

Indeed, the Milwaukee County district attorney did not charge conspiracy expressly against any of the eleven Italians whose trial is the heart of this book. But the Milwaukee prosecutor did select a conspiracy theory, which he announced the morning that the trial began. Each defendant learned only as jury selection began that he or she faced conviction not just for his or her own actions but for the actions of all ten other defendants, provided the prosecutor could convince the jurors that all acted in concert—that is, by agreement to commit at least the crime alleged in the charging document. Even if only one of the eleven committed assault with intent to murder, in other words, all eleven might be found guilty, if the jury but divined some agreement that they joined to work toward an assaultive outcome.

In these ways, the gossamer strands of conspiracy law made (and make now) an intricate and sticky web in which a skilled prosecutor may ensnare hangers-on whose actual roles in a crime are very minor, if not altogether imaginary. Truly innocent bystanders—the ones merely present or the ones who merely know what is under consideration, but who have not actually agreed to it—are supposed to be spared.[17] In the real world, though, these people on the far edges face considerable risk of being judged not just by the company they keep but by the company of anyone in their vicinity at exactly the wrong time.

With that quality of conspiracy prosecutions in mind, I included in chapter 5 a sketch of the 1918 federal prosecution of 166 IWW members in Chicago. This was a conspiracy trial to top all conspiracy trials and presented every risk of such trials in grotesque proportion. It included dozens upon dozens of minor players, many probably guilty of no more than radical thought. In fact, one striking surface irony of that case is that contemporaneous newspaper accounts sometimes described 166 defendants, other times 168 defendants. Who could keep track with so many? Yet for all it reveals about the dangers of huge trials and vast conspiracy allegations, the IWW trial mostly has escaped scholarly attention. That is surprising.

The IWW trial well may have been the first proceeding in American criminal justice that fairly could be labeled a "mass trial." It still stands as one of the largest, if not the largest, groups of criminal defendants an American court ever has attempted to try at one time. If only because of the sheer number of defendants, that trial strained beyond the breaking point the human and logistical capacities of the judicial system: the ability of jurors to keep evidence straight as to different defendants; the ability of lawyers to marshal and present evidence without omitting some of the people on trial; the ability of deputies to house and transport prisoners; the capacity of a courtroom to seat 166 defendants (and their lawyers, although the defendants actually tried dwindled) and still remain open to the public; and the ability of a judge to stay atop of evidentiary questions and rulings or simply to monitor the courtroom. The presiding judge himself was a personality of considerable interest. He was none other than Kenesaw Mountain Landis, who had something of a national reputation even before he left the federal bench in 1921 to continue as the first commissioner of major league baseball.

That 1918 Chicago IWW trial reflected the same hysteria about radicals and immigrants (groups that were seen as heavily overlapping, although not congruent) that had fueled the Milwaukee trial a few months earlier. The arrests for the Chicago trial shortly preceded the Italians' trial in Milwaukee, as the federal government sought to smother by force most war dissent in the summer and autumn of 1917. With the IWW arrests fresh in jurors' minds, the prosecutors in Milwaukee would impugn several of the eleven defendants by eliciting evidence or simply by insinuating that they were IWW members or "Wobblies."

Although only sketched here, the Chicago IWW trial is an important part of the backdrop for the Milwaukee case. In addition to the fear and suspicion that the mass arrests and trials of radicals fed, the Chicago IWW trial bears on the Milwaukee case more specifically. It reinforces the truth that the judicial debacle in Milwaukee was not isolated; rather, it was consistent with the prevailing judicial response to groups of radicals at the time. The literature of this era is much richer in discussion of executive responses to mass labor agitation and political violence—the use of army troops, sheriff's posses, Pinkertons, strikebreakers, or all of these to confront strikers and radical crowds—than in discussion of judicial responses. In the main, the slim literature on judicial reactions concerns Emma Goldman, Eugene Debs, Bill Haywood, and other major radical figures individually. The mass trial has received almost no attention.

Milwaukee's was a much smaller group than the Chicago federal trial, of course. But even a trial of eleven defendants (to say nothing of a trial of one hundred more than that) stretches to the breaking point or beyond the human capacities of jurors, a judge, witnesses, and lawyers simply to keep it all straight. To be blunt, individual defendants get lost in the mix. Oversight and confusion seem especially poor justifications for deprivation of liberty, yet those are about what mass trials inevitably offer. The forgotten defendant lumped into a guilty verdict with others does not do less time because of his innocence, let alone his anonymity.

Third Degree

In part, understanding either that IWW mass trial in Chicago or this story in Wisconsin depends upon grasping the complementary roles of four institutions in denying the humanity of the eleven people prosecuted here: the police, the prosecutor's office, the court itself, and the commercial newspapers. The lessons for today in this story stem largely from the ways in which these institutions and their agents may strip humanity from victims, witnesses, and defendants alike in the administration of criminal justice. In much earlier times, the techniques for doing that were outright torture: pincers, hot irons on the soles of feet, the rack, what have you. Over time, the methods became less crude and deadly but not less effective. The impulse to wrest confessions, to subjugate the wrongdoer completely, has remained unchanged. In the early decades of the twentieth century, the primary tools of the police in reducing the human dignity of suspects—and producing the desired confessions—were warrantless (which in practice meant nearly random) searches and arrests and then isolating detention punctuated by coercion. That coercion was "the third degree." And it was an open secret. Indeed, the police sometimes bragged about it.

They did in Milwaukee. In late autumn of 1917, Milwaukee's newspapers wrote frequently and admiringly of the police practice of applying "the third degree" to Italians in both the stationhouse and the jail. The term comes from Freemasonry and dates to the eighteenth century. A third-degree or Master Mason passed a rigorous oral examination to attain that status. Success set him apart in the lodges of that secret society from Apprentice (first-degree) and Fellow Craft (second-degree) Masons. Attaining the third degree was the basic goal of the Freemason.

By the later decades of the nineteenth century, the term had come to apply as well to rough police interrogation methods. It denoted then no specific method or methods; that remains true today. Rather, the term has applied to an elusive and changing list of stratagems and techniques designed to produce a confession by physical or psychological coercion and pressure. Generally, though, it entails prolonged interrogation, without formal charge, apart from friends and counsel in a stationhouse or jail, and often the accompanying threat or fact of physical attack. Courts long accepted the third degree in the sense that they simply ignored it and made use of its products.

Americans had spoken of the third degree in the context of police interrogation for decades before 1936, when the U.S. Supreme Court first considered the constitutional implications of relying in court on statements produced by isolation, threats, beatings, or worse. Understanding the reasons for the Supreme Court's long silence requires some background. The original thirteen states ratified the U.S. Constitution in 1789. That same year, the first Congress proposed ten amendments, a Bill of Rights. Those took effect in 1791, after eleven of the original states ratified them. Since then, the Fifth Amendment has promised that no person will be "compelled in any criminal case to be a witness against himself."[18] But the Fifth Amendment binds only the federal government, not the governments of the states.

Even as to the federal government, after the Bill of Rights another dozen years passed before the U.S. Supreme Court clearly asserted the judicial branch's power and right to tell the executive and legislative branches definitively what the Constitution requires or forbids them to do.[19] And at that, for a full century the Court said little if anything about a critical question of the Fifth Amendment's scope: does being a "witness" against oneself mean only giving testimony in a courtroom, in the formal sense, or does it embrace a defendant's statements to law enforcement officers who then might freely repeat those statements in court under a time-honored exception to the rule against hearsay? Not until 1892 did the Court even make clear that grand jury witnesses enjoy the Fifth Amendment's privilege against self-incrimination.[20] Police interrogations are at least one further step removed from a criminal trial than that investigative body, the grand jury, which calls witnesses by subpoena and operates in part under auspices of a court.

Well into the twentieth century, then, Americans had to guess what limits, if any, the Fifth Amendment imposed on interrogation by federal officers beyond the vague rule that only "voluntary" confessions win admission in court. Again, the Fifth Amendment placed not even that hazy limit on employees of states or their municipalities (which almost all police officers were) because the Fifth Amendment, like most of the federal Constitution, did not apply to them.

By the late nineteenth century, though, when the Supreme Court first began to consider confessions under compulsion, the Fifth Amendment was not the only constitutional provision bearing on the question. As the federal government re-grouped at the end of the Civil War, Congress sought to consolidate not just the union but the gains in perceived authority and legitimacy of the federal government itself. The so-called Civil War amendments, numbers thirteen through fifteen, were the first to impose direct and specific obligations on the states under the federal Constitution. Congress proposed the first of these amendments in winter 1865, in the waning days of the war. In 1869 it proposed the last. State ratification followed. The Thirteenth Amendment bars slavery; the Fifteenth addresses the right to vote regardless of race or former enslavement.

But easily the lengthiest and widest-ranging of these three amendments to the Constitution is the Fourteenth Amendment. It does not speak of compulsory self-incrimination directly. But it does promise that no state will deprive any person of life, liberty, or property "without due process of law."[21] In that regard, the Fourteenth Amendment echoes and extends to the states the federal government's obligations under the Fifth. Then and since, however, the notion of due process has been a riddle. What process exactly is "due"? To whom? When? And does this promise have substantive content (if so, what?) or just a procedural connotation?

These all are questions that have nettled American judges since the Fifth Amendment and its Due Process Clause took effect. In 1791 the phrase probably had the same import as Magna Carta's "law of the land,"[22] but that hardly clarified matters. At best, only sketchy answers had emerged by 1868, when a sufficient number of states ratified the Fourteenth Amendment.

Whatever the answers, the conscious parallel to the Fifth Amendment's Due Process Clause invited the argument that perhaps the Fourteenth Amendment sweeps within the same phrase some or all of the more explicit guarantees of the earlier amendment and the Bill of Rights of which it is a part. Maybe due process of law encompasses the right to a grand jury's consideration of a felony charge, or the privilege against compulsory self-incrimination, or protection from double jeopardy; the Fifth Amendment grants all of these in the clauses preceding its assurance of due process. Congress by the 1860s may have meant "due process" as shorthand for all of it—and maybe for all of the Bill of Rights, or even all of the common law's traditional protections and comforts of Englishmen. At least, so lawyers plausibly could, and still can, contend.

Sometimes the justices of the Supreme Court have agreed on the scope of the Fourteenth Amendment's Due Process Clause, sometimes not. For example, the Court decided relatively early that due process does not require states to charge felonies only by grand jury, as the federal government must.[23] The Court has stuck to that view. A state prosecutor alone may issue a felony charge, subject to later judicial assessment.

But the coercive, sometimes brutal methods of sheriffs or policemen eventually would call the Court to consider whether due process forbids wresting confessions by torment or outright torture. In 1936 the Supreme Court looked straight at the third degree—although not by name—for the first time. In that first case, it was black men, not Italians, who had faced the third degree.

The Court's discussion of the ordeal of three men in Kemper County, Mississippi, almost two decades after the bombing in Milwaukee, offered a front-row view of the barbaric methods that found a place in some American sheriffs' offices and police stations. The case was *Brown v. Mississippi*. Kemper County was and is rural, in Mississippi's pine belt. Cotton was its crop. Blacks outnumbered whites, as they still do. Poverty was pervasive. In the 1930s the county acquired the nickname "Bloody Kemper," because its rate of lynchings doubled the rest of Mississippi's.[24]

Following the murder of a white farmer in 1934, suspicion quickly fell on three black sharecroppers. Led by a deputy sheriff, a white mob soon descended on the shabby home of one of the three men. With the deputy's help, the crowd looped a rope around the man's neck and slung the end over a tree limb. They hoisted him into the air, strangling, then let him down to demand his confession, over and over again. He did not confess. That was only the beginning, though. Deputies soon arrested and whipped him repeatedly. Eventually he confessed and implicated the two others.

If anything, those two men fared worse in the sheriff's office. Deputies forced them to strip naked and bend over chairs. At that point, "their backs were cut to pieces with a leather strap with buckles on it." A deputy gave them "definitely to understand that the whipping would be continued unless and until they confessed, and not only confessed, but confessed in every matter of detail as demanded by those present." The men confessed, and the whipping did continue as necessary to make them "change . . . or adjust . . . their confession in all particulars of detail so as to conform to the demands of their torturers."[25]

With the dirty work done, the Kemper County sheriff, a neighboring sheriff, and a Methodist minister (the brother of one of the sheriffs) then came ceremonially to the jail to hear the confessions.[26] The night before, after the whipping stopped, the deputies had warned that the abuse would resume if any of the three men strayed from his rehearsed story. The three black men did not stray. In a "solemn farce," they repeated the stories obediently for the two sheriffs and the minister, all of whom soon would testify in court to the free and voluntary confessions.

Trial began just three days later. The district attorney was an ambitious young man named John C. Stennis, then not yet thirty-three years old but later a U.S. senator for almost forty-two years, from 1947 to 1989.[27] Throughout the short trial, the mark of the rope on the first man's neck remained obvious to all in the courtroom.[28] No evidence supported a conviction other than the confessions—to the voluntary quality of which the two sheriffs and the minister indeed testified piously. By the end of the second day of trial, after thirty minutes of deliberations, the jury convicted the three accused. The judge immediately sentenced them to hang.[29] Exactly one week had passed since neighbors had discovered the white farmer dying in his house next to a cottonseed pile.

When the case made its way to the U.S. Supreme Court from the Mississippi courts, Chief Justice Charles Evans Hughes wrote for a unanimous Court. The Court did not hold that the Fourteenth Amendment's Due Process Clause incorporated the privilege against self-incrimination. It acknowledged two earlier decisions that held otherwise. But those concerned only compulsory appearance as a witness at one's own trial. "Compulsion by torture to extort a confession is a different matter," Chief Justice Hughes declared.[30]

The torture that the Court confronted in *Brown* offended principles of justice "so rooted in the traditions and conscience of our people as to be ranked as fundamental."[31] Use of that evidence was so far contrary to the American sense of justice that it denied due process. It rendered the trial a "mere pretense,"[32] as if the state had replaced trial by jury with trial by ordeal or the witness stand with the rack.[33] For the first time the U.S. Supreme Court held that a state cannot rely upon coerced confessions in court. Simple due process, not the guaranty against compelled self-incrimination, was the reason.

Four years later, in 1940, the Supreme Court turned again to third-degree interrogation methods, this time in a case tried in Florida.[34] Someone robbed and killed an elderly white man on a Saturday evening in Pompano, Florida.[35] Suspicion evidently fell on the entire black population, for the police within a day arrested between twenty-five and forty black men without warrant or charge. What followed before the state charged four of them was an ugly sojourn through backwoods and sheriff's offices for days, different in its details but almost as harrowing as the experience of the Mississippi men in *Brown*.

Noting the conflicting testimony on whether police officers had physically abused the men, the Supreme Court assumed that officers had not. Still, "the haunting fear of mob violence was around them in an atmosphere charged with excitement and public indignation"; that rendered the confessions involuntary. Justice Hugo L. Black, who wrote for the Supreme Court to reverse the convictions and spare the men's lives, himself had been an active Ku Klux Klansman for a time before he left Birmingham, Alabama.[36]

The Court also took that occasion to comment expressly on the third degree. "The police practices here examined are to some degree widespread throughout our country," it observed, citing an American Bar Association report and other sources. "It has even been suggested that the use of the 'third degree' has lowered the esteem in which administration of justice is held by the public and has engendered an attitude of hostility to and unwillingness to cooperate with the police on the part of many people."[37] Those who always have suffered most from third-degree methods, Justice Black finished, have been "the poor, the ignorant, the numerically weak, the friendless, and the powerless."[38]

By then the Supreme Court was a decade behind the growing public disquiet over brutal police methods. President Hoover's National Commission on Law Observance and Enforcement, called the Wickersham Commission after its chair, former attorney general George W. Wickersham, had issued a rump report in 1931. The report documented "widespread" physical and psychological coercion in seeking confessions in at least fifteen major cities.[39] The Wickersham Commission issued thirteen other reports in 1931, and police misconduct was at best a lesser interest of the commission. Still, more than any other single alert, the Wickersham Commission report awakened the public to police violence and lawlessness.

The report was right. Rough, degrading, and coercive police methods were widespread. There can be no northern conceit that cases of third-degree methods arose only in the South, for example. Among many northern cases, a 1952 Illinois decision on third-degree interrogation reports a broken rib during a police beating, and a 1922 Wisconsin case details a suspect's deep bruises on his arms, back, and buttocks after a night of beating with police parade clubs.[40] In its landmark *Miranda* decision, in 1966, the Supreme Court listed other recent, geographically scattered examples of brutal third-degree tactics.[41]

But *Miranda* came almost fifty years after the events in Milwaukee in the autumn of 1917. No one was much concerned about police coercion at the time, least of all against a group of Italian malcontents. Indeed, the establishment newspapers of the day fairly crowed over police boasts of third-degree tactics.

Notes

Preface

1. An important recent book, Timothy Messer-Kruse's *The Trial of the Haymarket Anarchists: Terrorism and Justice in the Gilded Age* (New York: Palgrave MacMillan, 2011), makes that argument powerfully. Messer-Kruse did what earlier historians apparently did not: he read the actual trial transcript of the prosecution of the eight Haymarket defendants. Possibly he overestimates the likelihood that a better defense case actually would have mattered in the day and setting of that trial; it may be mistaken to think so. But he musters a solid showing that the proceedings at least were not the sham or travesty that many long have believed they were. And, whether rightly or wrongly, the eight defendants there were tried and convicted for the acts charged. The eleven Italian immigrants tried in Milwaukee in 1917, whose story this book tells, instead may have been convicted not so much for the acts charged but for later events that happened while they already were jailed awaiting trial and in which they could have had no active role.

2. Physical abuse in police stations by no means has disappeared entirely, though. For a prolonged, grotesque, and persistent example, see *Wilson v. City of Chicago*, 6 F.3d 1233 (7th Cir. 1993), and other accounts of the behavior of a former Chicago police lieutenant, Jon Burge, and others in his precinct. Today rogue police officers also may face a civil lawsuit or departmental discipline. Note specifically, too, that American interrogations on foreign soil of suspected terrorists or combatants often do not fit the domestic criminal justice paradigm, as the country has seen since 2001.

3. There are three straightforward reasons in many places for the close relationship between the judiciary and police agencies. First, many judges continue to come to the bench from prosecutors' offices, where they worked closely as allies with the police for years. Second, many American state court judges have to run for re-election or retention, and law enforcement officers (like lawyers) often are a critical voting bloc in those elections, which not infrequently have low turnout. And third, judges see police officers regularly: officers apply for warrants, testify in court frequently, and provide security in courtrooms and courthouses. Familiarity and dependence may foster a natural affinity (or, occasionally, contempt).

4. See, e.g., Richard A. Leo and Richard J. Ofshe, "The Consequences of False Confessions: Deprivations of Liberty and Miscarriages of Justice in the Age of Psychological Interrogation," *Journal of Criminal Law and Criminology* 88 (1997): 429; Steven A. Drizin and Richard A. Leo, "The Problem of False Confessions in the Post-DNA World," *North Carolina Law Review* 82 (2004): 891.

5. See, e.g., Jordan Abshire and Brian H. Bornstein, "Juror Sensitivity to the Cross-Race Effect," *Law and Human Behavior* 27 (October 2003): 471; Christian A. Meissner and John C. Brigham, "Thirty Years of Investigating the Own-Race Bias in Memory for Faces: A Meta-Analytic Review," *Psychology, Public Policy and Law* 7 (2001): 3; John P. Rutledge, "They All Look Alike: The Inaccuracy of Cross-Racial Identifications," *American Journal of Criminal Law* 27 (2001): 207; Elizabeth F. Loftus, *Eyewitness Testimony* (Cambridge, MA: Harvard University Press, 1996).

6. At present, thirty-four states retain the death penalty, to be exact. China, North Korea, Yemen, the United States, and Saudi Arabia now are the most common users of capital punishment. The rank order varies from year to year.

Chapter 1. What the Scrubwoman Found

1. "Nine Officers and 2 Others Are Victims," *Milwaukee Sentinel*, November 25, 1917, 1; see also G. L. McDonough, "Dynamite Death! Milwaukee's Appalling Police Massacre," *True Detective Mysteries* 18, no. 6 (September 1932): 104. Many details of the blast are included in the purported first-person account of G. L. McDonough, published some years later in *True Detective Mysteries* magazine. This account presents a problem. On the one hand, it stands as the only lengthy article by a contemporary observer that ties events in Bay View in August and September 1917 to the November 24, 1917, bomb blast—and in part it purports to recite personal observations. On the other hand, the magazine was pulpy and the article deliberately lurid, to say nothing of remarkably inaccurate in places. McDonough had been a police reporter with the *Milwaukee Free Press* newspaper. He claimed to have arrived at the central police station minutes after the bomb exploded. Whether that was true or not, his account of what occurred after the blast has a greater ring of accuracy than his description of the events that preceded it. Some of his details of the Bay View rallies and confrontations in late August and early September 1917 are flatly wrong, a few wildly so. In the end, I credit cautiously some of McDonough's version of what transpired after the bomb exploded but mostly discredit his secondhand version of events before, unless independently corroborated. McDonough agrees generally with the details in this paragraph. McDonough, "Dynamite Death!," 106. Incidentally, McDonough put the time that Kaiser's watch stopped at 7:33 p.m. McDonough, "Dynamite Death!," 106.

2. The *Milwaukee Leader* insisted that every window in the building broke. "Authorities Believe List of Dead in Crash Will Be Placed at 10," *Milwaukee Leader*, November 26, 1917, 1. The *Milwaukee Journal*, though, described the blast as breaking only the windows on the Oneida Street side of the building.

3. "Italians Find Bomb, Taking It to Station," *Milwaukee Sentinel*, November 25, 1917, 1.

4. "Nine Officers and 2 Others Are Victims," *Milwaukee Sentinel*, November 25, 1917, 1; "Italians Find Bomb, Taking It to Station," 1.

5. "Nine Officers and 2 Others Are Victims," 1; see also McDonough, "Dynamite Death!," 104–6.

6. The details of these two paragraphs come from "Thousands of Curious See Blast Scene," *Milwaukee Leader*, November 26, 1917, 1.

7. Milwaukee Police Department website, memorial page, www.ci.mil.wi.us/display.

8. "Nine Officers and 2 Others Are Victims," 1.

9. "Nine Officers and 2 Others Are Victims," 1. The condition of the bodies initially caused rescuers to believe that eleven had died. In fact, ten did. A photograph of O'Brien appeared with an article headlined "Officers Killed in Police Station Blast," *Milwaukee Sentinel*, November 25, 1917, 2.

10. "Gun Fight Occurs in Bay View," *Milwaukee Sentinel*, September 10, 1917, 1. More plausibly, perhaps, the same newspaper commented after Templin's death that he had reported for duty again a week after being shot. "25 Men Arrested in Big Roundup," *Milwaukee Sentinel*, November 25, 1917, 1.

11. "Nine Officers and 2 Others Are Victims," 1.

12. Ibid.

13. "Death Chamber Scene of Horror," *Milwaukee Sentinel*, November 25, 1917, 2.

14. *Milwaukee Leader*, November 24, 1917, masthead.

15. *Milwaukee Leader*, November 26, 1917, 5.

16. Victor Greene, "Dealing with Diversity: Milwaukee's Multiethnic Festivals and Urban Identity, 1840–1940," *Journal of Urban History* 31, no. 6 (September 2005): 820, 826, and n. 21.

17. In 1920, 36.1 percent of foreign-born white residents of Milwaukee were German, 21 percent were Polish, 5.4 percent Austrian, 4.4 percent Hungarian, and 3.7 percent Italian. 1920 U.S. Census, Table 6. Percentages of residents with foreign-born parents were similar.

18. See, e.g., "Old Settlers' Club Honors Judge James G. Jenkins," *Milwaukee Free Press*, September 30, 1917, 10 (recounting Judge Jenkins's reminiscences, which included the Third Ward fire that "drove the Irish out of the Third Ward and refilled it with Italians").

19. "Gun Fight Occurs in Bay View," 2.

20. "First Community Church," *The View* (June 1969) (a monthly bulletin of the Summerfield United Methodist Church in Milwaukee, with which Giuliani's Italian Evangelical Mission Church eventually merged), in *Protestant Evangelical Mission to the Italians*, an unpublished manuscript collection, MSS 1103 (one folder), Milwaukee County Historical Society Research Library.

21. Ibid.

22. The ship manifest is available at www.ellisislandrecords.org/search/shipManifest.

23. Biographical information on August Giuliani comes from *Protestant Evangelical Mission to the Italians*, MSS 1103, and from his petition for naturalization, petition no. 5597, vol. 27, p. 97 (1916), Milwaukee County Historical Society Research Library. Giuliani himself said that he landed in the United States on January 7, 1911. *State v. Bianchi*, no. A1338, Record at 189 (Milwaukee Municipal Court 1917) (subsequent citations are to Trial Abstract). The ship manifest is available at www.ellisislandrecords.org/search/shipManifest.

24. Although an occasional newspaper article of the day described Giuliani as a Lutheran, the Methodists rightly claim him. In 1969 his church merged with the Summerfield United Methodist Church in Milwaukee. Giuliani testified that he was a Methodist minister at the trial of the eleven defendants charged in the September 9, 1917, Bay View riot. Usually, accounts of the day refer to him generally as an evangelical Protestant. Trial Abstract 189.

25. Trial Abstract 145–46.

26. For an enlightening discussion of settlement houses and related church ministries and dogma, see Michael E. McGerr, *A Fierce Discontent: The Rise and Fall of the Progressive Movement in America* (New York: Oxford University Press, 2005) , 53–58, 64–69, 77–79, 94–104. This paragraph relies heavily on McGerr's book.

27. *Protestant Evangelical Mission to the Italians*, MSS 1103, October 13, 1916, postcard to Mrs. William Hauerwas, 643 East Conway Street, Milwaukee.

28. "Maud Richter Is Certain Bomb Is Anarchist Work," *Milwaukee Leader*, November 26, 1917, 1.

29. So claimed the *Milwaukee Leader*, which offered the closest to a first-person account when it quoted Maud Richter. Ibid., 1.

30. "In Grief over the Dead," *Milwaukee Journal*, November 25, 1917, 1.

31. "Maud Richter Is Certain Bomb Is Anarchist Work," 1. Richter gave a consistent description of the bomb to the *Milwaukee Sentinel*, too. "Bomb Meant for Pastor and Flock," *Milwaukee Sentinel*, November 25, 1917, 1.

32. "Maud Richter is Certain Bomb is Anarchist Work," 1.

33. "Third Ward Is 'in Bad' Again," *Milwaukee Journal*, November 25, 1917, 1.

34. The U.S. Census Bureau reported that the population of the city of Milwaukee was 373,857 in 1910 and 457,147 in 1920.

35. *Milwaukee Leader*, December 31, 1917, part 2, p. 2.

36. "Third Ward Is 'In Bad' Again."

37. "Bombs the Particular Weapon of Sicilians," *Milwaukee Journal*, November 25, 1917.

38. Ibid.

39. Ibid. The central police station logged Richter's call at 5:20 p.m. "Italian Consul Deplores Bomb Tragedy," *Milwaukee Sentinel*, November 26, 1917, 4. Richter lived at the YWCA, which stood at 384 Jackson Street. Trial Abstract 354.

40. His full name probably was Salvatore Mazzone. The Social Security Death Index lists a Salvatore Mazzone, date of birth unknown, as having a Social Security number issued in Wisconsin and dying in August 1961.

41. "Italian Consul Deplores Bomb Tragedy," 4.

42. "Scene of Explosion Charnel House," *Milwaukee Journal*, November 25, 1917, 1.

43. Ibid.

44. "Chief Calls It Murder," *Milwaukee Sunday Sentinel*, November 25, 1917, 1.

45. "Lawyer for Deputies Gets Death Threat following Central Station Blast," *Milwaukee Sentinel*, November 27, 1917, 1.

46. "Authorities Believe List of Dead in Crash Will Be Placed at 10," 1.

47. "Thousands of Curious See Blast Scene," 1.

48. Ibid.

49. Ibid. The attempted suicide of a custodian at the Pabst Theater is a detail from "Dynamite Death!," 104. I have no reason to doubt that particular detail.

50. Robert W. Wells, *This Is Milwaukee* (Garden City, NY: Doubleday, 1970). McDonough quoted Lieutenant Flood more colorfully as explaining to Detective Bert Stout, "A rat that she used to go around with is bothering her for money. Get her story and go out and pick up this fellow and bring him in. I'll take care of him." McDonough, "Dynamite Death!," 104.

51. "Authorities Believe List of Dead in Crash Will Be Placed at 10," 5.

52. The *Milwaukee Leader* was just one newspaper that referred that way to the bomb. "Authorities Believe List of Dead in Crash Will Be Placed at 10," 1.

53. "Scene of Explosion Charnel House," 1; "Authorities Believe List of Dead in Crash Will Be Placed at 10," 1.

54. "Nine Officers and 2 Others Are Victims," 1.

55. "Lawyer for Deputies Gets Death Threat following Central Station Blast," 1.

56. See McDonough, "Dynamite Death!," 11 (illustration showing cross-section of the bomb).

57. The details in these two sentences come from McDonough, "Dynamite Death!," 106. The report of the slug found in the bedroom one block away has only McDonough as its source.

58. McDonough, "Dynamite Death!," 105.

59. "Mangled, Chats with Friends," *Milwaukee Journal*, November 25, 1917, 1. McDonough wrote, in a slight variance, that Stecker was dead on arrival at the hospital. "Dynamite Death!," 105.

60. These were Kaiser, Stecker, Weiler, O'Brien, and Templin. "Five Milwaukee Women Whose Husbands, Detectives, Were Killed in the Central Station Bomb Blast," *Milwaukee Evening Sentinel*, November 26, 1917, 1.

61. "In Grief over the Dead," 1.

62. "Thousands of Curious See Blast Scene," 1. Just weeks earlier, on October 1, 1917, Flood had completed twenty-nine years of service.

Chapter 2. Eleven

1. "Flags to Fly at Half Mast," *Milwaukee Sentinel*, November 26, 1917, 4.

2. "Mass to Be Said for Bomb Victims," *Milwaukee Sentinel*, November 28, 1917, 4.

3. "Flags to Fly at Half Mast," 4.

4. Ibid.

5. "Possible Confession Seen in Drag-Net Use by Police Officials," *Milwaukee Leader*, November 27, 1917, 1.

6. "Death Chamber Scene of Horror," *Milwaukee Sentinel*, November 25, 1917, 2.

7. "Station Tragedy Baffles Police," *Milwaukee Sentinel*, November 29, 1917, 6.

8. "Operator's Widow Dazed," *Milwaukee Sentinel*, November 25, 1917, 2.

9. "Death Chamber Scene of Horror," 2.

10. "Possible Confession Seen in Drag-Net Use by Police Officials," 1.

11. "Police Seek Clue to Bomb Crash in Trial of Rioters," *Milwaukee Leader*, November 28, 1917, 10. On December 21, 1917, the *Milwaukee Leader* reported that a vaudeville benefit performance by local actors had raised another $7,500 from an audience of six thousand. "Benefit Performance for Bomb Victims' Kin Brings in $7,500 Total," *Milwaukee Leader*, December 21, 1917, 2.

12. "Mass to Be Said for Bomb Victims," 4.

13. "Flags at Half Mast," *Milwaukee Sunday Sentinel*, November 25, 1917, 2.

14. "Anarchist's Bomb Explodes in Police Station—Kills Eleven," *Milwaukee Sentinel*, November 25, 1917, 1. The theory persisted that supporters of alleged Italian rioters in Bay View planted the device. Even the new Progressive newspaper in Madison, Wisconsin, William T. Evjue's *Capital Times*, ran an Associated Press article after the trial that asserted simply, "The explosion of the bomb at the police station was a sequel to the Bay View riots." "11 Italians Held as Guilty," *Capital Times*, December 21, 1917, 2. Evjue's newspaper probably was dependent upon wire reports, though, as it had published its first issue just eight days earlier, on December 13, 1917.

15. Trial Abstract 355.

16. One trial witness then, Clarence Brunner, also played the accordion. Trial Abstract 517.

17. Newspaper reporters were aware of the sympathies of many Bay View Italians or surmised them. See, e.g., "Gun Fight Occurs in Bay View," *Milwaukee Sentinel*, September 10, 1917, 2 (asserting that sympathies of Bay View Italians are with Austria in the war).

18. Trial Abstract 152–53.

19. Trial Abstract 149, 158.

20. Trial Abstract 165.

21. Trial Abstract 163.

22. Trial Abstract 160.

23. Trial Abstract 161.

24. Trial Abstract 166.

25. "Chief Calls It Murder," *Milwaukee Sentinel*, November 25, 1917, 1.

26. *In re Cannon*, Grand Jury Investigation Transcript, 1922–23, at 8 (Wisconsin Historical Society, Archives Room; MADm/56/F6-7, Series 1769). Subsequent citations are to "GJ Tr."

27. "25 Men Arrested in Big Roundup," *Milwaukee Sentinel*, November 25, 1917, 1.

28. Ibid.

29. Ibid.

30. "Authorities Believe List of Dead in Crash Will Be Placed at 10," *Milwaukee Leader*, November 26, 1917, 1.

31. "Possible Confession Seen in Drag-Net Use by Police Officials," 1.

32. "Maker of Bomb Still at Large," *Milwaukee Sentinel*, November 28, 1917, 1.

33. Ibid.

34. "Hints at Clews in Bomb Case," *Milwaukee Journal*, November 28, 1917, 1.

35. Ibid.

36. In the 1910 U.S. Census, the twenty-eight-year-old Carchidi listed his occupations as tailor and musician. By the 1920 Census, he listed life insurance office work as his occupation; the same in 1930. The 1930 Census includes the barest hint of what the 1922–23 grand jury investigation suggested more directly about Carchidi's shady role for lawyers: Carchidi's eldest son, Franklin, still lived with his parents at age twenty-two and listed his occupation ambiguously as a "collector" for a law firm. But, as early as September 1918, when he registered for the draft, Carchidi listed his own occupation as insurance agent. GJ Tr. 2460.

37. GJ Tr. 2518. The census never shows the Carchidi family living that close to the Zabel family. But, of course, a census offers only a decennial snapshot, and the Carchidi family moved with some frequency. The Zabels also moved at least once between the 1910 and 1930 census counts. What census records do confirm is that the Carchidi family and the Zabel family lived in the same ward on the city's west side during most of the period 1910–30. In earlier years, the Carchidis lived in a more modest neighborhood on the city's near northwest side, at 6th Street and Chambers Avenue. 1910 U.S. Census.

38. The 1910, 1920, and 1930 census records all list Carchidi as born in Italy of Italian parents. His wife, Alice, by contrast, was born in Wisconsin of parents who also had been born in Wisconsin.

39. GJ Tr. 2520. Milwaukee's west side, where the Carchidi family lived in a series of apartments and homes, decidedly was not an Italian area or a recent immigrant's neighborhood at all. Eventually, the family settled in the suburb immediately west of Milwaukee's west side, Wauwatosa. 1930 U.S. Census. The 1930 census placed the value of the Carchidis' Wauwatosa home, which they owned, at $8,000. That would have been a substantial house in its day, although it was in the middle of the range of home values on that street, again according to 1930 census records.

40. GJ Tr. 2513.

41. GJ Tr. 2518–19.

42. "Bomb Meant for Pastor and Flock," *Milwaukee Sentinel*, November 25, 1917, 1.

43. *Milwaukee Leader*, 1.

44. "Gun Fight Occurs in Bay View," 2.

45. "Possible Confession Seen in Drag-Net Use by Police Officials," 1; see also "Police Seek Clue to Bomb Crash in Trial of Rioters," 1.

46. *Milwaukee Leader*, November 29, 1917, 1.

Chapter 3. American Anarchists

1. Consider generally Thomas More, *Utopia* (New York: Knopf, 1910), 59–107.

2. See, e.g., "Sixty-Three of U.S. Ship Crew Missing," *Milwaukee Sentinel*, November 28, 1917, 1, concerning the torpedoing of an American steamship, the *Actaron*, by a German U-boat.

3. Alice Wexler, *Emma Goldman: An Intimate Life* (New York: Pantheon, 1984), 227.

4. *Mother Earth* 12, no. 5 (July 1917): 140; see also Wexler, *Emma Goldman: An Intimate Life*, 234, quoting the same passage from Berkman's summation.

5. Emma Goldman, letter to Agnes Inglis, April 1917, Joseph Labadie Collection, University of Michigan, quoted in Wexler, *Emma Goldman: An Intimate Life*, 230.

6. Ibid., 230–32. Galleani vigorously opposed the war and boiled his view down to a slogan: "Against the war, against the peace, for the social revolution!" Paul Avrich, *Anarchist Portraits* (Princeton, NJ: Princeton University Press, 1988), 170.

7. William Godwin (1756–1836) laid out some of the foundational ideas of philosophical anarchism but did not describe himself as one. He was an Englishman and, eventually, the husband of Mary Wollstonecraft, an early feminist and radical two or three centuries ahead of her time.

8. Paul Avrich, *Anarchist Voices: An Oral History of Anarchism in America* (Princeton, NJ: Princeton University Press 1995), 313, 315–20.

9. Ibid., 316.

10. Ibid., 167–70.

11. Ibid., 316.

12. Ibid., 167, 168.

13. Ibid., 168, 166.

14. Trial Abstract 490.

15. Trial Abstract 693. The witness, Officer John F. Wesolowski, did not identify the journal by name. But he described it as published in Paterson, New Jersey, which all but certainly makes it *La Questione Sociale*. The newspaper was out of date, though, for *La Questione Sociale* stopped publication in 1916. *Cronaca Sovversiva* continued for more than a year. Galleani published it first in Barre, Vermont, and later in Lynn, Massachusetts.

16. See Beverly Gage, *The Day Wall Street Exploded* (New York: Oxford University Press, 2009), 48–49, 207–11; Avrich, *Anarchist Portraits*, 157, 273n65.

17. Hippolyte Havel, "Biographic Sketch of Emma Goldman," in Emma Goldman, *Anarchism and Other Essays* (New York: Dover, 1969), 15. For a short time in Paris, Havel and Goldman were lovers. Candace Serena Falk, *Love, Anarchy, and Emma Goldman* (New Brunswick, NJ: Rutgers University Press, 1990), 32.

18. Goldman, Preface, *Anarchism and Other Essays*, 42.

19. An example of just such a split in the ranks of socialists was ongoing in Minneapolis the weekend of the Bay View disturbance. Some socialists and labor leaders held a "loyalty

convention" there, urging support for America's war effort. "Call on Socialists to Uphold Nation," *New York Times*, September 10, 1917, 5. Samuel Gompers, president of the American Federation of Labor, was among the speakers. He told the *Times*, "We have sent out a spirit from one end of the land to the other to stamp out sedition and to confuse and confound the traitors who talk peace and anti-Americanism and say they are talking for the American working man." About this time, *Mother Earth* and *Mother Earth Bulletin* regularly reviled Gompers. The *New York Times* cited in the same article Milwaukee's own Victor L. Berger and the radical New York lawyer Morris Hillquit as two pacifist socialists whom the Minneapolis convention opposed.

20. The assessment of the causes of the Bay View riot and the perspective on the accused Italians that emerged in stories, headlines, and editorials in the *Milwaukee Leader* during autumn 1917 were different from those in the *Milwaukee Sentinel*. The other mainline Milwaukee newspaper of the day, the *Milwaukee Journal*, was similar to the *Sentinel*. Madison's progressive *Capital Times* had not begun publication in September 1917 and did not later give enough attention to the trial of the Bay View eleven to allow any strong impression of its editorial attitude toward the riot and its causes.

21. Emma Goldman, *Living My Life*, 2 vols. (1931; reprint, New York: Da Capo Press, 1970), 1:11.

22. Ibid., 1:7.

23. Ibid., 10. Professor James Green makes the same point, essentially, in his *Death in the Haymarket* (New York: Pantheon, 2006), 267–77.

24. Falk, *Love, Anarchy, and Emma Goldman*, 10, quoting William M. Reedy, "The Daughter of a Dream," *St. Louis Mirror*, November 5, 1908.

25. Wexler, *Emma Goldman: An Intimate Life*, 100–12.

26. Goldman, *Anarchism and Other Essays*, 49–50.

27. For a useful discussion of the notion of *Attentat* and its development among anarchists, see Green, *Death in the Haymarket*, 90–93, 128–44. For more assistance in understanding the German term *Attentat*, the author turned to Gary R. Geipel and Marcus J. Berghahn, both proficient German speakers.

28. Avrich, *Anarchist Portraits*, 34, 98–99, 200. Frick managed Andrew Carnegie's company, the Carnegie Steel Company. The shooting was in connection with the Homestead strike.

29. Goldman, *Living My Life*, 1:83, 86–103.

30. Goldman, "The Psychology of Political Violence," in *Anarchism and Other Essays*, 88.

31. Ibid., 62–63.

32. Goldman, "Minorities versus Majorities," in *Anarchism and Other Essays*, 70.

33. Ibid., 78.

34. Emma Goldman, *Voltairine de Cleyre* (Berkeley Heights, NJ: Oriole Press, 1932), an essay published in pamphlet form, in which Goldman calls de Cleyre "the most gifted and brilliant anarchist woman America ever produced"; Goldman, *Living My Life*, 2:504–5.

For the magazine's promotion of favored writers, see, e.g., the back page of *Mother Earth* 12, no. 3 (May 1917), under the heading "Anarchist Literature."

35. The May 1917 issue of *Mother Earth* includes a short quotation from Thoreau on page 96; on the same page appears an advertisement for Goldman's May 20, 1917, lecture praising both Thoreau and Emerson.

36. *Mother Earth Bulletin* 1, no. 1 (October 1917): 3.

37. See Emma Goldman, *Living My Life*, 1:56. The May 1917 issue of *Mother Earth* also advertised for sale two of Maxim Gorky's novels, *The Confession* and *The Spy*.

38. Goldman, "Minorities versus Majorities," 69.

39. Wexler, *Emma Goldman: An Intimate Life*, 276. Goldman delivered a speech at the University of Wisconsin in Madison in 1934 during her ninety-day tour on a visa.

40. Falk, *Love, Anarchy, and Emma Goldman*, 318.

41. Clarence Darrow spent most of his professional life in Chicago after moving there from Ashtabula County, Ohio, where he practiced as a young lawyer not far from his Kinsman birthplace. Goldman also spent much time in Chicago, in a sense the birthplace of anarchist activism in America thanks to the 1886 Haymarket Square tragedy and the subsequent hanging of four anarchists and the jailhouse suicide of a fifth. However, Darrow and Goldman seem more to have known of each other than to have known each other. As late as 1901, Goldman still had not met Darrow personally. Goldman, *Living My Life*, 1:303–4. Further, she spurned his help then as the government sought to implicate her in the assassination of President William McKinley. Darrow had sent an emissary from his office who angered Goldman. Ibid. In Goldman's two-volume autobiography, Darrow receives only one other mention, and a passing one at that: she notes that a group selected Darrow to represent John Turner in the U.S. Supreme Court. Ibid., 348. Turner was an English radical who either was first (according to Goldman) or among the first to face deportation under the 1903 Immigration Act. Darrow and his law partner at the time, Edgar Lee Masters (author of the *Spoon River Anthology*), did represent Turner in the Supreme Court and lost. *Turner v. Williams*, 194 U.S. 279 (1904).

42. 39 Stat. 874 (1917). The 1917 Act, like earlier immigration acts in 1903 (that one in response to President William McKinley's 1901 assassination by a supposed anarchist, Leon Czolgosz) and 1907, expressly excluded anarchists and persons convicted of crimes of moral turpitude, as well as those who advocated the violent or forceful overthrow of the U.S. government. It was the 1903 Act that first barred anarchists expressly. 32 Stat. 1213 (1903). But the 1917 Act also clarified the government's power to deport such aliens after their admission. Note that Emma Goldman denied that Czolgosz was an anarchist. Goldman, "The Psychology of Political Violence," in *Anarchism and Other Essays*, 88. Her denial must be taken together with the bitter experience of the federal government's sustained but unsuccessful effort to link her to McKinley's assassination.

43. *Mother Earth Bulletin* 1, no. 3 (December 1917): 4.

44. *Mother Earth Bulletin* 1, no. 2 (November 1917): 4.

45. *Mother Earth Bulletin* 12, no. 3 (May 1917): 71–72.

46. Nunzio Pernicone, *Carlo Tresca: Portrait of a Rebel* (New York: Palgrave Macmillan, 2005), 97.

47. *Mother Earth Bulletin* 1, no. 1 (October 1917): 7; *Mother Earth Bulletin* 1, no. 7 (April 1918): 4. After five months in trial, on August 31, 1918, the jury convicted Haywood and more than one hundred others. Haywood lost his appeal in October 1920, and in March 21 he jumped bond and decamped to the Soviet Union rather than surrender to serve his twenty-year prison sentence. Pernicone, *Carlo Tresca*, 98. Judge Landis was the first commissioner of major league baseball, serving from November 1920 until his death, in 1944.

48. "Hundred Suspects Arrested in Big Anarchist Drive," *Milwaukee Sentinel*, November 28, 1917, 1.

49. "Troops May Be Sent to Meet I.W.W. Acts," *Milwaukee Sentinel*, November 28, 1917, 1.

50. "Federal Officer Is Aiding Police," *Milwaukee Sentinel*, December 1, 1917, 2.

51. "Detroit Police Find Big Bomb in Station," *Milwaukee Sentinel*, December 1, 1917, 2. A bomb scare earlier that autumn in Detroit had turned out to be a false alarm. A supposed bomb in the headquarters of the IWW turned out on close inspection to be "nothing more than a piece of mechanism left in the place by workmen who did some carpenter job." "I.W.W. 'Bomb' Proves to Be Piece of Junk," *Milwaukee Leader*, September 12, 1917, 1.

52. On July 22, 1916, someone detonated a bomb at a San Francisco parade. Ten people died. Police initially suspected anarchists but soon arrested instead a labor leader, Thomas J. Mooney, and his associate, a shoemaker, Warren K. Billings. They also arrested Mooney's wife, Rena, Israel Weinberg, and Edward Nolan. Tom Mooney was a socialist, not an anarchist. At a trial marred by perjury, probably adduced deliberately by prosecutors, Mooney and Billings were convicted, with the former sentenced to death and the latter to life imprisonment. When solid evidence of perjury and a frame-up emerged, the California governor commuted Mooney's sentence to life imprisonment in 1918. Emma Goldman and other anarchists took up the cause of Mooney and Billings in 1917, only in part because the San Francisco district attorney, Charles M. Fickert, by then had indicted Alexander Berkman in the bombing. See "San Francisco's Sixth Victim," *Mother Earth Bulletin* 1, no. 1 (October 1917). Eventually, Fickert dropped the indictment against Berkman, as he did that against Nolan (Rena Mooney and Israel Weinberg were acquitted at trial). In spite of the near certainty that Mooney and Billings were framed, the two men spent more than twenty-two years in prison as successive California governors refused relief. A newly elected governor of California, Culbert Olson, finally released both men in 1939. In 1931, the Wickersham Commission, the first mainstream body to bring police brutality to the public's attention, also was critical of the Mooney and Billings trials.

53. *Mother Earth Bulletin* 1, no. 1 (October 1917): 7.

54. *Mother Earth Bulletin* 1, no. 5 (February 1918): 3.

55. *Mother Earth Bulletin* 1, no. 7 (April 1918): 4.

56. *Mother Earth Bulletin* 12, no. 6 (August 1917): 204.

57. "Will Urge Courts to Stop Sedition," *New York Times*, September 11, 1917, 13.

58. "Search Nearing Home for Seditious Papers," *New York Times*, September 13, 1917, 3. Scott Nearing remained a lifelong peace activist, author, and conservationist, dying at age one hundred in 1983.

59. "The *Masses* Again Barred from Mails," *New York Times*, September 15, 1917, 7. The more famous Judge Learned Hand, also at that time a judge on the U.S. District Court for the Southern District of New York (and a cousin of Augustus Hand), earlier had ordered the postmaster general to mail *The Masses*, but U.S. Attorney Francis Gordon Caffey secured a stay from the court of appeals. From 1929 to 1947, Caffey himself sat as an active federal district judge in the Southern District of New York. He died on senior status in 1951.

60. "Suspends German Edition," *New York Times*, October 16, 1917, 3.

61. For an account of the No-Conscription League, the trial, and its aftermath, see Wexler, *Emma Goldman: An Intimate Life*, 230–37.

62. *Goldman v. United States*, 245 U.S. 474 (1918). The government asked the U.S. Supreme Court days later to issue the mandate immediately so that Goldman would have no further right to bail pending appeal. The Supreme Court obliged ten days after issuing its opinion affirming the convictions. *Goldman v. United States*, 38 S. Ct. 222 (January 28, 1918) (mem.).

63. See Trial Abstract 1478–79 (Reverend Giuliani explaining in rebuttal the testifying defendants' explanations of their educational backgrounds); Trial Abstract 1485.

64. Trial Abstract 1390–91, 1405–19.

65. See Trial Abstract 1405–7, 1414–18. The portion most directly concerned with Bianchi's political views reads: "A socialist-anarchist is different from a socialist-democrat and the difference is the democrat socialist to the king by the vote and the socialist-anarchist is in favor of this war because after the war is through you will find that there is nothing left any more. By revolution I mean when the people is educated enough they don't need no revolution, the government I think is the people, if the people don't want no government the people govern it themselves. People will get control of the government when they read enough, when they get education enough. Certainly never by violence, you can't change nothing at all." The reader must bear in mind here that Bianchi was testifying in his second language (perhaps with the uncertain aid of an interpreter) and that court reporters at the time did not make verbatim records of testimony but rather made condensed narratives with some verbatim excerpts.

66. Trial Abstract 1362–70.

67. Trial Abstract 1300–10.

68. Trial Abstract 1428–34, 1438–50.

69. "Actors in Jail, Recital Is Off," *Milwaukee Sentinel*, September 11, 1917, 1.

70. Ibid. The hall still stands today. It remains in use as a tavern with a dance floor where an audience formerly might have gathered.

71. Ibid.

72. Emma Goldman letter to Harry Weinberger, January 8, 1918, provided to author by Alice Hall, Government Documents Editor, The Emma Goldman Papers, University of California, Berkeley.

73. Trial Abstract 1313–22, 219.

74. Trial Abstract 1333–45, 1409–12. If Giuliani's testimony at trial was correct, the defendants' descriptions of having received two or three years of schooling in Italy would not correspond exactly with completion of second or third grade in primary school in the United States. Giuliani likened it to a fifth- or sixth-grade education in the United States. Several of the defendants described leaving school at about age twelve, having completed two or three years. That at least would be consistent with Giuliani's rough estimate.

75. Trial Abstract 1272–84.

76. Trial Abstract 1263–64.

77. Trial Abstract 1250–54.

78. Trial Abstract 1346–48.

79. Trial Abstract 1353.

80. "Six Italians Admit Being Anarchists," *Milwaukee Evening Sentinel*, December 10, 1917, 1, 5.

81. For an authentic account of life in mining towns and camps, see Jack Conroy, *The Disinherited* (1933; reprint, Columbia: University of Missouri Press, 1991), 39–99.

82. Trial Abstract 1035.

83. Trial Abstract 1036–37.

84. Trial Abstract 1038.

85. Trial Abstract 1044.

86. Ibid.

87. Anarchists took it then and take it today as an article of faith that guards at Santo Stefano prison murdered Bresci. There appears, however, little reliable research either to prove suicide or to disprove it. See generally Pier Carlo Masini, *Storia Degli Anarchici Italiani Nell' Epoca Degli Attentati* (Milan: Rizzoli Editore, 1981), 171–72; Arrigo Petacco, *L'Anarchico che Venne Dall' America* (Milan: Arnoldo Mondadore Editore, 1969), 139–47.

88. Paul Avrich, *Sacco and Vanzetti: The Anarchist Background* (Princeton, NJ: Princeton University Press, 1991), 95.

89. Avrich, *Anarchist Portraits*, 168.

90. See, e.g., Goldman, "Anarchism," in *Anarchism and Other Essays*, 52–53, 56, 62–63.

91. Goldman, "The Hypocrisy of Puritanism," in *Anarchism and Other Essays*, 167–76.

Chapter 4. Doffed Hats and Honored Flags; Buttoned Coats, Pigs, and Rags

1. Avrich, *Sacco and Vanzetti*, 104.
2. Ibid., 62–65, 104–5.
3. Ibid., 62, 199. The execution of Sacco and Vanzetti, on August 23, 1927, after a palpably biased trial for their alleged roles in a murderous holdup in South Braintree, Massachusetts, remains controversial to this day.
4. Ibid., 153–54, 156, 169–73.
5. Trial Abstract 171. Note 13 in chapter 7 explains at length how this Trial Abstract is different from a full, verbatim transcript and why I cite it.
6. Trial Abstract 171–72.
7. "Gun Fight Occurs in Bay View," 1; Trial Abstract 523–24.
8. Trial Abstract 533.
9. Trial Abstract 529.
10. Avrich, *Sacco and Vanzetti*, 55; Paul Avrich, "Italian Anarchism in America: An Historical Background to the Sacco-Vanzetti Case" (lecture, www.recollectionbooks.com/bleed/Encyclopedia/SaccoVanzetti/essaypa.html).
11. Bartolo Testolin, for example, had returned to Milwaukee only one week earlier. He had wandered from Chicago to Belgium, Wisconsin, not quite forty miles north of Milwaukee along Lake Michigan. Trial Abstract 1347. The village then had a vast limestone quarry. At least one newspaper still listed Testolin's home as South Chicago. "Take Statements of Many Witnesses," *Milwaukee Journal*, September 10, 1917, 1.
12. Officer (and acting detective) John F. Wesolowski recalled it as "a bright sunshiny but chilly day." Trial Abstract 695.
13. *Milwaukee Leader*, September 10, 1917, 1.
14. Trial Abstract 1171, 1036.
15. Trial Abstract 1037.
16. Trial Abstract 1038.
17. Trial Abstract 264, 292, 426.
18. Trial Abstract 368.
19. Trial Abstract 355, 426.
20. See, e.g., Trial Abstract 1132, 1317.
21. Trial Abstract 221.
22. Trial Abstract 600, 604, 508.
23. Trial Abstract 292.
24. Trial Abstract 1362–63.
25. Trial Abstract 515–16.
26. Trial Abstract 179–80, 187, 368–69, 172–73, 1429, 1447–48.
27. Trial Abstract 176–77.
28. Trial Abstract 177.

29. Swedish-born Joe Hill (or Joe Hillstrom) gets credit for many IWW songs. He also was an organizer of the IWW and informally its cartoonist. The state of Utah executed him by firing squad in 1915 on a flimsy conviction of murder.

30. Trial Abstract 1303, 1309–10, 1364–65.

31. Trial Abstract 1285 (Amedeo Lilli).

32. Today, the reference to "America" would be ambiguous. Not so then. The abbreviated title surely meant the air known more fully as "America the Beautiful," the lyrics to which Katharine Lee Bates wrote in 1893, revised in 1904, and rendered in final draft in 1913. Samuel A. Ward supplied the score. Irving Berlin did not write "God Bless America" until 1918, the year following the events in Bay View.

33. Trial Abstract 205.

34. See, e.g., Trial Abstract 181–82.

35. A non-Italian who presented himself as a passerby on his way to the nearby South Shore Yacht Club, Trial Abstract 503, Robert Blackwood, commented at trial on the difference between the two groups: Giuliani's removing their hats when they sang "America" and the crowd on the other side of the street standing with caps in place. Trial Abstract 508–9.

36. Trial Abstract 1313.

37. Trial Abstract 152.

38. Trial Abstract 153.

39. Trial Abstract 154.

40. Trial Abstract 154–55.

41. Trial Abstract 219.

42. Trial Abstract 1315–16.

43. Trial Abstract 178, 276.

44. Trial Abstract 197–98, 179–80, 280–81.

45. Trial Abstract 182. This was Giuliani's testimony, which regularly sounded exaggerated or at least tinged with dramatic flourish.

46. Trial Abstract 446.

47. That is how nineteen-year-old Dominic Germanotta, of Giuliani's congregation, put it. Trial Abstract 670–71. Vincenzo Fratesi and others were shaking their fists menacingly. Trial Abstract 293.

48. Trial Abstract 170–71. Although Milwaukee had a small office of the fledgling Bureau of Investigation in the U.S. courthouse on East Wisconsin Avenue, under the direction of Special Agent Ralph Izard, there is no indication that the federal authorities offered Giuliani any help. They likely would have seen his request for police protection as purely a local matter, not one for federal intervention. Indeed, even after the melee and shooting on September 9, the U.S. Attorney, H. A. Sawyer, and Izard hesitated to move, probably because they still saw it as a local issue. "Actors in Jail, Recital Is Off," 1.

The federal agency had its roots in a small group of Department of Justice agents assembled in 1908 under President Theodore Roosevelt's attorney general, Charles J.

Bonaparte. Bonaparte's successor as attorney general under President William Howard Taft, George Wickersham, christened the agency the Bureau of Investigation in 1909. www.fbi.gov/libref/historic/history/origins.htm.

49. Trial Abstract 171–72.

50. Trial Abstract 292. Bear in mind, too, that the police detectives spoke no Italian, so they had limited ability to grasp the nuances of the interactions between the two groups.

51. Trial Abstract 336.

52. Trial Abstract 182.

53. Trial Abstract 182, 336.

54. Trial Abstract 449.

55. That was the consistent version of the police and the evangelists. Trial Abstract 183–84, 293–94, 336, 548, 668–69. But defendant Bartolo Testolin also acknowledged that Formaceo fired first. Trial Abstract 1353. So did Cornelius Pajot, an uncharged man who lived on that block and testified for the state. Trial Abstract 548. An apparently disinterested bystander also had Formaceo firing first. Trial Abstract 515–16.

56. Trial Abstract 336.

57. Trial Abstract 184.

58. "Gun Fight Occurs in Bay View," 1.

59. Trial Abstract 294. Templin's testimony was from the preliminary examination, because the November 24 explosion at the central police station took his life before trial. Weiler perished in that explosion, too.

60. Trial Abstract 294–95.

61. Trial Abstract 451; "Rigid Investigations into Bay View Riot Started by Officials," *Milwaukee Sentinel*, September 10, 1917, 1.

62. Trial Abstract 295.

63. Trial Abstract 724.

64. Trial Abstract 681.

65. Trial Abstract 669.

66. Trial Abstract 311, 681, 701.

67. Trial Abstract 294, 311, 313, 617–18. The police later found a revolver and a shotgun in a trunk in the home that the two Fratesi brothers shared with Maria and Pasquale Nardini, but Adolfo claimed ownership of those. Trial Abstract 1301. Maybe they were his, maybe not; Adolfo clearly was the less involved in the day's madness, and it would not be the first or the last instance of one brother taking the fall for another out of filial loyalty.

68. Trial Abstract 724.

69. Trial Abstract 336, 317.

70. "Postpone Cases against Italians," *Milwaukee Sentinel*, September 14, 1917, 1.

71. Trial Abstract 507, 682.

72. Trial Abstract 548, 506.

73. Trial Abstract 450.

74. Trial Abstract 507.

75. Trial Abstract 507.

76. Trial Abstract 724.

77. "Gun Fight Occurs in Bay View," 2.

78. Ibid.

79. Ibid. (missed less than one day's work). Inconsistently but more plausibly, the same newspaper reported after Templin's death that he had returned to work a week after being shot. "25 Men Arrested in Big Roundup," 1.

80. Trial Abstract 1352.

81. Trial Abstract 681, 1353.

82. "Second Victim of Anarchist Riot Dies," *Wisconsin State Journal*, September 15, 1917, 3.

83. Trial Abstract 1292–93.

84. Trial Abstract 1294.

85. Trial Abstract 681. Of the major newspapers, only the *Milwaukee Leader* bothered to name him. "Detectives Fight Bay View Rioters; One Dead, 6 Hurt," *Milwaukee Leader*, September 10, 1917, 1.

86. See Trial Abstract 700 (Detective Wesolowski testifying of the Austrian, "I do not know where he is, the last I heard of him he was in a hospital").

87. Trial Abstract 515–16.

88. Trial Abstract 466.

89. Trial Abstract 461–65.

90. "Postpone Cases against Italians," *Milwaukee Sentinel* 1 (September 14, 1917). The newspaper reported the results of the coroner's inquest into the shooting.

91. Trial Abstract 701.

92. "Second Italian Dies Result of Riot Shots," *Milwaukee Sentinel*, September 15, 1917, 1; Trial Abstract 701.

93. Trial Abstract 463–64, 467–68.

94. Trial Abstract 1291.

95. "Grave Situation Is Seen in Riot," *Milwaukee Sentinel*, September 11, 1917, 1.

96. "Second Victim of Anarchist Riot Dies," *Wisconsin State Journal*, September 15, 1917, 3; "Second Italian Dies Result of Riot Shots," 1; Trial Abstract 464.

97. "Second Victim of Anarchist Riot Dies," 3.

98. Trial Abstract 1318 (Gavino Denurra's testimony).

99. Ibid.

100. Trial Abstract 703–4, 1336, 1404.

101. Trial Abstract 1472. Witnesses elsewhere described Miles as having gold teeth.

102. Trial Abstract 1404.

103. Trial Abstract 506–7.

104. Trial Abstract 1336–37.

105. The *Milwaukee Leader* described "a score of detectives" raiding the clubhouse. "Detectives Fight Bay View Rioters; One Dead, 6 Hurt," 1.

106. Trial Abstract 368–69, 516, 521–22.

107. Trial Abstract 368–69, 436, 437, 575.

108. Trial Abstract 530–31.

109. Trial Abstract 1264.

110. Compare Trial Abstract 1338, 1318–19, 682–84, 1471.

111. Detective Wesolowski gave contradictory testimony on whether officers went first to the clubhouse and then to the Nardinis' house or the other way around. Trial Abstract 683, 707.

112. Trial Abstract 683, 706–7.

113. "Gun Fight Occurs in Bay View," 1.

114. "Take Statements of Many Witnesses," 1.

115. Ibid.

116. Ibid.

117. "Police Kill Two in I.W.W. Riot," *New York Times*, September 10, 1917, 4.

118. "Officials Start Probe of Sunday's Riot," *Milwaukee Journal*, September 10, 1917, 1. The slant in favor of a confrontation between patriots and anarchists was not limited to the conservative press. In Madison, eight days after William T. Evjue began to publish the progressive *Capital Times*, his newspaper explained, "The riots occurred during a patriotic mass meeting in the Italian district." "11 Italians Are Held as Guilty," 2.

119. "Detectives Fight Bay View Rioters; One Dead, 6 Hurt," *Milwaukee Leader* 1 (September 10, 1917).

120. "Anarchists Not Involved in Riot, Italians Assert," *Milwaukee Leader*, September 11, 1917, 1.

121. Ibid.

122. Ibid.

123. Ibid.

124. Ibid.

125. At least, so their lawyer later asserted. William B. Rubin, letter to Thomas Neacy, December 29, 1917.

126. "Verdict of Guilty Returned against Bay View Rioters," *Milwaukee Leader*, December 21, 1917, 3E.

127. "The Police Tragedy," *Milwaukee Leader*, November 25, 1917, 6.

128. "Possible Confession Seen in Drag-Net Use by Police Officials," 1.

129. Trial Abstract 1252, 1273, 1314, 1348, 1429–30, 1438. Their lawyer claimed that all but Vincenzo Fratesi and Pietro Bianchi attended a Roman Catholic church at least occasionally. These last two "had not attended church at all." William B. Rubin, letter to Thomas Neacy, December 29, 1917, 2.

130. Trial Abstract 1315, 1442.

131. See, e.g., Trial Abstract 570–72.

132. *Bianchi v. State*, 169 Wis. 75, 89, 171 N.W. 639, 645 (1919).

133. *Statistical Abstract of the United States* 40 (1917), Table 46. Religious affiliation was not then broken down by state or smaller political divisions.

134. Even today, the geographical area covered by the Archdiocese of Milwaukee is 31.1 percent Roman Catholic, significantly higher than the 22.9 percent of Americans nationwide who are Roman Catholic. *Official Catholic Directory* (2005) (numbers as of January 1, 2005), quoted in Matthew E. Bunson, *Catholic Almanac* (Huntington, IN: Our Sunday Visitor Pub. Div., 2006).

135. Were the police present at all on August 26 and September 2? The evidence is both scant and mixed, but they probably were not at the scene. True, Giuliani did warn some of the clubhouse crowd on August 26 not to announce their anarchist views out loud, as a police officer was near. Trial Abstract 154–55. But that may have been a ruse on Giuliani's part, a bit of quick thinking in an effort to avoid an escalation of the confrontation. Certainly no officer intervened or showed himself that day. Moreover, Giuliani later testified that he first arranged for a police escort after the September 2 rally. Trial Abstract 170–71. That action suggests strongly that September 9 marked the first appearance of the Milwaukee Police Department at Giuliani's gatherings. So Formaceo probably would not have been expecting the police when he came to the corner.

136. Trial Abstract 184.

137. Two letters found in Testolin's trunk, addressed but unmailed, may have suggested that he intended to issue a call to comrades elsewhere. The state offered them at trial and Giuliani translated them. Trial Abstract 728–29. Again, though, these letters were never mailed.

138. "Gun Fight Occurs in Bay View," 1.

139. "Anarchists Not Involved in Riot, Italians Assert," 1.

140. "Detectives Fight Bay View Rioters; One Dead, 6 Hurt," 1.

141. Ibid.; "Police Fail to Get Riot Facts from Italians," *Wisconsin State Journal*, September 11, 1917, 1.

142. "25 Men Arrested in Big Roundup," 1.

143. "Anarchists Not Involved in Riot, Italians Assert," 2; "Grave Situation Is Seen in Riot," 1.

144. "Anarchists Not Involved in Riot, Italians Assert," 2.

145. "Dozen Italians Charged with Grave Offenses," *Milwaukee Sentinel*, September 12, 1917, 1.

146. Trial Abstract 691.

147. "Detectives Fight Bay View Rioters; One Dead, 6 Hurt," 1.

148. Trial Abstract 726.

149. See Trial Abstract 821.

150. Trial Abstract 791–803, 804.

151. "Rigid Investigations into Bay View Riot Started by Officials," 1.

152. Katherine Eyerick Giuliani is buried in the Cleveland Street Cemetery, Amherst Township, in Lorain County, Ohio. That county abuts Lake Erie's southern shore, just west of Cleveland's Cuyahoga County.

153. Protestant Evangelical Mission to the Italians, Milwaukee County Historical Society, MSS 1103 (one folder), October 13, 1916, postcard to Mrs. William (Rose) Hauerwas, 643 East Conway Street, Milwaukee.

154. Trial Abstract 357.

155. Trial Abstract 355; Trial Abstract 149.

156. "Rigid Investigations into Bay View Riot Started by Officials," 1.

157. Ibid.

158. Trial Abstract 470–71.

159. *Bianchi v. State*, 169 Wis. 75, 94–95, 171 N.W. 639 (1919).

160. GJ Tr. 1459.

161. The Wisconsin Supreme Court acknowledged that point. *Bianchi v. State*, 169 Wis. 94–95, 171 N.W. 647.

162. More than one person made that general observation of Zabel under oath, and these people were unconnected. See GJ Tr. 1842–43, 2231–32, 2412, 2559–70.

163. See, e.g., Trial Abstract 1375–78 (Vincenzo Fratesi's renunciation of much of his purported statement and his complaint that requests for an interpreter other than Giuliani had gone ignored).

164. Trial Abstract 476.

165. GJ Tr. 2445. The witness testifying was Albert K. Stebbins, who later represented Carchidi in various scrapes with the law. Carchidi also retained William B. Rubin from time to time (see GJ Tr. 100–101, 2461–62) and drummed up business for Rubin's office.

166. "Dozen Italians Charged with Grave Offenses," 1. August Marinelli was among the twelve defendants, charged in case he made a miraculous recovery. He did not. After Marinelli died, the state dismissed the complaint against him on October 16, 1917, after the preliminary hearing. Pardon Papers, Series 98, Box 204 (1922), at Wisconsin Historical Society, Archives Room.

167. "Jury Convicts Italian after a Speedy Trial," *Milwaukee Sentinel*, September 12, 1917, 1.

Chapter 5. Chaos

1. See, e.g., "Bay View Anarchists Held under Heavy Bail," *Milwaukee Daily News*, September 14, 1917, 1; "Italians in Bay View Riot Are Bound Over," *Milwaukee Free Press*, October 17, 1917, 3. The latter story began, "Eleven Italians, alleged anarchists"; many articles and headlines did not bother even to offer the token "alleged."

2. "Postpone Cases against Italians," *Milwaukee Sentinel*, September 14, 1917, 1; "Bay View Anarchists Held under Heavy Bail," 1.

3. "Postpone Cases against Italians," *Milwaukee Sentinel*, September 14, 1917, 1; "Bay View Anarchists Held under Heavy Bail," 1.

4. "Riot Case Continued to Oct. 15," *Milwaukee Free Press*, September 29, 1917, 2.

5. "Blow at I.W.W., 168 Are Indicted; Scores Arrested," *New York Times*, September 29, 1917, 1, 11.

6. *Milwaukee Daily News*, September 28, 1917, 1.

7. "I.W.W. Leaders Are Jailed by U.S.," *Milwaukee Daily News*, September 29, 1917, 1; "Federal Agents Jail 45 I.W.W. Intriguers," *Milwaukee Daily News*, October 1, 1917, 1; "I.W.W. Trial Starts Today," *New York Times*, April 1, 1918, 20. Haywood had escaped the hangman in Idaho in 1907 when Clarence Darrow defended him successfully on a charge that he and others had murdered the former governor of Idaho, Frank Steunenberg. For a magnificent account of that trial and of much of American history in the decades immediately before, see J. Anthony Lukas, *Big Trouble* (New York: Simon and Schuster, 1997).

8. "Federal Agents Jail 45 I.W.W. Intriguers," *Milwaukee Daily News*, October 1, 1917, 1.

9. "Arrest Giovanitti and Miss Flynn," *New York Times*, October 1, 1917, 1.

10. Ibid.; "Police Kill Two in I.W.W. Riot," *New York Times*, September 10, 1917, 4. Citing only an unnamed source, the *Times* claimed that the two dead men had come from "Chicago and the East only a few days ago" and that they were "personal friends of Autrio Giovanti [*sic*], the I.W.W. leader of New York."

11. "103 I.W.W. Leaders Face Judge Landis," *New York Times*, December 16, 1917, 6.

12. "What Has Been Proved at I.W.W. Trial," *New York Times*, August 4, 1918, 40.

13. "Ton of Evidence Gathered," *New York Times*, September 29, 1917, 11; "U.S. Hurls Ton of Evidence at I.W.W.," *Milwaukee Daily News*, September 28, 1917, 1; see also Jules Archer, *Strikes, Bombs and Bullets* (New York: Simon and Schuster, 1972), 147.

14. "Ton of Evidence Gathered," 11.

15. "50 More Arrests in I.W.W. Roundup," *New York Times*, September 30, 1917, 1.

16. Ibid.; David Pietrusza, *Judge and Jury: The Life and Times of Judge Kenesaw Mountain Landis* (South Bend, IN: Diamond Communications, 1998), 119.

17. "Eight Places Raided by Agents in Chicago," *Milwaukee Sentinel*, September 6, 1917, 1–2.

18. *Haywood v. United States*, 268 F.795, 801 (7th Cir. 1920).

19. Many decisions of the U.S. Supreme Court recite the history of writs of assistance and their role in prompting adoption of the Fourth Amendment. For just one prominent and oft-cited example that antedates the *Haywood* case, see *Weeks v. United States*, 232 U.S. 383, 389–91 (1914). Historians and other authors have offered detailed examinations of the writs of assistance and their relationship to the Fourth Amendment, too. See, e.g., Nelson B. Lasson, *The History and Development of the Fourth Amendment to the United States Constitution* (Baltimore: Johns Hopkins University Press, 1937), 53–98; Telford Taylor, *Two Studies in Constitutional Interpretation* (Columbus: Ohio State University Press, 1969). Some of the Framers had personal, bitter experience with writs of assistance. Such a writ was used, for example, to seize John Hancock's sloop, the *Liberty*.

20. *Haywood*, 268 F. at 801.

21. "Nation-wide Raid Made on I.W.W.," *Milwaukee Sentinel*, September 6, 1917, 1.

22. Propaganda against War Causes Act," *Milwaukee Sentinel*, September 6, 1917, 1; "Federal Agents Raid 3 Places as I.W.W. Quarters," *Milwaukee Sentinel*, September 6, 1917, 1.

23. "Federal Agents Raid 3 Places as I.W.W. Quarters," 1.

24. Ibid.

25. Ibid.

26. All four counts of conviction for the many defendants were conspiracy charges. *Haywood*, 268 F. at 797–98.

27. "Police Kill Two in I.W.W. Riot," 4.

28. In order, the headlines appeared on the first pages of the *Milwaukee Evening Sentinel*, September 10, 1917; *Milwaukee Sentinel*, September 10, 1917; *Milwaukee Leader*, September 11, 1917; *Milwaukee Evening Sentinel*, November 28, 1917; *Milwaukee Evening Sentinel*, November 30, 1917; *Milwaukee Sentinel*, November 28, 1917; *Milwaukee Sentinel*, December 21, 1917.

29. Matthew S. Goldberg, "Death and Injury Rates of U.S. Military Personnel in Iraq," *Military Medicine* 175 (April 2010): 220, 221 Fig. 2.

30. www.census.gov/popest/archi.ves/1990s/popclockest.txt.

31. Ibid.

32. "Senate Appropriates 7 Billion War Fund," *Milwaukee Daily News*, October 4, 1917, 1.

33. "4,000 Demand Senator Resign," *Milwaukee Free Press*, September 28, 1917, 1.

34. Ibid. Even with his vitriol, Roosevelt's appearance in Racine was not quite so dramatic as his appearance at the Hotel Gilpatrick in Milwaukee five years earlier. On that occasion, the deranged John Flammang Schrank shot Roosevelt outside the hotel when the president arrived to deliver a campaign speech in his 1912 effort to return to the White House as the Progressive Party candidate. His folded speech and a steel eyeglass case in Roosevelt's breast pocket slowed the bullet and saved him. Shaken, bleeding, and pale, he still went ahead with the speech, reportedly shouting, "It takes more than that to kill a Bull Moose."

35. See generally Michael E. McGerr, *A Fierce Discontent: The Rise and Fall of the Progressive Movement in America, 1870–1920* (New York: Oxford University Press, 2005), 80–81, 88, 280–81.

36. "Death of Zabel Ends a Colorful Career," *Milwaukee Journal*, January 3, 1948, 3.

37. Nelson Algren, *Chicago: City on the Make* (Chicago: University of Chicago Press, 2011), 64.

38. Ibid., 62.

39. "I.W.W. Trial Starts Today," 20. Fitts was a seasoned fifty-one years old in 1917 and previously had served as attorney general of Alabama, where he was born.

40. See Pietrusza, *Judge and Jury*, 65–76, 95. Much of Landis's notoriety flowed from his effort to fine John D. Rockefeller's Standard Oil Company more than $29 million in 1907. A court of appeals later set aside that judgment as an abuse of discretion. *Standard Oil*

Co. of Indiana v. United States, 164 F. 376 (7th Cir. 1908). In 2006 dollars, the fine would have been more than $627.5 million.

41. Pietrusza, *Judge and Jury*, 95.

42. "Landis a National Figure," *New York Times*, November 13, 1920; "Landis Quits Bench for Baseball Job; Boomed for Mayor," *New York Times*, February 19, 1922, 3.

43. Pietrusza, *Judge and Jury*, 149.

44. "103 I.W.W. Leaders Face Judge Landis," 6. The same newspaper later would describe Vanderveer as from Seattle. "What Has Been Proved at I.W.W. Trial," 40. The handgun incident made news even in Milwaukee. "Find Revolver on Counsel for I.W.W.," *Milwaukee Sentinel*, December 16, 1917, 2.

45. *Haywood*, 268 F. at 802; Pietrusza, *Judge and Jury*, 120–31. The court of appeals described the trial as beginning in mid-April, while Pietrusza puts the start at April 1, 1918. Pietrusza also asserts that jury selection took a month. Pietrusza, *Judge and Jury*, 120. He writes that the trial ended abruptly on August 17. Ibid., 131.

46. "100 I.W.W.'s Guilty of War Plotting," *New York Times*, August 18, 1918, 9.

47. Ibid.; Pietrusza, *Judge and Jury*, 120.

48. Pietrusza, *Judge and Jury*, 132.

49. "80 I.W.W. Members Must Serve Terms," *New York Times*, April 12, 1921.

50. "100 I.W.W.'s Guilty of War Plotting," 1; Pietrusza, *Judge and Jury*, 132–33.

51. Quoted in "What Has Been Proved at I.W.W. Trial," 40.

52. "Hundred Suspects Arrested in Big Anarchist Drive," *Milwaukee Sentinel*, November 28, 1917, 1.

Chapter 6. Of Counsel

1. "Possible Confession Seen in Drag-Net Use by Police Officials," 1; see also "Police Seek Clue to Bomb Crash in Trial of Rioters," 1.

2. Milwaukee Manuscript Collection P, Biographical Note, Wisconsin Historical Society, Milwaukee Area Research Center, archives, University of Wisconsin–Milwaukee.

3. "T. E. Leahy, Lawyer, Dies," *Milwaukee Journal*, June 30, 1949, 1, 13.

4. Ibid.

5. William B. Rubin, letter to Hon. A. C. Backus, October 25, 1917. This letter, like those and other documents related to Rubin in this chapter, is included in the William B. Rubin Papers, Milwaukee Manuscript Collection P, Wisconsin Historical Society, Milwaukee Area Research Center archives. The repository is the Golda Meir Library at the University of Wisconsin–Milwaukee.

6. John P. Frey, letter to Hon. A. C. Backus, November 2, 1917.

7. William B. Rubin, letter to John P. Frey, November 12, 1917.

8. Ibid.

9. William B. Rubin, telegram to John P. Frey, November 22, 1917; William B. Rubin, letter to Joel Rubin, November 23, 1917.

10. William B. Rubin, letter to Abner J. Rubin, December 8, 1917.

11. "Stanch Champion of Rights, Bill Rubin to Ease Up a Bit at 83," *Milwaukee Journal*, August 31, 1956, part 2, pp. 1, 6; W. G. Bruce, *History of Milwaukee, Illustrated*, vol. 3 (Chicago: S.J Clarke, 1922), 852.

12. "Atty. William B. Rubin's Funeral to Be Held Today," *Milwaukee Journal*, February 4, 1959, part 1, p. 4.

13. Ibid.

14. Bruce, *History of Milwaukee, Illustrated*, 3:852.

15. William B. Rubin, letter to Abner J. Rubin, October 25, 1917.

16. Ibid.; William B. Rubin, letter to Beatrice Mesirow, December 11, 1917.

17. Milwaukee Manuscript Collection P, Biographical Note, University of Wisconsin–Milwaukee.

18. *Iron Molders' Union No. 125 v. Allis-Chalmers Co.*, 166 F. 45 (7th Cir. 1908), *affirming in part, vacating in part and modifying*, 150 F. 155 (E.D. Wis. 1906).

19. Milwaukee Manuscript Collection P, Biographical Note, University of Wisconsin–Milwaukee; *Milwauker Wochenblat*, August 24, 1917, 12. This newspaper was a weekly publication that appeared in English, Yiddish, and Hebrew. See also "Atty. William B. Rubin's Funeral to Be Held Today," part 1, p. 4.

20. E.g., William B. Rubin, letter to Samuel Gompers, October 13, 1917.

21. Ibid., 2.

22. *The Samuel Gompers Papers*, vol. 8, *Progress and Reaction in the Age of Reform, 1909–13*, ed. Peter J. Albert and Grace Palladino (Urbana: University of Illinois Press, 2001), 457–58, reprinting Samuel Gompers's letter to W. B. Rubin, February 17, 1913.

23. E.g., William B. Rubin, letters to John P. Frey, November 12, 1917, and Abner J. Rubin, December 8 and 14, 1917.

24. See William B. Rubin, letter to John P. Frey, December 2, 1918.

25. *Milwauker Wochenblat*, August 24, 1917, 12.

26. One of these was Joseph A. Padway, who himself would become a nationally prominent labor lawyer.

27. W. B. Rubin, Statement, as of October 1, 1918. Rubin's statement may have been prepared in connection with a tax dispute with the federal Commissioner of Internal Revenue.

28. "Atty. William B. Rubin's Funeral to Be Held Today," part 1, p. 4.

29. William B. Rubin, "A Tribute to Clarence Darrow," *Capital Times*, March 16, 1938, D2.

30. Ibid.

31. "Introduction of Clarence S. Darrow," William B. Rubin Papers, Milwaukee Manuscript Collection P, Wisconsin Historical Society, Milwaukee Area Research Center, archives.

32. There are several full accounts of Darrow's life, for different readers' tastes. All of them address Darrow's trials in Los Angeles. The first Darrow biography that centers on

the California charges against Darrow is Geoffrey Cowan, *The People v. Clarence Darrow: The Bribery Trial of America's Greatest Lawyer* (New York: Crown, 1993). It is a thorough and objective account of the McNamara trial and the proceedings against Darrow that followed, if not as sympathetic to Darrow as are some of his other biographers.

33. Ina Ten Eyck Firkins, *An Index to Plays, 1880–1926* (New York: H. W. Wilson, 1927), 162.

34. Quoted in Bruce, *History of Milwaukee, Illustrated*, 3:853.

35. See, e.g., William B. Rubin, letters to Samuel Gompers, October 13, 1917, and November 15, 1917.

36. William B. Rubin, second letter to Samuel Gompers, October 13, 1917; William B. Rubin, letter to Samuel Gompers, November 15, 1917, 2.

37. Compare "Let Berger Talk" with "The Case of Berger," both in the William B. Rubin Papers, Milwaukee Manuscript Collection P, Wisconsin Historical Society, Milwaukee Area Research Center, archives.

38. William B. Rubin, letter to Samuel Gompers, October 13, 1917, 2.

39. "Attorney William B. Rubin's Funeral to Be Held Today," part 1, p. 4.

40. Milwaukee Manuscript Collection P, Biographical Note, University of Wisconsin–Milwaukee.

41. Rubin was the subject of ambulance-chasing (more formally "champerty" if the issue was the lawyer rewarding the independent ambulance-chaser or "barratry" if the lawyer actually directed the chase) inquiries by the bar more than once. He avoided disbarment twice but was not exonerated either. See *State v. Rubin*, 201 Wis. 30, 229 N.W. 36 (1930); *State ex rel. Reynolds v. Milwaukee County Circuit Court, Branch 1*, 193 Wis. 132, 214 N.W. 396 (1927) (per curiam).

42. "Stanch Champion of Rights, Bill Rubin to Ease Up a Bit at 83," part 2, p. 6.

43. *In Memoriam Winfred C. Zabel*, Wis. 255 (1949): xxxii.

44. Ellis Baker Usher, *Wisconsin: Its Story and Biography, 1848–1913*, vol. 4 (Chicago: The Lewis Pub. Co., 1914), 832–34.

45. *In Memoriam Winfred C. Zabel*, xxxii.

46. Usher, *Wisconsin: Its Story and Biography*, 4:832–34.

47. Ibid.

48. Usher, *Wisconsin: Its Story and Biography*, 4:834; *In Memoriam Winfred C. Zabel*, xxxv.

49. See John W. Slayton, *Props to Capitalism* (1912), 9–10, a Socialist pamphlet.

50. *In Memoriam Winfred C. Zabel*, xxxv.

51. Slayton, *Props to Capitalism*, 9–10; Usher, *Wisconsin: Its Story and Biography*, 4:834.

52. GJ Tr. 1370–1416, 1719–25. A woman, Florence Wilmot, who admitted running a separate bordello testified independently that the same assistant district attorney had patronized her establishment. Her account indirectly supports the first story. GJ Tr. 1396–98.

53. GJ Tr. 1723–24.

54. A fawning biography of Zabel, in *Wisconsin: Its Story and Biography, 1848–1913*, makes that claim for him at p. 833. It may or may not be true.

55. "Sanity Board Named to Examine Schrank," *New York Times*, November 13, 1912, 9.

56. *In Memoriam Winfred C. Zabel*, xxxvii.

57. *In Memoriam Winfred C. Zabel*, xxxii.

58. "Death of Zabel Ends Colorful Career," *Milwaukee Journal*, January 3, 1948, 3.

59. Ibid.

60. "Death of Zabel Ends Colorful Career," 3. The encomium found at *In Memoriam Winfred C. Zabel*, xxxvii, places Zabel's final year in office at 1920, not 1922. But the 1921 Wisconsin Blue Book, p. 313, establishes that the newspaper, not the eulogy, was correct. Zabel served until the end of 1922.

61. GJ Tr. 76–82, 89–90, 1461–62.

62. GJ Tr. 2533–44.

63. GJ Tr. 1492.

64. GJ Tr. 6, 203, 1461–62, 1464–65, 3865.

65. GJ Tr. 1464–67.

66. GJ Tr. 2287–2301.

67. GJ Tr. 76–82, 1485.

68. GJ Tr. 2468–71.

69. GJ Tr. 2474–75, 2482–83.

70. So the Wisconsin Supreme Court later found, although not necessarily as to the same "investigator." *State v. Cannon*, 199 Wis. 401, 226 N.W. 385, 387 (1929).

71. GJ Tr. 1068.

72. GJ Tr. 2038, 2043.

73. "R.J. Cannon Indicted," *New York Times*, February 4, 1923, 5.

74. The charge was dismissed, eventually. The Wisconsin Reports demonstrate that the other lawyer, Raymond J. Cannon, continued to practice without interruption from 1923 until 1929, when the Wisconsin Supreme Court suspended his license for two years on different allegations. That petition made no mention of a bribery allegation, let alone a conviction. Dissenting in part, Justice Crownhart noted further that Cannon "has been found guilty of no crime." *State v. Cannon*, 199 Wis. 401, 226 N.W. 385, 391 (1929) (Crownhart, J., dissenting in part). Zabel's obituary in Milwaukee's most widely circulated newspaper noted the indictment in very general terms and explained only that the subsequent trial had "resulted in the exoneration of Mr. Zabel and the other defendants." Death of Zabel Ends Colorful Career," 3. Cannon himself is a fascinating character. He once had played professional baseball and served as a spring training pitcher in the major leagues. GJ Tr. 4075–76. He stayed involved in baseball and with baseball players and other athletes even after he quit the game and took up law. Cannon represented two ousted players, "Shoeless Joe" Jackson and Oscar "Happy" Felsch, in civil suits against the Chicago White Sox's owner, Charles Comiskey, after the 1919 World Series scandal. Cannon also formed a Ball Players

Union in an early attempt to organize major league baseball players to negotiate with owners. He even represented the boxer Jack Dempsey for a time. Eventually, Cannon would serve three terms in the U.S. House of Representatives, from 1933 to 1939, as a progressive Democrat. Voters swept him in with Franklin Delano Roosevelt as the nation wallowed at economic low tide in 1932. Wisconsin Blue Book (1935); Interview Thomas R. Cannon, January 24, 2011 (notes in author's possession).

75. "Death of Zabel Ends Colorful Career," 3.

76. GJ Tr. 2232.

77. GJ Tr. 2231.

78. GJ Tr. 1888–89.

79. GJ Tr. 1889, 1892.

80. GJ Tr. 1887–88.

81. GJ Tr. 1889–90.

82. GJ Tr. 2555–56.

83. GJ Tr. 2552–53.

84. GJ Tr. 2556–57.

85. GJ Tr. 2560–65.

86. GJ Tr. 2569–70.

87. GJ Tr. 2570.

88. GJ Tr. 3764–65.

89. GJ Tr. 3766.

90. GJ Tr. 2412.

91. GJ Tr. 2378.

92. "Tribute Paid at Bier of Well Known Milwaukee Woman," *Milwaukee Journal*, April 15, 1915, clipping contained in William B. Rubin Papers, Milwaukee Manuscript Collection P, Wisconsin Historical Society, Milwaukee Area Research Center, archives. Note that Rubin retained that clipping for the rest of his life. He also dedicated his 1916 book, *The Toiler in Europe: A Popular Psychological Insight into European Labor Conditions* (Cincinnati: S. Rosenthal & Co., 1916), to Sonia.

93. GJ Tr. 2378.

94. "Atty. William B. Rubin's Funeral to Be Held Today," part 1, p. 4; see also "William B. Rubin," the second editorial on the *Milwaukee Sentinel*'s editorial page the same day; "Stanch Champion of Rights, Bill Rubin to Ease Up a Bit at 83," part 2, pp. 1, 6.

95. "Zabel Dies as Voters Again Re-Elect Him," *Milwaukee Sentinel*, November 4, 1936, 1.

96. GJ Tr. 2381.

97. GJ Tr. 3875–80.

98. GJ Tr. 3880.

99. GJ Tr. 3880–81.

100. GJ Tr. 3881–82.

101. GJ Tr. 3884.

102. GJ Tr. 3884–85.

103. GJ Tr. 3888.

104. According to the Lake Park Friends' website, www.lakeparkfriends.org, the newly created Milwaukee Parks Commission began to acquire the land for Lake Park in 1889. The commission retained Olmsted. Work on the park continued through 1908. However, Olmsted himself grew senile and was confined to a hospital by 1895. He died there in 1903.

105. GJ Tr. 3882–83.

106. *In Memoriam Winfred C. Zabel*, xxxiii.

107. "Blizzard Snarls Milwaukee Traffic; Holiday Saves City from Knockout," *Milwaukee Sentinel*, January 2, 1948, 1.

108. "Death of Zabel Ends Colorful Career," 3.

109. *In Memoriam Winfred C. Zabel*, xxxii–xxxvi (1949); "Death of Zabel Ends Colorful Career," 3.

110. "Possible Confession Seen in Drag-Net Use by Police Officials," 1; see also "Police Seek Clue to Bomb Crash in Trial of Rioters," 1.

Chapter 7. "The Public Mind Has Become Violently Inflamed against All Italians"

1. "Italian Trials Postponed until Friday," *Milwaukee Evening Sentinel*, November 28, 1917, 1.

2. "Italians Salute the Flag," *Milwaukee Journal*, November 28, 1917, 1; "Italian Trials Postponed until Friday," 1.

3. "Italians Salute the Flag," 1; "Italian Trials Postponed until Friday," 1.

4. "Italians Salute the Flag," 1.

5. Woller had been the clerk of both the municipal and the district courts since 1890. Trial Abstract 99, in *Bianchi v. State*, no. 10 (October Term, 1918), 10.

6. "Women Lose Jury Right Fight in Chicago, Win in Wisconsin," *New York Times*, June 22, 1921, 1.

7. See generally R. C. Van Caenegem, *The Birth of the English Common Law*, 2nd ed. (Cambridge: Cambridge University Press, 1988), 68–84, for a scholarly but concise recounting of the fragmentary origins of the modern jury's precedents.

8. Richard P. McBrien, *Lives of the Popes* (New York: HarperCollins, 2000), 182.

9. Frederick Pollock and Frederic William Maitland, *The History of English Law before the Time of Edward I*, vol. 2 (Cambridge: Cambridge University Press, 1895), 597–602, 602n1; see also ibid., 2:630–39, 647, and vol. 1, 117–21, 128–29; Van Caenegem, *The Birth of the English Common Law*, 69, 132n15. Trials by ordeal included devices like the dunking chair (in which the suspect was tied to a chair and tossed into a river to see whether he sank or floated. Sinking indicated innocence but also meant likely drowning), jousting, or other actual physical combat. The eighteenth of seventy-one Constitutions adopted in the Fourth Lateran Council forbade clerics from participating in blood-shedding punishments or

purgations by ordeal. While Magna Carta also committed its signers to the jury, it did so only insofar as the jury otherwise was the "law of the land." At that point, trial juries were not generally the law of the land.

10. Van Caenegem, *The Birth of the English Common Law*, 71.

11. "A righteous man regardeth the life of his beast, but the tender mercies of the wicked are cruel." Prov. 12:10.

12. John G. Gregory, *History of Milwaukee*, vol. 3 (Chicago: S. J. Clarke, 1931), 811–12.

13. The pardon application for Amedeo Lilli appended an "exemplified copy" of the trial court record, including pleadings. It is stored at the Wisconsin Historical Society, Madison, and catalogued as Pardon Papers, Series 98, Box 204 (1922, LeClaire through Luther), MAD OS/13/M5–14/G4. Lilli's is Pardon Application no. 135 (1922), and his application also included Vincenzo Fratesi. Some of the court record also is reprinted in the appellate record for *Bianchi v. State*, no. 10 (October Term, 1918). One of the required filings of the defendants-appellants was the "Case," set in typescript and bound separately from the appellants' brief. The "Case" reproduces parts of the trial record relevant to the appeal, including an abstract of the trial testimony. The University of Wisconsin Law School, 975 Bascom Mall, Madison, is the repository of the appellate record.

Again, the court records butcher the defendants' names throughout. The proper spelling of the name of the first defendant in the Amended Information filed in Milwaukee Municipal Court probably was "Adolfo Fratesi."

Finally, the reader should understand that citations to the trial testimony and other statements at trial come from the abbreviated Trial Abstract that the lawyers compiled for purposes of appeal as part of the "Case," not from a verbatim trial transcript itself. A court reporter almost surely prepared a verbatim transcript, because the Abstract refers to page numbers consistent with a full transcript (I use those page numbers here, because they are more precise locators of the testimony and rulings I cite). But I was unable to find a transcript. The Wisconsin Historical Society does not have it. While the clerk of the Milwaukee County Circuit Court might, a deputy clerk explained that records from that era are spotty if they exist at all and are not organized or kept in any filing system. Many are missing or presumed missing. Part of the reason is that the court in which this case was tried, then called the Milwaukee Municipal Court, no longer exists. It was abolished and its jurisdiction transferred to the circuit court after a change in the law in 1961. See *City of Milwaukee v. Trzesniewski*, 35 Wis. 2d 487, 151 N.W.2d 109 (1967). From 1895 until then, the Milwaukee Municipal Court handled all felony cases. *State v. Krause*, 260 Wis. 313, 318, 50 N.W.2d 439, 441–42 (1951). While municipal courts exist today in Milwaukee and in all incorporated municipalities in Wisconsin, they are very different courts: they handle only minor, noncriminal violations of municipal ordinances.

If there was a full transcript, the Wisconsin Supreme Court would have had it while the appeal was pending in that court. But the clerk of the Wisconsin Supreme Court would have returned that transcript, with the rest of the municipal court record, to the Milwaukee Municipal Court after the supreme court's decision was final.

In short, the Abstract of the trial, which does include short segments of apparently verbatim testimony and comment, is the best available source I was able to discover for documenting the trial proceedings. I have preferred newspapers as sources only where a newspaper article signaled that it was quoting verbatim by putting words in quotation marks. But the essential cautionary note remains: the Abstract was by design not complete and was prepared by lawyers as a matter of advocacy to assist the supreme court on appeal. While lawyers could have faced judicial criticism or worse had they deliberately misled the supreme court on the content of the transcript, still we have no assurance that the Abstract is entirely fair and accurate.

14. Pardon Papers, Series 98, Box 204 (1922, LeClaire through Luther).

15. Pardon Papers, Series 98, Box 204 (1922, LeClaire through Luther).

16. *Bianchi v. State*, no. 10 (October Term, 1918), 8.

17. *Bianchi v. State*, no. 10 (October Term, 1918), 8.

18. *Bianchi v. State*, no. 10 (October Term, 1918), 3–4.

19. Pardon Papers, Series 98, Box 204 (1922, LeClaire through Luther).

20. The liverwurst is named after the city of Braunschweig, in Germany's north-central coal-mining region.

21. *Bianchi v. State*, no. 10 (October Term, 1918), 5–6, and Vincenzo Fratesi Affidavit.

22. *Bianchi v. State*, no. 10 (October Term, 1918), 7, and Vincenzo Fratesi Affidavit.

23. William B. Rubin, letter to Thomas Neacy, December 29, 1917, 7, William B. Rubin Papers, Milwaukee Manuscript Collection P, Wisconsin Historical Society, Milwaukee Area Research Center archives.

24. *Bianchi v. State*, no. 10 (October Term, 1918), 6, and Vincenzo Fratesi Affidavit.

25. "Sanity Board Named to Examine Schrank," 9.

26. *Haywood v. United States*, 268 F. 795, 802 (7th Cir. 1920); Pietrusza, *Judge and Jury*, 120–31.

27. *State v. Bianchi*, no. A1338 (Milw. Municipal Court), Record, in Pardon Papers, Series 98, Box 204 (1922, LeClaire through Luther); "Seeks to Shift Scene of Trials," *Milwaukee Evening Sentinel*, November 30, 1917, 1.

28. *State v. Bianchi*, no. A1338 (Milw. Municipal Court), Record, in Pardon Papers, Series 98, Box 204 (1922, LeClaire through Luther).

29. "Seeks to Shift Scene of Trials," 1.

30. "Venue Change for Italians Denied," *Milwaukee Sentinel*, December 1, 1917, 6.

31. "Seeks to Shift Scene of Trials," 1.

32. "Venue Change for Italians Denied," 6.

33. "Seeks to Shift Scene of Trials," 1.

34. Ibid.

35. Ibid.

36. Ibid.

37. "Court Receives New Complaint," *Milwaukee Evening Sentinel*, December 3, 1917, 6; *Bianchi v. State*, no. 10 (October Term, 1918), 8–10.

38. "Court Receives New Complaint," 6.

39. For a snapshot of the widespread practice of excluding wage laborers from American juries, either by law or by custom, see *Thiel v. Southern Pac. Co.*, 328 U.S. 217 (1946).

40. "State Accepts Two for Jury," *Milwaukee Evening Sentinel*, December 5, 1917, 1.

41. Ibid.

42. "Riot Case Jury Hard to Secure," *Milwaukee Sentinel*, December 6, 1917, 4.

43. "Jury Which Tried Italians in Municipal Court on the Charge of Being Implicated in Bay View Riot," *Milwaukee Sentinel*, December 21, 1917, 5.

44. "State Accepts Two for Jury," 1.

45. "Riot Case Jury Hard to Secure," 4.

46. "Jury Selected to Try Italians," *Milwaukee Evening Sentinel*, December 6, 1917, 1.

47. See "Jury Which Tried Italians in Municipal Court on the Charge of Being Implicated in Bay View Riot," 5 (photograph).

48. *Bianchi v. State*, no. 10 (October Term, 1918), 2–3.

49. "Declares Woman Urged Bloodshed," *Milwaukee Sentinel*, December 7, 1917, 5.

50. Ibid.

51. Ibid.

52. Trial Abstract 145, in *Bianchi v. State*, no. 10 (October Term, 1918), 10.

53. Trial Abstract 152, *Bianchi v. State*, no. 10 (October Term, 1918), 12.

54. Trial Abstract 160, *Bianchi v. State*, no. 10 (October Term, 1918), 14.

55. Trial Abstract 165–66, *Bianchi v. State*, no. 10 (October Term, 1918), 15.

56. Trial Abstract 166, *Bianchi v. State*, no. 10 (October Term, 1918), 15.

57. See, e.g., Trial Abstract 151, 158, 169, *Bianchi v. State*, no. 10 (October Term, 1918), 12, 14, 16.

58. Trial Abstract 188–89, *Bianchi v. State*, no. 10 (October Term, 1918), 20.

59. "Mrs. Bartelt Dies; Sought Voting Rights," *Milwaukee Journal*, May 14, 1964, part 1, p. 24.

60. See, e.g., Trial Abstract 188, 217, *Bianchi v. State*, no. 10 (October Term, 1918), 20, 27.

61. "Fail to Shake Pastor's Story of Fatal Riot," *Milwaukee Evening Sentinel*, December 7, 1917, 1.

62. Ibid.

63. *Bianchi v. State*, no. 10 (October Term, 1918), 35–36.

64. "Aver Meetings Were Patriotic," *Milwaukee Sentinel*, December 8, 1917, 4.

65. *Bianchi v. State*, no. 10 (October Term, 1918), 35.

66. *Bianchi v. State*, no. 10 (October Term, 1918), 35–37.

67. *Bianchi v. State*, no. 10 (October Term, 1918), 37.

68. See "State Rests in Italians' Trial," *Milwaukee Evening Sentinel*, December 12, 1917, 1, 2; "Alleged Rioters Are Identified," *Milwaukee Evening Sentinel*, December 8, 1917, 1, 9.

69. *Bianchi v. State*, no. 10 (October Term, 1918), 50.

70. "Alleged Rioters Are Identified," 1, 9.

71. Ibid.; "Witness Identifies Italian Rioters," *Milwaukee Sentinel*, December 9, 1917, part 2, p. 5.

72. "Jurors Make Music to Pass Their Idle Time," *Milwaukee Evening Sentinel*, December 10, 1917, 5.

73. "Silent Threat Used in Trial," *Milwaukee Evening Sentinel*, December 11, 1917, 5.

74. *Bianchi v. State*, no. 10 (October Term, 1918), 97; "Silent Threat Used in Trial," 5.

75. "Silent Threat Used in Trial," 5.

76. Ibid.

77. The exchange is at *Bianchi v. State*, no. 10 (October Term, 1918), 96.

78. *Bianchi v. State*, no. 10 (October Term, 1918), 117.

79. "State Rests in Italians' Trial," 1, 2; "Halts Trial of Alleged Rioters," *Milwaukee Sentinel*, December 13, 1917, 7.

80. "Arrest Italian Leaving Court," *Milwaukee Evening Sentinel*, December 15, 1917, 1, 3.

81. As to the indefinite detention and questioning, see "Arrest Witness at Trial of Rioters," *Milwaukee Sentinel*, December 16, 1917, part 2, p. 1; "Arrest Three More Italians," *Milwaukee Evening Sentinel*, December 17, 1917, 5. As to the later claim that the police had acted upon the request of federal authorities, see "Alleged Rioters Give Testimony," *Milwaukee Evening Sentinel*, December 18, 1917, 1, 2.

82. "Denies Release of Italian," *Milwaukee Journal*, December 18, 1917, 2.

83. "Arrest Italian Leaving Court," 1, 3.

84. Ibid.

85. Ibid.

86. Ibid.

87. "Arrest Three More Italians," 5.

88. GJ Tr. 2414.

89. *Bianchi v. State*, no. 10 (October Term, 1918), 91.

90. *Bianchi v. State*, no. 10 (October Term, 1918), 117. The state also used an Italian Presbyterian minister from Chicago, G. A. Lizzi, to translate a few of the documents. Ibid., 116. The spelling of the Chicago minister's last name comes from the record on appeal.

91. *Bianchi v. State*, no. 10 (October Term, 1918), 117.

92. "Six Italians Admit Being Anarchists," *Milwaukee Evening Sentinel*, December 10, 1917, 1, 5.

93. See, e.g., Trial Abstract 1375–78, in *Bianchi v. State*, no. 10 (October Term, 1918), 200–201 (Vincenzo Fratesi's renunciation of much of his purported statement and his complaint that requests for an interpreter other than Giuliani went ignored).

94. "Six Italians Admit Being Anarchists," 5.

95. Thomas Leahy, Frank Fawcett, and Bill Rubin all testified briefly too in the defense case. *Bianchi v. State*, no. 10 (October Term, 1918), 120–22.

96. Trial Abstract 475–77, in *Bianchi v. State*, no. 10 (October Term, 1918), 66–67.

97. "Rigid Investigations into Bay View Riot Started by Officials," 1.

98. GJ Tr. 209, 225 (F. F. Groelle).

99. GJ Tr. 207, 209–10, 220.

100. GJ Tr. 208–9.

101. Avrich, *Sacco and Vanzetti*, 105, 109–11.

102. Ibid.

103. Ibid., 109–11.

104. Ibid., 111–12, 113.

105. Ibid., 110.

106. GJ Tr. 207, 209, 225; GJ Tr. 2018 (Louis Koenig); "Two Bombs at Home of District Attorney," *Milwaukee Journal*, April 16, 1918, 1, 15.

107. Avrich, *Sacco and Vanzetti*, 112–13; "Two Bombs at Home of District Attorney," 1, 15.

108. Avrich, *Sacco and Vanzetti*, 113; "Two Bombs at Home of District Attorney," 1.

109. "Two Bombs at Home of District Attorney," 15.

110. GJ Tr. 219–20 (Groelle).

111. GJ Tr. 220; GJ Tr. 2018 (Koenig).

112. "Two Bombs at Home of District Attorney," 1.

113. See *Bianchi v. State*, no. 10 (October Term, 1918), 255–61 (index of witnesses).

114. "Halts Trial of Alleged Rioters," 7.

115. "Says Anarchy Not Violence," *Milwaukee Evening Sentinel*, December 14, 1917, 1; "Attorney Defends Socialists' Aims," *Milwaukee Sentinel*, December 15, 1917, 4.

116. *Bianchi v. State*, no. 10 (October Term, 1918), 121.

117. *Bianchi v. State*, no. 10 (October Term, 1918), 136.

118. See, e.g., *Bianchi v. State*, no. 10 (October Term, 1918), 145, 147.

119. "Aver Meetings Were Patriotic," 4.

120. See, e.g., *Bianchi v. State*, no. 10 (October Term, 1918), 160–62.

121. *Bianchi v. State*, no. 10 (October Term, 1918), 161.

122. "Arrest Three More Italians," 5.

123. See generally *Bianchi v. State*, no. 10 (October Term, 1918), 169–219.

124. *Bianchi v. State*, no. 10 (October Term, 1918), 211, 214.

125. *Bianchi v. State*, no. 10 (October Term, 1918), 214–19.

126. *Bianchi v. State*, no. 10 (October Term, 1918), 209.

127. *Bianchi v. State*, no. 10 (October Term, 1918), 201.

128. *Bianchi v. State*, no. 10 (October Term, 1918), 197, 202.

129. *Bianchi v. State*, no. 10 (October Term, 1918), Case at 203.

130. "Rioters' Trial Is Nearing End," *Milwaukee Evening Sentinel*, December 19, 1917, 1.

131. *Bianchi v. State*, no. 10 (October Term, 1918), 220–21; "Riot Case to Go to Jury Thursday," *Milwaukee Sentinel*, December 20, 1917, 6.

132. *Bianchi v. State*, no. 10 (October Term, 1918), 226–27.

133. *Bianchi v. State*, no. 10 (October Term, 1918), 226.

134. *Bianchi v. State*, no. 10 (October Term, 1918), 50, 92.

135. *Bianchi v. State*, no. 10 (October Term, 1918), 105, 17–18, 33, 22.

136. *Bianchi v. State*, no. 10 (October Term, 1918), 38, 96.

137. *Bianchi v. State*, no. 10 (October Term, 1918), 18, 23.

138. *Bianchi v. State*, no. 10 (October Term, 1918), 227–28.

139. *Bianchi v. State*, no. 10 (October Term, 1918), 228.

140. *Bianchi v. State*, no. 10 (October Term, 1918), 229.

141. Ibid.

142. Ibid.

143. *Bianchi v. State*, no. 10 (October Term, 1918), 240–47; "Bay View Rioters Found Guilty of Intent to Murder," *Milwaukee Sentinel*, December 21, 1917, 1.

144. *Bianchi v. State*, no. 10 (October Term, 1918), 247–49.

145. "Bay View Rioters Found Guilty of Intent to Murder," 1.

146. "Bay View Rioters Found Guilty of Intent to Murder," 1 (fewer than twenty minutes of deliberations, only one ballot); "See Lesson for Italian Gangs," *Milwaukee Evening Sentinel*, December 21, 1917, 6 (seventeen minutes of deliberations); "Verdict of Guilty Returned against Bay View Rioters," *Milwaukee Leader*, December 21, 1917, 1 (seventeen minutes); "Guard Italians Found Guilty," *Milwaukee Journal*, December 21, 1917, 4 (seventeen minutes).

147. "Bay View Rioters Found Guilty of Intent to Murder," 1.

148. Ibid.

149. Ibid.

150. Ibid.

151. "Guard Italians Found Guilty," 4.

152. "See Lesson for Italian Gangs," 6.

153. Ibid.

154. "Italians Get 25 Year Sentence," *Milwaukee Journal*, December 27, 1917, 2.

155. Ibid.

156. Ibid.

157. "Eleven Rioters Are Sentenced," *Milwaukee Evening Sentinel*, December 27, 1917, 1; "Eleven Italians Sent to Prison," *Milwaukee Sentinel*, December 28, 1917, 6. Rubin understood only Bianchi and Bartolo Testolin to speak and read English. William B. Rubin, letter to Bartolo Testolin and Pietro Bianchi, January 2, 1918, William B. Rubin Papers, Milwaukee Manuscript Collection P, Wisconsin Historical Society, Milwaukee Area Research Center archives.

158. "Italians Get 25 Year Sentence," *Milwaukee Journal*, December 27, 1917, 1, 2; "Eleven Rioters Are Sentenced," 1.

159. "Eleven Italians Sent to Prison," 6; "Italians Get 25 Year Sentence," 1.

160. "The Milwaukee Frame-Up," *Mother Earth Bulletin* 1, no. 4 (January 1918): 4 (listing Emma Goldman as the author of that article); see also "Boy Is Orphaned," *Milwaukee Sentinel*, December 28, 1917, 6.

161. "Boy Is Orphaned," 6.

Chapter 8. Darrow

1. William B. Rubin, letter to Arminio Conte, December 27, 1917, William B. Rubin Papers, Milwaukee Manuscript Collection P, Wisconsin Historical Society, Milwaukee Area Research Center archives. According to the clipping in Rubin's papers concerning Sonia Rubin's funeral, Conte had served as one of the pallbearers.

2. Emma Goldman, letter to Harry Weinberger, January 8, 1918, provided to author by Alice Hall, Government Documents Editor, The Emma Goldman Papers, University of California, Berkeley.

3. Ibid.

4. Sam Castagna, "In Milwaukee," *Mother Earth Bulletin* 1 (October 1917): 8.

5. Emma Goldman, letter to Harry Weinberger, January 2, 1918, Harry Weinberger Papers, Yale University Library, Department of Manuscripts and Archives, provided to author by Alice Hall, Government Documents Editor, The Emma Goldman Papers, University of California, Berkeley.

6. Emma Goldman, "The Milwaukee Frame-Up," *Mother Earth Bulletin* 1 (January 1918): 3.

7. Ibid.

8. Harry Weinberger, letter to Emma Goldman, January 9, 1918, provided to author by Alice Hall, Government Documents Editor, The Emma Goldman Papers, University of California, Berkeley.

9. Ibid.

10. See, e.g., Emma Goldman, letter to Kitty Beck, January 8, 1918, and Emma Goldman, letter to Harry Weinberger, January 8, 1918, both provided to author by Alice Hall, Government Documents Editor, The Emma Goldman Papers, University of California, Berkeley; Goldman, "The Milwaukee Frame-Up."

11. Leola M. Hirschman, letter to Emma Goldman, January 10, 1918, William B. Rubin Papers, Milwaukee Manuscript Collection P, Wisconsin Historical Society, Milwaukee Area Research Center archives.

12. William B. Rubin, letter to Bartolo Testolin and Pietro Bianchi, January 2, 1918, William B. Rubin Papers, Milwaukee Manuscript Collection P, Wisconsin Historical Society, Milwaukee Area Research Center archives. Rubin's cover letter to the warden at Waupun explained that Testolin and Bianchi (whom he described as Burt Testolin and Peter Bianchi) could speak and read English and requested that they be allowed to translate the letter for the others. A later letter places the meeting on New Year's Day. William B. Rubin, letter to S. Secchi, January 19, 1918, William B. Rubin Papers, Milwaukee Manuscript Collection P, Wisconsin Historical Society, Milwaukee Area Research Center archives.

13. *Goldman v. United States*, 245 U.S. 474 (1918); "Affirms Sentence on Emma Goldman," *New York Times*, January 15, 1918, 10.

14. Emma Goldman, letter to Kitty Beck, January 8, 1918, provided to author by Alice Hall, Government Documents Editor, The Emma Goldman Papers, University of California, Berkeley.

15. See, e.g., Emma Goldman, letter to Harry Weinberger, January 2, 1918, Harry Weinberger Papers, Yale University Library, Department of Manuscripts and Archives, provided to author by Alice Hall, Government Documents Editor, The Emma Goldman Papers, University of California, Berkeley; Leola M. Hirschman, letter to Emma Goldman, January 10, 1918, William B. Rubin Papers, Milwaukee Manuscript Collection P, Wisconsin Historical Society, Milwaukee Area Research Center archives.

16. Originally, the Field Museum, known first as the Columbian Museum, was on the grounds of the Columbian Exposition of 1892 in Jackson Park. It moved closer to downtown in 1921. See www.fieldmuseum.org/museum_info.

17. Emma Goldman, letter to Harry Weinberger, January 8, 1918, provided to author by Alice Hall, Government Documents Editor, The Emma Goldman Papers, University of California, Berkeley.

18. "Say Woman Posed as Federal Officer," *New York Times*, February 2, 1918, 6.

19. "Berkman and Goldman Going Back to Prison," *New York Times*, February 3, 1918, 6.

20. "Emma Goldman Again in Stripes," *New York Times*, February 7, 1918, 2.

21. In December 1919, not long after her release from prison, Goldman was deported with Berkman on the *Buford*. Although she later returned to America as a visitor, the government did not permit her to resume residency in the United States. After her death, in May 1940, it allowed her remains to return. She is buried at Chicago's Waldheim Cemetery near the Haymarket defendants who were hanged.

Even after she entered the Missouri State Prison at Jefferson City, Goldman remained interested in the plight of the eleven Milwaukee Italians. Surely at her prompting, the March 1918 issue of *Mother Earth Bulletin* carried an article urging readers, "Keep an eye on Milwaukee. Ten men and one woman were sentenced in that city to twenty-five years penitentiary each. The circumstances under which the arrest and conviction took place were related in a recent issue of the 'Bulletin.' They are of such a nature that even the worst pessimist would refuse to believe that the higher courts will sustain the sentence." *Mother Earth Bulletin* 1, no. 6 (March 1918): 5. The *Bulletin* also noted that William Judin still was collecting money for the appeal.

22. Leola M. Hirschman, letter to S. Secchi, January 10, 1918, William B. Rubin Papers, Milwaukee Manuscript Collection P, Wisconsin Historical Society, Milwaukee Area Research Center archives.

23. William B. Rubin, letter to S. Secchi, December 27, 1917, William B. Rubin Papers, Milwaukee Manuscript Collection P, Wisconsin Historical Society, Milwaukee Area Research Center archives.

24. Emma Goldman letter to Harry Weinberger, January 8, 1918, provided to author by Alice Hall, Government Documents Editor, The Emma Goldman Papers, University of California, Berkeley.

25. Goldman, *Living My Life*, 1:303–4.

26. Ibid., 1:303.

27. In addition to the mention in connection with Czolgosz, Goldman names Darrow as the lawyer chosen to represent the English anarchist John Turner before the U.S. Supreme Court, evidently with her blessing. Ibid., 1:348; Wexler, *Emma Goldman: An Intimate Life*, 118–19. Darrow and his partner at the time, Edgar Lee Masters, went on to lose Turner's case. *Turner v. Williams*, 194 U.S. 279 (1904). As reflected in her letters to and about Harry Weinberger and in correspondence about her own case, Goldman had a much more charitable view of left-leaning lawyers than of U.S. courts generally, so she likely would not have blamed Darrow for the loss.

28. Goldman, *Living My Life*, 1:304. If Goldman had a soft spot for Darrow, it may have been because of Voltairine de Cleyre, of whom Goldman wrote glowingly. She viewed de Cleyre as "this most gifted and brilliant anarchist woman America ever produced." Goldman, *Voltairine de Cleyre*, 1. And it was a chance occasion on which de Cleyre heard Darrow speak on socialism in Pennsylvania that de Cleyre described as a pivotal point in her development as a radical. Goldman, *Voltairine de Cleyre*; Sharon Presley and Crispin Sartwell, eds., *Exquisite Rebel: The Essays of Voltairine de Cleyre* (Albany: SUNY Press, 2005), 34.

29. William B. Rubin, letter to S. Secchi, January 19, 1918, William B. Rubin Papers, Milwaukee Manuscript Collection P, Wisconsin Historical Society, Milwaukee Area Research Center archives.

30. William B. Rubin, letter to S. Secchi, January 23, 1918, William B. Rubin Papers, Milwaukee Manuscript Collection P, Wisconsin Historical Society, Milwaukee Area Research Center archives.

31. William B. Rubin, letter to Victoria Licci, January 23, 1918, William B. Rubin Papers, Milwaukee Manuscript Collection P, Wisconsin Historical Society, Milwaukee Area Research Center archives.

32. William B. Rubin, letter to S. Secchi, January 23, 1918, William B. Rubin Papers, Milwaukee Manuscript Collection P, Wisconsin Historical Society, Milwaukee Area Research Center archives.

33. See *Bianchi v. State*, 169 Wis. 75, 171 N.W. 639 (1919).

34. Bruce, *History of Milwaukee, Illustrated*, 3:682–85; "A. C. Umbreit, Attorney, Dies," *Milwaukee Sentinel*, June 29, 1927.

35. Arthur Weinberg and Lila Weinberg, *Clarence Darrow: A Sentimental Rebel* (New York: Atheneum, 1987), 18; Clarence Darrow, *The Story of My Life* (1932; reprint, Boston: Da Capo Press, 1996), 12, 13.

36. Weinberg and Weinberg, *Clarence Darrow: A Sentimental Rebel*, 23.

37. Ibid., 21.

38. Darrow, *The Story of My Life*, 14, 15; Weinberg and Weinberg, *Clarence Darrow: A Sentimental Rebel*, 18.

39. Darrow, *The Story of My Life*, 40–41, 377–79; Weinberg and Weinberg, *Clarence Darrow: A Sentimental Rebel*, 20–21. The Weinbergs note that Ammirus Darrow gave Clarence the middle name "Seward" as a tribute to the abolitionist politician William H. Seward, a Republican who later served as President Lincoln's secretary of state.

40. Darrow, *The Story of My Life*, 13.

41. There are several biographies of Darrow. One, Charles Yale Harrison's *Clarence Darrow* (New York: Jonathan Cape, 1931), had the cooperation of Darrow and his second wife, Ruby. The first biographer who wrote after Darrow's death, Irving Stone, was mostly uncritical but important. Stone's sentimental book captures nicely the sentimental man who is its subject. Irving Stone, *Clarence Darrow: For the Defense* (New York: Doubleday, Doran, 1941). Darrow's most scholarly and prolific biographers were Lila Weinberg and Arthur Weinberg. Their work is sympathetic but also more rigorously tied to primary and secondary sources. Arthur Weinberg, *Attorney for the Damned* (Chicago: University of Chicago Press, 1957); Arthur Weinberg and Lila Weinberg, eds., *Clarence Darrow: Verdicts Out of Court* (Chicago: Ivan R. Dee, 1963); Arthur Weinberg and Lila Weinberg, *Clarence Darrow: A Sentimental Rebel* (New York: Putnam, 1980). Kevin Tierney's 1979 biography does not explore much new ground but is quite readable. Kevin Tierney, *Darrow: A Biography* (New York: Thomas Y. Crowell, 1979). Darrow's least sympathetic—but not unfair—biographer is Cowan, *The People v. Clarence Darrow: The Bribery Trial of America's Greatest Lawyer.*

For his part, Darrow's autobiography, *The Story of My Life*, originally published by Scribner's in 1932 and reissued by Da Capo Press in 1996, has the strengths and weaknesses of most or all autobiographies: a firsthand account, yes, but styled to shape the readers' image of the author as the author would have it. Darrow asks himself few tough questions in his autobiography. He also wrote an earlier, highly autobiographical novel, *Farmington* (Chicago: A. C. McClurg, 1904).

Finally, Darrow appears at length in books about his significant trials. Recent examples are Edward L. Larson, *Summer for the Gods* (New York: Basic Books, 1997), a Pulitzer Prize–winning book on the Scopes trial in Dayton, Tennessee, in 1925; Kevin Boyle, *Arc of Justice: A Saga of Race, Civil Rights, and Murder in the Jazz Age* (New York: Henry Holt, 2004), a National Book Award recipient on the trials of Ossian Sweet and his family members in Detroit; and the unmatchable J. Anthony Lukas, *Big Trouble*, detailing the trial of Big Bill Haywood and others for the 1905 assassination of former Idaho governor Frank Steunenberg.

42. As to baseball, Darrow was emphatic. "[N]ever has life held for me anything quite so entrancing as baseball." Darrow, *The Story of My Life*, 17.

43. Ibid., 31–32.

44. Weinberg and Weinberg, *Clarence Darrow: A Sentimental Rebel*, 24; Darrow, *The Story of My Life*, 27.

45. Weinberg and Weinberg, *Clarence Darrow: A Sentimental Rebel*, 25.

46. Ibid.

47. See *University of Michigan General Catalogue of Officers and Students, 1837–1911* (Ann Arbor: University of Michigan Press, 1912), available online at the University of Minnesota Law Library's extraordinary Clarence Darrow Digital Collection, www.darrow.law.umn.edu/trials.php. The General Catalogue also lists Ammirus Darrow as having attended the law school, in 1864–65.

48. Darrow, *The Story of My Life*, 29–30; Weinberg and Weinberg, *Clarence Darrow: A Sentimental Rebel*, 26–27.

49. Darrow, *The Story of My Life*, 29–30; Weinberg and Weinberg, *Clarence Darrow: A Sentimental Rebel*, 26–27. At the time, it was very common for lawyers to be admitted to the bar without graduating from or even attending law school. Aspirants would "read" law in a lawyer's office, a position that today we might call a legal intern or a law clerk. In Darrow's day, this path probably was the norm. As late as 1941 President Franklin D. Roosevelt appointed to the U.S. Supreme Court a lawyer who had no college degree and only one year of law school, Justice Robert H. Jackson. Today, states require both a law degree (usually a J.D.) and a satisfactory score on a two- or three-day bar examination for admission to the bar. Wisconsin alone continues to grant bar admission to graduates of its in-state law schools, who need not sit for the bar exam.

50. Darrow's first wife, Jessie Ohl, was from Kinsman, although her family had moved to Sharon, Pennsylvania, by the time she married Darrow, in 1880. Jessie bore a son, Paul, in late 1883. He would be Darrow's only child. Weinberg and Weinberg, *Clarence Darrow: A Sentimental Rebel*, 27–28.

51. Darrow, *The Story of My Life*, 30.

52. Ibid., 32.

53. See Weinberg and Weinberg, *Clarence Darrow: A Sentimental Rebel*, 23–24.

54. Darrow, *The Story of My Life*, 16.

55. Ibid., 32.

56. Ibid., 34.

57. Ibid., 39, 41.

58. In addition to the anecdote about the home purchase that fell through, Darrow admitted Everett's influence on the decision to move to Chicago. Ibid., 39–40.

59. Ibid., 41–48. As to the single tax and Henry George's political economy, see generally Henry George, *Poverty and Progress* (New York: D. Appleton, 1880).

60. Darrow, *The Story of My Life*, 46–48.

61. Ibid., 381.

62. Ibid., 42.

63. Ibid., 36.

64. Ibid., 49–51.

65. Ibid., 51–52, 57.

66. Ibid., 57.

67. Ibid., 57, 58–59, 62.

68. Weinberg and Weinberg, *Clarence Darrow: A Sentimental Rebel*, 50–55.

69. Darrow, *The Story of My Life*, 59–60.

70. Ibid., 61; Weinberg and Weinberg, *Clarence Darrow: A Sentimental Rebel*, 54–55.

71. Darrow, *The Story of My Life*, 61; Weinberg and Weinberg, *Clarence Darrow: A Sentimental Rebel*, 54.

72. Weinberg and Weinberg, *Clarence Darrow: A Sentimental Rebel*, 69–71; Darrow, *The Story of My Life*, 33.

73. Darrow, *The Story of My Life*, 33; Weinberg and Weinberg, *Clarence Darrow: A Sentimental Rebel*, 70–71. A second marriage, to Ruby Hamerstrom in 1903, lasted the rest of Darrow's life, although he philandered occasionally when it suited him. Weinberg and Weinberg, *Clarence Darrow: A Sentimental Rebel*, 115, 122, 154–57.

74. See the very helpful online library of Darrow's correspondence that the University of Minnesota Law Library has assembled: The Clarence Darrow Digital Collection, http://darrow.law.umn.edu.

75. Weinberg and Weinberg, *Clarence Darrow: A Sentimental Rebel*, 269.

76. Darrow, *The Story of My Life*, 50.

77. Ibid., 74.

78. Ibid., 75–76.

79. Ibid., 66.

80. Ibid., 68.

81. Weinberg and Weinberg, *Clarence Darrow: A Sentimental Rebel*, 77–79; Darrow, *The Story of My Life*, 74–75.

82. Weinberg and Weinberg, *Clarence Darrow: A Sentimental Rebel*, 79; Darrow, *The Story of My Life*, 75.

83. Weinberg and Weinberg, *Clarence Darrow: A Sentimental Rebel*, 78. With judicious editing, most of Darrow's summation in the Kidd prosecution is reprinted in Weinberg, *Attorney for the Damned*, 269–326.

84. Darrow, *The Story of My Life*, 64.

85. See generally Weinberg and Weinberg, *Clarence Darrow: A Sentimental Rebel*, 91–104, 127–52, 162–67; Darrow, *The Story of My Life*, 112–71; for the trials that followed Steunenberg's murder, along with much else about nineteenth-century and early twentieth-century America, see Lukas, *Big Trouble*.

86. Weinberg and Weinberg, *Clarence Darrow: A Sentimental Rebel*, 172–74; Darrow, *The Story of My Life*, 184–86; Cowan, *The People v. Clarence Darrow*, 255–65.

87. Weinberg and Weinberg, *Clarence Darrow: A Sentimental Rebel*, 249.

88. Ibid., 206–7, 213.

89. Ibid., 269. Masters originally published *Spoon River Anthology* in 1915.

90. Ibid., 269; Darrow, *The Story of My Life*, 203–4.

91. Darrow, *The Story of My Life*, 203.

92. Weinberg and Weinberg, *Clarence Darrow: A Sentimental Rebel*, 269.

93. Ibid., 269–70; Stone, *Clarence Darrow: For the Defense*, 346–49.

94. See generally Weinberg and Weinberg, *Clarence Darrow: A Sentimental Rebel*, 270–78; Darrow, *The Story of My Life*, 203–9.

95. Weinberg and Weinberg, *Clarence Darrow: A Sentimental Rebel*, 270. As to his intimate relationship with Mary Field, see 154–55.

96. Kevin Boyle's *Arc of Justice* covers the Henry and Ossian Sweet trials thoroughly.

97. As to the Scopes trial, see for example Larson, *Summer for the Gods*. There are many other accounts as well, and a transcript of Darrow's cross-examination of Bryan as an

expert on the Bible remains readily available. The Scopes trial was the basis of Jerome Lawrence and Robert E. Lee's 1950 play *Inherit the Wind* (which opened on Broadway almost five years later, in 1955) and of Stanley Kramer's 1960 movie with the same name. Both are good drama and provide a nice allegory for the anti-intellectual mood and Communist fear of the early 1950s, although outside that context they render unfair, flat caricatures at least of Bryan and perhaps of the creationist side of the debate.

98. The Leopold and Loeb case also has produced an extensive literature, including nearly verbatim reprints of Darrow's closing arguments. Secondary accounts include Hal Higdon, *The Crime of the Century: The Leopold and Loeb Case* (New York: G. P. Putnam's Sons, 1975); and, more recent, Simon Baatz, *For the Thrill of It: Leopold, Loeb, and the Murder That Shocked Chicago* (New York: Harper, 2008). The Leopold and Loeb case was treated fictionally in Meyer Levin, *Compulsion* (New York: Simon and Schuster, 1956), and in Orson Welles's 1959 movie of the same title.

99. Cowan, *The People v. Clarence Darrow*, 444.

100. To that effect, Cowan quotes letters from both Mary Field's younger sister, Sara, and the journalist Lincoln Steffens, who covered the McNamara trial and Darrow's own trials and was a sympathetic but perceptive friend. Cowan, *The People v. Clarence Darrow*, 442, 444.

101. Weinberg and Weinberg, *Clarence Darrow: A Sentimental Rebel*, 26.

102. Weinberg and Weinberg, *Clarence Darrow: Verdicts Out of Court*, 110.

103. Ibid., 115.

104. *Are We Machines?*, Little Blue Book no. 509 (Girard, KS: Haldeman-Julius Co., n.d.); *Is Man a Machine?* (New York: League for Public Discussion, 1927).

105. Clarence Darrow, *Crime and Criminals: Address to the Prisoners in the Cook County Jail* (Chicago: Charles H. Kerr, 2000), 15.

106. Ibid., 11.

107. Darrow, *The Story of My Life*, 86.

108. Ibid., 96–104.

109. Ibid., 96–111.

110. *United States ex rel. Turner v. Williams*, 194 U.S. 279 (1904).

111. Weinberg and Weinberg, *Clarence Darrow: A Sentimental Rebel*, 355–56.

112. Helen Keller, letter to Clarence Darrow, August 19, 1931, in the Clarence Darrow Digital Collection, University of Minnesota Law Library, http://darrow.law.umn.edu.

113. Victor L. Berger, "The Flag Superstition," *Broadsides* (Milwaukee: Social-Democratic Publishing Company, 1912), 97–98.

114. Some of Darrow's biographers overlook the appeal of the eleven Milwaukee Italians, but Stone and Tierney cover it briefly. Stone devotes four pages to the case and does not dig deep. His account includes some inaccuracies, although none of great significance. Stone, *Clarence Darrow: For the Defense*, 360–63. Tierney offers less than two pages on the case, again discussing only the broad outline, but gets the facts right. Tierney, *Darrow: A Biography*, 306–7.

115. Darrow certainly did handle a number of appeals, though. Indeed, he represented a noted anarchist, John Turner, in the U.S. Supreme Court and also appealed to that court on behalf of two of the defendants in the Idaho trial following the murder of former governor Frank Steunenberg. See *United States ex rel. Turner v. Williams*, 194 U.S. 279 (1904); *Pettibone v. Nichols*, 203 U.S. 192 (1906); *Stewart v. Ramsay*, 242 U.S. 128 (1916). He handled several appeals in the federal court of appeals in Chicago. See, e.g., *Crimp v. McCormick Constr. Co.*, 71 F. 356 (7th Cir. 1896); *United States v. St. John*, 254 F. 794 (7th Cir. 1918). And the case of the eleven Italians was not his only appeal to the Wisconsin Supreme Court. He was involved in a second appeal to the Wisconsin Supreme Court several years later. *Eckman v. State*, 191 Wis. 63, 209 N.W. 715 (1926). Darrow also handled a smattering of appeals in other state supreme courts over his long career.

116. Weinberg and Weinberg, *Clarence Darrow: A Sentimental Rebel*, 282–85; Darrow, *The Story of My Life*, 210–17.

117. Weinberg and Weinberg, *Clarence Darrow: A Sentimental Rebel*, 288–89; Darrow, *The Story of My Life*, 218–20.

118. Weinberg and Weinberg, *Clarence Darrow: A Sentimental Rebel*, 294–95; Darrow, *The Story of My Life*, 218–19.

119. Weinberg and Weinberg, *Clarence Darrow: A Sentimental Rebel*, 288.

120. Ibid., 285.

121. Edgar Lee Masters, *Clarence Darrow* (poem, 1922). As to the hot-and-cold relationship between Darrow and Masters, see *Kessinger's Mid-West Review* 5, no. 2 (August 1925): 2–6; Weinberg and Weinberg, *Clarence Darrow: A Sentimental Rebel*, 122–25.

122. Clarence Darrow's 1918 remarks are reprinted in *Response of Clarence Darrow to Birthday Greetings* (Greeley, CO: Tribune-Republican Pub. Co., 1947), 22, 26–27, 29, 31.

123. "Two Bombs at Home of District Attorney," 1, 15.

Chapter 9. May It Please the Court

1. Ward Stone Ireland, an American, invented the first modern shorthand machine capable of recording several letters or a whole word in a single stroke of several fingers in 1910. He called his invention the stenotype machine. According to the website of the National College of Court Reporting, an official court reporter first made use of a reporting machine in a 1935 trial—that of Richard "Bruno" Hauptmann, convicted in the kidnapping and death of the infant son of Charles and Anne Lindbergh. See http://nccr.com.au/whatis-machinesh/brief-history.html.

2. I refer throughout to an "appeal" because that is the generic term that modern readers will understand. Here I note only that, at the time, the Wisconsin Supreme Court and some other courts actually reviewed criminal convictions on writ of error. WIS. STAT. §§ 3043, 4724 (1917). The technical differences between an appeal of an order, see WIS. STAT. § 3069 (1917), and a writ of error to review a final judgment in a case tried to a jury are not important here.

3. Wis. Stat. § 3070 (1917).

4. Wis. Stat. § 4720 (1917).

5. Wis. Stat. § 4720 (1917).

6. Rogers had represented Darrow in the first trial on juror bribery charges in Los Angeles in 1912. The two eventually had a falling out, in part because of Darrow's ego and Rogers's struggles with alcohol. Rogers did not represent Darrow at the second trial.

7. *Brief and Argument for Plaintiffs in Error*, no. 10 (October Term, 1918), 47–48.

8. Ibid., 49.

9. Ibid., 74–75. I take minor liberties with punctuation in both of these extended quotations from the defense brief.

10. See *Brief for Defendant in Error*, no. 10 (October Term, 1918); GJ Tr. 216.

11. Wisconsin Department of Administration, *Wisconsin State Capitol* (brochure, revised September 2005), and *Wisconsin State Capitol Tour Narration* (March 2006).

12. Most of Darrow's biographers devote some attention to this trial, which Darrow won. See, e.g., Weinberg and Weinberg, *Clarence Darrow: A Sentimental Rebel*, 77–79; Stone, *Clarence Darrow: For the Defense*, 103–12.

13. The second was *Eckman v. State*, 191 Wis. 63, 209 N.W. 715 (1926).

14. The phrase appears in the official reports of the Supreme Court of the United States at least as early as 1864. See *Providence Tool Co. v. Norris*, 69 U.S. (2 Wall.) 45, 51 (1864). But it was in vogue much earlier than that. For example, Edmund Randolph, counsel for Aaron Burr, addressed the court in that fashion in Burr's treason trial in 1807, over which Chief Justice John Marshall presided. *United States v. Burr*, 25 F. Cas. 55, 68 (C.C. Va. 1807) (No. 14,693).

15. Stone, *Clarence Darrow: For the Defense*, 362.

16. See www.wicourts.gov/courts/supreme/justices/retired/winslow.htm.

17. Rowberg File microfiches 1440–1552, vols. 1–68 (obituary in Norwegian), Naeseth Library, Madison, Wisconsin.

18. Aad J. Vinje, letter to Henry Goddard Leach, May 17, 1928, Wisconsin Historical Society.

19. *Bianchi v. State*, 169 Wis. 75, 88, 171 N.W. 639 (1919).

20. *Bianchi v. State*, 169 Wis. at 89.

21. *Bianchi v. State*, 169 Wis. at 90.

22. *Bianchi v. State*, 169 Wis. at 90–91. I have left the names of the defendants as the state supreme court spelled them.

23. *Bianchi v. State*, 169 Wis. at 91, 97.

24. *Bianchi v. State*, 169 Wis. at 91.

25. Since statehood, Wisconsin has elected its judges, from those who serve on local municipal courts up through those on the Wisconsin Supreme Court.

26. *Bianchi v. State*, 169 Wis. at 92.

27. *Bianchi v. State*, 169 Wis. at 92.

28. *Bianchi v. State*, 169 Wis. at 94–95.

29. The Wisconsin Supreme Court applied harmless error doctrine to the admission of an involuntary statement, a potentially controversial choice and one that arguably favors an authoritarian interest in societal stability over a libertarian interest in limited governmental power. Not until 1991, seventy-two years later, did the U.S. Supreme Court follow that same course, when it finally faced the issue squarely. See *Arizona v. Fulminante*, 499 U.S. 279, 310 (1991) (Rehnquist, J.).

30. *Bianchi v. State*, 169 Wis. at 96.

31. *Bianchi v. State*, 169 Wis. at 96–97.

32. "Court Frees Seven Men in Riot Case," *Milwaukee Evening Sentinel*, April 2, 1919, 1; "Court Frees 7 in Riot Cases," *Milwaukee Journal*, April 2, 1919, 1, 15.

33. "Darrow Wins Acquittal of Seven Rioters," *Capital Times*, April 2, 1919, 3.

34. "Decision of Court Surprise to District Attorney," *Milwaukee Journal*, April 2, 1919, 15.

35. "Scores Easy Victory over His Opponent," *Milwaukee Evening Sentinel*, April 1, 1919, 1.

36. Incidentally, the *Milwaukee Sentinel* thought it notable that the three supreme court candidates together had spent more than $5,000 on that race. Rosenberry, the incumbent, was the big spender, with a campaign expenditure of $4,940.39. "Over $5,000 Spent in Supreme Court Race," *Milwaukee Sentinel*, April 3, 1919.

37. The song dates to the Civil War, but Americans returned to it with each new war at least through World War II. See http://lcweb2.loc.gov/diglib/ihas/loc.natlib.ihas.200000024/default.html.

38. Clarence S. Darrow, letter to Paul Darrow, May 2, 1919, in the Clarence Darrow Digital Collection, University of Minnesota Law Library, http://darrow.law.umn.edu.

Chapter 10. Infernal Machine

1. "May Deport Freed Italians," *Milwaukee Sentinel*, April 3, 1919, 5.

2. Robert Tanzilo, *Milwaukee 1917: Uno Scontro Tra Italoamericani* (Foligno, Italy: Editoriale Umbra, 2006), 111–17; Robert Tanzilo, "Politics, Protest and Proselytization: A Struggle among Italian-Americans in 1917 Milwaukee" (2006 manuscript, updated February 2009), 132–38 (copy in author's possession).

3. Pardon Papers, Series 98, Box 204 (1922, LeClaire through Luther), Wisconsin Historical Society.

4. Author's conversation with Robert Tanzilo, who has spoken extensively with Areno's daughter.

5. Tanzilo, "Politics, Protest and Proselytization," 137–38. According to Tanzilo, Pasquale Nardini was deported earlier.

6. "Death of Zabel Ends a Colorful Career," 3.

7. Tanzilo, "Politics, Protest and Proselytization," 134–36.

8. Winfred C. Zabel, letter to Gov. John J. Blaine, March 3, 1921, 1, in Pardon Papers, Series 98, Box 204 (1922, LeClaire through Luther), Wisconsin Historical Society.

9. Gov. John J. Blaine, letter to Howard D. Ebey, Acting Inspector in Charge, U.S. Department of Labor, Immigration Service, November 22, 1921, in Pardon Papers, Series 98, Box 204 (1922, LeClaire through Luther), Wisconsin Historical Society. The core of that hospital remains to this day as part of the Dodge Correctional Institution, a few blocks west of the prison at Waupun.

10. Gov. John J. Blaine, letter to H. R. Landis, U.S. Department of Labor, Immigration Service, October 5, 1921, in Pardon Papers, Series 98, Box 204 (1922, LeClaire through Luther), Wisconsin Historical Society.

11. Pardon Petition to Gov. John J. Blaine, March 1, 1921, 2–3, in Pardon Papers, Series 98, Box 204 (1922, LeClaire through Luther), Wisconsin Historical Society.

12. Ibid., 3.

13. Winfred C. Zabel, letter to Gov. John J. Blaine, March 3, 1921, 5, in Pardon Papers, Series 98, Box 204 (1922, LeClaire through Luther), Wisconsin Historical Society.

14. Ibid., 5–6.

15. Ibid., 6.

16. "John J. Blaine, Former U.S. Senator and Governor, Dies," *Fennimore Times*, April 18, 1934. Blaine left his papers to the Wisconsin Historical Society. Wis. Mss Pl, MAD 3/36/A6-B5.

17. GJ Tr. 18.

18. *Bianchi v. State*, 169 Wis. at 88.

19. Clarence Darrow, letter to Gov. John J. Blaine, April 19, 1921, in Pardon Papers, Series 98, Box 204 (1922, LeClaire through Luther), Wisconsin Historical Society.

20. Ibid.

21. John J. Blaine, letter to Clarence Darrow, April 21, 1921, in Pardon Papers, Series 98, Box 204 (1922, LeClaire through Luther), Wisconsin Historical Society.

22. See Gov. John J. Blaine, letter to H. R. Landis, October 5, 1921; Howard D. Ebey, letter to Gov. John J. Blaine, October 7, 1921; Gov. John J. Blaine, letter to Howard D. Ebey, November 22, 1921; Howard D. Ebey, letter to Gov. John J. Blaine, November 30, 1921; Howard D. Ebey, Western Union telegram to Gov. John J. Blaine, December 9, 1921; Howard D. Ebey, letter to Gov. John J. Blaine, February 2, 1922, all in Pardon Papers, Series 98, Box 204 (1922, LeClaire through Luther), Wisconsin Historical Society.

23. Warden Robert M. Coles, letter to Gov. John J. Blaine, February 9, 1922, in Pardon Papers, Series 98, Box 204 (1922, LeClaire through Luther), Wisconsin Historical Society.

24. Tanzilo, "Politics, Protest and Proselytization," 137–38.

25. Ibid., 138 and n. 322.

26. *Mother Earth* magazine had its last offices at 20 East 125th Street in Harlem. See *Mother Earth* 12, no. 3 (May 1917). The Nardinis lived at 241 East 120th Street. Tanzilo, "Politics, Protest and Proselytization," 137 and n. 320.

27. Tanzilo, "Politics, Protest and Proselytization," 138 and n. 323.

28. Social Security Death Index; see also ibid., 137.

29. Wexler, *Emma Goldman: An Intimate Life*, 276; Falk, *Love, Anarchy, and Emma Goldman*, 318.

30. Wisconsin Historical Society, Wisconsin Name Index, Record no. 3206.

31. *In Memoriam Winfred C. Zabel*, xxxiii; "Death of Zabel Ends a Colorful Career," 3.

32. "Zabel Dies as Voters Again Re-Elect Him," 1; "Death of Zabel Ends a Colorful Career," 3.

33. *State v. Rubin*, 201 Wis. 30, 229 N.W. 36, 39 (1930) ("This affidavit made by Mr. Rubin also contained most fulsome praise of himself"; quotations of Rubin's aggrandizement of himself follow).

34. W. B. Rubin, *The Bolshevists: A Comedy Drama* (Boston: Cornhill, 1921).

35. See *State v. Rubin*, 201 Wis. 30, 229 N.W. 36 (1930) (finding professional misconduct but censuring rather than suspending Rubin from practice); *Rubin v. State*, 194 Wis. 207, 216 N.W. 513 (1927) (affirming contempt finding); *Rubin v. State*, 192 Wis. 1, 211 N.W. 926 (1927) (affirming a separate criminal contempt finding and $25 fine); "Stanch Champion of Rights, Bill Rubin to Ease Up a Bit at 83," part 2, pp. 1, 6.

36. "Atty. William B. Rubin's Funeral to Be Held Today," part 1, p. 4.

37. "First Community Church," *The View* (June 1969), 2–4 (bulletin of the Summerfield United Methodist Church and the First Community United Methodist Church, available at "Protestant Evangelical Mission to the Italians," MSS-1103, Milwaukee County Historical Society); "Crowd Fills Church for Double Rite," *Milwaukee Sentinel*, November 29, 1929, 7.

38. Tanzilo, "Politics, Protest and Proselytization," 151–52; "Alleges Church Fight in Suit," *Milwaukee Journal*, April 16, 1922, part 2, p. 1.

39. GJ Tr. 1.

40. http://www.wisbar.org/AM/Template.cfm?Section=History&Template= /CustomSource/History/presidents.cfm.

41. GJ Tr. 1–2.

42. GJ Tr. 13–23.

43. GJ Tr. 202. Groelle's professional activities after he left the district attorney's office are lost. He died of heart disease on March 2, 1941, in Pewaukee, Wisconsin, about twenty miles west of Milwaukee, and is buried in Evergreen Cemetery in Manitowoc. Death information comes from the cemetery's records.

44. GJ Tr. 202, 204.

45. GJ Tr. 211–12, 226.

46. GJ Tr. 203, 205, 205–6.

47. GJ Tr. 203, 205–6.

48. GJ Tr. 206, 209.

49. GJ Tr. 207, 207–9.

50. GJ Tr. 211 (Zabel discussing resigning), 220 (Zabel practically a nervous wreck, considering resigning), 219 (Groelle's reaction and fear).

51. GJ Tr. 209.

52. GJ Tr. 215.

53. GJ Tr. 214–15.

54. GJ Tr. 209.

55. WIS. STAT. § 4720 (1917).

56. GJ Tr. 211, 214.

57. GJ Tr. 217.

58. GJ Tr. 218.

59. GJ Tr. 214.

60. GJ Tr. 223.

61. GJ Tr. 210.

62. GJ Tr. 210.

63. GJ Tr. 212.

64. GJ Tr. 211.

65. GJ Tr. 216.

66. GJ Tr. 20.

67. GJ Tr. 13–14. Groelle later disputed in part Hardgrove's version of their conversation. GJ Tr. 212–13.

68. GJ Tr. 2381.

69. GJ Tr. 219, 221, 225.

70. GJ Tr. 221.

71. GJ Tr. 226–27.

72. GJ Tr. 2017.

73. GJ Tr. 2018.

74. GJ Tr. 2519.

75. GJ Tr. 2520.

76. GJ Tr. 2520.

77. GJ Tr. 2530–32.

78. GJ Tr. 221.

79. *State v. Carchidi*, 187 Wis. 438, 204 N.W. 473 (1925).

80. "Death of Zabel Ends Colorful Career," 3.

81. *State v. Carchidi*, 187 Wis. 438, 204 N.W. 473 (1925).

82. *Bianchi v. State*, 169 Wis. at 90.

83. *Bianchi v. State*, 169 Wis. at 90–91.

84. *Bianchi v. State*, 169 Wis. at 91.

85. See, e.g., "Declares Woman Urged Bloodshed," 5.

86. Recent biographers have explored Darrow's dark side more fully than earlier ones. See, e.g., John A. Farrell, *Clarence Darrow: Attorney for the Damned* (New York: Doubleday, 2011).

87. "Clarence Darrow Is Dead in Chicago," *New York Times*, March 14, 1938, 15.

88. Avrich, *Sacco and Vanzetti*, 104–5.

Appendix

1. In *Wolf v. Colorado*, 338 U.S. 25, 27–28 (1949), the Supreme Court held that the Fourth Amendment applies to the states through the Fourteenth Amendment's due process

clause. But the Court specifically refused to require states to adopt the federal "exclusionary rule," dating to 1914, that usually forbade the federal government to make use at trial of evidence obtained in violation of the Fourth Amendment. Only in 1961, with *Mapp v. Ohio*, 367 U.S. 643, 654–55 (1961), did the Supreme Court require states also to apply the exclusionary rule to Fourth Amendment violations.

2. See Percy Henry Winfield, *The History of Conspiracy and Abuse of Legal Procedure* (Cambridge: Cambridge University Press, 1921), 92–96; Francis B. Sayre, "Criminal Conspiracy," *Harvard Law Review* 35 (1922): 393, 395–96. Sayre places the year of enactment at 1285.

3. Winfield, *The History of Conspiracy*, 93.

4. Sayre, "Criminal Conspiracy," 398–99.

5. Ibid.

6. I William Hawkins, *Pleas of the Crown*, c. 72, § 2 (1716).

7. Here, abuse of process may have included the acts of lawyers or officials intentionally stirring up or financially supporting litigation with the hope of sharing in its proceeds, called "maintenance," although that is murky, like much else in the early common law era. If maintenance warranted a conspiracy charge, then so did its included subset, champerty (splitting the proceeds of litigation with someone who procured the client). See Winfield, *The History of Conspiracy*, 138–50.

8. IV William Blackstone, *Commentaries on the Laws of England*, c. 10, § 15, at 136 (1769).

9. *Harrison v. United States*, 7 F.2d 259, 263 (2d Cir. 1925) (L. Hand, J.).

10. Formally, the act in furtherance—which England, like America after it, called an "overt act"—provided the "*locus poenitentiae*," or location of the offense, and some corroboration of the existence of the criminal agreement. For an abbreviated discussion of those two functions of the overt act requirement, see *Braverman v. United States*, 317 U.S. 49, 53 (1942). The overt act also served the function of identifying the specific point in time before which a conspirator could withdraw from the conspiracy and face no criminal liability. See *United States v. Britton*, 108 U.S. 199, 204 (1883).

11. For a good discussion of the so-called overt act requirement, see Note, "Developments in the Law of Criminal Conspiracy," *Harvard Law Review* 72 (1959): 920, 945–49.

12. *Braverman v. United States*, 317 U.S. 49, 53 (1942).

13. See generally Note, "Developments in the Law of Criminal Conspiracy," 925–35.

14. Ibid., 957–60.

15. The classic case is *Pinkerton v. United States*, 328 U.S. 640 (1946).

16. That is true only as to an actual offense of conviction. It is not true as to hearsay statements that might be used to prove an offense. The prosecution may offer so-called co-conspirators' statements against a defendant as an exception to the hearsay rule to prove another crime, even if the formal charges do not include conspiracy. See *St. Clair v. United States*, 154 U.S. 134, 149–50 (1894), and, for one of many modern applications of that rule, *United States v. Lara*, 181 F.3d 183, 196 (1st Cir. 1999).

17. There are many cases to this effect, and most federal circuits now have pattern jury instructions that except from criminal liability those with "mere knowledge" of the conspiracy or those who were associated with conspirators by "mere presence." For a general discussion of the underlying theoretical and practical issues related to this proof of actual agreement, see Note, "Developments in the Law of Criminal Conspiracy," 930–33.

18. U.S. Const. amend. V.

19. The decision generally credited with establishing the Supreme Court's preeminence in constitutional interpretation is *Marbury v. Madison*, 5 U.S. (1 Cranch) 137 (1803).

20. *Counselman v. Hitchcock*, 142 U.S. 547, 562–64 (1892).

21. U.S. Const. amend. XIV.

22. So the Supreme Court held. *Murray's Lessee v. Hoboken Land & Improvement Co.*, 59 U.S. (18 How.) 272 (1855).

23. *Hurtado v. California*, 110 U.S. 516 (1884).

24. Richard C. Cortner, *A "Scottsboro" Case in Mississippi: The Supreme Court and Brown v. Mississippi* (Jackson: University Press of Mississippi, 1986), 4 and nn. 4–5.

25. Ibid.

26. Ibid., 21.

27. Ibid., 158. John Stennis replaced a very short-lived successor to Judge Sturdivant in 1937 and served as circuit judge until he ran successfully for the U.S. Senate. Ibid., 157–58.

28. *Brown v. State*, 173 Miss. 542, 161 So. 465, 471 (1935) (Griffith, J., dissenting).

29. Cortner, *A "Scottsboro" Case in Mississippi*, 10.

30. *Brown v. Mississippi*, 297 U.S. 285.

31. Ibid.

32. Ibid., 286.

33. Ibid., 285.

34. *Chambers v. Florida*, 309 U.S. 227 (1940).

35. Ibid., 229.

36. Roger K. Newman, *Hugo Black: A Biography* (New York: Pantheon Books, 1994), 91–100. Black's membership was not just a youthful indiscretion. He joined at age thirty-seven, according to Newman. Later in life, Black generally explained his membership as necessary for an aspiring politician in the Clay County and Birmingham of that day.

37. *Chambers v. Florida*, 309 U.S. at 240 n. 15.

38. Ibid., 238.

39. National Commission on Law Observance and Enforcement, *Report on Lawlessness in Law Enforcement* (Washington, DC: U.S. Government Printing Office, 1931).

40. *People v. Sloss*, 412 Ill. 61, 70, 104 N.E.2d 807, 812 (1952); *Lang v. State*, 178 Wis. 114, 189 N.W. 558, 560–62 (1922).

41. *Miranda v. Arizona*, 384 U.S. 436, 445–46, and 446n7 (1966), citing examples.

Index

Page references in italics indicate illustrations. Unless otherwise indicated, businesses, organizations, and events are in Milwaukee. In subentries, "Darrow" refers to Clarence Darrow, "Giuliani" refers to August Giuliani, and "Zabel" refers to Winfred Zabel.

Ball Players Union, 232–33n74

Bartelt, Arthur H., 107, 162–64, 177, 184

Bates, Katharine Lee, 221n32

Bay View (Wisconsin): geography of, 7; houses in, 45–46; map of, 7. *See also* Italians of Bay View

Bay View riot (1917), 4; anarchism's role in, 37, 41–42, 53–57, 224n118; Avrich on, 43; caps on and coats buttoned, significance of, 46–47; casualties of, 49–52; causes of, 18–19, 53–57, 215n20; eleven Italians arrested/jailed in, 19, 22, 43 (*see also* Bay View riot trial); Giuliani blamed for, 58; Giuliani's church group at the rally, 42–45, 53–55, 57; gun battle at, 48–49, 222n55; IWW linked to, 63–65, 199; LaDuca's audience confronts Giuliani's group, 45–48, 221n35, 221n47; LaDuca's speech before, 44–45; linked to bombing at police station, 55, 133; media coverage of, 52–56, 215n20, 224n118; police presence at, 47–49, 51, 57, 221n48, 222n50, 222n55; police presence at previous rallies, 56–57, 225n135; religion's role in, 54–56; weather conditions during, 44, 220n12

Bay View riot appeal: bill of exceptions in, 159–60, 184; Darrow's role in, 140–41, 151, 154, 159–60, 163–64, 183–84; defendants treated as individuals in, 167–70; defense briefs in, 160–62; defense fund for, 138, 140, 242n21; Goldman's role in, 138–41, 242n21; grand jury investigation into corruption of, 181–90, 192, 253n67; media coverage of, 171; oral argument scheduled, 162; public reaction to the decision, 170–71; Rubin's role in, 139–42; Sissman's role in, 141, 155, 159–60; state's brief in, 162; supreme court justices in, 165; supreme court's decision in, 166–70, 173, 188–89, 250n29; Vinje's remarks on Backus, 169; Zabel agrees with bill of exceptions, 160; Zabel's oral argument in, 164; Zabel's reaction to the decision, 171, 190

Bay View riot investigation: Carchidi as informant during, 61–62; Giuliani as translator in, 60–61, 126–27; Italian community's silence during, 57–58; police roundup of Italians, during, 57–58; police searches/seizures, 58–59, 64; police target the Nardini home, 52, 224n111; suspects detained/interrogated without being charged, 61, 169, 226n161; warrantless searches/arrests in, 58; Zabel files charges against the suspects, 58, 62, 65; Zabel's handling of, 59–61, 169, 226nn161–62

Bay View riot trial, 70; anarchist books and pamphlets as evidence in, 124, 126–27; Backus calls the case, 109–10; Backus instructs the jury, 133, 189; Backus orders spectators frisked, 107, 113; Backus's bias in, 113–15, 123; Backus's sentencing in, 135–36; bomb or death threats against prosecutors and judge during, 128–29, 156, 182, 185–86; the "Case," 235n13; change of venue requested and denied, 111–16; charges against the defendants, 110, 133, 197–98; convictions in, 134–35; court records for, 235–36n13; courtroom for, *101*; defendants' backgrounds, 35–37, 130–31, 218n65, 219n74; defendants' bail set, 63; defendants identified as anarchists, 23, 25, 27, 34–35, 37, 40, 63, 135–37; defendants identified as conspirators, 110, 133, 135–36; defendants' imprisonment following, 136–37; defendants linked to police station bombing, 55, 133; defendants photographed on way to court, 107–8; defendants' religion, 55, 131, 224n129; defendants salute the flag, 108; defendants' testimony in, 130–31; defense attorneys' testimony in, 238n95; defense witnesses arrested during, 124–26, 130; defense witnesses in, 128–29; evidence against the defendants, 132; Giuliani cross-examined by Rubin, 120–21; and Giuliani's patriotic vs. religious motives at the rally, 120–21, 129–30; Giuliani's testimony at, 119–21, 127, 132, 221n45; Goldman's support of the defendants, xiii, 31–32, 137–39, 179; Groelle accuses Testolin of threatening a juror, 122; Groelle questions Zabel in, 127; Groelle's summation, 132; Groelle threatened during, 128, 182; jury deliberation in, 134; jury selection in, 108–9, 114–18; media coverage of, 35, 116–17; media influences perception of

Galleani, Luigi, 25–26, 40–41, 43, 214n6
Gayety Theater, 82–83
George, Henry, 144
Geraghty, Josephine, 74
German immigrants, 6, 209n17
Germanotta, Dominic, 221n47
Giovannitti, Arturo, 63–65, 227n10
Giuliani, August: appearance of, 9, *94*, *103*, 119; arrival in United States, 9, 210n23; background of, 9; Bay View riot, role in (*see under* Bay View riot); on causes of the riot, 53; conversion to Methodism, 9, 210n24; death of, 181; evangelical work of, 9–10, 16–18, 59, 181 (*see also* Bay View riot; Italian Evangelical Mission Church); marriage to Katherine, 9–10, 59, 181; personality of, 10; politics and patriotism of, 17–18, 59; reports to police after the riot, 59; on riot defendants as anarchists, 37; on riot defendants' education, 219n74; self-importance of, 59–60; sexual impropriety suspected of, 120–21, 181; shakes Denurra's hand, 47; testimony of (*see under* Bay View riot trial); as translator, 60–61, 126–27
Giuliani, Katherine Eyerick, 9–10, 59, 181, 226n152
Giuliani, Waldo August, 59, *94*
Glanvill, Ranulf de, 194
"God Bless America," 221n32
Godwin, William, 214n7
Goldman, Emma ("E.G."): anarchism of, 26–27, 29–30, 137; appearance of, 28; background of, 27–28; and Berkman, 29–30; on capitalist wars, 25; causes championed by, 29; Czolgosz supported by, 29–30, 141, 216n42; and Darrow, 32, 140–41, 216n41, 243nn27–28; death and burial of, 31, 179, 242n21; on de Cleyre, 215n34, 243n28; defendants in Bay View riot trial supported by, xiii, 31–32, 137–39, 179; deportation of, xiii, 31–32, 34, 242n21; fame of, 39; feminism of, 31; and Havel, 214n17; on the Haymarket Square bombing, 27–28; "The Hypocrisy of Puritanism," 42; imprisonment of, 140; *Living My Life*, 31; on Marxism, 30; "The Milwaukee

Frame-Up," 138–39; "Minorities *versus* Majorities," 30–31; Mooney and Billings supported by, 217n52; *Mother Earth* founded and published by, 28, 31 (see also *Mother Earth*); on Areno Nardini, 137; on Maria Nardini, 36, 137; personality of, 28; prosecuted for No-Conscription League role, 34, 139, 218n62; on religion, 42; role after McKinley's assassination, 29, 216nn41–42; role in Bay View riot appeal, 138–41, 242n21; travels outside the United States, 32; on the United States, 31; on violence and the *Attentat*, 29–30, 56; visit to United States after deportation, 31, *106*, 179, 216n39, 242n21; writers admired by, 31, 215–16nn34–35
Gompers, Samuel, 71, 74–75, 78, *98*, 150, 180, 215n19
Great War. *See* World War I
Groelle, Frederick F., 162; career of, 182; Darrow's Chicago meeting with, 183–84, 187; death of, 252n43; role in trial of Bay View eleven, 71, 107; testimony in grand jury investigation of Zabel, 182–90, 192, 253n67. *See also* Bay View riot trial

Hale, Sir Matthew, 195
Hamilton, Alexander, 40
Hancock, John, 227n19
Hand, Augustus N., 34
Hand, Learned, 196, 218n59
Hardgrove, J. Gilbert, 184, 253n67
harmless error doctrine, 250n29
Harrison, Charles Yale: *Clarence Darrow*, 244n41
Hartman, Louis, 13
Hauptmann, Richard ("Bruno"), 248n1
Havel, Hippolyte, 26, 214n17
Hawkins, Sir William, 195
Haymarket Square bombing (Chicago, 1886): media coverage of, 68; vs. Milwaukee bombing (1917), xi, xiv, 14; surviving defendants pardoned, 153; trial and executions following, xi–xii, 27–28, 207n1, 216n41
Haywood, William D. ("Big Bill"), 33, 63–64, 149–50, 199, 217n47, 227n7, 244n41
hearsay rule, 121, 201, 254n16

La Follette, Robert Marion, 66–67, 165

Lake Park, 234n104

Landis, Kenesaw Mountain, 33, 68–69, 114, 128, 198, 217n47, 228–29n40

Larson, Edward L.: *Summer for the Gods*, 244n41

law of the land, 202

Lawrence, Jerome: *Inherit the Wind*, 247n97

lawyers, 154–55, 245n49. *See also individual lawyers*

Leach, Henry Goddard, 166

Leahy, Thomas, 71, 107–8, 111–12, 117, 121, 238n95

Lee, Robert E.: *Inherit the Wind*, 247n97

Leopold (Nathan) and Loeb (Richard) trial, 151, 247n98

Levin, Meyer: *Compulsion*, 247n98

Lilli, Amedeo: arrested after the riot, 51–52; background of, 36; at the Bay View riot, 45, 47–48; charges against, 110; deportation of, 174, 178; Giuliani's testimony about, 51–52; gun fired during riot, 49, 132; imprisonment of, 174; pardon petition for, 175–78, 190–91, 235n13; politics of, 47; shot during riot, 50; witness testimony on, 132; Zabel's interrogation of, 61. *See also* Bay View riot appeal; Bay View riot trial

lineups, procedures for, xv

Little, Frank, 32–33

Living My Life (Goldman), 31

Lizzi, G. A., 238n90

Lloyd, William Bross, 155

loan-sharking, 80

Longobardi, Gabriel, 20

loyalty convention (Minneapolis, 1917), 214–15n19

Lukas, J. Anthony: *Big Trouble*, 244n41

lynchings, 202–3

Magna Carta, 109, 202, 235n9

Magunik, Michael, 50–51, 223n86

maintenance, as a form of conspiracy, 254n7

Malatesta, Errico, 25–26, 41

Mangert, Henry, 13

Marbury v. Madison, 255n19

Marinelli, August, 48–52, 62, 64, 132, 226n166, 227n10

Marshall, John, 249n14

Marshall, Thomas Riley, 32

Marx, Karl, 26

Marxism, 31

The Masses, 34, 218n59

Masters, Edgar Lee, 150, 155–56, 216n41, 243n27

Mazzone, Sam, 12, 17, 21–22, 45, 210n40

McDonough, G. L., 208n1, 211n57, 211n59

McKinley, William, 29, 216n41–42

McNamara (James B. and John J.) juror bribery case (1912), xiii, 76–77, 150, 190, 249n6

McPherran, Ralph S., 13

Messer-Kruse, Timothy, 207n1

Miles, Officer, 51, 223n101

Milwaukee: brick homes in, 45–46; description of, 4–5; immigrant population of, 5–7, 209n17; murder rate in, 11; population of, 20, 210n34; religions represented in, 56, 225nn134; socialism in, 6

Milwaukee Daily News, 66

"The Milwaukee Frame-Up" (Goldman), 138–39

Milwaukee Free Press, 208n1

Milwaukee Journal, 11, 53–54, 171, 208n2, 215n20

Milwaukee Leader, 6; on anarchists, 27; on the Bay View riot, 53–55, 58, 215n20; on the bomb, 208n2, 210n29, 211n52; on bombing investigation, 22; on bombing trial, 35; politics of, 27

Milwaukee Municipal Court, 235n13

Milwaukee Parks Commission, 234n104

Milwaukee Police Department: informers for (*see* Carchidi, Frank J.); Italian distrust of police, 22; third degree used by, 200; ties to immigrant neighborhoods, 20–21

Milwaukee police station bombing (1917): Bay View riot linked to, 55, 133; blast-damage descriptions, 3–4, 13–14, 208nn1–2, 211n57; bomb's arrival at station, 11–12 (*see also* Richter, Maud); bomb's description, 13; death toll from, xi, xiv, 3–4, 209n9; Deckert brings bomb to squad room, 12–13; families of victims of, 16, 212n11; firemen's search following, 3; funerals for victims of, 15, 109; vs. Haymarket Square bombing, xi, xiv, 14; injuries from, 13; location of police station, 12, 9*1*; media coverage of, 4, 16, 114, 208nn1–2, 211n52, 212n14; police routine following,

Vinje, Arthur M., *105*
Volstead Act, 152

Walker, Catherine, 4, 12–15, 211n50
war, anarchists on, 24–25, 41, 214n6
Ward, Samuel A., 221n32
Weiler, Paul J., 4, 15, 47–49, 57, 121, 211n60,
    222n59
Weinberg, Israel, 217n52
Weinberg, Lila and Arthur, 143, 155, 243n39,
    244n41
Weinberger, Harry, 138–40
Welles, Orson: *Compulsion*, 247n98
Wesolowski, John F., 48–50, 52, 61, 121, 214n15,
    220n12, 223n86, 224n111
West Allis (Wisconsin), 13, 74
Western Federation of Miners, 149–50
"When Johnny Comes Marching Home Again,"
    171, 250n36
Whitman, Walt, 31
Wickersham, George, 204, 222n48
Wickersham Commission (National Commission
    on Law Observance and Enforcement),
    204–5, 217n52
William the Conqueror, 194
Wilmot, Florence, 231n52
Wilson, Woodrow: Espionage Act signed by, 32;
    Italian immigrants' antipathy toward, 9;
    radicals arrested, imprisoned, and deported
    under, 32–34, 217n52; wartime support for,
    5, 17–18
Winslow, John B., 165
Wisconsin Evening News, 88–89
Wisconsin State Capitol, *103*, 163
Wisconsin Supreme Court, *103*; on the Bay View
    riot, 55; on the Bay View riot trial, 134–
    35; election of judges to, 249n25; hearing
    room of, 163; on Zabel's handling of riot
    suspects, 61, 226n161; on Zabel's prosecu-
    tion of Schrank, 81. *See also* Bay View riot
    appeal
Wobblies. *See* IWW

Woller, John W., 108, 234n5
Wollstonecraft, Mary, 214n7
Women's Missionary Society, 9
workers, 37–40
World Series scandal (1919), 171–72, 232n74
World War I: as a capitalist war, 25; fear of immi-
    grants and radicals produced by, 179, 199;
    Italy joins the Allies in, 9, 18, 41; media
    coverage of, 24; opposition to, 33–34; sup-
    port for, 5, 66–67, 155, 214–15n19; U.S.
    casualties in, 66; U.S. entry into, 9, 17–18;
    U.S. expenditures on, 66
writs of assistance, 64–65, 227n19
wrongful convictions, xv–xvi

Zabel, Clothilde, 79
Zabel, William, 79, 82, 87, 180
Zabel, Winfred C.: appearance of, 79, *95*; back-
    ground of, 79; and Borstad, 84–86; bribery
    allegations against, 82–83, 232n74; bullying
    and misconduct by, 83–87, 123–24; and
    Carchidi, 82–83; Darrow's Chicago meeting
    with, 183–87, 190; death of, 90, 180; as district
    attorney, final year, 82, 232n60; early law
    career of, 79; education of, 79; elected dis-
    trict attorney, 79–81; on first day of the riot
    trial, 107; at funeral of bombing victims, 15;
    grand jury investigation into corruption of,
    181–90, 192, 253n67; Indiana indiscretion
    of, 89–90; marriage of, 79; pardon petition,
    response to, 175–77, 190–91; politics of,
    79–80, 81; with prostitutes, 80, 231n52; on
    prostitution, 80; publicity sought by, 59–
    60; relationship with women, 83; reputa-
    tion of, 81–83; retirement from trial work,
    180; riot investigated by (*see under* Bay View
    riot investigation); Rubin's feud with, 72,
    87–90, *104*; Schrank prosecuted by, 81, *91*.
    See also Bay View riot appeal; Bay View riot
    trial
Zabel family, 21, 213n37
Zawec, Steve, 36, 39, 42, 44–45, 51–52, 54, 124